INVERTING
THE
PYRAMID

INVERTING THE PYRAMID

THE HISTORY OF SOCCER TACTICS

JONATHAN WILSON

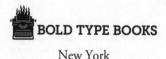 BOLD TYPE BOOKS

New York

First published in 2009, 2013 in Great Britain by The Orion Publishing Group

Copyright © 2013, 2018 by Jonathan Wilson
Designed by Jetdesignltd.com
Cover image © Mark Henderson / Alamy

Bold Type Books
116 East 16th Street, 8th Floor New York, NY 10003
www.boldtypebooks.org
@BoldTypeBooks

Printed in the United States of America

First published in 2009, 2013 in Great Britain by The Orion Publishing Group
Second Trade Paperback Edition: August 2018

Published by Bold Type Books, an imprint of Perseus Books, LLC,
a subsidiary of Hachette Book Group, Inc.

Bold Type Books is a co-publishing venture of the Type Media Center and
Perseus Books.

The Hachette Speakers Bureau provides a wide range of authors for speaking events. To find out more, go to www.hachettespeakersbureau.com or call (866) 376-6591.

The publisher is not responsible for websites (or their content)
that are not owned by the publisher.

Print book interior design by Trish Wilkinson

The Library of Congress has cataloged the original trade paperback edition as follows:

Wilson, Jonathan.
    Inverting the pyramid : the history of soccer tactics / Jonathan Wilson.
        pages   cm
    Includes bibliographical references and index.
    ISBN 978-1-56858-738-7 (pbk.) — ISBN 978-1-56858-963-3
(e-book) 1. Soccer. 2. Soccer—Defense. 3. Soccer—Coaching.
I. Title.
GV943.W555 2013
796.334'2—dc23   2013010268

ISBNs: 978-1-56858-738-7 (trade paperback original);
978-1-56858-919-0 (paperback reissue); 978-1-56858-926-8 (ebook)

LSC-C

Printing 6, 2022

CONTENTS

Felix qui potuit rerum cognoscere causas

VERGIL, GEORGICS, NO. 2, L490

ACKNOWLEDGMENTS
TO THE FIRST EDITION

In writing this, I have been humbled by just how generous so many people have been with their time and thoughts. This is a long list, but that should not diminish how vital a role each of the people included in it played.

In Ukraine, Hungary, and Russia, my thanks to Taras Hordiyenko, Sándor Laczkó, and Vladimir Soldatkin, who were as enlightening and thorough as ever. Thanks also to Aliaksiy Zyl and his coterie of Dinamo fans in Minsk for their advice (and thanks to Chris Fraser for introducing us. Dima: the polonium night at the Emirates will never be forgotten).

In Argentina, my thanks to Marcela Mora y Araujo for introducing me to her vast circle of friends, to Rodrigo Orihuela, Féderico Mayol, Neil Clack, and Klaus Gallo for their help in setting up interviews, translating, research, and ferrying me around, and to Araceli Alemán for opening up her vast library of material, the regular disquisitions on the superiority of Juan Román Riquelme to, well, everything, and, of course, the extended walking tour.

In Brazil, my thanks to Ivan Soter, Roberto Assaf, Paulo Émilio, and Alberto Helena Junior for sharing their time and learning so freely, to Cassiano Gobbet, Robert Shaw, and Jordana Alvarez dos Santos for their efforts in research, translation, and logistics, and also to Aidan Hamilton and Alex Bellos for sketching out the background and putting me in touch with experts on the ground.

Thanks to Gabriele Marcotti for all his assistance with the Italian sections, for being such an informed and robust sounding board, but most particularly for allowing me finally to participate in one of those restaurant debates in which bowls of hummus, tabouleh, and tzatziki become the Udinese defense. I'd still like my time-share on the quiz trophy, though.

Thanks to Philippe Auclair for his help in France, to Christoph Biermann, Raphael Honigstein, and Uli Hesse-Lichtenberger for their assistance with all matters German, to Simon Kuper and Auke Kok for their words of wisdom on Dutch soccer, and to Sid Lowe and Guillem Balagué for their advice on Spain. Thanks also to Brian Glanville for his unfailing generosity of spirit and for putting me right on a number of historical matters.

Thanks to Richard McBrearty of the Scottish Football Museum at Hampden and Peter Horne at the National Football Museum in Preston for sharing their expertise in the origins of soccer, and to the staff of the British Library at St. Pancras, the Mitchell Library in Glasgow, and the British Newspaper Library at Colindale.

Thanks also, for their various help in reading over sections of the manuscript, translation, and suggesting avenues of research to Jon Adams, David Barber, Maurício Ribeiro Barros, Hanspeter Born, Duncan Castles, Marcus Christenson, James Copnall, Graham Curry, Sorin Dumitrescu, Dave Farrar, Igor Goldes, Luke Gosset, Gavin Hamilton, Georg Heitz, Paul Howarth, Emil Ianchev, Maciej Iwanski, Richard Jolly, John Keith, Thomas Knellwolf, Jim Lawton, Andy Lyons, Ben Lyttleton, Dan Magnowski, Emma McAllister, Kevin McCarra, Rachel Nicholson, Vladimir Novak, Gunnar Persson, Andy Rose, Paul Rowan, Ljiljana Ruzić, Milena Ruzić, Dominic Sandbrook, John Schumacher, Hugh Sleight, Rob Smyth, Graham Spiers, György Szepesi, Eric Weil, Duncan White, Axel Vartanyan, Shinobu Yamanaka, and Bruno Ziauddin.

Thanks to my agent, David Luxton, and my editor at Orion, Ian Preece, for their unflagging support and helpful interventions, and to the copyeditor, Chris Hawkes, for his diligence.

And thanks, finally, to Ian Hawkey for spending so much of the Cup of Nations sharing his expertise in matters of punctuation, and to Network Rail for the points failure that led to the long wait just north of Durham during which the flaw in Reep's theory became apparent to me.

ACKNOWLEDGMENTS
TO THE REVISED EDITION

Many of those who helped with the first edition were of great assistance also with this revised version so, again, I owe a debt of gratitude to them. But I must also thank Alexander Jackson of the National Football Museum for his wisdom on all things pre-war and his generosity in sharing research; Martin Cloake for his help with the additional material on the Spurs teams of Peter McWilliam and Arthur Rowe; Esteban Bekerman, Ed Malyon, Martin Mazur, Ezequiel Fernández Moores, Joel Richards, and Pablo Vignone for their advice in Argentina; and Tim Vickery for sharing his vast knowledge of the Brazilian game.

Additional thanks are due to Rob Smyth for his obsession with the Denmark team of the eighties and his generosity in sharing his analysis of them.

And thanks to Nick Wehmeier for coming up with the "Total Recall" chapter title.

I should, of course, reiterate my gratitude to my agent, David Luxton. At Orion, my thanks to Alan Samson and Paul Murphy for their help with this edition, and of course to my editor Ian Preece and the copyeditor John English. Thanks to Carl Bromley at Nation Books and to copyeditor Carrie Watterson and project editor Melissa Veronesi for their help with the US edition.

And huge thanks, as ever, to Kat Petersen, for her help and support and for essentially seeing subediting as a way of life.

FOREWORD TO THE REVISED EDITION

When, in 2005, I wrote the article for *FourFourTwo* that would lead to the thoughts that led to the pitch that led to *Inverting the Pyramid*, tactics were on the periphery of British soccer coverage. Thirteen years on, they have long since moved into the mainstream. If not for the majority of English fans, then at least for a significant minority, watching Jamie Carragher and Gary Neville dissecting the weekend's action on a giant interactive screen on Monday night has become essential. Every newspaper carries regular tactical columns, there are dozens of tactics blogs, and terms like *false nine* and *inverted winger* have become commonplace.

Inverting the Pyramid has been part of that movement. It didn't, as some have suggested, cause it; rather it caught a wave that was rising anyway and perhaps helped provide a historical context for those with an interest in analyzing what they were watching. English soccer can still feel Luddite at times, but its consumption is growing in sophistication every day. In fact, it may be that, for some, the interest in tactics has gone too far and become an obsession.

I made the point in the prologue when the book was first published in 2008, but it's worth reiterating given that so many seem to cast me as some kind of tactical fundamentalist: I don't believe tactics are the only thing that determines how a side plays, and I don't believe tactics are always the most important aspect in how a game works out. Rather they are one aspect among many—a neglected one perhaps, but just one thread, alongside ability, fitness, motivation, power, and luck, in an immensely complex tapestry. Not only that, but I don't believe tactics can be separated from the other aspects: a physically fit team must play in a different way than a tired team, a team low on confidence perhaps needs to play in a more cautious style, a team that includes dilettantish players must set up in a way to cover those deficiencies. Everything is related.

Equally, designations of formations can at times seem a little arbitrary. Just how far behind the main striker does the second striker have to play for 4–4–2 to become 4–4–1–1? And how advanced do the wide midfielders have to be for that to become a 4–2–3–1? And if the support striker then pulls a little deeper and the wide men advance, is that still 4–2–3–1 or has it become 4–2–1–3 or even 4–3–3? Given that full-backs often push high, so their average position places them level with the holding midfielders, why don't we term some 4–2–3–1s as a 2–4–3–1? The terms essentially are shorthand, often rooted in convention as much as actuality, a useful if slightly crude way of giving a basic idea of a lineup.

In tactics, there are few absolutes. There certainly is no "best" formation, something I've been asked about repeatedly in the past decade. While there must be a basic balance of attack and defense, everything depends on circumstance: on the players available, on their physical and mental state, on the conditions, on form, on what a side wants from a game—and, of course, on the opposition and their players, formation, and physical and mental state. Not merely is everything related; everything is relative.

The first edition of this book closed with some observations on the strikerless formations deployed by Roma and Manchester United and cited Carlos Alberto Parreira's theory that 4–6–0 would be the formation of the future. He didn't use the term *false nine* but that is what we've now learned to call the player who drops deep from the position in which an orthodox center-forward used to operate, and the fact that the term *false nine* is now used so freely, is so instantly understood, suggests both how common the trend is and how interest in tactical analysis has grown over the past ten years.

In that time, Pep Guardiola turned Barcelona into the greatest side the world has known for at least two decades and, in doing so, altered the tactical landscape. The second edition considered the origins and implementation of his philosophy and examined, in far greater detail than the original, the evolution of that passing style from Queen's Park through Newcastle and Tottenham to Ajax and Barcelona. It looked at how Total Football evolved under Louis van Gaal and Marcelo Bielsa and also tried to place Barcelona in context, looking at the origins of the Spanish game and how *la furia* became the ideal in Spain before the arrival of Vic Buckingham and Rinus Michels.

But there were additions everywhere—offering more nuanced interpretations, refining, and expanding. There was far more detail, for instance, on the British game in the Edwardian age, which I had perhaps given the impression was universally obsessed by a robotic 2–3–5. Similarly, the birth of the back three in the 1920s was a much slower and more complicated process than I'd acknowledged; astonishingly, C. B. Fry was discussing it as early as 1897. There was a lot more as well about the return of the back three in the early eighties: where I'd previously credited the development to Carlos Bilardo and Franz Beckenbauer, I now realize that Sepp Piontek and Ćiro Blažević have at least as good a claim.

And there were the smaller details yielded by further research—and particularly by readers getting in touch to point out omissions or suggest alternative interpretations. I had been vaguely aware, for instance, that there was probably an Argentinian equivalent of Dori Kürschner, the Hungarian who took the W-system of defending to Brazil. Sure enough, reading through a file of articles from Argentinian newspapers of the thirties given to me by the historian Esteban Bekerman, I realized that Emerigo Hirschl, who won the double with River Plate in 1936 and who I'd assumed was Argentinian, was actually Imre or Emerich Hirschl, a Hungarian who'd (probably) emigrated in 1929. Further research indicated he had developed a W-defense but that it had taken three years to be fully acknowledged. Like Kürschner, Hirschl was Jewish, which hints at how profoundly the development of soccer was shaped by rising anti-Semitism in the thirties.

This third edition continues that process of revision, correcting, and refining, but also picks up on what has happened since Guardiola left Barcelona. Even those who never attempted to replicated his style—or who actively opposed it—have been influenced by him. Every top side now plays with the knowledge of what was possible with the right manager and the right players at the right club at the right time, but the soccer world is no longer governed by *guardiolisme*. Rather it is one among a number of competing strategies: those born in Germany from the belated adoption of pressing, and those that stem from the Argentinian tradition of *anti-fútbol* and José Mourinho's inversion of the same Cruyffian principles. It's that development that is the major new material in this edition.

The more you research, of course, the more connections start to emerge, the more you begin to see the networks of influence that underlie the development of tactics. Take for instance the fact that the two Englishmen to have managed Barcelona since the Second World War both played under coaches who played at Spurs under Peter McWilliam in the late thirties—Terry Venables under Bill Nicholson and Bobby Robson under Vic Buckingham, the man who laid the foundations of the modern passing game at Camp Nou. Perhaps that's just a coincidence, but it hints at a nexus of tradition and core philosophy that provides a framework for the whole game. Soccer tactics are always evolving; so too must its history.

London, January 2018

PROLOGUE

A tapas bar in the Bairro Alto in Lisbon, the evening after England beat Switzerland 3–0 in the 2004 European Championship. The rioja had been flowing, and a multinational group of journalists was discussing whether Sven-Göran Eriksson had been right to stick with an orthodox 4–4–2, or whether, as it had been suggested he would, he should have switched to a midfield diamond. Had player-power, a late-night delegation of midfielders, forced the unexpected reversion to the flat four in midfield?

"Oh, what's the difference?" an English colleague protested. "They're the same players. The formation isn't important. It's not worth writing about."

There was a splutter of indignation. As I raised a drunken finger to jab home my belief that people like him shouldn't be allowed to watch soccer, let alone talk about it, an Argentinian, probably wisely, pulled my arm down. "The formation is the only thing that's important," she said. "It's not worth writing about anything else."

And there, in a moment, was laid bare the prime deficiency of the English game. Soccer is not about players—or at least not just about players; it is about shape and about space, about the intelligent deployment of players and their movement within that deployment. (I should, perhaps, make clear that by "tactics" I mean a combination of formation and style: one 4–4–2 can be as different from another as Steve Stone from Ronaldinho). The Argentinian was, I hope, exaggerating for effect, for heart, soul, effort, desire, strength, power, speed, passion, and skill all play their parts, but, for all that, there is also a theoretical dimension, and, as in other disciplines, the English have on the whole proved themselves unwilling to grapple with the abstract.

That is a failing, and it is something that frustrates me, but this is not a polemic about the failure of English soccer. Apart from anything else, unless we are making comparisons with the interwar era, I'm not convinced that English soccer *is* failing. Sven-Göran Eriksson was derided by the end, but only Alf Ramsey had previously guided England to the quarterfinals of three successive international tournaments. Whether Steve McClaren's failure to get England through a Euro 2008 qualifying group that was far tougher than the xenophobes imagined represents a blip or the beginning of a prolonged slide only history will tell, but it seems perverse to start arranging the wake when England would have qualified had Steven Gerrard converted a simple chance four minutes after half-time in Moscow.

Look at Uruguay, look at Austria: that is decline (even taking into account the Oscar Washington Tabárez–inspired spike in performances in 2010 and 2011). Look at Scotland, still punching heroically above their weight despite the restrictions imposed by a population of only five million. Look, most of all, at Hungary, the team who, in November 1953, rang the death knell for English dreams of superiority. By the time Ferenc Puskás, the greatest player of that most glorious of teams, died in November 2006, Hungary had slumped so far that they were struggling to remain in the top one hundred of the FIFA world rankings. *That* is decline.

Nonetheless, for English soccer, the 6–3 defeat to Hungary at Wembley stands as the watershed. It was England's first defeat at home to continental opposition, and, more than that, the manner in which they were outplayed annihilated the idea that England still ruled the world. "The story of British football and the foreign challenge," wrote Brian Glanville in *Soccer Nemesis*, his reaction to that defeat, "is the story of a vast superiority, sacrificed through stupidity, short-sightedness, and wanton insularity. It is a story of shamefully wasted talent, extraordinary complacency and infinite self-deception." And so it was.

And yet, thirteen years later, England became world champions. The vast superiority may have been squandered, but England were evidently still among the elite. In the past half century, I'm not sure that much has changed. Yes, perhaps we do have a tendency to get carried away before major tournaments, which makes a quarterfinal exit sting rather more than it probably ought, but England remain one of the eight or ten sides who have a realistic chance of winning a World Cup or European Championship (freakish champions like Denmark or Greece notwithstanding). The question then is why that opportunity has not been taken. Perhaps a more coherent structure of youth coaching, an increased focus on technique and tactical discipline, limits on the number of foreign players in the Premiership, snapping players out of their complacent bubbles, or any of the other hundred panaceas that have been suggested would improve England's chances, but success is a nebulous quarry. Luck retains its place in soccer, and success can never be guaranteed, particularly not over the six- or seven-game span of an international tournament.

A theory has grown up that winning the World Cup in 1966 was the worst thing that could have happened to English soccer. Rob Steen, in *The*

Mavericks, and David Downing, in his books on England's rivalries with Argentina and Germany, argue that that success set England back because it established deep in the English soccer consciousness the notion that the functionality of Alf Ramsey's side was the only way to achieve success. I don't fundamentally disagree with either of them—although the trait predates Ramsey—but it seems to me that the real problem is not so much the way Ramsey's England played as the fact that, in the minds of generations of fans and coaches in England, it laid out a "right" way of playing. Just because something was correct in a particular circumstance, with particular players, and at a particular stage of soccer's development, does not mean it will always be effective. If England in 1966 had tried to play like Brazilians, they would have ended up like Brazil: kicked out of the tournament in the group stage by physically more aggressive opponents—in fact they would have been worse off, for they had few, if any, players with the technical attributes of the Brazilians.

If there is one thing that distinguishes the coaches who have had success over a prolonged period—Sir Alex Ferguson, Valeriy Lobanovskyi, Bill Shankly, Boris Arkadiev—it is that they have always been able to evolve. Their teams played the game in very different ways, but what they all shared was the clarity of vision to successfully recognize when the time was right to abandon a winning formula and the courage to implement a new one. What I want to make clear is that I don't believe there is a "correct" way to play. Yes, from an emotional and aesthetic point of view, I warmed more to the passing of Arsène Wenger's Arsenal than to the pragmatism of José Mourinho's Chelsea, but that is a personal preference; it is not to say one is right and one is wrong.

I am well aware, equally, that compromises have to be made between theory and practice. On a theoretical level, I respond to Lobanovskyi's Dynamo Kyiv or the AC Milan of Fabio Capello. Yet on the pitch, when at university I had for two years the chance to influence the style of my college side (well, the seconds and thirds at least), we played highly functional soccer. Admittedly, we weren't very good, and we probably got the best out of the players available, but I suspect we could have played more aesthetically pleasing soccer than we did. Amid the beer-soaked celebrations that followed a title each year, I'm not sure anybody was too bothered.

It is not even so simple, though, as to say that the "correct" way of playing is the one that wins most often, because only the dourest of Gradgrinds would claim that success is measured merely in points and trophies; there must also be room for romance. That tension—between beauty and cynicism, between what Brazilians call *futebol d'arte* and *futebol de resultados*—is a constant, perhaps because it is so fundamental not merely to sports but also to life: to win or to play the game well? It is hard to think of any significant actions that are not in some way a negotiation between the two extremes of pragmatism and idealism.

The difficulty, then, is in isolating of what that extra quality comprises. Glory is not measured in absolutes, and what constitutes it changes with circumstance and time. British crowds soon grow tired of patient buildup, but in, for instance, Capello's first spell at Real Madrid, crowds booed when Fernando Hierro hit long accurate passes for Roberto Carlos to run onto. To the modern sensibility, it is baffling that the early amateur soccer players considered passing unmanly, and yet it may be in time to come—as indeed it already is in certain cultures—that the present-day British distaste for diving seems just as naively irrelevant.

Even acknowledging that soccer is about more than simply winning, though, it would be ludicrous to deny the importance of victory. Wenger can be frustratingly quixotic at times, but, as his negative tactics in the 2005 FA Cup final showed, even he at times acknowledges the need to win. To condemn Ramsey, when he brought the only international success England has known is a luxury English fans cannot afford; to accuse him of ruining English soccer rather than saluting his tactical acuity seems willfully perverse.

I'm not saying we should discount them entirely, but it is dangerous, anyway, to read too much into performances at the major international tournaments. The achievements of Spain have skewed the perspective, but it is rare that there is one outstanding side in the world, rarer still that they actually win the World Cup. The example of Brazil in 2002, casually brushing aside the opposition, is almost unique, and even then, particularly given their lethargic qualifying campaign, it seemed almost supremacy by default as the other contenders capitulated in the heat. France probably were the best side in the 1998 tournament, but they only really showed that in the final. Two years later, they were significantly the best side at Euro 2000 and yet were within a minute of losing the final to Italy.

In fact, two of the greatest sides of all time, the Hungarians of 1954 and the Dutch of 1974, lost in the final—both to West Germany, which may or may not be coincidence. A third, the Brazil of 1982, didn't even get that far. 1966 aside, England's best performance in a World Cup came in 1990, a tournament so beloved for Gazza's tears and an England penalty shoot-out defeat—a trope that would become tediously familiar but which, back then, carried the resonance of tragic failure—that it helped kick-start the 1990s boom. Yet England's preparation for that tournament was awful: they scraped through qualifying; their manager Bobby Robson was pilloried in the press on an almost daily basis, the media was expelled from the training camp after revelations about the relationship between various players and a local PR rep, and the whole thing was played out in the shadow of hooliganism. Against the Republic of Ireland and Egypt, England were dire, and against Belgium and Cameroon they were lucky; only against Holland and West Germany, neither of which games they won, did they play well. In fact, the only team England defeated in ninety minutes was Egypt. And this, somehow, led to soccer's middle-class revolution.

Over the course of a league season, luck, momentum, injuries, errors by players, and errors by referees even themselves out—if not absolutely, then certainly far, far more than they do over seven games in a summer. That England have gone more than fifty years without winning a trophy is annoying—and for that various managers, players, officials, and opponents bear a degree of responsibility—but it does not equate to a fundamental decline. It is possible that there is a fundamental flaw in the way England play the game, and an almost self-conscious Luddism hasn't helped, but it would be hard to make a serious case for a total overhaul of the English game on the basis of results in major tournaments alone.

Globalization is blurring national styles, but tradition, perpetuated by coaches, players, pundits, and fans, is strong enough that the styles remain distinguishable. What became apparent in the writing of this book is that every nation came fairly quickly to recognize its strengths and that no nation seems quite to trust them. Brazilian soccer is all about flair and improvisation, but it looks yearningly at the defensive organization of the Italians. Italian soccer is about cynicism and tactical intelligence, but it admires and fears the physical courage of the English. English soccer is about tenacity and energy, but it believes it ought to mimic the technique of the Brazilians.

The history of tactics, it seems, is the history of two interlinked tensions: aesthetics versus results on the one side and technique versus physique on the other. What confuses the issue is that those who grow up in a technical culture tend to see a more robust approach as a way of getting results, while those from a physical culture see pragmatism in technique; and beauty—or at least what fans prefer to watch—remains very much in the eye of the beholder. British fans may admire (although most seemed not to) the cerebral jousting of, say, the 2003 Champions League final between AC Milan and Juventus, but what they actually want to see is the crash-bang-wallop of the Premier League. That is not entirely fair, for Premier League soccer is far more skillful now than it was even ten years ago, but it remains quicker and less possession driven than any other major league. Judging by the figure paid for overseas television rights, the rest of the world thinks it has found a happy balance.

The midfifties saw the publication of a rash of books that tried to come to terms with England's declining status. Glanville's was probably the angriest, but just as revealing is *Soccer Revolution* by Willy Meisl, the younger brother of the great Austrian coach Hugo Meisl. As staunchly Anglophile as only an immigrant can be, his work is more of a lament. For them, blaming the unapologetic conservatism of the English game made sense, and, with the benefit of hindsight, it can be seen as part of a more general cultural attack on an establishment that had overseen the end of empire but was yet to find an appropriate role. England's blinkeredness *was* at fault for the loss of soccer superiority. Yes, the rest of the world would have caught up at some point, for, as Glanville wearily notes, pupils have a habit of overcoming their masters; but these masters, through their arrogance and insularity, were complicit in their own downfall.

That, though, was then. England's fall from her pedestal is no longer news. In that, by tracing the tactical evolution of the game, it attempts to explain how we got to where we are now, this book belongs to the same family as *Soccer Nemesis* and *Soccer Revolution*, but it sets out from a very different present, with England failing to rise rather than falling. It is, anyway, a history, not a polemic.

A NOTE ON TERMINOLOGY

In Britain, the term *center-half* is regularly used to describe a central defender. There are historical reasons for this, which are explained at the beginning of Chapter 4, but, for the sake of clarity, I have used *center-half* specifically to describe the central midfielder in the 2–3–5 formation. Hopefully the terms used for other positions are less ambiguous.

1

FROM GENESIS TO THE PYRAMID

In the beginning there was chaos, and soccer was without form. Then came the Victorians, who codified it, and after them the theorists, who analyzed it. It wasn't until the late 1920s that tactics in anything resembling a modern sense came to be recognized or discussed, but as early as the 1870s there was an acknowledgment that the arrangement of players on the field made a significant difference to the way the game was played. In its earliest form, though, soccer knew nothing of such sophistication.

Various cultures can point to games that involved kicking a ball, but, for all the claims of Rome, Greece, Egypt, the Caribbean, Mexico, China, or Japan to be the home of soccer, the modern sport has its roots in the mob game of medieval Britain. Rules—inasmuch as they existed at all—varied from place to place, but the game essentially involved two teams trying to force a roughly spherical object to a target at opposite ends of a notional field. It was violent, unruly, and anarchic, and it was repeatedly outlawed. Only in the early nineteenth century, when the public schools—their thinking shaped by advocates of muscular Christianity—decided that sports could be harnessed for the moral edification of their students, did anything approaching what we would today recognize as soccer emerge. Before there could be tactics, though, there had, first of all, to be a coherent set of rules.

Even by the end of the nineteenth century, when the earliest formations began to emerge, it was rare to subject them to too much thought. In soccer's earliest days, the notion of abstract consideration of tactics, of charts with crosses and arrows, would have been all but inconceivable, and yet the development of the game is instructive in what it reveals of the mind-set of soccer, the unseen, often unacknowledged hard wiring from which stemmed British conceptions of how it should be played (and, for forty years after the rules were first drawn up, there was nothing but a British conception).

The boom came in the early Victorian era and, as David Winner demonstrates in *Those Feet*, was rooted in the idea that the empire was in decline and that moral turpitude was somehow to blame. Team sports, it was thought, were to be promoted because they discouraged solipsism, and solipsism allowed masturbation to flourish, and there could be nothing more debilitating than that. The Reverend Edward Thring, headmaster of Uppingham School, for instance, insisted in a sermon that it would lead to "early and dishonoured graves." Soccer was seen as the perfect antidote, because, as E. A. C. Thompson would write in *The Boys' Champion Story Paper* in 1901, "There is no more manly sport than football. It is so peculiarly and typically British, demanding pluck, coolness and endurance."

There are very good politico-economic reasons for the coincidence, but there is also a neat symbolism in the fact that, after soccer had been used to shore up the empire, Britain's ultimate decline as an imperial power coincided with the erosion of the home nations' dominance in soccer. Soccer soared in popularity through the first half of the nineteenth century, but in those early days rules varied from school to school, largely according to conditions. At Cheltenham and Rugby, for instance, with their wide, open fields, the game differed little from the mob game. A player could fall on the ground, be fallen upon by a great many of his fellows, and emerge from the mud relatively unscathed. In the cloisters of Charterhouse and Westminster, though, such rough-and-tumble play would have led to broken bones, so it was there that the dribbling game developed. That outlawed— or at least restricted—handling of the ball, but the game still differed radically from modern soccer. Formations were unheard of, while the length of the game and even the numbers of players on each side were still to be established. Essentially, prefects or older pupils would run with the ball at their feet, their teammates lined up behind them (backing up) in case the ball bounced loose in a tackle, while the opposition players—or, at certain schools, fags (that is, younger pupils who were effectively their servants)— would try to stop them.

Interplay among forwards, if it happened at all, was rudimentary, and from that sprouted certain fundamentals that would shape the course of early English soccer: the game was all about dribbling; passing, cooperation, and defending were perceived as somehow inferior. Head-down charging, certainly, was to be preferred to thinking, a manifestation, some would say, of the English attitude to life in general. In the public schools, thinking tended to be frowned upon as a matter of course. (As late as 1946, the Hungarian comic writer George Mikes could write of how, when he had first arrived in Britain, he had been proud when a woman called him "clever," only to realize later the loadedness of the term and the connotations of untrustworthiness it carried.)

The differing sets of rules frustrated efforts to establish soccer at universities until, in 1848, H. C. Malden of Godalming, Surrey, convened a meeting in his rooms at Cambridge with representatives of Harrow, Eton, Rugby, Winchester, and Shrewsbury—and, remarkably, two nonpublic schools—at which were collated what might be considered the first unified Laws of the Game. "The new rules were printed as the 'Cambridge Rules,'" Malden wrote. "Copies were distributed and pasted up on Parker's Piece [an area of open grassland in the center of the city], and very satisfactorily they worked, for it is right to add that they were loyally kept and I never heard of any public school man who gave up playing for not liking the rules."

Fourteen years later the southern version of the game took another step towards uniformity as J. C. Thring—the younger brother of Edward, the Uppingham headmaster—having been thwarted in an earlier attempt to draw up a set of unified rules at Cambridge, brought out a set of ten laws entitled "The Simplest Game." The following October, another variant, the "Cambridge University Football Rules," was published. Crucially, a month later, the Football Association was formed, and it immediately set about trying to determine a definitive set of laws of the game, intending still to combine the best elements of both the dribbling and the handling game.

It failed. The debate was long and furious but, after a fifth meeting at the Freemason's Tavern in Lincoln's Inn Fields in London, at 7:00 p.m. on December 8, 1863, carrying the ball by hand was outlawed, and soccer and rugby went their separate ways. The dispute, strangely, was not over the use of the hand but over hacking; that is, whether kicking opponents in the shins should be allowed. F. W. Campbell of Blackheath was very much in favor. "If you do away with [hacking]," he said, "you will do away with all the courage and pluck of the game, and I will be bound to bring over a lot of Frenchmen who would beat you with a week's practice." Sports, he appears to have believed, were about pain, brutality, and manliness; without that, if it actually came down to *skill*, any old foreigner might be able to win. A joke it may have been, but that his words were part of a serious debate is indicative of the general ethos, even if Blackheath did end up resigning from the association when hacking was eventually outlawed.

The dribbling game prevailed, largely because of Law 6, the forerunner of the offside law: "When a player has kicked the ball, anyone of the same side who is nearer to the opponent's goal-line is out of play, and may not touch the ball himself, nor in any way whatever prevent any other player from doing so, until he is in play." In other words, passes had to be either lateral or backward; for Englishmen convinced that anything other than charging directly at a target was suspiciously subtle and unmanly, that would clearly never do.

Dribbling itself was rather different from modern conceptions of the art. In his history of the FA Cup, Geoffrey Green, the late soccer correspondent of the *Times* of London, quotes an unnamed writer of the 1870s:

A really first-class player . . . will never lose sight of the ball, at the same time keeping his attention employed in the spying out of any gaps in the enemy's ranks, or any weak points in the defence, which may give him a favourable chance of arriving at the coveted goal. To see some players guide and steer a ball through a circle of opposing legs, turning and twisting as the occasion requires, is a sight not to be forgotten. . . . Skill in dribbling . . . necessitates something more than a go-ahead, fearless, headlong onslaught of the enemy's citadel; it requires an eye quick at discovering a weak point, and *nous* to calculate and decide the chances of a successful passage.

In terms of shape, it sounds rather like an elementary form of modern rugby union, only without any handling.

Tactics—if that is not too grand a word in the circumstances—were similarly basic, even after the number of players had been fixed at eleven. Teams simply chased the ball. It wasn't even until the 1870s that the goalkeeper became a recognized and universally accepted position, not until 1909 that he began to wear a different colored shirt than the rest of his team, and not until 1912 that he was restricted to handling the ball only in his own box—a rule change implemented to thwart the Sunderland goalkeeper Leigh Richmond Roose's habit of bouncing the ball to the halfway line. If there were a formation at all in those earliest days, it would probably have been classified as two or three backs, with nine or eight forwards.

Even when Law 6 was changed in 1866, following Eton's convention and permitting a forward pass provided there were at least three members of the defensive team between the player and the opponent's goal when the ball was played (i.e., one more than the modern offside law), it seems to have made little difference to those brought up on the dribbling game. As late as the 1870s, Charles W. Alcock, a leading early player and administrator (and the first man to be caught offside after the 1866 law change), was writing evangelically of "the grand and essential principle of backing up. By 'backing up,' of course, I shall be understood to mean the following closely on a fellow-player to assist him, if required, or to take on the ball in the case of his being attacked, or otherwise prevented from continuing his onward course." In other words, even a decade after the establishment of the FA, one of the founding fathers of the game considered it necessary to explain to others that if one of their teammates were charging head down at goal, it might be an idea to go and help him—although expecting to receive the ball from him volitionally seems to have been a step too far.

That, at least, is how it was in the south. The north was making its own advances, particularly in south Yorkshire, where a combination of Old Harrovian teachers at Sheffield College and the traditional folk games of Holmfirth and Penistone led to the establishment of the Sheffield Club on October 24, 1857, initially as a way for cricketers to stay fit during the winter. On Boxing Day that year, the world's first interclub match was played as they beat Hallam Football Club 2–0. The sport grew rapidly: within five years crowds of several hundred were common, and fifteen clubs had been established in the area. The Sheffield Club drew up its own set of rules, published in 1862, which, significantly, although showing the influence of Harrow, Rugby, and Winchester, made no mention of offside.

There appears, though, to have been some regulation, because when Sheffield's secretary William Chesterman wrote to the newly founded Football Association on November 30, 1863, submitting the club's subscription and his contribution to the debate over laws, he noted, "We have no printed rule at all like your *No. 6*, but I have written in the book a rule, which is always played by us." Exactly what that was remains unclear. Sheffield's formal acceptance of offside came only in 1865, as part of horse trading over rules ahead of a game against Notts County, and even then it required only one defensive player to be goal side of the forward when the ball was played for him to be onside. That, clearly, made passing far more viable, although it is debatable to what extent the opportunities it provided were taken up.

The FA failed to respond to Sheffield's overtures, and so for several years two codes—or rather, two basic codes, because there were also variations in Nottingham and other cities—existed. They met for the first time in 1866, with a match between London and Sheffield in Battersea Park on March 31, 1866. London won 2–0, with contemporary reports suggesting they were the more skillful side but had been unsettled by Sheffield's physicality.

After much back and forth over whose regulations to play by, Alcock brought a London team to Sheffield in December 1871. Playing under Sheffield rules, the home team won 3–1, their victory generally being attributed to their organized formation. That, taken in conjunction with their more liberal offside law, might suggest a passing game, but it seems Sheffield were rather more rooted in dribbling even than London. According to Percy M. Young in *Football in Sheffield*, the Sheffield players found "the dribbling skill of Alcock quite outside their range of experience. Moreover, Alcock was alive to the virtues of the well-placed pass (the local players adopted the simpler and more direct method of ignoring their own colleagues and making straight for goal on every possible occasion) and the delicate combination between himself and Chenery was a revelation to 2,000 delighted spectators." There would be eighteen further meetings before Sheffield finally came into the FA fold in 1878.

There may not have been a culture of passing in Sheffield, but it does seem they would punt the ball long to clear their lines. In *Soccer: The World Game*, Geoffrey Green notes that when Sheffield players arrived in London for an exhibition match in 1875 and began "butting the ball with their heads," the crowd regarded it as "something for amusement rather than admiration." In a pure dribbling game, of course, there would have been no need for the ball ever to leave the ground, other—perhaps—than to lift it over a challenging foot. Only if the ball were played a significant distance in the air would heading have been necessary.

The Scottish Football Association annual's report of an 1877 match between Glasgow and Sheffield makes the point clearly:

> That the game was a very well contested one, and victory has rested with the best side, no one will deny; but that it was a pretty game, abounding in fine displays of combined dribbling, which has frequently distinguished a Scottish team above all others, few will admit. . . . The fact cannot be hidden . . . that the tactics pursued by the Sheffield team on Saturday were partially responsible for this inasmuch as they play a different set of rules from those of the English and Scottish Associations, and to them our "off-side" rule is next to a dead letter. In this manner, long kicking was largely indulged in on Saturday on their side; and in order to meet the same style of play, the Glasgow men actually lost that united action which had led them on to victory in many a harder fought field.

The spread of passing itself—that "united action"—can be traced back to one game, soccer's first international, played between England and Scotland at the West of Scotland Cricket Ground, Partick, in 1872. England's lineup comprised a goal, a three-quarter back, a half-back, a fly-kick, four players listed simply as "middle," two as "left side," and one as "right side," which, to try to apply modern notation, sounds like something approximating a lop-sided 1–2–7. "The formation of a team as a rule," Alcock noted, " . . . was to provide for seven forwards, and only four players to constitute the three lines of defence. The last line was, of course, the goalkeeper, and in front of him was only one full-back, who had again before him but two forwards, to check the rushes of the opposing forwards."

Scotland were represented by the Queen's Park club, which, until the foundation of the Scottish FA in 1873, governed the Scottish game—functioning much like the Marylebone Cricket Club in cricket or the

First International: Scotland 0 England 0, Partick, 30 November 1872

Royal and Ancient in golf. Crucially, they were about eighteen pounds per man lighter than England. It is indicative of the physicality of early soccer that most pundits seemed to have expected that weight advantage would give England a comfortable victory, but what it actually did was to stimulate the imagination. Although direct evidence is sketchy, it seems probable that, as Richard McBrearty of the Scottish Football Museum argues, Queen's Park decided they had to try to pass the ball around England rather than engage in a more direct man-to-man contest in which they were likely to be outmuscled, and their formation was very definitely a 2–2–6. The ploy paid off. England, with a more established tradition and a far larger pool of players from which to select, were firm favorites, but they were held to a goalless draw. "The Englishmen," the report in the *Glasgow Herald* said, "had all the advantage in respect of weight, their average being about two stones heavier than the Scotchmen [a slight exaggeration], and they also had the advantage in pace. The strong point with the home club was that they played excellently well together."

That success may have confirmed the notion of passing as superior to dribbling—north of the border at least—but it could never have worked had passing not been part of the game in Scotland almost from the start. When the Queen's Park club was established in 1867, the version of the offside law they adopted held that a player was infringing only if he were both beyond the penultimate man and in the final fifteen yards of the field. That, clearly, was legislation far more conducive to passing than either the FA's first offside law or its 1866 revision. Queen's Park accepted the three-man variant when they joined the FA on November 9, 1870, but by then the idea of passing was already implanted. In Scotland the ball was there to be kicked, not merely dribbled, as H. N. Smith's poem celebrating Queen's Park's victory over Hamilton Gymnasium in 1869 suggests:

> *The men are picked—the ball is kicked,*
> *High in the air it bounds;*
> *O'er many a head the ball is sped . . .*

Robert Smith, a Queen's Park member and Scotland's right-winger in that first international, remarked after playing in the first of the four matches Alcock arranged between England and a team of London-based Scots that were the forerunners to proper internationals. "While the ball was in play," he wrote in a letter back to his club, "the practice was to run or dribble the ball with the feet, instead of indulging in high or long balls."

One of Queen's Park's motivations in joining the English association was to try to alleviate the difficulties they were having finding opponents who would agree to play by a standard set of rules. In the months leading up to their acceptance into the FA, they played games of ten, fourteen, fifteen and sixteen a side, and in 1871–1872 they managed just three games. "The club, however," Richard Robinson wrote in his 1920 history of Queen's Park, "never neglected practice." Their isolation and regular matches among themselves meant that idiosyncrasies became more pronounced—as they would for Argentina in the thirties—and so the passing game was effectively hot housed, free from the irksome obstacle of bona fide opponents. "In these [practice] games," Robinson went on,

> the dribbling and passing . . . which raised the Scottish game to the level of fine art, were developed. Dribbling was a characteristic of English play, and it was not until very much later that the Southerners came to see that the principles laid down in the Queen's Park method of transference of the ball, accompanied by strong backing up, were those that got the most out of the team. Combination was the chief characteristic of the Queen's Park's play. These essentials struck Mr C. W. Alcock and in one of his earlier Football Annuals formed the keynote for a eulogium on Scottish players, accompanied by earnest dissertations advocating the immediate adoption by English players of the methods which had brought the game to such a high state of proficiency north of the Tweed.

Alcock, in fact, was nowhere near as convinced as that. Although he professed himself intrigued by the "combination game"—and for all the prowess he had shown at Sheffield—he expressed doubt in that annual of 1879 as to whether "a wholesale system of passing pays." Passing, he evidently believed, was all very well as an option, but should never be allowed to supplant the dribbling game.

Nonetheless, it quickly spread, particularly in Scotland, where the influence of Queen's Park was all encompassing, leading ultimately to the highly romanticized "pattern-weaving" approach, characterized by strings of short passes zigzagging between the forward and half lines. Queen's Park organized the Scotland side for the first two internationals and even after the foundation of the Scottish Football Association remained a powerful voice in shaping the sport. They acted as evangelists, traveling across the country to play exhibition games. Records of a match against Vale of Leven, who became one of the early powerhouses of Scottish soccer, describe the game being stopped at regular intervals so the rules and playing methods could be described, while a game in Edinburgh in 1873 kick-started soccer in the capital. It is perhaps indicative of the impact of those matches that the Borders remain a rugby stronghold: a missionary game Queen's Park were scheduled to play there had to be canceled because of

FA Cup commitments, so soccer's seeds were never sown. As McBrearty points out, Scotland's demographics, with the majority of the population living in the central belt between the Glasgow and Edinburgh conurbations, made it far easier for one particular style to take hold than it was in England, where each region had its own idea of how the game should be played.

Queen's Park's tactics in the first international raised eyebrows in England, but the southward spread of the passing game can be attributed largely to two men: Henry Renny-Tailyour and John Blackburn, who played for Scotland in their victory over England in the second international. Both were lieutenants in the army and both played their club soccer for the Royal Engineers, carrying the Scottish style with them to Kent. "The Royal Engineers were the first football team to introduce the 'combination' style of play," W. E. Clegg, a former Sheffield player, wrote in the *Sheffield Independent* in 1930. "Formerly the matches Sheffield played with them were won by us, but we were very much surprised that between one season and another they had considered 'military football tactics' with the result that Sheffield was badly beaten by the new conditions of play."

The passing approach was implanted in school soccer by the Reverend Spencer Walker, as he returned as a master to Lancing College, where he had been a pupil, and set about turning "a mere bally-rag into a well-ordered team." "The first thing I fell upon," he wrote, "was the crowding of all the forwards on the leading forward. They crowded round him wherever they went. So I made Rule 1: Fixed places for all the forwards, with passing the ball from one to the other. You should have seen the faces of our first opponents, a sort of 'Where do we come in?' look."

For all Alcock's skepticism, it gradually became apparent that passing was the future. The Old Carthusians side that beat the Old Etonians 3–0 in the 1881 FA Cup final was noted for its combinations, particularly those between E. M. F. Prinsep and E. H. Parry, although the following year the Old Etonian goal that saw off Blackburn Rovers, the first northern side to reach the final, stemmed, Green wrote in his history of the FA Cup, from "a long dribble and cross-pass" from A. T. B. Dunn that laid in W. H. Anderson. Still, the Etonians were essentially a dribbling side.

The final flourish of the dribbling game came in 1883. For the first time the cup received more entries from outside London than from within, and for the first time the cup went north as Blackburn Olympic beat Old Etonians in the final. The amateur era—at least in terms of mind-set—was over; something acknowledged two years later when the FA legalized professionalism.

All the Olympic side had full-time jobs, and it caused something of a stir when their half-back and de facto manager, Jack Hunter, took them to

Blackpool for a training camp before the final. This was very evidently not the effortless superiority to which the amateurs aspired. Early in the game, injury reduced the Etonians to ten men, but it is doubtful whether they would have been able to cope with Olympic's unfamiliar tactic of hitting long sweeping passes from wing to wing. The winning goal, scored deep in extra time, was characteristic of the game as a whole: a cross-field ball from Tommy Dewhurst (a weaver) on the right found Jimmy Costley (a spinner) advancing in space on the left, and he had the composure to beat J. F. P. Rawlinson in the Etonian goal.

In Scotland, the superiority of passing was old news. "Take any club that has come to the front," the columnist "Silas Marner" wrote in the *Scottish Umpire* in August 1884, "and the onward strides will be found to date from the hour when the rough and tumble gave place to swift accurate passing and attending to the leather rather than the degraded desire merely to coup an opponent." Not that everybody was convinced. Two months later, after Jamestown Athletics had been beaten 4–1 in the Scottish Cup by Vale of Leven, "Olympian" was scathing of their combination game in his On the Wing column in the *Umpire*. "'Divide and Conquer' was a favourite dictum of the great Machiavelli when teaching princes how to govern. . . . What shall I say of the Jamestown's attempt to, I suppose, verify the truth of the aphorism. Their premises were right, but then they went sadly wrong with the conclusion. They made the grave mistake of dividing *themselves* instead of their opponents and so paid the penalty. And what a penalty! Tell it not in Gath. Publish it not in Askelon. Strategy can never take the place of eleven good pairs of nimble legs."

Well, it can and it did and, to the consternation of traditionalists in both England and Scotland, it meant one of the two center-forwards— who, it was found, tended to replicate each other's role in a passing game— slipping back into a deeper position, eventually becoming, over the course of the 1880s, a center-half in a 2–3–5 formation: the pyramid. There is a widespread belief as expressed by, for instance, the Hungarian coach Arpad Csanadi in his immense and influential coaching manual *Soccer*, that the 2–3–5 was first played by Cambridge University in 1883, but there is evidence to suggest they may have been using the system as much as six years before that. Nottingham Forest, equally, were enthusiastic advocates of the system by the late 1870s, inspired in their experiments by their captain Sam Widdowson, who also invented the shinpad.

Certainly Wrexham were employing a center-half when they faced Druids in the Welsh Cup final in 1878; their captain and fullback Charles Murless, a local real estate agent, deciding to withdraw E. A. Cross from the forward line, seemingly because he believed that the pace of the center-forward who remained, John Price, was sufficient to cover for any resulting

Wrexham 1 Druids 0, Welsh Cup final, Acton, 30 March 1878

shortfall in attack. He was vindicated as James Davies settled a tight game with the only goal two minutes from time.

The gradual spread of the 2–3–5 meant that the center-half soon developed into the fulcrum of the team, a figure far removed from the dour stopper he would become. He was a multiskilled, all-rounder, defender and attacker, leader and instigator, goal scorer and destroyer. He was, as the great Austrian soccer writer Willy Meisl put it, "the most important man on the field."

Intriguingly, the *Sheffield Independent,* in its report on the first floodlit game—an exhibition between the "Reds" and the "Blues" played in October 1878—listed each team with four backs, a half, and five forwards. There is, though, no other evidence of any side playing with more than two defenders for another three decades, so it seems probable that what is actually being described is a 2–3–5, with the wing-halves whose job it would become to pick up the opposing inside-forwards, listed not as halves but as backs.

A sense of the outrage prompted by even the idea of defending is given by a piece in the *Scottish Athletic Journal* of November 1882 condemning the habit of "certain country clubs" of keeping two men back twenty yards from their own goal, there merely, the writer tartly suggests, "to keep the goalkeeper in chat." Similarly, Lugar Boswell Thistle, a club from Ayrshire, were deplored for attacking with a mere nine men. The reactionaries, though, were fighting a losing battle, and it was with a 2–3–5 that Dumbarton beat Vale of Leven in the Scottish Cup final in 1883.

It was the success of Preston North End in the 1880s that confirmed the pre-eminence of the 2–3–5. Initially a cricket and rugby club, they played a "one-off" game under association rules against Eagley in 1878. No positions were recorded for that game, but, in November of the following year, they met Halliwell, with a team listed in the classic 2–2–6: that is, with two full-backs, two half-backs, two right-wingers, two left-wingers, and two center-forwards. Preston joined the Lancashire Football Association for the 1880–1881 season, and, although they initially struggled, the arrival of a host of Scottish players—professionals in all but name—transformed the club. By 1883 the rosters were for the first time showing Preston lining up in a 2–3–5 system. Exactly whose idea that was is unclear, but it is known that James Gledhill, a teacher and doctor from Glasgow, gave a series of lectures "showing by blackboard what might be done by a team of selected experts," as David Hunt put it in his history of the club. It was with that system that Preston went on to win the first two Football League titles, the first of them, in 1887–1888, without losing a game.

England played a 2–3–5 for the first time against Scotland in 1884, and, by October that year, the system was common enough that when Notts

County went north for a friendly against Renfrewshire, the *Umpire* listed their team in 2–3–5 formation without comment. The Scotland national side first used a pyramid in 1887, prompting much grumbling about their aping of what was initially an English tactic. The tone of a profile of Celtic's James Kelly, published in the *Scottish Referee* in 1889, though, makes clear that by the end of the decade the debate was over. "There are many people who believe that when Scotland adopted the centre half-back position she sacrificed much of her power in the game," it read. "We do not share altogether this opinion, and if the players who fill this space in our clubs were men of Mr Kelly's calibre there would be no difference of opinion on the matter, nor would we have any cause to regret having followed England in this matter."

For the three and a half decades that followed, not much changed. In Britain at least, the 2–3–5 remained the default, but that's not to say that there weren't variations. Although it would be misleading to suggest there was a wealth of abstract or sophisticated discussion about tactics, in the years leading up to the First World War there was a growing interest in how the game should be played; Edwardian soccer certainly wasn't about each team turning up and playing in exactly the same way week after week.

Between 1907 and 1914, for instance, a total of sixty-four instructional columns appeared in the *Sheffield Telegraph and Star Sports Special*, although Peter J. Seddon's *Football Compendium* lists twelve books or handbooks on how to play the game published between 1898 and 1912, of which nine were written by or involved the input of professional players. There was also a series of columns by "Looker-On"—usually the Scottish journalist Bruce Campbell—entitled Leaves from My Notebook, that discussed elements of tactics and style and often incorporated interaction with readers. As Alex Jackson of the National Football Museum, an expert in soccer of the period leading up to the First World War, points out, underlying almost every debate is the fundamental difference between the Scottish short-passing game and the more direct passing common in England.

But Scottish versus English, short passing versus long passing, science versus physique was only part of it. The third of the instructional columns in the *Sheffield Telegraph and Star Sports Special* was written in 1907 by the Woolwich Arsenal center-half Percy Sands and asked, "Is Football Becoming More Scientific?" In it he reflected that such was the level of thought devoted to how the game should be played that "one hears of the adoption of various combinations such as the open game, the short passing game, the triangular movement, the kick and rush method, the individual method, and so on."

Abstract thought, slowly, was beginning to take hold. It was in the Danubian coffeehouses during the following decade that tactical debate entered the intellectual mainstream, but it was going on to an extent in Edwardian England. In 1913, in a piece entitled "Left Half-Back Play," Sheffield United's George Utley reflected on Barnsley's FA Cup triumph the previous year. "It was not by thoughtless football that Barnsley gained their successes," he wrote.

> Many a time—and invariably before a match with a big team—we debated our tactics at length in the dressing room and elsewhere, and settled on certain lines of action. Once when we were at Lytham, preparing for the Cup Final, we had begun to talk in this way after dinner. Up jumped the trainer. He collected twenty-two lumps of sugar and set them all out on the table, in the positions of a couple of football elevens, and with moves this way and that preceded to show us how [George] Lillycrop would score the first goal, and how we should win by 2–0.

Actually Barnsley drew 0–0 against West Brom before winning the replay 1–0 with a Harry Tufnell goal two minutes from the end of extra time, but the general point stands: Barnsley, for all they were seen as the exemplars of the traditional English style, modified their approach according to the opposition.

Tom Boyle, who captained both Burnley and Barnsley, was adamant that

> The side which indulges in the best tactics will win in the end and the captain of the team largely decides the tactics to be adopted by his side. There is no end of scope for the strategical business in a football team. The captain must be on the look-out for the weak points in the opposition and by directing play to that portion of the field make the utmost of the revealed weaknesses. If on one flank the opposition seems too strong for the men he has on that side of the field, then he will send forth the order to keep the play on the weak part in the armour of his opponents. It is by tactics that the games of the future will be won more than anything else, and lucky will be the team that has a genius for a captain—the man who can shoulder the cares.

His words raise two vital issues. First, it was the captain rather than the coach or manager who determined tactics, his role being far more akin to a modern captain in cricket than in soccer. And, second, he was modifying the 2–3–5; Boyle would shift play to one flank or the other rather than making wholesale positional changes. At the same time, his thinking seems very modern in his recognition that there are few absolutes in tactics: "In football," he said, "the tactics adopted must always be in relation to the ability of the men on the side to carry them out successfully. Because of this, it is hard to lay down hard and fast rules."

The Preston side that won the first two league titles, the Sunderland and Aston Villa teams that dominated English soccer in the 1890s, and the Newcastle team of the 1900s were heavily reliant on Scottish imports and, logically enough, played a Scottish-style short-passing game. "The forwards tip-tap the ball here and there, making headway by short, sharp, transfers from one man to another," explained Frank Buckley, a full-back for Birmingham and Derby and later an innovative manager of Wolves.

The great Newcastle captain Colin Veitch credited the introduction of the style there to the signing of the forward R. S. McColl from Queen's Park (better known as Toffee Bob because of the chain of newsstands he had established with his brother). Also in that side was the left-half Peter McWilliam, who had joined from Inverness Thistle a year earlier. He would go on to be a hugely influential manager of Tottenham Hotspur and offered a description of McColl's playing style that was reprinted by Looker-On. A "fine first touch" was the starting point, after which,

> a quick glance over the field and he seemed to take in the whole position. The same instant went away a beautifully judged pass, always along the ground to his team mate in the best position, while he took up the most dangerous position for the return pass. He seemed to see several "moves" in once, just as in a game of draughts. Very often I have seen him give a pass, then take up a position for the return transfer, knowing that before it came to him the ball required to be played by probably two or more of his side.

That was the core of the Scottish game, essentially a minor evolution of the pass and move approach first sprung on an unsuspecting England in 1872. A variation on the passing approach popularized at Newcastle was the so-called triangular game, which involved passing moves between the half-back, inside-forward, and winger on one or both flanks. Newcastle's Bob Hewison, who occupied a number of roles on the left side of the field, termed it "the three cornered triangular, or sixth forward play," which suggests its attacking nature. "The critics," he said, "regard it as the essence of pure football, the science and art of the pastime." It was comparatively rare, though, largely because it was so difficult to get right. "Too much importance cannot be attached to individuality, brains, adaptability, speed," Hewison wrote. "The demands are so great that only the real artist is able to play it. But there is no reason why there should not be a cultivation of the art, since it is the pure football."

That may have seemed obvious to him, or to anybody else exposed to the Scottish game, but in southern England the sense persisted that the more muscular form of the game was the purer one. Corinthians, defiantly amateur and, in their own minds at least, the defenders of the best traditions of the game, continued to encourage dribbling and physicality. The club had been established by Nicholas Lane Jackson, the FA official who had led the campaign against Preston's use of professionals, and he insisted that "passing forward on the run" should be the defining feature of their style. "The whole line of forwards is on the run together and, until it loses the ball or shoots at goal, does not stop," said C. B. Fry who, among his many sporting achievements, turned out for Corinthians. "Much of the scientific and exceedingly clever short passing of professional forwards involves stopping and dodging backwards, a method which often retains the ball but also retards the wave of attack."

That may sound unsubtle, yet, by the late 1890s, Corinthians had in G. O. Smith a center-forward who was more focused on distributing the ball to his wingers and teammates than on scoring himself—the first intimation, perhaps, of the false nine. As the prolific Steve Bloomer, who played alongside Smith for England, said, he "transformed the role of the centre-forward from that of an individual striker into a unifier of the forward line, indeed the whole team."

At professional level the more direct approach tended to manifest as open or wing play. "The most dangerous form of forward play is the swinging, open style, with long passes from the centre to the wings, and from the inside men of one wing to the flankers of the other," explained the Sheffield Wednesday inside-left Andrew Wilson. "If you put the ball about like this the defenders don't know where to have you. They can smother forwards who stick to the ball, but when it is turned this way and that, with speed, they are in a quandary." As the Wednesday inside-right Billy Gillespie put it, the tactic involved "sweeping passes from the inside man of one wing to the outside man of the other, with long transfers from the centre-forward to each side."

The style had been practiced by the likes of Blackburn Olympic and was then developed by West Bromwich Albion in the mid-1880s. They lost in the 1886 and 1887 FA Cup finals and few gave them much hope when they faced the mighty Preston, 26–0 winners over Hyde earlier in the competition, in the 1888 final. So confident were Preston that they asked the referee, Major Francis Marindin, if they could be photographed with the cup before kick-off. "Hadn't you better win it first?" he replied.

Preston's players later complained that they'd gotten stiff standing on the banks of the Thames watching the University Boat Race earlier in the day, but, whatever the reason, in front of a crowd of seventeen thousand, the first sellout in soccer history, "the long passing and open game of West Bromwich," as Geoffrey Green described it, prevailed 2–1. Key to their win was the diminutive right-winger W. I. Bassett, who was selected that evening for the England side to face Wales and remained a regular for the national team for the following eight years. "In his day wing players would make for the corner flags before lobbing their centres into the goalmouth but Bassett was never a slave to these methods," said Green. "He believed in making ground rapidly (his acceleration was terrific) and releasing the ball as accurately and as quickly as possible before the defence had had time to recover."

Very early on there was a sense that the short-passing style was for the grandees and a longer game was for those perhaps less skilled and trying to make the most of limited ability. "Here was a side of purely local Stafford-shire extraction with a wage-bill of no more than £10 a week," Green wrote, "facing the might of Preston, a team of highly paid artists, many of them celebrated Scottish experts."

In Scotland, though, there was absolutely no doubt that the pure form of the game was the short-passing style, something perhaps best seen in the op-position to the long-ball style of the Dumbartonshire clubs—Renton, Vale of Leven, and Dumbarton—from the Glasgow press. When Renton, the Scottish Cup winner, beat West Brom, the FA Cup winners, in the so-called Champions of the World match in 1888, their play was so rough that the Scottish press, explicitly advocating for Queen's Park's passing soccer, ex-pressed sympathy for West Brom. Given West Brom's reputation for direct play, that gives some indication just how far from the Queen's Park template Renton's style must have been.

So well known was Dumbartonshire's predilection for the long ball that when Barnsley went to Glasgow to play Celtic in a friendly in 1912, the preview in the *Scottish Umpire* contrasted the "short and artistic" style of Celtic with "the bold, daring old Renton game by Barnsley." The game fin-ished 1–1, leading the Referee's Notebook column to reflect that

we have been accustomed in the past to marvel at the machine like pass-ing of Aston Villa, and the brilliant individualism of some of the West Bromwich players, but never before have we seen just such a combina-tion of artistic ability, unbounded enthusiasm and dare-devil tactics as that furnished by the Yorkshiremen. Some people seemed not to like the dare-devil part of the game, but it is the new English style . . . the game was worth going a long way to see if only for the contrast in styles. Celtic deserve credit for the way they stood up to such resolutely deter-mined opponents. This was Barnsley's first game of the season and it says much for the quality of their training that the men left the field almost as fresh as when they emerged from the pavilion.

There was a perception, as Alex Jackson points out, that neat, passing soccer was fine for the league but that a side needed to be uncompromising if they were to win the cup, in which the slightest slipup could mean elimination. In an article in Issue Three of the *Blizzard*, he outlined how Newcastle, having lost in three of the previous five FA Cup finals, changed their approach to a tougher, more direct style before beating Barnsley in a replay in the 1910 final. "This more direct style was also favoured in cup-ties in England," Jackson wrote in another article on early tactics, "with the demands and rewards of cup-football encouraging an extra emphasis on vigour, tackling, speed which contributed to the particularly physical nature of English football."

In that regard, it's intriguing that Percy Sands should have spoken also of "kick-and-rush" soccer when listing the various styles of play. It's surely not a version of the game any coach would consciously advocate, and Jackson found no example of any player describing his own team as playing in that way, yet it seems to hint at the increasing pace and aggression of the game in the years leading up to the First World War: precisely that intensity found in Cup-tie soccer.

The problem of excessive speed was particularly acute in England. The issue would become a major concern in the two following decades, but even before the First World War there was an awareness that the English game was beginning to emphasize pace, perhaps to a detrimental extent. "After a considerable experience of both Scottish and English football I have no hesitation in saying the Scottish game is actually slower, although to my mind the Scots achieve the same result as the English with less exertion," wrote Looker-On in 1910 (although he was, of course, a Scot).

That first-class football in Scotland is more calculated, more methodical, and consequently slower than English football is something which practically every Scotsman will admit, and I may say . . . that as a rule the Caledonians are very proud of the fact. Country clubs in Scotland play a game very like the average English League game, and in first-class circles in Scotland this is usually referred to with contempt as "the country kick and rush game." Scotsmen apart from football are as quite fast as Englishmen, but when playing Soccer they seem to play a "thinking game" to a greater extent than the Saxons.

Three years later, Looker-On refined his argument, noting that the difference in the speed and emphasis of the game in England and Scotland wasn't just down to the players but also to the wider culture of the game. "In Scotland," Looker-On wrote,

> . . . the game is slower, because the Scottish crowds understand that when a man starts to take the ball half-way round the field, he is not necessarily doing all that work for the sole purpose of appearing smart. The Scottish crowds are quite aware that at the end of such a dribble the operator may have drawn away most of the opposing defence towards himself, with the result that when he makes a pass a colleague is left with an open goal. In England the man who attempts anything of that kind is left in no doubt as to the opinion of the spectators. He is advised to get rid of the ball or told to get one for himself, and the Scottish game would not be popular in England for a very long time, not until English crowds began to understand it. Several times people have said to me, "What success [Johnny] Walker or [Jimmy] McMenemy would have been in England," and I have always disagreed. The two great forwards just mentioned would have been barracked into disgust on almost any ground in England, simply because the crowd would not have understood what they were trying to do.

Players were aware that speed was having a negative impact. "To say that a player lacks pace is tantamount to utter condemnation of him in the eyes in the majority of followers in game," the West Brom winger A. C. Jephcott commented in 1914, and the result of that was that "craft and cleverness, in tactics and in ball control, seem to be relegated to a secondary place." The winger Jocky Simpson, who was born in Lancashire but moved to Scotland at an early age and played for both Falkirk and Blackburn Rovers, was in no doubt that the English game was quicker, something he blamed for the declining number of goals in the years leading up to the war. "In my opinion the terrific speed at which the game in England is played is largely responsible for the poor scoring," he said. "Too much appears to me to be sacrificed to the mere idea of 'getting forward.'"

But quick or slow, with passing short, triangular, or wing to wing, or even with old-style dribbling, the pyramid would remain the global default until the change in the offside law in 1925 led to the development, in England, of the W-M. Just as the dribbling game and all-out attack had once been the "right"—the only—way to play, so 2–3–5 became the touchstone.

2

THE WALTZ AND THE TANGO

It wasn't only Britain that found football irresistible; almost everywhere the British went in search of trade and commerce they left the game, and that didn't just include parts of the empire. There was money to be made exporting copper from Chile, guano from Peru, meat, wool, and hide from Argentina and Uruguay, and coffee from Brazil and Colombia, and there was banking to be done everywhere. By the 1880s, 20 percent of Britain's foreign investment was in South America, and by 1890 there were forty-five thousand Britons living in the Buenos Aires area, along with smaller, but still significant, communities in São Paulo, Rio de Janeiro, Montevideo, Lima and Santiago. They ran their businesses, but they also established newspapers, hospitals, schools, and sporting clubs. They exploited South America's natural resources, and in return they gave soccer.

In Europe, it was a similar story. If there was a British community—whether centered on diplomacy, banking, trade, or engineering—soccer soon followed. The first Budapest club was Újpest, established at a gymnasium in 1885, and MTK and Ferencváros weren't far behind. Vienna was the center of the British presence in central Europe, and soccer, having initially been played among the staff of the embassy, banks, and various trading and engineering companies, soon took hold. The first match in Austria took place on November 15, 1894, between the Vienna Cricket Club and gardeners from Baron Rothschild's estate, but local interest was so great that by 1911 the cricket club had become Wiener Amateure. Among Czechs, soccer had to compete with *Sokol*, a local variant of *Turnen*, the nationalistic gymnastics popular in Germany, but, with increasing numbers of young intellectuals in Prague turning to London and Vienna for guidance, the game soon took root there as well. The inauguration of the Challenge Cup in 1897, open to any side from the Habsburg Empire, prompted a further upsurge in interest.

Anglophile Danes, Dutch, and Swedes were equally quick to adopt the game, Denmark proving good enough to take silver at the 1908 Olympics. There was never any sense, though, of trying to do anything different from the British, whether from a tactical or any other point of view. To look at photographs of Dutch sporting clubs of the late nineteenth century is to look at a pastiche of Victorian Englishness, all drooping moustaches and studied indifference. As a participant quoted by Maarten van Bottenburg and Beverley Jackson in *Global Games* put it, the purpose of sport was to play "on English grounds, with all their English customs and English strategies . . . amid the beautiful Dutch landscape." This was about imitation; invention didn't come into it.

It was in central Europe and South America, where attitudes toward the British were more skeptical, that soccer began to evolve. The 2–3–5 formation was retained, but shape is only part of the matter; there is also style. Where Britain, despite the acceptance of passing and the spread of 2–3–5, generally persisted in ruggedness and physicality, others developed subtler forms of the game.

What set soccer in central Europe apart was the speed at which it was taken up by the urban working class. Although tours by the likes of Oxford University, Southampton, Corinthians, Everton, and Tottenham and the arrival of various coaches meant a British influence remained, those playing the game had not been inculcated in the beliefs of the English public schools and so had no preconceived notions of the "right" way of doing things.

They were fortunate, also, that it was Scots who made the biggest impression, ensuring that the focus of the game was on quick, short passing. In Prague, for instance, the former Celtic inside-left John Madden—"the ball artist of his day with all the tricks" according to Jim Craig in *A Lion Looks Back*—coached Slavia between 1905 and 1938, while his compatriot John Dick, once of Airdrieonians and Arsenal, had two stints in charge of Sparta between 1919 and 1933. In Austria, meanwhile, a conscious effort was made to copy the style of the Rangers side that had toured in 1905.

The greatest teacher of the Scottish game, though, was an Englishman of Irish descent: Jimmy Hogan. Born and raised in Burnley in a staunchly Catholic family, in his teens he toyed with the idea of entering the priesthood, but he turned to soccer and went on to become the most influential coach there has ever been. "We played football as Jimmy Hogan taught us," said Gusztáv Sebes, the coach of the great Hungary side of the early fifties. "When our football history is told, his name should be written in gold letters."

Defying his father's wish for him to become an accountant, Hogan joined the Lancashire side Nelson as a sixteen-year-old and, developing into what he described as "a useful and studious inside-right," went on to Rochdale and then Burnley. He was, by all accounts, a difficult character, haggling repeatedly for better wages and showing a wholly alien devotion to self-improvement.

His teammates nicknamed him the Parson in recognition of his meticulous, almost ascetic, disposition. At one point Hogan and his father devised a primitive exercise bike—essentially a bicycle mounted on a rickety wooden stand—on which he would cycle thirty miles a day until he realized that, far from making him quicker, he was merely tightening his calf muscles.

The ideal of effortless superiority may have belonged to the early amateurs, but it carried over into the professional game. Training, as such, was frowned upon. Players were expected to run, perhaps even practice their sprints, but ball work was seen as unnecessary, possibly even deleterious. Tottenham's training schedule for 1904, for instance, shows just two sessions a week with the ball, and they were probably more enlightened than most. Give a player a ball during the week, ran the reasoning, and he would not be so hungry for it on a Saturday: a weak metaphor turned into a point of principle.

After one match, in which he had dribbled through a number of challenges to create an opportunity only to shoot disappointingly over the bar, Hogan asked his manager, Spen Whittaker, what had gone wrong. Had the position of his foot been wrong? Had he been off balance? Whittaker was dismissive, telling him just to keep trying, that to score one out of ten was a decent return. Others would have shrugged off the incident but, perfectionist that he was, Hogan dwelled on it. Surely, he thought, it was not a matter of luck but of technique. "From that day I began to fathom things out for myself," he said. "I coupled this with seeking advice from the truly great players. It was through my constant delving into matters that I became a coach later in life. It seemed the obvious thing, for I had coached myself as quite a young professional."

Hogan felt frustrated by Burnley's primitive approach, but it was a financial dispute that finally persuaded him, at the age of twenty-three, to leave Lancashire for the first time, enticed to Fulham by their manager, Harry Bradshaw, whom he had known briefly at Burnley. Bradshaw had no playing pedigree and was a businessman and administrator rather than a coach, but he had clear ideas about how soccer should be played. No fan of kick and rush, he employed a series of Scottish coaches schooled in the close-passing game, ensured a hefty Scottish representation among the playing staff, and left them to get on with it.

The policy was undeniably successful. Hogan helped Fulham to the Southern League championship in both 1906 and 1907 and, having joined the Second Division of the Football League in 1907–1908, they reached the semifinal of the FA Cup, losing to Newcastle United. It was Hogan's last match for the club. He had been struggling for some time with a knee injury, and Bradshaw, business head firmly in place, decided that to retain him was an unjustifiable risk. Hogan briefly joined Swindon Town before representatives of Bolton Wanderers, having waited for him outside church after evensong one Sunday, persuaded him back to the northwest.

His career there was disappointing, ending in relegation, but a preseason trip to the Netherlands made Hogan aware of Europe's potential and its players' desire to learn. English soccer may have dismissed coaching as unnecessary, but the Dutch were begging for it. Following a 10–0 win over Dordrecht, Hogan vowed that one day he would "go back and teach those fellows how to play properly." He also, crucially, became good friends with James Howcroft, an engineer from Redcar who was a leading referee. Howcroft regularly officiated games overseas and, as a result, knew several foreign administrators. One evening, Howcroft mentioned to Hogan that he had heard that Dordrecht were looking for a new coach and hoped to employ somebody with an expertise in the British game. The coincidence was remarkable and the opportunity not to be missed; Hogan applied, and, at the age of twenty-eight, a year after making his vow, he was back in Holland to fulfill it, accepting a two-year contract.

Hogan's players were amateurs, many of them students, but he began to train them as he believed British professionals should have been trained. He improved their fitness, certainly, but he believed the key was to develop their ball control. He wanted his team, he said, to replicate "the old Scottish game," to play in "an intelligent, constructive and progressive, on-the-carpet manner." Crucially, because many of them came from the universities, his players were keen to study, and Hogan introduced lessons, outlining in chalk on a blackboard how he thought soccer should be played. Tactics and positioning began to be understood and explained not in an ad hoc manner on the pitch but via diagrams in a classroom.

Hogan was successful and popular enough that he was asked to take charge of the Dutch national side for a game against Germany, which they won 2–1. Still only thirty, though, he felt he had more to give as a player so, when his contract at Dordrecht was up, he returned to Bolton, who had retained his registration. He played a season there, helping them to promotion, but his future, he knew, lay in coaching. He began looking for work again in the summer of 1912, and again Howcroft proved instrumental, putting him in touch with the great pioneer of Austrian soccer, Hugo Meisl.

Meisl was born in the Bohemian city of Maleschau in 1881 to a middle-class Jewish family who moved to Vienna while he was still very young. He became obsessed by soccer and played with limited success for the Cricket Club. His father, though, wanted him to go into business and found him work in Trieste, where he became fluent in Italian and began to pick up other languages. Returning to Austria to perform his military service, he accepted his father's request that he should secure employment at a bank, but he also started working for the Austrian soccer federation. Initially his job was concerned largely with fund-raising, but Meisl, like Hogan an intelligent inside-forward, had firm ideas on how the game should be played and was determined to shape the future of Austrian soccer. Slowly, his role expanded until, as the de facto head of the Austrian federation, he gave up banking altogether.

In 1912, Austria drew 1–1 against Hungary in a game refereed by Howcroft. Meisl was frustrated by the outcome and asked Howcroft where his side was going wrong. Howcroft replied that he thought they needed a proper coach, somebody who could develop their individual technique, somebody, in other words, like his old friend Jimmy Hogan. Meisl promptly hired him on a six-week contract, partly to work with leading Austrian clubs but mainly to prepare the Austria national squad for the Stockholm Olympics.

Hogan's first training session did not go well. The Austrian players found him difficult to understand and thought he was concentrating rather too much on basics. Meisl, though, was impressed, and he and Hogan talked long into the night about their vision of soccer. Tactically, neither saw anything wrong with the 2–3–5, which had, after all, formed the basis of all soccer for more than thirty years—but they believed that movement was necessary, that too many teams were too rigid and so predictable. Both believed that it was essential to make the ball do the work, that swift combinations of passes were preferable to dribbling, and that individual technique was crucial, not for the slaloming individual runs that would become such a feature of the game in South America but for the instant control of an incoming pass to allow a swift release. Hogan was also keen to stress the value of the long pass to unsettle opposing defenses, provided it was well directed and not an aimless upfield punt. Meisl was a romantic, but what is fascinating about Hogan is that his beliefs were, essentially, pragmatic. He was not an evangelist for the passing game through any quixotic notion of what was right; he simply believed that the best way to win matches was to retain possession.

Austria hammered Germany 5–1 in Stockholm but went down 4–3 to Holland in the quarterfinals. Still, Meisl was convinced, and, when the

German soccer federation asked him to give Hogan a reference, he instead offered Hogan a job, putting him in charge of Austria's preparations for the 1916 Olympics. "To leave my dark, gloomy, industrial Lancashire for gay Vienna was just like stepping into paradise," Hogan said. He worked with the Olympic side twice a week and spent the rest of the time coaching the city's top club sides, finding himself so much in demand that he was forced to begin his sessions with Wiener FC at 5:30 in the morning. Austria warmed to Hogan and Hogan warmed to Austria. Their soccer, he said, was like a waltz, "light and easy," and Meisl was optimistic of success in 1916. War, though, destroyed that dream.

Realizing the probability of conflict, Hogan approached the British consul and asked whether it would be advisable to return swiftly with his family to Britain. He was told there was no imminent danger but within forty-eight hours war had been declared. A day later, Hogan was arrested as a foreign national. The US consul managed to get Hogan's wife and children back to Britain in March 1915. Hogan was released the day before he was due to be sent to an internment camp in Germany after the Blythe brothers, who owned a department store in Vienna, agreed to act as guarantors for him. For almost eighteen months he worked for them, teaching their children how to play tennis, but, 130 miles to the east, moves were afoot to bring him back into soccer. Baron Dirstay, the Cambridge-educated vice president of the Budapest club MTK, had heard of Hogan's plight and, after pulling various diplomatic strings, secured him a position coaching his side, provided he agreed to report regularly to the local police.

Hogan readily accepted. With most of the senior team away at the front, his first task was to assemble a squad. He turned, naturally, to youth, picking up two of the club's most popular players, György Orth and Jozsef "Csibi" Braun, after spotting them in a kickabout as he strolled through Angol Park. "I pounced on them and said 'they are mine, my very own,'" he explained. "They were both intelligent lads attending high school in Budapest. Every day after school I had them on the field, instructing them in the art of the game." Clever and eager to learn, Orth and Braun were typical both of the sort of player central Europe produced and of the sort of player with whom Hogan loved to work, which is, of course, why he felt so at home in both Vienna and Budapest. "The great advantage which continental football has over British soccer," Hogan said, "is that boys are coached in the art of the game at a very tender age."

His methods brought spectacular success. MTK won the title in 1916–1917, the first official championship after a brief hiatus for the war, and held on to it for nine years. As the war came to an end, a combined Budapest side gave notice of the growing strength of the continental game by hammering Bolton 4–1. Hogan, though, presided over just two of MTK's triumphs. As soon as he could when the war was over, he left for Britain. "The time I spent in Hungary was almost as happy as my stay in Austria. Budapest is a lovely city—in my opinion, the most beautiful in Europe," he said, but he had seen neither his wife nor his son in almost four years. Hogan was succeeded by one of his senior players, Dori Kürschner, who, twenty years later, would be crucial to the development of the game in Brazil.

Hogan returned to Lancashire and found a job in Liverpool working as a dispatch foreman for Walker's Tobacco. Money, though, remained tight, and he was advised to ask for a handout from the Football Association, which had established a fund to support professionals financially disadvantaged by the war years.

It proved a watershed in his career. Hogan believed he was due £200 and borrowed £5 to cover his traveling expenses to London. The FA secretary, Frederick Wall, though, treated him with disdain. The fund, Wall said, was for those who had fought. Hogan pointed out that he had been interned for four years and so had had no chance to sign up. Wall's response was to give him three pairs of khaki socks, sneering that "the boys at the front were very glad of those." Hogan was furious, never forgave the FA, and his talent—not that his ideas would have been well received in conservative England anyway—was lost to English soccer.

In Vienna, Meisl retained Hogan's template, although his faith was tested by a 5–0 defeat Austria suffered to Southern Germany shortly after the end of the war. On a frozen, rutted pitch in Nuremberg, their close-passing game proved impractical, and a despondent Meisl spent the return trip discussing with his players whether they should abandon their approach for something more direct and physical. Absolutely not, came their response, and so were set in stone the principles from which grew the *Wunderteam* of the early thirties, the first of the great unfulfilled national sides. Under Meisl, Brian Glanville wrote, "soccer became almost an exhibition, a sort of competitive ballet, in which scoring goals was no more than the excuse for the weaving of a hundred intricate patterns."

The pyramid remained as the basic shape, but the style of the game as a radicalized extension of the Scottish passing game was so different from that found in England that it became recognized as a separate model: the Danubian school. Technique was prized over physicality but was harnessed into a team structure. In South America, the game came to diverge even more sharply from the original model. Again technique was prized, but in Uruguay and, particularly, Argentina, it was individuality and self-expression that were celebrated.

The Football Association's Laws of the Game arrived in Argentina in 1867, where they were published by an English-language newspaper, the *Standard*. Later that year the Buenos Aires Football Club was founded as an offshoot of the cricket club, but the seeds fell on stony ground and six years later it switched to rugby. Only in the 1880s did soccer really take off, thanks largely to Alexander Watson Hutton, a graduate of the University of Edinburgh, who came to Argentina to teach at St. Andrew's Scotch School. He resigned when the school refused to extend its playing fields and established the English High School in 1884, where he employed a specialist games master to teach soccer. When the Argentinian Association Football League was reformed in 1893, Hutton was a central figure. Alumni, a team made up of old boys from the English High School, took their place in the First Division and came to dominate it in the early part of the twentieth century, while the school team itself played lower down the league pyramid. They were far from the only school to take soccer seriously, and six of the first seven titles were won by teams out of the prestigious Lomas de Zamora boarding school.

It was a similar story across the River Plate in Uruguay, where young British professionals founded cricket and rowing clubs that developed soccer sections, and British schools pushed the game. William Leslie Poole, a teacher at the English High School in Montevideo, was Hutton's counterpart, forming the Albion Cricket Club in May 1891, the soccer section of which was soon playing against teams from Buenos Aires.

In those early days, as a quick glance at the rosters demonstrates, the players were largely British or Anglo-Argentinian, and so was the ethos. In his history of amateur soccer in Argentina, Jorge Iwanczuk speaks of the goal being "to play well without passion" and of the importance of "fair play." In a game against Estudiantes de la Plata, Alumni even refused to take a penalty because they believed it had been incorrectly awarded. It was all about doing things the "right way," a belief that extended into tactics: 2–3–5 was universal. The *Buenos Aires Herald*'s extensive coverage of Southampton's 3–0 victory over Alumni in 1904—the first game played on Argentinian soil by a British touring side—makes clear how public school values prevailed. Britain's pre-eminence, an editorial claimed, was the result of "an inherent love of all things manly."

Gradually, though, British dominance waned. The Argentinian Football Association (AFA) adopted Spanish as its language of business in 1903 and the Uruguayan FA did likewise two years later. Alumni were wound up in 1911, and the following year AFA became the Asociación del Football Argentina, although it would take until 1934 before *football* became *fútbol*. Uruguayans and Argentinians, uninfected by British ideals of muscular Christianity, had no similar sense of physicality as a virtue in its own right, no similar distrust of cunning. The shape may have been the same, but the style was as different as it was possible to be. The anthropologist Eduardo Archetti insists that, as the influence of Spanish and Italian immigrants began to be felt, power and discipline were rejected in favor of skill and sensuousness—a trend that reached across a range of disciplines.

"Like the tango," wrote the Uruguayan poet and journalist Eduardo Galeano, "football blossomed in the slums." Different conditions necessitate a different style. Just as the game of the cloisters differed from the game of the playing fields in English public schools, so, in the tight, uneven, restricted spaces of the poorer areas of Buenos Aires and Montevideo, other skills developed and a new style was born: "a home-grown way of playing football," as Galeano put it, "like the home-grown way of dancing which was being invented in the *milonga* clubs. Dancers drew filigrees on a single floor tile, and football players created their own language in that tiny space where they chose to retain and possess the ball rather than kick it, as if their feet were hands braiding the leather. On the feet of the first Creole virtuosos, *el toque*, the touch, was born: the ball was strummed as if it were a guitar, a source of music."

Prioritizing different virtues, the two styles could not comfortably coexist, and so, inevitably, when old and new met, there was conflict. That was apparent as early as 1905, when the physicality of Nottingham Forest against a representative XI—made up largely of Anglo-Argentinians—in the sixth game of their tour led to considerable bad blood. The *Herald*, pro-British as ever, even was moved to issue a magnificently grand rebuke to those who had dared to criticize Forest's approach: "a game especially intended to improve the stamina and try the strength of young men in the prime of life is not necessarily a parlour game."

Acrimony became a feature of subsequent tours, caused largely by a fundamental disagreement on the part the shoulder-charge had to play in the game. Swindon Town's tour of 1912 was one of the few that could be judged a success, and from that came a realization that the British might perhaps have something to learn. Samuel Allen, the Swindon manager, was generally approving, saying he had seen no better soccer between amateur sides, but even he expressed a concern that local players "look on individual exploits as the main thing, and every time there was a chance to show clever work single-handed, it was taken." Even traditionalists within Argentina were skeptical about the creolization of the game. Jorge Brown, a former Alumni player of British origin, protested in the early 1920s that the new style of soccer "was weakened by an excess of passing close to the goal. It is a game that is more fine, perhaps more artistic, even apparently more intelligent, but it has lost its primitive enthusiasm." It was a criticism that would become increasingly familiar; until Hungary in 1953 settled the debate decisively at Wembley, Britain labored under the delusion that the rest of the world suffered from a lack of directness in front of the goal.

Nobody who watched Uruguay in the 1924 Olympics could have been so misguided. Argentina chose to stay at home, but Uruguay went to Paris and wrote one of the great stories of early soccer. Galeano has a tendency to overromanticize, but his evident glee in his country's gold medal is hard to begrudge. This was, first and foremost, a team of workers, including, among other professions, a meat-packer, a stonecutter, a grocer, and an ice salesman. They traveled to Europe in steerage and played to pay for their board, winning nine friendlies in Spain before they even reached France. Uruguay were the first Latin American side to tour Europe, but they attracted little attention—at least initially—only around two thousand turned up to watch them eviscerate Yugoslavia 7–0 in their opening game in the Olympics.

"We founded the school of Uruguayan football," said Ondino Viera, who would go on to manage the national side and who had a turn of phrase only marginally less colorful than Galeano's:

> without coaches, without physical preparation, without sports medicine, without specialists. Just us alone in the fields of Uruguay, chasing the leather from the morning to the afternoon and then into the moonlit night. We played for twenty years to become players, to become what players had to be: absolute masters of the ball . . . seizing the ball and not letting it go for any reason. . . . It was a wild football, our game. It was an empirical, self-taught, native style of football. It was a football that was not yet within the canons of the management of football in the Old World, not remotely. . . . That was our football, and that's how we formed our school of play, and that's how the school of play for the entire continent of the New World was formed.

In Paris, word soon got around. "Game after game," Galeano wrote, "the crowd jostled to see those men, slippery as squirrels, who played chess with a ball. The English squad had perfected the long pass and the high ball, but these disinherited children from far-off America didn't walk in their father's footsteps. They chose to invent a game of close passes directly to the foot, with lightning changes in rhythm and high-speed dribbling."

Chess with a ball? Charles Alcock would scarcely have recognized it, although he would presumably have appreciated the goal-scoring ability of the center-forward Pedro Petrone, even if he did refuse to head the ball for fear of disturbing his heavily brilliantined hair. Those who were there, though, were enraptured as Uruguay maintained their form through the competition, scoring a total of seventeen goals and conceding two in their four games before beating Switzerland 3–0 in the final. The reaction of the French essayist and novelist Henry de Montherlant was typical. "A revelation!" he wrote. "Here we have real football. Compared with this, what we knew before, what we played, was no more than a schoolboy's hobby."

Gabriel Hanot, who would go on to edit *L'Équipe* but was then coming to the end of a distinguished playing career, offered a less emotional response. Uruguay, he wrote, showed "marvellous virtuosity in receiving the ball, controlling it and using it. They created a beautiful football, elegant but at the same time varied, rapid, powerful and effective." As to the thought that British soccer might still be superior, Hanot was dismissive: "It is like comparing Arab thoroughbreds to farm horses."

Uruguay returned home and were promptly challenged to a game by Argentina, who insisted that their subsequent 3–2 aggregate win—achieved thanks to a 2–1 second-leg victory in Buenos Aires in a game halted early by crowd trouble—demonstrated that they would have been Olympic champions, if only they had turned up. Perhaps, perhaps not; it is impossible to say, but the Buenos Aires side Boca Juniors certainly impressed on a tour of Europe in 1925, losing just three of nineteen games.

Argentina did travel to Amsterdam for the Olympics four years later and, fittingly, met Uruguay in the final, losing 2–1 after a replay. Two years later, the two sides met again in the first World Cup final and again Uruguay was triumphant, winning 4–2. As far as it is possible to judge from contemporary reports, Uruguay's advantage seems to have been that, for all their artistry and for all Viera's claims of a raw spontaneity, they were able to retain a defensive shape, whereas Argentina's individualism led at times to confusion. According to the Italian journalist Gianni Brera in *Storia critica del calcio Italiano*, the 1930 World Cup final was evidence that "Argentina play football with a lot of imagination and elegance, but technical superiority cannot compensate for the abandonment of tactics. Between the two *rioplatense* national teams, the ants are the Uruguayans, the cicadas are the Argentinians." This is a fundamental: it could be said that the whole history of tactics describes the struggle to achieve the best possible balance of defensive solidity with attacking fluidity. So grew up the theory of *la garra charrúa*—*charrúa* relating to the indigenous Charrúa Indians of Uruguay and *garra* meaning literally "claw" or, more idiomatically, "guts" or "fighting spirit." It was that, supposedly, that gave a nation with a population of only three million the determination to win two World Cups, and it was also what gave a tenuous legitimacy to the brutality of later Uruguayan teams.

Romanticized as that theory may have been—there was, after all, next to no Charrúa involvement in soccer—what was obvious to everybody outside of Britain was that the best soccer in the world was being played on the River Plate estuary and that it was a game far advanced from the predictable

32

Uruguay 4 Argentina 2, World Cup final, El Centenario, Montevideo, 30 July 1930

2–3–5 as practiced in Britain. "The Anglo-Saxon influence has been disappearing, giving way to the less phlegmatic and more restless spirit of the Latin," a piece in the Argentinian newspaper *El Grafi* in 1928 asserted. "They soon began modifying the science of the game and fashioning one of their own. . . . It is different from the British in that it is less monochrome, less disciplined and methodical, because it does not sacrifice individualism for the honour of collective values. . . . River Plate football makes more use of dribbling and generous personal effort, and is more agile and attractive."

Imagination was prized to the extent that certain players were lionized as the inventors of certain skills or tricks: Juan Evaristo was hailed as the inventor of the *marianella*—the volleyed backheel, Pablo Bartolucci of the diving header, and Pedro Calomino of the bicycle kick, although this last example is disputed. Some say the bicycle kick was invented in Peru in the late nineteenth century; most seem to credit Ramón Unzaga Asla, a native of Bilbao who emigrated to Chile and first used it in 1914 (hence the use of term *chilena* throughout Spanish-speaking South America, although it might refer to David Arellano, a Chilean who popularized the technique on a tour of Spain in 1920), while others follow Leônidas, the Brazilian forward of the thirties, in attributing it to Petronilho de Brito. Weirdly, the former Aston Villa chairman Doug Ellis also claimed to have invented the bicycle kick, even though he never played soccer to any level and was not born until ten years after the first record of Unzaga performing the trick. Who actually invented it is less important in this context than what the arguments show of the value set on imagination around the River Plate estuary in the twenties. The shaming aspect for British soccer is that the game's homeland was so ill disposed to innovation that it is just about conceivable that Ellis *was* the first man to perform a bicycle kick on British soil.

Argentinian soccer developed its own foundation myth, based largely on the visit of the Hungarian side Ferencváros in 1922, which, exposing locals to the style of the Danubian school, supposedly revolutionized their thinking on the game. Given that the process of creolization had been going on for at least a decade, though, it seems probable that the tour simply confirmed changes that were already afoot, that in their early stages the Danubian and *rioplatense* games were similar and almost simultaneously shifted away from the physicality of the British style toward something based more on individual technique.

With the technical experimentation came a willingness to tinker—albeit gently—with tactics. "South American teams treated the ball better and were more tactical in outlook," said Francisco Varallo, Argentina's inside-right in the first World Cup final. "It was the era when we had five forwards with the No.8 and the No.10 dropping back and wingers sending in passes." Those inside-forwards came to be seen as the key to creativity, and the game developed a cult of the *gambeta*, the slaloming style of dribbling. In both Argentina and Uruguay, the story is told of a player skipping through the opposition to score a goal of outrageous quality and then erasing his footsteps in the dust as he returned to his own half so that no one should ever copy his trick.

Mythic, clearly, but indicative of the prevailing system of values that became even more pronounced as Argentinian soccer drifted into reclusiveness. Undermined by the emigration of players ahead of the 1934 World Cup—there were four Argentinians on the Italy side that won it—they were beaten in the first round by Sweden and then refused to send a team to France in 1938 after their own bid to host the tournament was turned down. As the Second World War took hold, and then Juan Perón led the country into isolation, Argentina did not appear again on the world stage until 1950 and in the interim enjoyed a golden age. A professional league began in 1931, big stadiums brought big crowds, and newspaper and radio coverage both tapped and fueled the nationwide interest in the game. So central did soccer become to Argentinian life that when Jorge Luis Borges, who hated the sport, and Adolfo Bioy Casares, who loved it, collaborated on the short story "Esse est percipi," it was soccer they chose to demonstrate how perceptions of reality could be manipulated, as they imagine a fan's disillusionment as he learns from a conversation with a club chairman that all soccer is staged, with results preordained and players played by actors.

The style that had begun to emerge in the twenties developed into something even more spectacular, *la nuestra*—"ours" or "our style of play"—which was rooted in the *criolla viveza*—"native cunning." The term itself seems to have been popularized in the aftermath of Argentina's 3–1 victory over an England XI in 1953: *la nuestra*—"our style"—could beat the style of the *gringos* (although technically that was only a representative game, not a full international). What it describes, though, is the whole early philosophy of Argentinian soccer, which was founded on the joy of attacking. Between September 1936 and April 1938, there was not a single goalless draw in the Argentinian championship. Yet goals were only part of the story. In a much-cited anecdote from his novel *On Heroes and Tombs* (annoyingly missing from the English translation), Ernesto Sabato discusses the spirit of *la nuestra* as the character Julien d'Arcangelo tells the hero, Martin, of an incident involving two Independiente inside-forwards of the twenties, Alberto Lalín and Manuel Seoane (nicknamed both la Chancha and el Negro), who were seen as embodying the two different schools of thought on how soccer should be played. "'To show you what those two modalities were,' D'Arcangelo says to Martin, 'I am going to share with you an illustrative anecdote. One afternoon, at half-time, la Chancha was saying to Lalín: "Cross it to me, man, and I can go in and score." The second half starts, Lalín crosses and sure enough el Negro gets to it, goes in and scores. Seoane returns with his arms outstretched, running towards Lalín, shouting: "See, Lalín, see?!" and Lalín answered, "Yes, but I'm not having fun." There you have, if you like, the whole problem of Argentinian soccer.'" The tricks, entertainment, came to rival winning in importance. Half a century earlier, Britain had herself had the argument: to keep playing the "right way," to keep dribbling (albeit in a far less flamboyant manner), or to adopt the style that won matches. In its twenty-year cocoon, in a culture obsessed by *viveza* and with few games against outsiders that might have brought defeat and a tactical rethink, the exuberant style flourished. It might not have been for the long-term good of Argentinian soccer, but it was fun while it lasted.

3

THE THIRD BACK

Part of soccer's enduring fascination is that it is a holistic game, that the slightest change in one part of the field can have unexpected and radical effects elsewhere. When the home associations persuaded the international board in 1925 to liberalize the offside law, it was to answer the specific issue of a lack of goals. Notts County had begun the trend, but by then several clubs, most notably Newcastle United with their full-back pairing of Frank Hudspeth and Bill McCracken, had become so adept at setting an offside trap that games would be compressed into a narrow sliver either side of the halfway line. When Newcastle drew 0–0 at Bury in February 1925, it came as the final straw. It was Newcastle's sixth goalless draw of a season that produced what at the time was an unthinkably low average of 2.58 goals per game. The soccer was boring, attendances were falling and the FA, for once, not merely recognized that something needed to be done but set about doing it.

The offside law that demanded that, for a forward to be onside, three opposing players (usually a goalkeeper and two defenders) had to be between him and his opponent's goal, had not gone unchanged since 1866, reacting largely to the increasing application of the offside trap. In April 1906, for instance, in a game between Scotland and England at Hampden Park, the England captain, S. S. Harris of Corinthians, responded to an injury to the left-half Harry Makepeace not by withdrawing a forward into the half line, as would have been normal, but by pushing the left-back, Herbert Burgess, forward and operating a high offside line. Robert Crompton, the right-back, sat deep to pick up long balls and breakaways, while the rest of the team pushed up to twenty yards from the Scotland goal line, effectively pinning them in their own goal area. "After Harris passed word back to play for safety the game became a farce," fumed a contemporary report quoted in Brian James's 1970 book *England v Scotland*. "The crowd seriously resented the change of front. It irritated them to see Crompton lying back and the English defence mingling among the Scottish forwards and putting them frequently offside within twenty yards of their own goal."

England lost 2–1, but there was an outcry from the soccer establishment. "The one-back game adopted by England is at all times an objectionable feature in club football," read another report. "But it is questionable if it is sportsmanlike for an international team to resort to this desperate move to keep down the scoring." Harris, who had captained England in all three of the matches they played in 1906, never played for his country again, and the following year the offside law was changed so no player could be offside in his own half.

Once the idea of an offside trap was out of the bottle, though, there was no putting it back, and the years before the First World War saw the ploy become increasingly common. The Notts County full-back pairing of Herbert Morley and Jock Montgomery were pioneers, but the offside trap became particularly associated with the Newcastle United full-back Bill McCracken, who was depicted in contemporary cartoons clapping his hands with glee at getting another offside call in his favor.

To a modern mind, the notion of an offside trap conjures images of the Arsenal back-four under George Graham, all perfectly in line, arms raised. Before 1925, though, it worked on a very different principle because the two full-backs rarely, if ever, played in line. The prime exponents of this staggered system were West Brom's Jesse Pennington and Blackburn's Bob Crompton, who played together a staggering twenty-three times for England before the First World War. "While Crompton goes well back, the West Bromwich man goes up the field—quite a considerable distance sometimes until he has the appearance of a fourth half-back," the Aston Villa forward Charlie Wallace explained. "His is the bold type of full-back play, and though it sometimes means that he has to do a sprint to catch up a player, his methods of working, in conjecture with the safe tactics of Crompton often enable the pair to break up an attack at its very source, because Pennington is in the place where the forward least expects him to be."

With the offside law stipulating that three defensive players were required to play a forward onside, that meant forwards had to take their position from the more advanced full-back; the other was thus always able to act effectively as a sweeper behind him. McCracken had numerous partners over the years, the most noted of them being Frank Hudspeth. "No doubt that I shall be told that the McCracken methods have not been for the good of the game, his originality has been the means of spoiling many a match," he wrote in defense of the offside trap in the *Sheffield Telegraph and Star Sports Special*. "But here is where the mistake is made. It is not the methods of McCracken which spoil the match. Games are spoilt because the opposing forwards will not take the trouble to think out schemes for the nullifying of these offside tactics. There is one splendid saving clause about this offside rule which forwards seem continually and wilfully to forget. If they keep behind the ball they cannot be offside, no matter whether McCracken runs forward or whatever else he does."

The authorities, though, were anxious, and in 1921 there came another tweak to the law, making it impossible for a player to be offside from a throw-in. By 1925, it had become apparent that even more drastic action was required. The FA came up with two possible solutions—either to require only two players to be in advance of the forward, or to add a line in each half forty yards from goal behind which a forward could not be offside—and set about testing them in a series of exhibition games, with one half being played under one alternative, and the second under the other.

At a meeting in London in June, the FA decided they preferred the version requiring only two defending players to play a forward onside. The Scottish FA soon adopted the amendment as well, and it was they who presented the proposed rule change to the international board, the new variant being implemented ahead of the 1925–1926 season. Previously a side looking to play the offside trap had been able to retain one full-back as cover as his partner stepped up to try to catch the forward; the new legislation meant that a misjudgment risked leaving the forward one on one with the goalkeeper.

On the face of it, the amendment was an immediate success, with the average number of goals per game shooting up to 3.69 the following season, but it brought about significant changes in the way the game was played and led directly to Herbert Chapman's development of the "third back" or W-M formation. And that, it is widely held, was what precipitated the decline and increasing negativity of English soccer.

The argument is put most strongly by Willy Meisl, the younger brother of Hugo, in *Soccer Revolution*, which was written in horrified response to England's 6–3 defeat at home to Hungary in 1953. Meisl, it should be said, had been a devout Anglophile even before he fled rising anti-Semitism in Austria to settle in London, and his book reads as a lament for a past he experienced only secondhand and probably idealized. He became a respected figure in sports journalism, writing mainly on English soccer for foreign publications, but *Soccer Revolution*, for all its fine phrase making, is (to modern eyes at least) a strikingly eccentric work. For him, the change in the offside rule was soccer's version of the Fall, the moment at which innocence was lost and commercialism won out.

Perhaps it was, but it was the very thin end of what is now a gargantuan wedge.

As he saw it, for he was no less a romantic than his brother, blinkered directors looking no further than their balance sheets had blamed the laws for soccer's failings without ever considering that they may be "guilty of a wrong approach to the game." And so they pressed ahead with a policy that "might have appeared to the layman a slight revision in the Laws of the Game" but that "turned out to be the crack of a shot that started an avalanche."

And here again the divide is reached between those who seek to win and those who wish simply to play well. These days the debate often feels perfunctory, but in the twenties it was sufficiently alive that the notion of a league itself—"an incubus" roared Brian Glanville—began to be questioned. "The average standard of play would go up remarkably if the result were not the all-important end of matches," Chapman admitted. "Fear of defeat and the loss of points eat into the confidence of players. . . . What it comes to is that when circumstances are favourable, the professionals are far more capable than may be believed, and it seems that, if we would have better football, we must find some way of minimising the importance of winning and the value of points." Winning and losing in soccer, though, is not about morality any more than it is in life. Even those who agree most wholeheartedly with the former Tottenham manager Danny Blanchflower's dictum that "the great fallacy is that the game is first and last about winning; it is . . . about glory, it is about doing things in style and with a flourish" would surely not have it decided in the manner of figure-skating, by a panel of judges awarding marks out of ten. It is a simple but unfortunate fact that eventually those who are looking to win games will toy with negativity. After the glorious excesses of *la nuestra*, it came to the Argentinians; and, for all the self-conscious aestheticism of the Austrians, it would just have surely have come to them had Fascism not gotten there first. Golden ages, almost by definition, are past: gleeful naivety never lasts forever.

The most obvious immediate effect of the change in the offside law was that, as forwards had more room in which to move, the game became stretched and short passing began to give way to longer balls. Some sides adapted better than others, and the beginning of the 1925–1926 season was marked by freakish results. Arsenal, in particular, seemed unable to settle into any pattern of consistency and, after beating Leeds United 4–1 on September 26, they were hammered 7–0 by Newcastle United on October 3.

Charlie Buchan, the inside-right and probably the team's biggest star, was furious and told Chapman he was retiring and wanted to stay in the northeast, where he had enjoyed considerable success with Sunderland. This Arsenal, he said, was a team without a plan, a team with no chance of winning anything. Chapman must have seen his life's project begin to crumble, and Buchan's words would have had a particular sting because, if nothing else, Chapman was a planner.

He had been born in Kiveton Park, a small colliery town between Sheffield and Worksop, and, but for soccer, he would have followed his father into mining. He played first for Stalybridge, and then for Rochdale, then Grimsby, Swindon, Sheppey United, Worksop, Northampton Town, Notts County, and, finally, Tottenham. He was a journeyman player, good enough to stay out of the pits but little else, and, if that part of his career was notable at all, it was for the pale yellow calfskin boots he wore in the belief they made him easier for teammates to pick out, an early indication of the inventiveness that would serve him so well as a manager.

His managerial career did not exactly begin with a fanfare. He was lying in the bath after playing in a friendly for Tottenham's reserve side in the spring of 1907 when his teammate Walter Bull mentioned that he had been approached to become player-manager of Northampton but wanted to prolong his full-time playing career. Chapman said that he would be interested, Bull recommended him, and Northampton, after failing to attract the former Stoke and Manchester City half-back Sam Ashworth, gave him the job.

A fan of the Scottish passing game, as was apparently anyone who gave the matter any thought, Chapman wanted his side to reproduce the "finesse and cunning" he saw as integral to that conception of soccer. After a couple of promising early results, though, Northampton faded, and a home defeat to Norwich in November saw them fall to fifth from last in the Southern League.

That was Chapman's first crisis, and he responded with his first great idea, a recognition that "a team can attack for too long." He began to encourage his team to drop back, his aim being less to check the opposition forwards than to draw out their defenders and so open up attacking space. By Christmas 1908, Northampton were top of the Southern League; they went on to win the title with a record ninety goals.

Chapman moved on to Leeds City in 1912 and, in the two seasons before the First World War, took them from second from last of Division Two to fourth. He also hit upon one of his most notable innovations, instituting team talks after watching players arguing passionately over a game of cards. The war interrupted their progress there, but just as damaging to Chapman and the club were accusations that the club had made illegal payments to players. He refused to hand over the club's books, which led to Leeds City being expelled from the league and Chapman being banned from soccer for life in October 1919.

Two years later, though, while he was working for the Olympia oil and cake works in Selby, Chapman was approached by Huddersfield Town to become the assistant to their manager Ambrose Langley, who had played alongside his late brother Harry before the war. Chapman was intrigued and appealed to the FA, noting that he had been away from the club working at the Barnbow arms factory when the supposed illegal payments had been made.

The FA showed mercy, Chapman took the job and, when Langley decided a month later that he would rather be running a pub, he found himself installed as manager. He advised the directors that they had a talented young squad, but that they needed "a general to lead them." Clem Stephenson of Aston Villa, he decided, was just the man. Stephenson was thirty-three and, crucially, given Chapman's belief in the value of counterattacking, had developed a way of breaking the offside trap by dropping into his own half before springing forward. Performances and gates improved rapidly, while Chapman, always looking at the bigger picture, returfed the field and renovated the press seats at Leeds Road. In 1922, despite their stuffed donkey mascot catching fire in the celebrations that followed the semifinal victory over Notts County, Huddersfield won the FA Cup, Billy Smith converting a last-minute penalty in the final at Stamford Bridge to see off Preston North End.

The authorities, though, were not impressed. The game had been a poor one, littered with niggling fouls, leading the FA to convey its "deep regret" at the behavior it had witnessed and to express a hope that "there will not be any similar conduct in any future final tie." Huddersfield asked what was meant, to which the FA replied that the club should recognize indecency when it saw it, the lack of clarification prompting many to believe that Chapman was being censured for having deployed his center-half, Tom Wilson, deeper than usual so that, in the words of the *Huddersfield Examiner*, he acted as "a great spoiler."

It is impossible at this remove to determine whether the FA had anything so specific in mind, but again what is apparent is the perception that there was a "right way to play" from which Chapman was deemed to have deviated. Equally, the deployment of Wilson with a brief, if not to manmark, then certainly to check Billy Roberts, the opposing center-forward, suggests that the stopper center-half was on its way and may have come into existence even without the change in the offside law.

With hindsight, in fact, the stopper center-half seems implicit in the pyramid formation, even if it took time for that to be universally accepted. When two 2–3–5s met, in terms of attributing responsibility, the game could essentially be seen as five forwards facing five defenders. The center-half would always pick up the center-forward, but some teams preferred to have their full-backs marking the opposing wingers with the half-backs picking up the inside-forwards and some vice versa. W. H. Brelsford, the Sheffield United right-half, noted that if the full-back picked up the winger then "there is a tendency to a scattering of the defence" but acknowledged that half-backs were able to close down the opposing inside-forwards more quickly. As with so much else, in other words, there were advantages and disadvantages with both systems, and which of the two was preferable depended on circumstance.

With either system, from a very early stage, the center-half had at least some defensive responsibility, and the need for a balanced half-back line was well established. "Sometimes I doubt whether it really pays to have three half-backs in a team able to feed their forwards to perfection," Brelsford wrote in January 1914. "They all get to enjoy that part of the game so much that the defensive part is apt to suffer. The best middle line in my opinion is one which has a good blend of vigour and skill about it, but not with all three men playing exactly the same type of game. If you've a couple of tip-top feeds, then you want a determined breaker-up in their company; if you've two strong spoilers, well, it is imperative to have a third who can feed in first-class style."

Some center-halves, even in the years immediately before the war, specialized in defending. Newcastle, for instance, who had been noted for their attacking half-back line, signed the center-half Wilf Low from Aberdeen in 1909, seemingly to provide cover for the more creative players alongside him. A retrospective piece in the *Sheffield Telegraph and Star Sports Special* in 1914 spoke of how "all that season [1910–1911] he had been wrecking the reputation of almost every centre-forward he met."

The tendency was certainly for the center-half to be more defensive than the wing-halves. The Sheffield United full-back Bernie Wilkinson wrote that "the centre-half back should pay the greater attention to defence and the wing halves to attack," while the Bristol City center-half Billy Wedlock explained that "the centre-half should watch the opposing centre-forward. If he does and does his work well, the best centre-forward in the world cannot shine so long as he is haunted by the terrier tackler."

As early as 1897, C. B. Fry had referred to the tactic of using the center-half in a purely defensive capacity. "Sometimes," he wrote in the *Encyclopaedia of Sport and Games*, "when a side is a goal or two ahead, and it is thought advisable to play a purely defensive game, a third-back is added by diminishing the number of forwards . . . with regard to the shift of withdrawing a forward and putting an extra back, there is much to be said: that three backs are extremely hard to get through . . . but unless the players thus moved are versatile and capable of performing satisfactorily the duties of their altered positions . . . it is certainly unwise to play a third back, unless the extra man is a capable player in that position."

Withdrawing a forward, of course, is different from pushing the center-half deeper, but the fact that even somebody as traditionalist in approach as Fry was prepared to countenance adding a defender suggests the 2–3–5 was not quite as sacrosanct as it can at times seem. From the first decade of the twentieth century it seems to have been not uncommon for teams to push the center-half back for difficult away games. The former Chelsea manager David Calderhead, for instance, in an interview with *Thomson's Weekly* in 1933, said, "I remember the third-back game being a very effective operation away back in my own playing days. One of the finest exponents of it was Herbert Dainty, the ex-Notts County and Dundee centre-half."

Although there were incidents of clubs fielding their center-half with a specific defensive brief, what was unique about Chapman's Huddersfield was less the fact that they coupled that with a distinctive style, based around their manager's distrust of the wing play that was so revered in Britain. Inside passing, Chapman argued, was "more deadly, if less spectacular" than the "senseless policy of running along the lines and centring just in front of the goalmouth, where the odds are nine to one on the defenders." As the *Examiner* noted in 1924 after Huddersfield had wrapped up the league title, "the low passing and the long-field play of the Leeds Road team has become famous."

What was significant was not merely that Chapman had a clear conception of how soccer should be played, but that he was in a position to implement that vision. He was—at least in Britain—the first modern manager, the first man to have complete control over the running of the club, from signings to selection to tactics to arranging for gramophone records to be played over the public-address system to keep the crowd entertained before the game and at half-time. With Huddersfield on their way to defending their title in 1925, the *Sporting Chronicle* asked: "Do clubs realise to the full today the importance of the man who is placed in control? They are ready to pay anything up to £4,000 and £5,000 for the services of a player. Do they attach as much importance to the official who will have charge of the player? . . . The man behind the scenes who finds players, trains talent, gets the best out of the men at his command is the most important man in the game from the club's point of view."

The following year Huddersfield completed a hat trick of league titles, but by then Chapman was gone, enticed south by what he saw as even the greater potential of Arsenal. It was not, it must be said, obvious. Arsenal were struggling to stay up and, in Sir Henry Norris, laboring under an idiosyncratic and domineering chairman. Leslie Knighton, Chapman's predecessor, had been forbidden to spend more than £1,000 on a player in an age in which £3,000 fees were becoming common, and there was a ban on bringing in players measuring less than 5'8". When Knighton defied the height restriction to sign the 5'0" Hugh "Midget" Moffatt from Workington in 1923, Norris off-loaded the player to Luton Town before he had played a single league game. Knighton was dismissed at the end of the

1924–1925 season, with Norris citing poor results, although Knighton claimed it was because the club wanted to avoid paying him a bonus he was due from a benefit match.

Chapman, warning that it would take him five years to win anything, took the job only on condition he would face no such restrictions, something to which Norris reluctantly agreed. His first signing was Charlie Buchan. Sunderland valued him at £4,000, which their manager, Bob Kyle, insisted represented value for money, as the inside-forward would guarantee twenty goals a season. If he was so confident, Norris replied, then the fee should be structured according to Buchan's scoring record: a £2,000 initial payment, plus £100 for each goal scored in his first season. Kyle went along with it, Buchan scored twenty-one, and Sunderland gratefully accepted £4,100.

Not that such a thing seemed likely that September after the defeat at Newcastle. Buchan was an awkward character who had walked out on his first day at Arsenal because he thought the uniform was inadequate and then refused to train on his second because he found a lump of congealed Vaseline in his supposedly freshly laundered sock. Some managers might have seen that as willful obstructiveness or an unrealistic finickiness; Chapman seems instead to have regarded it as evidence of high standards. He also admired in Buchan an independence of thought about the game, something that was far from common among players of the age. John Lewis, a former referee, had noted in 1914 that "our professionals evince no great anxiety to learn anything of the theory of the sport. . . . In most teams there is no evidence of pre-conceived tactics or thought-out manoeuvres," and, for all Chapman's efforts to encourage debate, not much had changed.

Buchan had been alerted to the effectiveness of using a defensive center-half by his Sunderland teammate Charlie Thomson, who had begun his career as a center-forward before becoming a center-half who could drop into the back line, and from the beginning of the season he had argued that the change in the offside rule meant the center-half had to take on a more defensive role. It was notable that in Arsenal's defeat at St. James' the Newcastle center-half Charlie Spencer stayed very deep. He offered little in an attacking sense but repeatedly broke up Arsenal attacks almost before they had begun, allowing Newcastle to dominate possession and territory. Chapman, in the end, was convinced, but the mystery is why, given his natural inclination to the counterattack, he had not done so earlier. He was not a man readily cowed by authority, but perhaps the FA's words after the 1922 Cup final, coupled with his recognition of what they had done for him in lifting his life ban, had an effect.

Others had already come to the same conclusion. Although the lack of interest in and awareness of tactical aspects of the game means evidence is piecemeal, it's fairly clear that the third back long predated the change in the offside law. What that change did, though, was to raise a spirit of tactical experimentation, leading teams to investigate the secondary effects of using a third back elsewhere on the field.

On October 3, 1925, for instance, the day of Arsenal's revelatory defeat at Newcastle, under the headline "the W formation," George White wrote in the Cherry Blossom column in the *Southampton Football Echo* that

> the Saints were beaten by Bradford City at the Dell on Saturday [September 26] by tactics. The home team, to my mind, had more of the play than the City, and put up the better exhibition of football, that is, as the game was played before the offside law was altered. But the City were very smart indeed on the ball, and their tactics did the rest, so that they scored two goals, while the Saints could reply only once. There is a lot of talk in the dressing rooms at the moment over what is known as the W formation in attack to deal with the changed conditions of play. In this formation the centre-forward and the two extreme wingers go well up the field—staying only a yard or so onside—and the two inside wing-forwards remain behind, acting as five-eighths, or in other words operating in a sphere of play near the half-backs and behind the three advanced forwards.

That would be remarkable enough if White were talking about the Bradford manager David Menzies as a lone tactical maverick, but he concludes that use of the W-system was widespread: "The goal-scoring figures up to date go to suggest that this is the method mostly adopted, for there have been scarcely any cases of the inside wing-forwards running riot in the goal-scoring sense, while on the other hand, five, four and three goals in a match have been credited the centre-forwards with startling frequency, and the extreme wing men have also figured largely in the goal-scoring department."

Chelsea—like Southampton, a Second Division side at the time—were one of the major beneficiaries of the new law, the aging Scotland international Andy Wilson reveling in the withdrawn inside-forward role in which his declining pace was less of an issue than it had been when playing higher up the field the previous season. "With this disposition of the attack," White went on, "the inside wing-forwards help, when their side is on the defensive, as additional half-backs, and practically throughout the game the centre-half-back becomes a third back."

White urged Southampton to adopt the W-formation against Port Vale that afternoon. They did so and achieved a creditable away draw and then used it again in beating Darlington 4–1 at home that Monday. The Cherry Blossom column the following Saturday—that is, a week after Southampton's draw at Port Vale and Arsenal's defeat at Newcastle—highlighted Dave Morris of Raith Rovers as the model of the modern deep-lying center-half. "He positions himself," White wrote, "a little in front of the backs and midway between them, whilst the wing half-backs look after the opposing wing-forwards, leaving the backs and the centre-half-back to deal with the three inside-forwards of the opposition [the terminology here is a little confusing—he means the centre-forward, the inside-right and the inside-left]. In this formation the inside-forwards work closer to the centre-half-back than formerly, and the pivot feeds these two, who in turn open the attack where they see an opportunity."

The W-formation evidently spread rapidly—astonishingly so, given the absence of television coverage. If teams as diverse as Southampton and Raith were using it by early October, it seems to have been a nationwide phenomenon within seven or eight games of the new season. Arsenal were certainly not the first club to come to the conclusion that the center-half had to become a third back, but they did employ the new formation more consistently and with greater success than anyone else.

Buchan initially argued, and Chapman agreed, that withdrawing the center-half left a side short of personnel in midfield, and so he proposed that he should drop back from his inside-right position, which would have created a very loose and slightly unbalanced 3–3–4—a halfway house between the 2–3–5 and the W. Chapman, though, valued Buchan's goal-scoring abilities too highly to compromise them and so instead gave the role of withdrawn inside-forward to Andy Neil. Given Neil was a third-team player, that came as something of a surprise, but it proved an inspired choice and an emphatic endorsement of Chapman's ability to conceptualize and compartmentalize, to recognize what specific skills were needed where. Tom Whittaker, who went on to become Chapman's trusted number two, recalled his boss describing Neil as being "as slow as a funeral" but insisting it didn't matter because "he has ball-control and can stand with his foot on the ball while making up his mind."

With Jack Butler asked to check his creative instincts to play as the deep-lying center-half, the new system had an immediate effect, and, two days after the debacle at Newcastle, Arsenal, with Buchan re-enthused by the change of shape, beat West Ham United 4–1 at Upton Park. They went on to finish second behind Huddersfield that season, at the time the highest league position ever achieved by a London club. The next season, though, began poorly, partly because success had brought overconfidence, and partly because opposing sides had begun to exploit Butler's lack of natural defensive aptitude. Some argued for a return to the traditional 2–3–5, but Chapman decided the problem was instead that the revolution had not gone far enough: what was needed at center-half was a player entirely without pretension. He found him, characteristically unexpectedly, in the form of Herbie Roberts, a gangling ginger-haired wing-half he signed from Oswestry Town for £200.

According to Whittaker, "Roberts's genius came from the fact that he was intelligent and, even more important, that he did what he was told." He may have been one dimensional, but it was a dimension that was critical. His job, Whittaker wrote, was "to intercept all balls down the middle, and either head them or pass them short to a team-mate. So you see how his inability to kick a ball hard or far was camouflaged." Bernard Joy, the last amateur to play for England and later a journalist, joined Arsenal in 1935 as Roberts's deputy. "He was a straightforward sort of player," Joy wrote in *Forward Arsenal!* "well below Butler in technical skill, but physically and temperamentally well suited to the part he had to play. He was content to remain on the defensive, using his height to nod away the ball with his red-haired head and he had the patience to carry on unruffled in the face of heavy pressure and loud barracking. This phlegmatic outlook made him the pillar of the Arsenal defence and set up a new style that was copied all over the world." And that, in a sense, was the problem. Arsenal became hugely successful, and their style was copied by sides without the players or the wherewithal to use it as anything other than a negative system.

Arsenal lost the FA Cup final to Cardiff in 1927, but it was after Norris had left in 1929 following an FA inquiry into financial irregularities that success really arrived. Buchan had retired in 1928, and his replacement, the diminutive Scot Alex James, signed from Preston for £9,000, made Chapman's system come alive. The club's official history cautions that "nobody should underestimate James's contribution to the successful Arsenal side of the 1930s. He was simply the key man." Economic of movement, he was supremely adept at finding space to receive the ball—preferably played rapidly from the back—and had the vision and the technique then to distribute it at pace to the forwards. Joy called him "the most intelligent player I played with. . . . On the field he had the knack of thinking two or three moves ahead. He turned many a game by shrewd positioning near his own penalty area and the sudden use of a telling pass into the opponents' weak point."

By the time Arsenal won the FA Cup in 1930—their first silverware, as Chapman had promised, coming in the fifth season after his arrival—the W had been adopted, and the new formation had taken clear shape. The fullbacks marked the wingers rather than inside-forwards, the wing-halves sat on the opposing inside-forwards rather than on the wingers, the center-half, now a center-back, dealt with the center-forward, and both inside-forwards dropped deeper: the 2–3–5 had become a 3–2–2–3, the W-M. "The secret," Joy wrote, "is not attack, but counter-attack. . . . We planned to make

Arsenal 2 Huddersfield Town 0, FA Cup final, Wembley, London, 26 April 1930

the utmost use of each individual, so that we had a spare man at each moment in each penalty area. Commanding the play in midfield or packing the opponents' penalty area is not the object of the game. . . . We at Arsenal achieved our end by deliberately drawing on the opponents by retreating and funnelling to our own goal, holding the attack at the limits of the penalty box, and then thrusting quickly away by means of long passes to our wingers."

Trophies and modernization tumbled on together, the one seeming to inspire the other. The FA, instinctively conservative, blocked moves to introduce shirt numbers and floodlit matches, but other innovations were implemented. Arsenal's black socks were replaced by blue-and-white hoops, a clock was installed at Highbury, Gillespie Road tube station was renamed Arsenal, white sleeves were added to their red shirts in the belief that white was seen more easily in peripheral vision than any other color, and, perhaps most tellingly, after training on Fridays, Chapman had his players gather round a magnetic tactics board to discuss the coming game and sort out any issues hanging over from the previous game. At Huddersfield he had encouraged players to take responsibility for their positioning on the field; at Arsenal he instituted such debates as part of the weekly routine. "Breaking down old traditions," a piece in the *Daily Mail* explained, "he was the first manager who set out methodically to organise the winning of matches."

It worked. Arsenal won the league in 1931 and 1933 and were beaten in the 1932 Cup final only by a highly controversial goal. Glanville wrote of them "approaching the precision of a machine," and, in their rapid transition from defense to attack, the unfussy functionalism of their style, there was a sensibility in keeping with the art deco surroundings of Highbury. The machine analogy is telling, recalling as it does Le Corbusier's reference to a house as "a machine for living in"; this was modernist soccer. William Carlos Williams, similarly, in a phrase that would become almost a slogan for his version of modernism, described a poem as "a machine made of words . . . there can be no part, as in any other machine, that is redundant." Chapman's Arsenal were very much of their age. "It was," Joy said of their style, "twentieth-century, terse, exciting, spectacular, economic, devastating."

Perhaps that is not surprising. Chapman was, after all, part of the first wave of beneficiaries of Forster's Education Act of 1870, which made schooling compulsory up to the age of twelve and allowed unprecedented numbers of working-class men to fill the managerial vacancies opened up by the First World War. They may not have had Ezra Pound's command to "make it new" ringing in their ears, but it is fair to suggest that the new managerial class was more open to innovation than its tradition-bound predecessors. Chapman, it is worth remembering, was a near contemporary of another modernist genius of Nottinghamshire mining stock, D. H. Lawrence.

Within soccer there were doubters, perhaps the most astute of them Carruthers in the *Daily Mail*, who, after the 1933 championship, commented, "If it were thought that other clubs would try to copy them, their example might, I'm afraid, be unfortunate. There is only one Arsenal today, and I cannot conceive another simply because no other club has players fit to carry on the same ideas."

The ideas, anyway, were imperfectly understood, as was demonstrated when England's selection committee picked Roberts for a friendly against Scotland in 1931. He was the first stopper to be called up for his country, but neither of the full-backs, Fred Goodall and Ernie Blenkinsop, was accustomed to the W-M. As a result, Scotland "picnicked happily in the open spaces," as L. V. Manning put it in the *Daily Sketch*, winning 2–0.

In Scotland, opinion was just as divided between those who recognized the efficacy of the more modern system and those who remained romantically tied to the short-passing game. The last hurrah of the pattern-weaving approach came on March 31, 1928, when the Scotland side, who would become immortalized as the Wembley Wizards, hammered England, Alex Jackson scoring three and Alex James two in a 5–1 win. In his report in the *Evening News*, Sandy Adamson described Jackson's first goal as "a zigzag advance which ought to go down in posterity as a classic of its kind" and went on to describe how "exultant Scots engaged in cat-and-mouse cantrips. . . . From toe to toe the ball sped. The distracted enemy was bewildered, baffled and beaten. One bit of weaving embraced eleven passes and not an Englishman touched the sphere until [Tim] Dunn closed the movement with a sky-high shot over the bar."

The *Glasgow Herald* was more restrained. "The success of the Scots," its report said, "was primarily another demonstration that Scottish skill, science and trickery will still prevail against the less attractive and simpler methods of the English style in which speed is relied upon as the main factor." Jimmy Gibson and Jimmy McMullan, the wing-halves, and Dunn and James, the inside-forwards, clearly did combine to devastating effect on a wet field, but it should be borne in mind that the game was effectively a play-off for the wooden spoon in the Home International Championship. The supposedly self-evident superiority of the Scottish style hadn't been apparent in the 1–0 defeat to Northern Ireland or the 2–2 draw against Wales.

It is significant too that eight of the Scotland eleven were based at English clubs: for all their passing ability, it evidently helped to have players used to the pace of the English game. Stylistically, anyway, this was not quite the throwback some would suggest. Tom Bradshaw, the center-half, was given a defensive role, marking Dixie Dean, so although they may not have been playing a full-blown W-M, neither was their system a classic 2–3–5.

The W-M's arrival in the club game was patchy. The former Rangers player George Brown recalled a charity game between a Rangers-Celtic XI and a Hearts-Hibs XI from "about 1930": "Davie Meiklejohn was at right-half, I was at left-half and Celtic's Jimmy McStay was at centre-half," he said. "Things did not go very well for us in the first half and by the interval we were one goal down. So during half-time, Meiklejohn said to McStay, 'All the trouble is coming through the middle because you are too far up the field. We play with Jimmy Simpson well back and this leaves the backs free.' McStay agreed to try this and we eventually ran out comfortable winners. So from then on he played the same type of game for Celtic." Like Jack Butler at Arsenal, though, McStay was no natural defender, and a run of nine seasons without a title was brought to an end only when the stopper center-half Willie Lyon was signed from Queen's Park.

And that, in a sense, was the problem: it was simply easier to be a good defensive center-half than a good attacking one. The creative part of Chapman's equation was even harder to fulfill. Inside-forwards of the ability of Alex James were rare but phlegmatic Herbie Roberts–style stoppers abounded. "Other clubs tried to copy Chapman," Jimmy Hogan said, "but they had not the men, and the result was, in my opinion, the ruination of British football, with the accent on defence and bringing about the big kicking game which put to an end the playing of constructive football. Through this type of game our players lost the touch and feeling for the ball."

The seeds of that decline may have predated the change in the offside law, but they were nurtured by Chapman's response to it. The effect of the third-back game, as Glanville said, was "to reinforce and aggravate weakness which already existed" because it encouraged a mental laziness on the part of coaches and players. It is far less arduous, after all, to lump long balls in the general direction of a forward than to endure the agonies of creation. Chapman, though, remained unapologetic. "Our system, which is so often imitated by other clubs, has lately become the object of criticism and discussion," he told Hugo Meisl. "There is only one ball in play and only one man at a time can play it, while the other twenty-one become spectators. One is therefore dealing only with the speed, the intuition, the ability and the approach of the player in possession of the ball. For the rest, let people think what they like about our system. It has certainly showed itself to be the one best adapted to our players' individual qualities, has carried us from one victory to another. . . . Why change a winning system?"

Chapman himself never had to, nor did he have to deal with the transition from one generation of players to the next. On January 1, 1934, he caught a chill during a game at Bury but decided to go anyway the next day to see Arsenal's next opponents, Sheffield Wednesday. He went back to London with a high temperature and, ignoring the advice of club doctors, went to watch the reserves play at Guildford. He retired to bed on his return, but by then pneumonia had set in, and he died early on January 6, two weeks shy of his fifty-sixth birthday.

Arsenal went on to win the title and made it three in a row the following year. A few months after his death, a collection of Chapman's writings was published. In it, intriguingly, he too seemed to express regret for the passing of a less competitive age. "It is no longer necessary for a team to play well," he said. "They must get goals, no matter how, and the points. The measure of their skill is, in fact, judged by their position in the league table."

This, now, seems all but axiomatic; it is a measure of how pervasive the amateur inclinations of the game remained that even Chapman seems to have considered it necessary to apologize for winning. "Thirty years ago," he went on, "men went out with the fullest licence to display their arts and crafts. Today they have to make their contribution to a system." And so, finally, resolved to winning, soccer recognized the value of tactics, the need for individuality to be harnessed within the framework of a team.

4

HOW FASCISM DESTROYED
THE COFFEEHOUSE

Herbert Chapman was one man, making one change to answer a specific problem. English soccer followed him because it saw his method worked, but the coming of the third-back game did not herald the coming of a generation of English tacticians. "Unfortunately," as Willy Meisl wrote, "the plaster cast remained, no soccer sorcerer or professor was here to smash it to pieces and cast it in another mould." If anything, the preference was to try to pretend the tactical change had not happened, that the sacred pyramid remained intact. When the FA made shirt numbering compulsory in 1939, they ignored later developments and stipulated that the right-back must wear 2, the left-back 3, right-half 4, the center-half 5, the left-half 6, the right-winger 7, the inside-right 8, the center-forward 9, the inside-left 10, and the left-winger 11, as though the 2–3–5 were still universal or at least the basis from which all other formations were mere tinkerings. That meant that teams using the W-M lined up, in modern notation, 2, 5, 3; 4, 6; 8, 10; 7, 9, 11, which is why *center-half* is—confusingly—used as a synonym for *center-back* in Britain.

Newspapers, similarly, ignored the reality, continuing to print team lineups as though everybody played a 2–3–5 until the 1960s. Even when Chelsea played the Budapest side Vörös Lobogó in 1954, and—alerted to tactical nuances by the fallout from England's 6–3 defeat to Hungary at Wembley a year earlier—made the effort to print the Hungarian formation correctly in the match program, they persisted with the delusion that their own W-M was actually a 2–3–5. So overwhelmingly conservative was the English outlook that the manager of Doncaster Rovers, Peter Doherty, enjoyed success in the fifties with his ploy of occasionally having his players switch shirts, bewildering opponents who were used to recognizing their direct adversary by the number on his back.

Numbering in a 2–3–5

Numbering in a W-M (England)

For the importance of tactics fully to be realized, the game had to be taken up by a social class that instinctively theorized and deconstructed, that was as comfortable with planning in the abstract as it was with reacting on the field, and, crucially, that suffered none of the distrust of intellectualism that was to be found in Britain. That happened in central Europe between the wars. What was demonstrated by the Uruguayans and Argentinians was explained by a—largely Jewish—section of the Austrian and Hungarian bourgeoisie. The modern way of understanding and discussing the game was invented in the coffeehouses of Vienna.

Soccer boomed in Austria in the twenties, with the establishment of a two-tier professional league in 1924. That November the *Neues Wiener Journal* asked, "Where else can you see at least 40–50,000 spectators gathering Sunday after Sunday at all the sports stadiums, rain or shine? Where else is a majority of the population so interested in the results of games that in the evening you can hear almost every other person talking about the results of the league matches and the club's prospects for the coming games?" The answer was easy: Britain aside, nowhere in Europe.

But where in Britain the discussion of games took place in the pub, in Austria it took place in the coffeehouse. In Britain soccer had begun as a pastime of the public schools, but by the 1930s it had become a resolutely working-class sport; in central Europe, it had followed a more complex arc, introduced by the Anglophile upper middle classes, rapidly adopted by the working classes, and then, although the majority of the players remained working class, seized upon by intellectuals.

Soccer in central Europe was an almost entirely urban phenomenon, centered on Vienna, Budapest, and Prague, and it was in those cities that coffeehouse culture was at its strongest. The coffeehouse flourished towards the end of the Habsburg Empire, becoming a public salon, a place where men and women of all classes mingled, but which became particularly noted for its artistic, bohemian aspect. People would read newspapers there, pick up mail and laundry, play cards and chess. Political candidates used them as venues for meetings and debates, while intellectuals and their acolytes would discuss the great affairs of the day: art, literature, drama, and, increasingly in the twenties, soccer.

Each club had its own café, where players, supporters, directors, and writers would mix. Fans of Austria Vienna, for instance, met in the Café Parsifal; Rapid fans in the Café Holub. The hub of the soccer scene in the interwar years, though, was the Ring Café. It had been the hangout of Anglophile cricketers, but by 1930 it was the center of the broader soccer community. It was, according to a piece written in the *Welt am Montag* after the Second World War, "a kind of revolutionary parliament of the friends and fanatics of football; one-sided club interest could not prevail because just about every Viennese club was present."

The impact of soccer on the wider culture is made clear by the career of the Rapid center-forward Josef Uridil. He came from the suburbs—in the Vienna of the time edgy, working-class districts—and his robust style of play was celebrated as exemplifying the proletarian roots of the club. He was the first soccer hero of the coffeehouse and in 1922 became the subject of a song by the noted cabaret artist Hermann Leopoldi, "Heute spielt der Uridil," which was so popular that it spread his fame even to those with no interest in soccer. He began advertising a range of products from soap to fruit juice, and by February 1924 he was appearing as an emcee at a music hall while at the same time *Pflicht und Ehre*, a film in which he appeared as himself, was showing in theaters.

It was into that environment that Hugo Meisl's *Wunderteam* exploded. The trend through the late twenties was upward and, despite a poor start, Austria narrowly missed out on the inaugural Dr. Gerö Cup, a thirty-month league tournament also featuring Czechoslovakia, Hungary, Italy, and Switzerland that began in 1927. After losing three of their opening four games, they hammered Hungary 5–1 and the eventual winners Italy 3–0, finishing runners-up by a point. In the Ring, they weren't satisfied and agitated for the selection of Matthias Sindelar, a gifted, almost cerebral, forward from Austria Vienna, a club strongly associated with the Jewish bourgeoisie.

He was a new style of center-forward, a player of such slight stature that he was nicknamed *Der Papierene*—"the Paper-man." There was an air of flimsy genius about him that led writers to compare his creativity to theirs: a fine sense of timing and of drama, a flair for both the spontaneous and the well crafted. According to Friedrich Torberg, one of the foremost of the coffeehouse writers and author of a 1978 collection *Die Erben der Tante Jolesch*, "He was endowed with such an unbelievable wealth of variations and ideas that one could never really be sure which manner of play was to be expected. He had no system, to say nothing of a set pattern. He just had . . . genius."

Hugo Meisl, though, was doubtful. He had given Sindelar his international debut as a twenty-three-year-old in 1926, but, for all that he stood in the vanguard of the new conception of soccer, Meisl was, at heart, a conservative. Everything he did tactically could be traced back to a nostalgic attempt to re-create the style of the Rangers tourists of 1905: he insisted on the pattern-weaving mode of passing, ignored the coming of the third back, and retained a sense that a center-forward should be a physical totem, somebody, in fact, like Uridil.

Uridil and Sindelar were both from Moravian immigrant families, both grew up in the suburbs, and both became celebrities (Sindelar too played himself in a film and supplemented his soccer player's income by advertising wristwatches and dairy products), but they had little else in common. As Torberg put it, "They can only be compared as regards popularity; in terms of technique, invention, skill, in short, in terms of culture, they were as different from each other as a tank from a wafer."

Finally, in 1931, Meisl succumbed to the pressure and turned to Sindelar, installing him as a fixture in the team. The effects were extraordinary, and on May 16, 1931, Austria thrashed Scotland 5–0. Two and a half years after the Wembley Wizards' 5–1 demolition of England, Scotland found themselves just as outmaneuvered by the same game, taken to yet greater heights. They were, admittedly, without any Rangers or Celtic players, fielded seven debutants, and lost Daniel Liddle to an early injury, while Colin McNab played on as a virtual passenger after suffering a blow to the head towards the end of the first half, but the *Daily Record* had no doubt about what it had witnessed: "Outclassed!" it roared. "There can be no excuses." Only the heroics of John Jackson, the goalkeeper, prevented an even greater humiliation.

Given England had been beaten 5–2 by France in Paris two days earlier, that week now seems to stand as a threshold, as the moment at which it became impossible to deny that the rest of the world had caught up with Britain (not that that stopped the British newspapers and soccer authorities from trying). The *Arbeiter-Zeitung* caught the mood perfectly: "If there was an elegiac note in watching the decline of the ideal the Scots represented for us, even yesterday, it was all the more refreshing to witness a triumph that sprang from true artistry. . . . Eleven footballers, eleven professionals—certainly, there are more important sides to life, yet this was ultimately a tribute to Viennese aesthetic sense, imagination and passion."

For the *Wunderteam*, that was just the beginning. Playing a traditional 2–3–5 with an elegant attacking center-half in Josef Smistik—but with an unorthodox center-forward who encouraged such fluidity that their system became known as the Danubian Whirl—Austria won nine and drew two of their next eleven games, scoring forty-four goals and winning the second edition of the Dr. Gerö Cup in the process. The coffeehouses were jubilant: their way had prevailed, largely because of Sindelar, a player who was, to their self-romanticizing eye, the coffeehouse made flesh. "He would play football as a grandmaster plays chess: with a broad mental conception, calculating moves and counter-moves in advance, always choosing the most promising of all possibilities," the theater critic Alfred Polgar wrote in his obituary in the *Pariser Tageszeitung*, an article remarkable for how many fundamental themes it drew together.

There was the analogy to chess Galeano had used to describe the Uruguayans of the twenties and, later still, Anatoliy Zelentsov would apply to Valeriy Lobanovskyi's Dynamo Kyiv. The influence of Hogan and his obsession with the instant control of the ball was apparent, as Polgar went on: "He was an unequalled trapper of a ball, and a stager of surprise counter-attacks, inexhaustibly devising tactical feints which were followed by the true attacking move that his deception had made irresistible, the opponents having been cunningly fooled by a flash of skill."

And, then, perhaps most strikingly, he pre-empts the thinking of the evolutionary biologist Stephen Jay Gould on "the universality of excellence." "I don't deny the differences in style and substance between athletic and conventional scholarly performance," Gould wrote, "but we surely err in regarding sports as a domain of brutish intuition. . . . The greatest athletes cannot succeed by bodily gifts alone. . . . One of the most intriguing, and undeniable, properties of great athletic performance lies in the impossibility of regulating certain central skills by overt mental deliberation: the required action simply doesn't grant sufficient time for the sequential processing of conscious decisions." Polgar said of Sindelar, "In a way he had brains in his legs, . . . and many remarkable and unexpected things occurred to them while they were running. Sindelar's shot hit the back of the net like the perfect punch-line, the ending that made it possible to understand and appreciate the perfect composition of the story, the crowning of which it represented."

And then, in December 1932, came the *Wunderteam*'s greatest test: England. They were not the best side in the world, far from it, but the world respected them for their influence over the development of the game and, at home, they remained unbeaten against foreign opposition. Spain had exposed England's vulnerability by beating them in Madrid in 1929, but two years later they felt the full force of the backlash, being hammered 7–1 at Highbury. Buoyed by the victory over Scotland, many in Austria were exuberantly hopeful, but Meisl, who always tended toward pessimism, was concerned and turned to his old friend and mentor, Jimmy Hogan.

Disenchanted with England, Hogan had moved to Switzerland in 1921, spending three years with Young Boys of Berne and then Lausanne, before returning to Budapest with MTK in their new guise as FC Hungaria. He then moved to Germany, working as an advisor to the soccer federation, coaching SC Dresden—where one of his pupils was Helmut Schön, who was assistant to Sepp Herberger when West Germany won the World Cup in 1954, and led them to victory himself in 1974—and generally evangelizing for a technically adept style of soccer that would ensure English soccer was soon overhauled by Europe.

He was initially greeted with suspicion and, when various local coaches complained about his lack of fluency in German, the German FA asked Hogan to prove himself by delivering a lecture without a translator. It began badly, as Hogan inadvertently presented himself as "a professor of languages, not a master of football" and got steadily worse. Attempting to stress the importance of the mind in soccer, he told his bemused audience that it was a game not merely of the body, but also of the committee.

Faced with laughter and derision, Hogan called for a ten-minute intermission and left the stage. When he returned, he was wearing his Bolton Wanderers uniform. He removed his cleats and his socks and, telling his audience that three-quarters of German players could not kick the ball properly, smashed a right-footed shot barefoot into a wooden panel fifteen yards away. As the ball bounced back to him he noted the value of being two-footed and let fly with another shot, this time with his left foot. This time the panel split in two. His point proven, Hogan undertook a lecture tour, in one month alone speaking to five thousand soccer players in the Dresden area. When he died in 1974, the then-secretary of the German Football Federation (DFB), Hans Passlack, wrote to Hogan's son, Frank, saying that Hogan was the founder of "modern football" in Germany.

Uneasy about the political situation, Hogan left Germany for Paris, sewing his savings into the seams of his plus-fours to avoid restrictions on the export of currency, but he struggled to maintain discipline there among a team of stars and returned to Lausanne, where he never came to terms with a chairman who believed that players should be fined for missing chances. When Meisl came calling, he was desperate for a challenge.

Austria, it must be said, seem to have been in need of him or at least in need of some outside confirmation of their talents. Two weeks before the game in London, with Sindelar unwell and playing far below his best, Austria had struggled to beat a scratch Vienna side 2–1. Nerves, evidently, were an issue, while there were fitness concerns over Adolf Vogl and Friedrich Gschweidl. Nonetheless, Austria was agog. Crowds gathered in the Heldenplatz to listen to commentary relayed over three loudspeakers, while the Parliamentary Finance Committee adjourned to follow the game.

The *Wunderteam* did not begin well, and within twenty-six minutes England were two up, both goals coming from the Blackpool forward Jimmy Hampson. Austria pulled one back six minutes into the second half, Sindelar and Anton Schall combining to set up Karl Zischek. Walter Nausch hit a post amid a welter of pressure, but then, as England rallied, an Eric Houghton free kick deflected off the ducking Schall and past Rudi Hiden in the Austria goal. Sindelar, with consummate control and a cool finish, made it 3–2, but almost as soon as he had done so a long-range effort from Sam Crooks put England back in charge. With England baffled by their opponents' habit of dropping behind the ball when out of possession, Austria continued to dominate, spinning their webs of passes, but their lack of thrust was to cost them. Zischek bundled in a corner with five minutes remaining, but it was too late. They lost 4–3, but their performance captured the imagination. "A revelation," said the *Daily Mail*, while the *Times* awarded Austria the "moral victory" and rhapsodized about their "passing skills."

Two years later, what was essentially the Austria national team played Arsenal at Highbury, although they were presented as a Vienna XI, matches between club and national sides being frowned upon by FIFA at the time. They lost 4–2, prompting Roland Allen to write in the *Evening Standard*, "It looks fine, it is fine: when the Austrians have learned how to turn all their cleverness into something that counts: when . . . they have organised the winning of football matches as highly as they have organised the taming of a football, they will make [everyone] sit up and take notice." The writing was on the wall, but nobody in England was minded to read it.

Instead, the two games were taken as confirmation of the cliché that continental European teams lack punch in the final third. Applied to the Austrians, there was a certain truth to it, but the wider point about ball retention was obscured, a situation that wasn't helped by Meisl's habit of talking in idealistic terms. "To us Middle Europeans," he said, "the attacking play of the British professional, seen from an aesthetic point of view, seems rather poor. Such play consists of assigning the job of scoring goals to the centre-forward and the wings, while to the inside-forwards is allotted the task of linking attackers and defenders, and more as half-backs than as attacking players. . . . The centre-forward, who, among us in Europe, is the leading figure, because of his technical excellence and tactical intelligence, in England limits his activity to exploiting the errors of the opposing defence."

He did, though, laud the pace at which the British played the game, saying it had left his own players "confused and disoriented": "Although their passing, swift and high, is rather lacking in precision, the English players compensate for this by the rare potency and great rapidity of their attacks." The familiar battle lines were drawn: England, physical, quick, and tough; the continent, technical, patient, and probably lacking in moral fiber.

Austria finally enjoyed the victory over England Meisl so craved in Vienna in May 1936. When he presented his team to Hogan, the Englishman questioned the stamina of the inside-forwards, to which Meisl replied that he expected to take a decisive lead in the first twenty minutes and spend the rest of the game defending it. He was right. Sindelar repeatedly dragged the center-half John Barker out of position—foreshadowing Harry Johnston's travails against Hungary's Nándor Hidegkuti seventeen years later—and England soon found themselves two down. George Camsell pulled one back early in the second half but, for all Meisl's bowler-hatted nervousness on the touchline, Austria's superiority was obvious. "We didn't know whether we were coming or going," Jack Crayston admitted. "And it was disgustingly hot." When the heat makes manic charging unsustainable and prioritizes possession, British teams have never prospered.

By then, though, the *Wunderteam* was in decline, and the Austrians had ceded their European supremacy to Italy. In terms of formation, the Italians—almost inadvertently—took up a middle ground between the English W-M and the 2–3–5 of the Danubians, but what set them apart was their ethos. "Technically less brilliant than its European rival," Glanville wrote, Italian soccer "compensated . . . by its greater forcefulness and the excellent physical condition of its players." A belief in the primacy of athleticism was perhaps natural under Fascism, but it corresponded too to the inclinations of Vittorio Pozzo, the bushy-haired visionary who became the presiding genius of interwar Italian soccer. Born near Turin in 1886, Pozzo had shown great promise as a runner, winning the 400m at the Piedmont Student Games, but was converted to soccer after a friend of his, Giovanni Goccione, who would go on to play at center-half for Juventus, mocked him for "running like a motor car" and suggested he should try running with "a ball in front of him."

No great player, Pozzo remained in academia, studying at the International School of Commerce in Zurich, where he learned English, French, and German, and then in London. Tiring of the expat community in the capital, he moved north to Bradford, where his father's influence found him a position studying the manufacture of wool. England, and soccer, suddenly gripped him. So determined did he become to understand his new home that, although a Catholic, he began to attend Anglican services. His weeks soon fell into the English routine: church on Sunday, work for five days, soccer on Saturday. His parents called him home to help with his brother's engineering firm, but he refused. His father cut off his allowance, but still he stayed, making ends meet by teaching languages.

Manchester United became Pozzo's favorite team, largely because of the style of their fabled half-back line of Dick Duckworth, Charlie Roberts, and Alec Bell. He took to hanging around by the players' exit at Old Trafford after matches and, one week, having finally plucked up the courage, he approached Roberts, told him what an admirer he was, and said how much he would appreciate the opportunity to talk with him about the game. It was the start of a lengthy friendship, from which grew the style

Pozzo would have his Italy side play twenty years later. He abhorred the third-back game, and demanded his center-half, like Roberts, be capable of sweeping long passes out to the wings. It was a belief he held fundamental and led, for instance, to his decision, having been rehired *comisario tecnico* in 1924, immediately to drop Fulvio Bernardini, an idol of the Roman crowds, because he was a "carrier" rather than a "dispatcher."

Pozzo finally went back to Italy to attend his sister's wedding, after which his family prevented him from returning to England. He soon found a position as secretary of the Italian Football Federation and was asked to take the national team to Sweden for the 1912 Olympics, becoming *comisario tecnico* for the first time. Having lost narrowly to Finland and then beaten Sweden, Italy were hammered 5–1 by Austria. The defeat was disappointing, if not unexpected, but it was significant in precipitating a first meeting between Pozzo and Meisl. They became friends and would be rivals for the rest of their lives.

Pozzo quit after a 3–1 defeat to Austria the following December and resumed his travels. He served as a major in the Alpine Regiment during the First World War and was made *comisario tecnico* for the second time following a 4–0 defeat to Austria shortly before the 1924 Olympics. They showed promise in Paris, beating Spain and Luxembourg before a narrow defeat to Switzerland, but Pozzo's wife died soon after, and he resigned again. For five years he served as a director of Pirelli, spending his spare time walking with his Alsatian in the mountains. In 1929, the Italian Federation came calling again. He served it for twenty years, turning Italy into the best side in Europe and probably the world.

When Pozzo had taken the job the first time, he had found a bloated league of sixty-four clubs, several of whom disestablished from the federation when he tried to form a more streamlined first division. By the time of his third coming, there was a professional league, and the Fascist government, having recognized the utility of sports as a propaganda tool, was eagerly investing in stadiums and infrastructure. "Whether beyond or within the borders, sporting or not, we Italians . . . shook and still shake with joy when seeing in these thoroughbred athletes, that overwhelm so many noble opponents, such a symbol of the overwhelming march of Mussolini's Italians," as Londo Ferretti, Mussolini's press officer, put it in *Lo Sport Fascista* after Italy's 1938 World Cup triumph.

The level to which Pozzo bought into Fascist ideology remains unclear. His associations with Mussolini led to him being shunned in the fifties and sixties and meant that the Stadio delle Alpi, the stadium built just outside Turin for the 1990 World Cup, was not named after him, but later in the nineties evidence emerged to suggest he had worked with the anti-Fascist resistance, taking food to partisans around Biella and helping Allied prisoners of war escape.

What is certainly true is that he made full use of the prevailing militarism to dominate and motivate his side. "More than one selector leads to compromise," he said, "and no great football team was ever built on that." He was an astute man-manager, developing a stern, paternalistic style to deal with players often idolized by fans of their clubs. He would, for instance, referee all practice games played in training, and if he thought a player refused to pass to a teammate because of some private grudge, he would send him off. If he picked two players who were known not to get along, he would force them to room together. It was his nationalism, though, that was most controversial. On the way to Budapest for a friendly against Hungary that Italy won 5–0, to take just one example, he made his players visit the First World War battlefields of Oslavia and Gorizia, stopping at the monumental cemetery at Redupiglia. "I told them it was good that the sad and terrible spectacle might have struck them: that whatever would be asked of us on that occasion was nothing compared with those that had lost their lives on those surrounding hills," he wrote in his autobiography. At other times, he would march at the head of his players singing the patriotic song "La Leggenda del Piave."

For all that, Pozzo was Anglophile enough to hark back to a golden age of fair play, fretting about the deleterious effects of the win bonuses that soon became a feature of the national league. "It is win at all costs," he said. "It is the bitter grudge against the adversary, it is the preoccupation of the result to the ends of the league table." He inclined, similarly, to a classical 2–3–5, but he lacked a center-half of sufficient mobility and creativity to play the formation well. Pozzo turned instead to Luisito Monti, who had played for Argentina in the 1930 World Cup. He joined Juventus in 1931 and became one of the *oriundi*, the South American players who, thanks to Italian heritage, qualified to play for their adopted country. Already thirty when he signed, Monti was overweight and, even after a month of solitary training, was not quick. He was, though, fit and became known as *doble ancho* (double-wide) for his capacity to cover the ground. Pozzo, perhaps influenced by a formation that had already come into being at Juventus, used him as a *centro mediano*, a halfway house—not quite Charlie Roberts, but certainly not Herbie Roberts either. He would drop when the other team had possession and mark the opposing center-forward but would advance and become an attacking fulcrum when his side had the ball. Although he was not a third back—Glanville, in fact, says it was only in 1939 with an article Fulvio Bernardini wrote after Pozzo's side had drawn 2–2 against England in Milan that the full implications of the W-M (the *sistema*, as Pozzo called it, as opposed to the traditional *metodo*) were fully appreciated in Italy—he played deeper than a traditional center-half, and so the two inside-forwards retreated to support the wing-halves. The shape was thus a 2–3–2–3, a W-W. At the time it seemed, as the journalist Mario Zappa put it in *La Gazzetta dello Sport*, "a model of play that is the synthesis of the best elements of all the most admired systems."

Shape is one thing; style is another, and Pozzo, despite his qualms, was fundamentally pragmatic. That he had a technically accomplished side is not in doubt, as they proved, before Monti had been called into the side, in a 3–0 victory over Scotland in 1931. "The men are fast," the *Corriere della Sera* reported of the hapless tourists, "athletically well prepared, and seem sure enough in kicking and heading, but in classic play along the ground, they look like novices." That would be stern enough criticism for any side, but for players brought up in the finest pattern-weaving tradition, it is damning.

Back then, the great center-forward Giuseppe Meazza, who had made his debut in 1930, was regularly compared to a bullfighter, although a popular song of the time claimed "he scored to the rhythm of the foxtrot." That sense of fun and élan, though, was soon to fade. Meazza remained a stylish forward, and there was no doubting the quality of the likes of Silvio Piola, Raimundo Orsi, and Gino Colaussi, but physicality and combativeness became increasingly central. "In the tenth year of the fascist era," an editorial in *Lo Stadia* noted in 1932, "the youth are toughened for battle, and for the fight, and more for the game itself; courage, determination, gladiatorial pride, chosen sentiments of our race, cannot be excluded."

Pozzo was also one of the earliest exponents of man marking, a sign that soccer had become not merely about a side playing its own game but about stopping the opposition playing theirs. In a friendly against Spain in Bilbao in 1931, for instance, he had Renato Cesarini mark Ignacio Aguirrezabala on the logic that "if I succeeded in cutting off the head with which the eleven adversaries thought, the whole system would collapse."

That raised concerns among the purists, but it was at the 1934 World Cup that questions really began to be asked about the ethics of Pozzo's Italy. Having drawn 1–1 with England—who were still persisting in their policy of isolation—a year earlier, Italy, playing at home, were always going to be among the favorites, particularly given the sense that the *Wunderteam* was past its peak. For once Meisl's pessimism seemed justified as he complained of the absence of Hiden, his goalkeeper, and of players exhausted by foreign tours with their club sides, although he also claimed, apparently accepting the English criticism that his side lacked punch, that

Italy 1 Austria 0, World Cup semifinal, San Siro, Milan, 3 June 1934

if he could have borrowed the Arsenal center-forward Cliff Bastin, they could have walked to victory.

Italy and Austria, Pozzo and Meisl, met in the semifinal, but by then the tournament had already begun to slink into disrepute. Austria were far from innocent, having been involved in a brawl in their quarterfinal victory over Hungary, but it was the 1–1 draw between Italy and Spain at the same stage that marked the descent of the tournament into violence. Monti, for all his ability, was quite prepared to indulge in the darker arts, while Ricardo Zamora, the Spain goalkeeper, was battered so frequently that he was unable to play in the replay the following day. Sources vary on whether three or four Spaniards were forced to leave the field through injury, but, either way, Spain were left feeling aggrieved as a diving header from Meazza gave Italy a 1–0 win.

The anticipated clash of styles in the semifinal was a damp squib. Sindelar was marked out of the game by Monti, Austria failed to have shot in the first forty minutes and Italy won by a single goal, Meazza bundling into Hiden's replacement, Peter Platzer, and Enrique Guaita, another of the *oriundi*, forcing the loose ball over the line. It was left to Czechoslovakia, who had beaten Germany in the other semi, to defend the honor of the Danubian school. At times they threatened to embarrass Italy and took a seventy-sixth-minute lead through Antonín Puč. František Svoboda hit a post and Jiří Sobotka missed another fine chance, but, with eight minutes remaining, Orsi equalized with a drive that swerved freakishly past František Plánička. Seven minutes into extra time, a limping Meazza crossed from the right, Guaita helped it on and Angelo Schiavio, who later spoke of having been driven by "the strength of desperation," beat Josef Čtyřoký to fire in the winner. Mussolini's Italy had the victory it so desired, but elsewhere the strength of that desire and the methods to which they were prepared to stoop to achieve it left a sour taste. "In the majority of countries the world championship was called a sporting fiasco," the Belgian referee John Langenus said, "because beside the will to win all sporting considerations were non-existent and because, moreover, a certain spirit brooded over the whole championship."

A meeting with England that November—the so-called Battle of Highbury—only confirmed the impression, as Italy reacted badly after Monti broke a bone in his foot in a second-minute challenge with Ted Drake. "For the first quarter of an hour there might just as well not have been a ball on the pitch as far as the Italians were concerned," said Stanley Matthews, the winger who was the first winner of the Ballon d'Or and was for a long time considered England's greatest ever player. "They were like men possessed, kicking anything and everything that moved." England capitalized on their indiscipline to take a 3–0 lead, but after Pozzo had calmed his side at half-time, they played stirringly to come back to 3–2 in the second half.

Beneath the aggression and the cynicism, Italy were unquestionably talented, and they retained the World Cup in 1938 with what Pozzo believed was his best side. Again, the focus was on defensive solidity. "The big secret of the Italian squad is its capacity to attack with the fewest men possible, without ever distracting the half-backs from their defensive work," Zappa wrote. Austria had been subsumed by Germany by then, but a team formed by the two semifinalists of the previous competition fared poorly and lost after a rematch to Karl Rappan's Switzerland in the first round. Czechoslovakia went out to Brazil in the last eight, but Hungary progressed to the final for the last showdown between the Danubian school and Pozzo. Italy proved too quick and too athletic and, with Michele Andreolo, another *oriundo* who had replaced Monti as the *centro mediano*, keeping a check on György Sárosi, the Hungarian center-forward, Meisl's conception of the game was made to look sluggish and old-fashioned. It did not pass without lament—"How shall we play the game?" the French journalist Jean Eskenazi asked. "As though we are making love or catching a bus?"—but pass it did.

Other Fascist countries followed a similar path. Soccer had begun in Spain in much the same way it had begun everywhere: it was introduced by the British. Specifically it was introduced by workers at a mining settlement in Minas de Rio Tinto in southwestern Spain where a British investor named Hugh Matheson had bought a moribund copper mine in 1873, paying £3.5 million, the first payment of which was made in gold coins transported by train and then oxcart.

The first recorded game, played in 1887 by two teams made up entirely of non-Spaniards on a field that now lies under an enormous slag-heap, marked the feast day of San Roque. The main entertainment would traditionally have been bullfighting, but the mining company had knocked the stadium down three years earlier claiming it had become a focal point for prostitutes and drunks. Myth has it that the match represented the British reaching out to the Spanish, a sporting event engaging both sides, but that, Jimmy Burns said, was far from the truth. Rather, the game confirmed the differences between British and Spanish. "One can imagine the local crowd being unimpressed initially . . . the game . . . lacked both the creativity and brinksmanship of the one popular local entertainment they could claim as their own." The histories of soccer and bullfighting in Spain have been intertwined ever since.

British involvement in mining also took the game to Bilbao, and it was there that it really took hold. The first purpose-built soccer stadium in Spain was the San Mamés, built in Bilbao in 1913, and that became the cradle of the Spanish game. Its personality was tough, energetic, and rooted in the values of British industry.

Athletic Club, the first superpower of the Spanish game, was founded in 1903 from a temporary merger of two pre-existing teams: one made up of British workers in the city and one that had been established by students at the Gymnasium Zamacois, who had learned the game while studying in England. Their first manager, unsurprisingly given the esteem in which British soccer was held, was an Englishman, Mr. Shepherd. Although the rule stipulating that only those of Basque descent could play for Athletic was soon implemented, the club remained Anglophile. It was backed financially by the De la Sota industrial and shipping conglomerate that supported the Allies during the First World War, continuing to trade with them throughout the conflict, and it stuck both with the English form of the name and with a policy of employing English coaches.

Shepherd was succeeded in 1914 by Billy Barnes, who had scored the winning goal for Sheffield United in the 1902 FA Cup final replay before going on to play for West Ham, Luton, and Queen's Park Rangers. He won two Copas del Rey, went back to Britain to sign up for service in the First World War, and returned to the club in August 1920. "Basque football has progressed a lot since I was last here," he said. "When I first came it was a patient, slow game of short passing—elegant to watch but totally unpractical, Scots style. I introduced at Athletic a fast game with long passing, taking the ball from wing to wing, and fast players in the centre capable of scoring goals. Today I find most clubs have a tendency to play this way whereas Athletic seems to have lost its way."

That same month, at the 1920 Olympic Games, Athletic's energetic approach was reified as the Spanish style. Spain went to Antwerp without any great expectation and with a team made up largely of players from the northern sides—because they played on grass, while those from the center and south tended to play on parched mud. They beat Denmark 1–0 in their first game but then lost 3–1 to the eventual gold-medalists Belgium in the quarterfinal. That wasn't the end of their tournament, though, as they entered a complicated repechage system that became a contest for the silver medal when Czechoslovakia were disqualified after storming off the field in the final in protest at the British referee's handling of the game.

Spain beat Sweden 2–1 and Italy 2–0 to set up a match for silver against the Netherlands. Félix Sesúmaga scored twice as Spain won that play-off 3–1, but it was another Basque who returned as the hero. At half-time in the game against Sweden, Spain trailed 1–0. Six minutes into the second half, they equalized through José María Belauste, a battered figure, his nose flattened by frequent blows, swollen ears pinned back by the knotted handkerchief he wore on his head to disguise his incipient alopecia. Two minutes after that, Domingo Acedo got the winner. It was Belauste's goal, though, the goal that began the recovery, that seemed to sum up the Basque style. "When play resumed after half-time," wrote Manolo de Castro, using the pseudonym Handicap, "Spain seemed to rally behind a call to battle and launched an attack of such ferocity that within two minutes it had secured a free-kick just outside the penalty area." Belauste launched himself at a chipped cross and took a number of Swedes with him as he bundled the ball into the net. It was, Handicap said, "a Herculean goal." The following day, a Dutch newspaper, comparing Spain's play to the ferocity of the Spanish troops that had sacked Antwerp in 1576, coined the term *la furia*. Spain happily adopted it.

The goal was mythologized as the incarnation of *la furia* and exaggerated; the great goalkeeper Ricardo Zamora later claimed Bellauste had carried the ball into the net on his chest with four Swedes clinging to his shirt. And so Spain became convinced that their way of playing, the right way to play, was *la furia*, defined by Burns as "a particularly muscular and aggressive style of football, blessed with nobility of intent and execution, over which the Basques at club level had already claimed a kind of copyright but which was absorbed into the broader national psyche."

Yet almost as soon as *la furia* had been accepted, its limitations were exposed. In June 1921, a Basque team featuring many Spain internationals, Belauste among them, set off for a tour of South America. They went first to Argentina, where they were beaten 4–0 by a Buenos Aires XI, unable for all their running to get the ball from opponents who played neat, coherent, technical soccer. They went on to Rosario, to Montevideo and São Paulo and everywhere found themselves struggling against more skillful opposition, eight games on tour yielding two wins, a draw, and five defeats.

There was change too in Bilbao. Barnes stayed for just a season, winning another Copa del Rey. Athletic advertised in the *Daily Mail* and the *Sporting Life* for a replacement and, from hundreds of enthusiastic applicants, selected a Mr. Burton. He had been in the job for just two months, though, when his lungs, weakened by poison gas during the war, collapsed. A committee of two former players and the captain ran the side for a while before Athletic were saved by Fred Pentland, who would become the most revered of all the British coaches to work in Spain between the wars.

The son of the lord mayor of Birmingham, Pentland had been an outside-right for Blackburn, QPR, and Middlesbrough, who had won five caps for England. He retired as a player in 1913 and moved to Berlin to accept an offer to become coach of the Germany national team—the job

Jimmy Hogan turned down to work with Austria. When the First World War began, he was interned in the civilian prisoner of war camp at Ruhleben, a racetrack six miles to the west of Berlin. Conditions at first were dreadful. Prisoners slept on straw in lice-infested horse trailers. They washed at a single standpipe and wore wooden clogs and coats charitably donated by locals. Their daily ration consisted of a ladleful of watery porridge and a lump of blood sausage.

Eventually, the German authorities allowed the prisoners to run their own affairs. What happened next was, as Barney Ronay put it in Issue Three of the *Blizzard*, "a love letter to the resourcefulness of a certain strain of British organisational pluck, and an expression of the creative cultural eclecticism often overlooked in the dubious legacy of empire." A whole society grew up, complete with postal service, police force, magazine, and library. A map of the camp shows tennis courts, a YMCA, a casino, a post office, a tea house, office buildings, wash houses and two full-sized soccer fields.

The population was entirely male but otherwise astonishingly diverse. "From the manor house to the slum, scarcely a breed or profession was unrepresented," one prisoner wrote in a pamphlet published shortly after the war. "All were jammed together in a small stableyard—company directors and seamen, concert musicians and factory workers, science professors and jockeys. . . . We were indeed a mixed crowd. I have walked along to the kitchen with the Earl of Perth (nicknamed Pearl of the earth), a coloured and a fireman."

The camp was overflowing with personalities and eccentrics. There was F. Charles Adler, a world-renowned conductor who had studied under Gustav Mahler; Sir James Chadwick, a Nobel Prize–winning physicist who had been the first to conceive the idea of the nuclear bomb; Prince Monolulu, a horse-racing tipster and probably the biggest black celebrity in Britain at the time; "Bertie" Smylie, the alcoholic editor of the *Irish Times* who usually sported a sombrero; and Geoffrey Pyke, who invented aircraft carriers made out of ice, once demonstrating them to Winston Churchill in his bath.

And, as along with Pentland, there was a remarkable number of soccer players and former soccer players. There was his former Middlesbrough teammate Steve Bloomer, who scored twenty-eight goals in twenty-three matches for England and had been named as coach of Britannia Berlin 92 in July 1914; his former Blackburn teammate, the full-back Sam Wolstenholme, who had become manager of the North German Football Association's representative side in spring 1914; Fred Spiksley, a former Sheffield Wednesday outside-left, who would win national titles as a coach in Sweden, Mexico, and Germany; the former Scotland international and Tottenham manager John Cameron, the coach of Dresdner SC; John Brearley, who had played for Cameron at Spurs and had become coach of Viktoria 89 Berlin; and the Germany international Edwin Dutton, whose parents had emigrated to Germany from South Shields.

Without the usual pressures of life, the prisoners set about educating themselves and having fun. "Activities were extended, improved, subdivided and elaborate to the point where Ruhleben became a world in itself," the journalist Israel Cohen, another of the inmates, noted. "It was a necessity if we were to maintain our physical fitness and save ourselves from ennui and inertia." There were classes on calculus, elementary physics, inorganic chemistry, organic chemistry, radioactivity, heredity, biology, music, literature, German literature (in German), Italian literature (in Italian), Shakespeare, and Euripides. A theater was established with a standing orchestra, and music hall shows were put on, with the female impersonators proving hugely popular.

Within a day of the camp opening it had seen its first kickabout and within two weeks teams called Tottenham Hotspurs, Manchester Rangers, and Bolton Wanderers had been set up. "There was only one football and none too robust," Cohen noted, while goals were marked out with "piled-up jackets." The camp commander, General von Kessel, disapproved of the games, and, with the onset of winter, the burgeoning league was abandoned. Over the winter, though, Von Kessel seems to have had a change of heart. He commandeered a field adjacent to the camp, on which the two soccer fields were marked out. The Ruhleben Football Association was established by Pentland, Bloomer, and Cameron, with the first game played under their regulations between Ruhleben, captained by Bloomer, and "The Rest," captained by a Mr. Richards on March 29. "The form in this game was so good," the camp magazine reported, "that everyone could see with practice the play could reach a pretty high standard." On May 2 an England XI featuring Pentland, Wolstenholme, and Bloomer took on a World XI captained by Cameron. Each of the fourteen barracks entered two teams into a league, which was so keenly contested and followed that crowds of more than a thousand were common.

In September 1915, the Ruhleben Football Association published its handbook. Printed in Berlin "at great cost" it ran to forty-eight pages and featured biographies of players, interviews with captains, and some tactical discussion. "It is also," Ronay wrote, "in its own way a first: the first time anything close to a coaching manual or a tactical guide had been written. Decanted out of the heady intellectualism of Ruhleben's multi-discipline school, the Ruhleben FA had caught the literary bug. The handbook is a suggestion of what might have followed had English football been able to re-absorb a hint of the furious progressiveness of peak-era Ruhleben." Pentland came to favor a short-passing game, something he supposedly picked up at Blackburn. As Ronay points out, though, there's little evidence for that, and it's at least as probable that he came to his conclusions about how the game should be played in the radical atmosphere of Ruhleben where there was little pressure for results and no crowds bellowing for the ball to be humped forward.

Pentland returned to Britain after the war and, while recuperating in the West Country, married his nurse, a war widow who was working with a Voluntary Aid Detachment. He soon returned to the continent, though, taking charge of the France side at the 1920 Olympics. After beating Italy in the quarterfinal, they lost to Czechoslovakia in the semifinals and had gone home before Czechoslovakia's expulsion, which might have offered them a route to the silver that was eventually won by Spain.

It was to Spain that Pentland then headed, first to Racing Santander and then, drawn by a salary of 10,000 pesetas a month, to Athletic. At his first training session, his first act was to teach his players how to tie their laces properly: "Get the basics right," he said, "and the rest will follow." He dismantled the long-ball approach of which Barnes had been so proud and instead instilled a passing game. It may still have been infused with the tenacity and determination of *la furia*, but it was soccer played with more thought and less urgency. Pentland would smoke cigars while training and refused to let the climate compromise his sense of what constituted proper dress. A photograph of him from *El Norte Deportivo* in 1928 shows a stern figure in a heavy suit accessorized with a spotted tie and an impeccably folded pocket handkerchief, with just a hint of an ironic smile drifting beneath his moustache and unyielding stare. And on his head, of course, is the trademark bowler hat from which he drew his nickname, *El Bombín*. He was idiosyncratic and demanding—and he was hugely successful.

Athletic, playing with slightly withdrawn inside-forwards, won back-to-back Biscay titles under Pentland as well as the 1923 Copa del Rey. Athletic players would celebrate major victories by snatching Pentland's hat from his head and jumping on it until it was destroyed. "Only three minutes left for you, bowler hat!" Pentland is said to have shouted as the final of the Copa del Rey drew to a conclusion.

He went to Athletic Madrid (the Atlético form was adopted only in 1941) in 1925, led them to the final of the Copa the following year, had a season with Real Oviedo, then returned to Athletic Madrid, winning El Campeonato del Centro in 1927. When England came to play at the Estadio Metropolitano in Madrid in 1929, he worked as an advisor to José María Mateos and helped mastermind a 4–3 victory for Spain—England's first defeat to continental opposition. Pentland left Madrid for Bilbao later in 1929; by the time he returned to Bilbao in 1933, he had collected two la Liga titles, four further Copas, and three more Biscay titles—and had seen his side beat Barcelona 12–1, still their record defeat. With the civil war approaching, Pentland left Spain in 1936, working briefly as assistant manager of Brentford before taking on his only first-team coaching job in England, with Barrow. As with so many of the early pioneers—most notably Hogan—Pentland remained unappreciated at home. At Athletic, though, he is regarded as the man who made the club. In 1959 he was invited back to Bilbao for a testimonial game against Chelsea at which he was given a Distinguished Members medal. When he died three years later, Athletic held a memorial service at San Mamés.

The English tradition was continued in Bilbao by William Garbutt, who had enjoyed success in Italy with Genoa and Napoli. He won la Liga in 1935–1936 but returned to Italy at the outbreak of the civil war. Franco's victory had profound consequences for Athletic. They were forced to change their name to Atlético and to abandon their policy of selecting only Basques, but Franco didn't hate them, far from it; until Real Madrid came to dominate Europe in the late fifties, Atlético Bilbao were his favorite team.

Franco's attitude toward the Basques was complex. Although he refused to allow any sense of the Basques as a nation, he and other right-wingers accepted that the roots of the "true Spain" lay in the Basque country, bound up with Catholicism and notions of empire and surviving against the odds. Basques were seen as being part of Spain's warrior class: as Burns put it, their "essential values, steeped in virility, are bravery, self-sacrifice, obedience to leaders and a sense of honour." Those qualities were central to the educational ideals of the Jesuit order, which had been founded by the Basque solider Ignatius of Loyola in the sixteenth century. The Jesuit schools, like the English public schools, saw sports as an essential part of building character. It was at one such school that Rafael Moreno Aranzadi, better known as Pichichi, the "Little Duck," developed his love of soccer. Another who played in a knotted handkerchief, he was a prolific striker for Athletic and a hero of the 1920 Olympic side. It was less for his goal-scoring feats, though, than because he was the embodiment of Catholic-Basque-Spanishness that the Francoist *Marca* chose to name the award for the top scorer in the Spanish league after him when they established the prize in 1953. While attempting to eradicate Basque nationalism, Franco lionized Basque soccer players as the epitome of Spanishness: the *furia española* was resurrected, only this time it was specifically infused with the spirit of the dictatorship.

That was most obvious in the case of Athletic Madrid, who in 1939 merged with Aviación National, a team that had been founded by members of the air force during the civil war. Given that they were struggling with a huge debt and that eight of their players had died in the conflict, there was a certain logic to the merger, but a number of Athletic fans were appalled. The club, after all, had been established by Basques as a Madrid offshoot of Athletic of Bilbao; it was an outsiders' team, not the club of the establishment. The ethos of the club on the field changed to reflect the club's new military leadership, something made clear by criticisms made by a general to Zamora, Atlético's coach, in 1939–1940, the first season after the resumption of the league. "What's lacking in this team," he said, "is *cojones*, a lot of *cojones* . . . the team has to run more and throw everything at the opposition . . . a coach needs to have a bit of spunk, impose discipline, use the whip now and again." Zamora evidently managed to implant the necessary *cojones* and Athletic Aviación de Madrid won the league that season and defended their title the following year.

In fact, to an extent *la furia* was the spirit of the dictatorship, promoted as part of the propaganda of Franco's New Spain, part of the tradition that had seen the Muslims expelled from Granada and the conquistadors set off across the Atlantic and into which Don Quixote was co-opted as exemplary of the Spanish refusal to compromise. "The *furia española* is present in all aspects of Spanish life, to a greater extent than ever," said an editorial in the Falangist newspaper *Arriba* in 1939. "In sport, the *furia* best manifests itself in football, a game in which the virility of the Spanish race can find full expression, usually imposing itself, in international contests, over the more technical but less aggressive foreign teams." Soccer, for Franco's Spain as much as Mussolini's Italy, became a martial pursuit.

As Sindelar reached the end of his career and with Meisl aging, the Danubian style of soccer may have faded away anyway, but the rise of Fascism made sure of it. With the Anschluss came the end of the central European Jewish intelligentsia, the end of the spirit of the coffeehouse, and the death of Sindelar. As the thirties went on, the great center-forward had increasingly withdrawn from the national team, but he allowed himself to be picked for what was dubbed a Reconciliation Game between an Ostmark XI and a German lineup on April 3, 1938.

Soccer in Germany was not so advanced as in Austria, but it was improving. Otto Nerz, the first national coach, who was hired on July 1, 1926, was an early advocate of the W-M, but something of Hogan's teaching lived on through Schalke 04, who reached nine of the ten championship playoff finals between 1933 and 1942, winning six. Their coach, Gustav Wieser, was an Austrian, and under him they practiced a version of the whirl that became known as *der Kreisel*—the "spinning top." According to the defender Hans Bornemann, it was not the man with the ball but those out of possession running into space who determined the direction of their attacks. "It was only when there was absolutely nobody left you could pass the ball to that we finally put it into the net," he said. Hogan may have admired their style, but he would have questioned their ethos.

Such excess troubled Nerz, and he refused to pick both Schalke's feted inside-forwards, Ernst Kuzorra and Fritz Szepan, for the national team. (He did, in fact, call up Szepan for the 1934 World Cup but bafflingly played him at center-half.) "Nerz," Kuzorra explained, "said to me: 'Let me tell you something: your odds and ends football at Schalke, all that passing around, doesn't impress me one bit. If you and Szepan play together it'll just be fiddling and dribbling around.'"

Germany were the semifinalist in Italy in 1934, which encouraged thoughts that they might win gold on home soil at the 1936 Olympics. Instead they lost, humiliatingly, 2–0 to Norway in what, unfortunately for Nerz, was the only soccer match Hitler ever attended. Sepp Herberger, an assistant to Nerz and the man who would lead West Germany to victory at the 1954 World Cup, was not at the game, having gone to watch Italy play Japan in another quarterfinal. He was eating a dinner of knuckle of pork and sauerkraut at the team camp when another coach brought him news of Germany's defeat. Herberger pushed his plate away and never touched knuckle of pork again. He succeeded Nerz after the tournament and immediately switched to a more Danubian model, bringing in Adolf Urban and Rudi Gellesch from Schalke and deploying the elegant, hard-drinking Mannheim inside-forward Otto Siffling as a central striker. The result was a team of greater flexibility that reached its peak on May 16, 1937, with an 8–0 friendly victory over Denmark in Breslau (what is now Wrocław). "The robot style people like to pin on Germany sank into the realm of legend," the journalist Gerd Kramer wrote. "Artistic football triumphed."

Still, they were neither as talented nor as artistic as the Austrians, and the Ostmark XI dominated the reconciliation game. Fact has become rather obscured by subsequent myths, but what is clear is that Sindelar missed a series of chances in the first half. Given how frequently he rolled the ball a fraction wide of the posts, even contemporary reports wondered whether he had been mocking the Germans—and supposed orders not to score—by missing on purpose. Eventually, midway through the second half, he knocked in a rebound, and when his friend Schasti Sesta looped a second from a free kick, he celebrated by dancing in front of a directors' box packed with high-ranking Nazis.

In the months that followed, Sindelar, who never made any secret of his Social Democratic leanings, repeatedly refused to play for Herberger's united German team. In August he bought a café from Leopold Drill, a Jew forced to give it up under new legislation—paying DM20,000, which was either a very fair price or disgracefully opportunistic, depending which account you choose to believe—and was censured by the authorities for his reluctance to put up Nazi posters. To claim he was a dissident, though, as some have, is to take things too far.

On the morning of January 23, 1939, his friend Gustav Hartmann, looking for Sindelar, broke down the door of a flat on Annagasse. He found him, naked and dead, lying alongside the unconscious form of his girlfriend of ten days, Camilla Castignola. She died later at the hospital, the victim, like Sindelar, of carbon monoxide poisoning caused by a faulty heater. Or at least that was what the police said, as they ended their enquiries after two days. The public prosecutor, though, had still not reached a conclusion six months later when the Nazi authorities ordered the case be closed. In a 2003 BBC documentary, Egon Ulbrich, a friend of Sindelar, claimed a local official was bribed to record his death as an accident, which ensured that he would receive a state funeral. Others came up with their own explanations. On January 25, a piece in the Austrian newspaper *Kronen Zeitung* claimed that "everything points towards this great man having become the victim of murder through poisoning." In his "Ballad on the Death of a Footballer," Torberg suggested suicide by a man who felt "disowned" by "the new order." There were later rumours that Sindelar or Castignola or both were Jewish. It is true that Sindelar played for Austria Vienna, the club of the Jewish bourgeoisie, and had been born in Moravia, a region from which many Jews had emigrated to the capital, but his family was Catholic. It is just about conceivable that Castignola, an Italian, may have had Jewish origins, but they were well enough hidden that she had been allowed to become co-owner of a bar in the week before her death. Most tellingly, neighbors had complained a few days earlier that one of the chimneys in the block was defective.

The available evidence suggests Sindelar's death was an accident, and yet the sense that heroes cannot mundanely die prevailed. What, after all, at least to a romantic liberal mind, could better symbolize Austria at the point of the Anschluss than this athlete-artist, the darling of Viennese society, being gassed alongside his Jewish girlfriend? "The good Sindelar followed the city, whose child and pride he was, to its death," Polgar wrote in his obituary. "He was so inextricably entwined with it that he had to die when it did. All the evidence points to suicide prompted by loyalty to his homeland. For to live and play football in the downtrodden, broken, tormented city meant deceiving Vienna with a repulsive spectre of itself. . . . But how can one play football like that? And live, when a life without football is nothing?"

To its end, the soccer of the coffeehouse remained heroically romantic.

5

ORGANIZED DISORDER

The soccer boom came late to the USSR and, perhaps because of that, it rapidly took on a radical aspect, uninhibited by historically rooted notions of the "right" way of doing things. British sailors had played the game by the docks in Odessa as early as the 1860s. A description in the *Hunter* magazine gives some idea of the chaos and physicality of the game: "it is played by people with solid muscles and strong legs—a weak one would only be an onlooker in such a mess," wrote their apparently bemused and disapproving reporter.

It was only in the 1890s that the sport began to be properly organized. In Russia, as in so many other places, the British had a decisive role, first in St. Petersburg, and later in Moscow, where Harry Charnock, general manager of the Morozov Mills, established the club that would become Dinamo Moscow in an attempt to persuade his workers to spend their Saturdays doing something other than drinking vodka. When Soviet myth making was at its height, it was said that the Dinamo sports club, which was controlled by the Ministry of the Interior and ran teams across the USSR, chose blue and white as their colors to represent water and air, the two elements without which man could not live. The truth is rather that Charnock was from Blackburn and dressed his team in the colors of the Blackburn Rovers.

Further west, the influence was naturally more central European. The city of Lviv was still part of the Austro-Hungarian Empire when, in 1894, it hosted the first soccer match played on what is now Ukrainian soil, a brief exhibition during a demonstration of sports by the Sokol Sports Club. By the time a national league was established in 1936, the British were long gone (the expatriate dominance ended in 1908 when Sport, a Russian team, won the Aspeden Cup, the local St. Petersburg competition), but the early 2–3–5 lingered as the default. The modification of the offside law in 1925 seems to have made little difference tactically and, with the USSR's isolation from FIFA restricting meetings with foreign opposition largely to games against amateur sides, there was little to expose how far the Soviets were falling behind.

All that changed in 1937. The coming of the national league might have led to more sophisticated analysis of the game anyway, but the trigger for development was the arrival of a Basque side on the first leg of a world tour aimed at raising awareness of the Basque cause during the Spanish Civil War. Because of their rarity, matches against foreign sides were always eagerly anticipated, all the more so in 1937 after the release the year before of *Vratar* (The Keeper), Semyon Timoshenko's hugely popular musical comedy. It features a young working-class boy—played by the matinee idol Grigori Pluzhnik—spotted catching a watermelon as it fell from a cart and selected for a local side to play against a touring team. Predictably, if ridiculously, after making a series of fine saves, the hero runs the length of the field in the final minute to score the winner. The film's most famous song rams home the obvious political allegory: "Hey, keeper, prepare for the fight / You are a sentry in the goal. / Imagine there is a border behind you."

The real-life tourists, though, featuring six members of the Spain squad from the 1934 World Cup, were no patsies for Soviet propaganda and, employing a W-M formation, hammered Lokomotiv 5–1 in their first game. Dinamo were then beaten 2–1, and, after a 2–2 draw against a Leningrad XI, the Basques returned to Moscow to beat the Dinamo Central Council's Select XI 7–4. Their final game in Russia saw them face Spartak, the reigning champions. Determined to end the embarrassment, the head of Spartak's coaching council, Nikolai Starostin, called up a number of players from other clubs, including the Dynamo Kyiv forwards Viktor Shylovskyi and Konstantyn Shchehotskyi, who had starred in a Kyiv Select XI's 6–1 victory over Red Star Olympic—a rare game against professionals on a tour of Paris in 1935. Starostin decided to match the Basques shape for shape, converting his center-half into a third back to try to restrict the influence of Isidro Lángara, the Basque center-forward. As Starostin records in his book *Beginnings of Top-Level Football*, the move was far from popular, with the most vocal opponent being the center-half, his brother Andrei. "'Do you want me to be famous across the whole Soviet Union?' he asked. 'You are denying me room to breathe! Who will help the attack? You are destroying the tactic that has been played out for years.'"

This was not, though, Spartak's first experiment with a third back. A couple of years earlier, injuries on a tour of Norway had forced them to tinker with their usual 2–3–5. "Spartak used a defensive version of the W-M by enhancing the two backs with a half-back," Alexander Starostin, another of the brothers, said. "When necessary, both the insides drew back." Impressed by the possibilities of the system, Spartak briefly continued the third-back experiment as they prepared for the 1936 spring season. "That thought, brave but unpopular in the country, was ditched after a 5–2 defeat to Dinamo [Moscow] in a friendly," Nikolai Starostin said. "Now came the second attempt, again in a friendly, but this time in a very important international encounter. It was a huge risk."

And not just from a sporting point of view. The authorities took the game so seriously that, in the buildup, Ivan Kharchenko, the chairman of the Committee of Physical Culture; Alexander Kosarev, the head of Comsomol (the organization of young Communists); and various other party officials slept at Spartak's training base at Tarasovka. "Spartak was the last hope," Nikolai Starostin wrote in his autobiography, *Football Through the Years*. "All hell broke loose! There were letters, telegrams, calls giving us advice and wishing us good luck. I was summoned to several bosses of different ranks and they explained that the whole of the country was waiting on our victory."

The day did not begin auspiciously, as Spartak were caught in a traffic jam, causing the kickoff to be delayed. Twice in the first half they took the lead, only for the Basques to level, but, after Shylovskyi had converted a controversial fifty-seventh-minute penalty, they ran away with it, Vladimir Stepanov completing a hat trick in a 6–2 win. Nikolai Starostin later insisted his brother's performance in an unfamiliar role had been "brilliant," although the newspapers and the goalkeeper, Anatoly Akimov, disagreed, pointing out that Lángara had dominated him in the air and scored one of the Basque goals.

That defeat proved an aberration. The Basques went on to beat Dynamo Kyiv, Dinamo Tbilisi and a team representing Georgia, prompting a furious piece in *Pravda*. Under the demanding headline "Soviet Players Should Become Invincible," it laid down what had become obvious: "The performances of Basque Country in the USSR showed that our best teams are far from high quality. . . . The deficiencies of Soviet football are particularly intolerable as there are no young people like ours in other countries, young people embraced by the care, attention and love of the party and government." Amid the bombast, there was some sense. "It is clear," the piece went on, "that improving the quality of the Soviet teams depends directly on matches against serious opponents. The matches against the Basques have been highly beneficial to our players (long passes, playing on the flanks, heading the ball)."

Four days later, the Basques rather proved *Pravda*'s point by completing the Soviet leg of their tour with a 6–1 victory over a Minsk XI. The lessons of the Basques, though, were not forgotten. It took time for the calls for increased involvement in international sports to be heeded, but it had been recognized that the W-M offered a number of intriguing possibilities.

The man who seized upon them most eagerly was Boris Arkadiev. Already highly regarded, he gradually established himself as the first great

Soviet theorist of soccer. His 1946 book, *Tactics of Football*, was for years regarded as a bible for coaches across Eastern Europe.

Born in St. Petersburg in 1899, Arkadiev moved to Moscow after the revolution, where, alongside a respectable playing career, he taught fencing at the Mikhail Frunze Military Academy. It was fencing, he later explained, with its emphasis on parry-riposte, that convinced him of the value of counterattacking. Having led Metallurg Moscow, one of the capital's smaller clubs, to third in the inaugural Supreme League in 1936, Arkadiev took charge of Dinamo Moscow, who had won that first title. There, his restless mind and fertile imagination—not to mention his habit of taking his players on tours of art galleries before big games—soon gained him a reputation for eccentric brilliance. His first season brought the league and cup double, but he had to rethink his tactics as the lessons of the Basques revolutionized Soviet soccer.

"After the Basque tour, all the leading Soviet teams started to reorganise in the spirit of the new system," Arkadiev wrote. "Torpedo moved ahead of their opponents in that respect and, having the advantage in tactics, had a great first half of the season in 1938 and by 1939 all of our teams were playing with the new system." The effect on Dinamo was baleful, as they slipped to fifth in 1938 and a lowly ninth the year after. With Lavrenty Beria, the notorious head of the KGB and the patron of the club, desperate for success, drastic action was required.

Others might have gone back to basics, but not Arkadiev: he took things further. He was convinced that the key was less the players he had than the way they were arranged, and so, in February 1940, at a preseason training camp at the Black Sea resort of Gagry, he took the unprecedented step of spending a two-hour session teaching nothing but tactics. His aim, he said, was a refined variant of the W-M. "With the third-back, lots of our and foreign clubs employed so-called roaming players in attack," Arkadiev explained.

> This creative searching didn't go a long way, but it turned out to be a beginning of a radical *perestroika* in our football tactics. To be absolutely honest, some players started to roam for reasons that had nothing to do with tactics. Sometimes it was simply because he had great strength, speed or stamina that drew him out of his territorial area, and once he had left his home, he began to roam around the field. So you had four players [of the five forwards] who would hold an orthodox position and move to and fro in their channels, and then suddenly you would have one player who would start to disrupt their standard movements by running diagonally or left to right. That made it difficult for

the defending team to follow him, and the other forwards benefited
because they had a free team-mate to whom they could pass.

The season began badly, with draws against Krylya Sovetov Moscow and
Traktor Stalingrad and defeat at Dinamo Tbilisi, but Arkadiev didn't waver.
The day after the defeat in Tbilisi, he gathered his players together, sat them
down, and made them write a report on their own performance and that of
their teammates. The air cleared, the players seemed suddenly to grasp
Arkadiev's intentions. On June 4, playing a rapid, close-passing style, Dinamo beat Dynamo Kyiv 8–5. They went on to win the return in Ukraine
7–0, and then, in August, they hammered the defending champions Spartak 5–1. Their final seven games of the season brought seven wins, with
twenty-six goals scored and just three conceded. "Our players worked to
move from a schematic W-M, to breathe the Russian soul into the English
invention, to add our neglect of dogma," Arkadiev said. "We confused the
opposition, leaving them without weaponry with our sudden movements.
Our left-winger, Sergei Ilyin, scored most of his goals from the centre-
forward position, our right-winger, Mikhail Semichastny, from inside-left
and our centre-forward, Sergei Soloviov, from the flanks."

The newspapers hailed the "organised disorder," while opponents
sought ways of combating it. The most common solution was to impose
strict man-to-man marking, to which Arkadiev responded by having his
players interchange positions even more frequently. "With the transition of
the defensive line from a zonal game to marking specific opponents," he
wrote, "it became tactically logical to have all the attackers and even the
midfielders roaming, while having all the defenders switch to a mobile system, following their opponents according to where they went."

It is important here to clarify exactly what Arkadiev meant by a "zonal
game." What he did not mean was the integrated system of "zonal marking" that Zézé Moreira introduced in Brazil in the early fifties and that
Viktor Maslov would later apply with such success at Dynamo Kyiv. He
was speaking rather of the transition from the simple zonal game of the
2–3–5, in which one full-back would take the left side and one the right,
to the strict system of the W-M, in which each player knew clearly which
player he was supposed to be marking (the right-back on the left-wing, the
left-half on the inside-right, center-back on center-forward, etc.). In England this had happened almost organically as the W-M developed; with
the W-M arriving fully formed in the USSR, there was inevitably a period
of confusion as the defensive ramifications were taken on board.

Very gradually, one of the halves took on a more defensive role, providing
extra cover in front of the back three, which in turn meant an inside-forward

dropping to cover him. It was a slow process, and it would be taken further more quickly on the other side of the globe, but 3–2–2–3 was on the way to becoming 4–2–4. Axel Vartanyan, the esteemed historian of Soviet soccer, even believes it probable that Arkadiev was the first man to deploy a flat back-four.

As war caused the dissolution of the league, Arkadiev left Dinamo for CDKA (the forerunner of CSKA) in 1943, and went on to win the championship five times before the club was disbanded because Stalin held them responsible for the USSR's defeat to Yugoslavia at the 1952 Olympics. Dinamo, meanwhile, continuing to apply Arkadiev's principles, beguiled Britain with their short-passing style—*passovotchka*, as it became known—as they came on a goodwill tour following the end of hostilities in 1945.

The buildup to their first game, against Chelsea at Stamford Bridge, was marked by political concerns and, more practically, fears that "charging" might become as great a source of dispute as it had been for British sides on those early tours of South America. Chelsea were only eleventh in the Southern Division—a full resumption of the league program still being several months away—and struggled to a fortuitous 3–3 draw, but their comparative lack of sophistication was clear. Just as Sindelar had tormented England by dropping deep, just as Nándor Hidegkuti would, so Konstantin Beskov bewildered Chelsea by refusing to operate in the area usually occupied by a forward.

The most striking aspect of Dinamo's play, though, was their energy and the intelligence with which they used it. "The Russians were on the move all the time," the Chelsea left-back Albert Tennant complained. "We could hardly keep up with them." Davie Meiklejohn, the former Rangers captain, wrote in the *Daily Record*: "They interchanged positions to the extent of the outside-left running over to the right-wing and vice versa. I have never seen football played like it. It was a Chinese puzzle to try to follow the players in their positions as it [*sic*] was given in the programme. They simply wandered here and there at will, but the most remarkable feature of it all, they never got in each other's way."

As Dinamo went on to thrash Cardiff 10–1, beat Arsenal 4–3, and draw 2–2 at Rangers, appreciation of their methods became ever more effusive. In the *Daily Mail*, Geoffrey Simpson spoke of them playing "a brand of football which, in class, style and effectiveness is way ahead of our own. As for its entertainment value—well, some of those who have been cheering their heads off at our league matches must wonder what they are shouting about." The question then was, was their style related to ideology?

There was talk—again—of their soccer being like chess and suggestions that much of Dinamo's soccer was based around preplanned moves. It may be an easy metaphor to speak of Communist soccer being built

Chelsea 3 Dinamo Moscow 3, friendly, Stamford Bridge, London, 13 November 1945

around the team as a unit with the players mere cogs within it, as opposed to the British game that allowed for greater self-expression, but that does not mean there is no truth to it. Alex James, the former Arsenal inside-forward, wrote in the *News of the World* that Dinamo's success "lies in teamwork to which there is a pattern. There is no individualist in their side such as a [Stanley] Matthews or a [Raich] Carter. They play to a plan, repeating it over and over again, and they show little variation. It would be quite easy to find a counter-method to beat them. This lack of an individualist is a great weakness." Or maybe their great individuals—and nobody would have denied that the likes of Beskov, Vsevolod Bobrov and Vasili Kartsev were fine, technically gifted players—simply utilized their gifts in a different way.

Mikhail Yakushin, who had replaced Arkadiev as coach of Dinamo, seemed just as anxious to peddle the ideological line as the British press. "The principle of collective play is the guiding one in Soviet football," he said. "A player must not only be good in general; he must be good for the particular team." What about Matthews? "His individual qualities are high, but we put collective football first and individual football second, so we do not favour his style as we think teamwork would suffer," Yakushin replied.

In Britain, this was a revolutionary thought, and it raises an intriguing theory. Broadly speaking, although Bob McGory attempted to replicate the *passovotchka* style at Stoke City to little success—perhaps not surprisingly, given Matthews's presence in his side—the lessons of the Dinamo tour were ignored. Now, given British soccer had ignored or patronized developments in South America and central Europe, it is unlikely—even in the revolutionary years immediately following the war—it would ever have cast off its conservatism entirely, but it may have been more open to innovation if it hadn't been blessed at the time with a glut of great wingers. Why change a formation that allowed the likes of Matthews, Tom Finney, and Len Shackleton in England, or Willie Waddell, Jimmy Delaney, and Gordon Smith in Scotland, to give full rein to their talents?

Matthews's finest hour, perhaps the high point of English wing play, came in the 1953 FA Cup final, when his jinks and feints inspired Blackpool to come from 3–1 down to beat Bolton 4–3. Six months later, on the same field, Hungary destroyed England 6–3, and the *Daily Mirror*'s headline proclaimed the "Twilight of the (Soccer) Gods." In terms of the reliance on wingers to provide the artistry, it was right.

The irony, of course, is that Herbert Chapman, the progenitor of the W-M, had been deeply suspicious of wing play. His system, the first significant tactical development in the English game in almost half a century, initially circumvented wingers, and yet it ended up being set in stone by them: the very aspect with which his innovation had done away returned to preclude further innovation. For managers with such players, sticking with the tried and tested was the logical thing to do. England's record in the years immediately following the war was good; they went almost two years without defeat from May 1947, a run that included a 10–0 demolition of Portugal in Estoril and a 4–0 victory over Italy, still the world champions, in Turin. Scotland's form was patchier, but even they could take comfort in six straight victories from October 1948. The problem was that the glister of those wingers ended up blinding Britain to the tactical advances being made elsewhere, and it would be eight years after the Dinamo tour before England's eyes were—abruptly—opened.

6

THE HUNGARIAN CONNECTION

The experience of the *Wunderteam* and Dinamo Moscow's *passovotchka* tour had hinted at the future but it was only in 1953 that England finally accepted the reality that the continental game had reached a level of excellence for which no amount of sweat and graft could compensate.

The visit of the *Aranycsapat*, Hungary's Golden Squad, to Wembley on November 25 that year—the Olympic champions, unbeaten in three years, against the mother of soccer, who still considered herself supreme—was billed as the Match of the Century. That might have been marketing hyperbole, but no other game has so resonated through the history of English soccer. England had lost to foreign opposition before—most humiliatingly to the United States in the World Cup three years earlier—but, other than a defeat to the Republic of Ireland at Goodison Park in 1949, never at home, where climate, conditions, and refereeing offered no excuse. They had certainly never been so outclassed. Hungary's 6–3 victory was not the moment at which English decline began but it was the moment at which it was recognized. Tom Finney, injured and watching from the press box, was left reaching for the equine metaphor Gabriel Hanot had used thirty years earlier. "It was," he said, "like cart-horses playing race-horses."

For the first half of the twentieth century, from both a soccer and a political point of view, Hungary had existed in the shadow of Austria. Their thinking had, inevitably, been influenced by Hugo Meisl and the Danubian Whirl, but the crucial point was that it was *thinking*. In Budapest, as in Vienna, soccer was a matter for intellectual debate. That was why Arthur Rowe was invited there to lecture on the W-M in 1940, presumably, given his later commitment to push and run, focusing on rather more subtle aspects of the system than simply the stopper center-half that so dominated the thoughts of English coaches of the time.

Aside from the negativity to which it lent itself, the major effect of the prevailing conception of the W-M was to shape the preferred mode of center-forward. Managers quickly tired of seeing dribblers and darters physically dominated by the close attentions of stopper center-halves and so turned instead to the sort of big battering ram–style center-forward still referred to today in Britain as the classic number 9; "the brainless bull at the gate" in Glanville's characterization. If Matthias Sindelar represented the cerebral central European ideal, it was Arsenal's Ted Drake—strong, powerful, brave, and almost entirely unthinking—who typified the English model.

But, just as there would have been no place for *Der Papierene* in England in the thirties, so beefy target men were thin on the ground in 1940s Hungary. That was troublesome, for 2–3–5 had yielded to W-M in the minds of all but a few idealists: there was a need either for Hungary to start developing an English style of center-forward or to create a new system that retained the defensive solidity of the W-M without demanding a brawny focal point to the attack.

It was Mártón Bukovi, the coach of MTK (or Vörös Lobogó as they became after nationalization in 1949), who hit upon the solution after his "tank," the Romanian-born Norbert Höfling, was sold to Lazio in 1948. If you didn't have the right style of center-forward, rather than trying to force unsuitable players into the position, he decided, it was better simply to do away with him altogether. He inverted the W of the W-M, developing what was effectively an M-M.

Gradually, as the center-forward dropped deeper and deeper to become an auxiliary midfielder, the two wingers pushed on to create a fluid front four. "The centre-forward was having increasing difficulties with a marker around his neck," explained Nándor Hidegkuti, the man who tormented England from his deep-lying role at Wembley.

So the idea emerged to play the No. 9 deeper where there was some space.

At wing-half in the MTK side was a fine attacking player with very accurate distribution: Péter Palotás. Péter had never had a hard shot but he was never expected to score goals and, though he wore the No. 9 shirt, he continued to play his natural game. Positioning himself in midfield, Péter collected passes from his defence, and simply kept his wingers and inside-forwards well supplied with passes. . . . With Palotás withdrawing from centre-forward, his play clashed with that of the wing-halves, so inevitably one was withdrawn to play a tight defensive game, while the other linked with Palotás as midfield foragers.

Hidegkuti played as a winger for MTK so, logically enough, when Gusztav Sebes decided to employ the system at national level, it was Palotás he picked as his withdrawn striker. He retained him through Hungary's Olympic triumph of 1952, when Hidegkuti played largely on the right, but that September, Palotás was substituted for Hidegkuti with Hungary 2–0 down in a friendly against Switzerland. Sebes had made the switch before, in friendlies against Italy and Poland, leading the radio commentator György Szepesi to conclude that he was experimenting to see whether Hidegkuti, by then thirty, was fit enough to fulfill the withdrawn role. Hungary came back to win 4–2, and so influential was Hidegkuti that his position became unassailable. "He was a great player and a wonderful reader of the game," said Ferenc Puskás. "He was perfect for the role, sitting at the front of midfield, making telling passes, dragging the opposition defence out of shape and making fantastic runs to score himself."

Hidegkuti was almost universally referred to as a withdrawn center-forward, but the term is misleading, derived largely from his shirt number. He was, in modern terminology, simply an attacking midfielder. "I usually took up my position around the middle of the field on [József] Zakariás's side," he explained,

> while [József] Bozsik on the other flank often moved up as far as the opposition's penalty area, and scored quite a number of goals, too.
>
> In the front line the most frequent goal scorers were Puskás and [Sándor] Kocsis, the two inside-forwards, and they positioned themselves closer to the enemy goal than was usual with . . . the WM system. . . . After a brief experience with this new framework Gusztáv Sebes decided to ask the two wingers to drop back a little towards midfield, to pick up the passes to be had from Bozsik and myself, and this added the final touch to the tactical development.

It was Hidegkuti, though, who destroyed England. Their players had, after all, grown up in a culture where the number denoted the position. The right-winger, the number 7, lined up against the left-back, the number 3; the center-half, the number 5, took care of the center-forward, the number 9. So fundamental was this that the television commentator Kenneth Wolstenholme felt compelled in the opening minutes of the game to explain the foreign custom to his viewers. "You might be mystified by some of the Hungarian numbers," he said in a tone of indulgent exasperation. "The reason is they number the players rather logically, with the centre-half as 3 and the backs as 2 and 4." They numbered them, in other words, as you would read them across the pitch, rather than by archaic custom: how was an Englishman to cope? And, more pertinently, what was a center-half to do if the center-forward kept disappearing off towards the halfway line? "To me," Harry Johnston, England's center-half that day, wrote in his autobiography, "the tragedy was the utter helplessness . . . being unable to do anything to alter the grim outlook." If he followed him, it left a hole between the two full-backs; if he sat off him, Hidegkuti was able to drift around unchallenged, dictating the play. In the end Johnston was caught between the two stools, and Hidegkuti scored a hat trick. Syd Owen, Johnston's replacement for the rematch in Budapest six months later, fared no better, and England were beaten 7–1.

It wasn't just Hidegkuti who flummoxed England, though. Their whole system and style of play was alien. It was, Owen said, "like playing people from outer space." Billy Wright, England's captain, admitted, "We completely underestimated the advances that the Hungarians had made." It says much about the general technical standard of English soccer at the time that Wolstenholme was enraptured by Puskás nonchalantly performing half a dozen keepie-ups while he waited to kick off. If that sends a shudder of embarrassment down the modern English spine, it is nothing to what Frank Coles wrote in the *Daily Telegraph* on the morning of the game. "Hungary's superb ball-jugglers," he asserted with a touching faith in the enduring powers of English pluck, "can be checked by firm tackling." Little wonder Glanville spoke of it as a defeat that "gave eyes to the blind."

And yet it wasn't just about technique; perhaps it wasn't even primarily about technique. Yes, Hungary had, in Puskás, Hidegkuti, Kocsis, Bozsik, and Zoltán Czibor, five of the greatest players of the age and, in Sebes, an inspirational and meticulous coach but, as Hungary's right-back Jenő Buzánszky acknowledged, "It was because of tactics that Hungary won. The match showed the clash of two formations and, as often happens, the newer, more developed formation prevailed." Perhaps it is wrong to divide the two, for although the tactics permitted the technique to flourish, without the technique the tactics would have been redundant. England were slow to react to the problems (and certainly negligent in failing to address them ahead of the rematch in Budapest six months later), but it is hard to argue that their manager Walter Winterbottom picked the wrong tactics on the day. The problem, rather, was endemic.

England, Geoffrey Green wrote in the *Times* the following morning,

> found themselves strangers in a strange world, a world of flitting red spirits, for such did the Hungarians seem as they moved at devastating pace with superb skill and powerful finish in their cherry bright shirts. One has talked about the new conception of football as developed by the continentals and South Americans. Always the main criticism against the style has been its lack of a final punch near goal. One has

England 3 Hungary 6, friendly, Wembley, London, 25 November 1953

thought at times, too, that perhaps the perfection of football was to be found somewhere between the hard-hitting, open British method and this other more probing infiltration. Yesterday, the Hungarians, with perfect teamwork, demonstrated this mid-point to perfection.

Not that Sebes saw his Hungary as the midpoint of anything. Having organized a labor dispute at the Renault factory in Paris before the war, his Communist credentials were impeccable and, although he was assuredly saying what his government wanted to hear, there is no reason to believe he was not also voicing his own opinion as he insisted Hungary's success, so obviously rooted in the interplay of the team as opposed to the dissociated individuality of England, was a victory for socialism. Certainly that November evening, as the flags hung limp in the fog above the Twin Towers, themselves designed to reflect the work of Lutyens in New Delhi, it didn't take a huge leap of the imagination to recognize empire's symbolic defeat.

Soccer, of course, is not played on the blackboard. However sound the system, success on the field requires compromise between—in the best case, stems from a symbiosis of—the theory and the players available. Bukovi's idea was perfect for Hungary, because four front men and a withdrawn center-forward permitted a fluidity of attack that suited the mind-set of their forwards. It is revealing watching a video of the game today that, midway through the first half, Wolstenholme observes, in a tone somewhere between amusement and amazement, that "the outside-*left* Czibor came across to pick up the ball in the outside-right position."

Fluidity is all very well, but, of course, the more fluid a team is, the harder it is to retain the structures necessary to defend. That is where Sebes excelled. He was so concerned with detail that he had his side practice with the heavier English balls and on a training field with the same dimensions as Wembley, and his notebook shows a similar care for the tactical side of the game. He encouraged the two full-backs, Buzánszky and Mihály Lantos, to advance, but that meant the center-half, Gyula Lóránt, dropping even deeper, into a position not dissimilar to the sweeper in Karl Rappan's *verrou* system. Puskás had license to roam, while Bozsik, notionally the right-half, was encouraged to push forwards to support Hidegkuti. That required a corresponding defensive presence, which was provided by the left-half, Zakariás, who, in the tactical plan for the game Sebes sketched in his notebook, appears so deep he is almost playing between the two full-backs. Two full-backs, two central defensive presences, two players running the middle and four up front: the Hungarian system was a hair's breadth from 4–2–4.

And yet the *Aranycsapat* remained forever unfulfilled. After thirty-six games undefeated, Hungary threw away a two-goal lead to lose 3–2 to

West Germany in the 1954 World Cup final, undone, in the end, by ill luck, a muddy pitch that hampered their passing game, a touch of complacency, and the German manager Sepp Herberger's simple ploy of sitting Horst Eckel man to man on Hidegkuti. A system thought up to free the center-forward from the clutches of a marker fell down when the marker was moved closer to him.

Perhaps, though, they paid as well for a defensive frailty. Even allowing for the attacking standards of the time, the Hungarian defense was porous. The three they conceded to West Germany meant they had let in ten in the tournament, while in 1953 they leaked eleven goals in a six-game run that culminated in the 6–3 win at Wembley. Just about everybody agreed that the three flattered England, an observation taken at the time to emphasize Hungary's superiority, but it could just as well be interpreted as a criticism of their laxity.

The problem with three at the back is that the defense operates on a pivot, with the left-back tucking in alongside the center-back if attacks come down the right and vice versa, rendering it vulnerable to being "turned" by a smart cross-field ball that, at the very least, gave the winger on the opposite flank acceleration room. Zakariás, still notionally a midfielder, did not play deep enough to provide the extra cover that would have allowed a full-back to remain tighter to the winger he was supposed to be marking.

Whatever the cause of the defeat in Berne, the response in Hungary was one of fury. When they had returned after beating England at Wembley, the *Aranycsapat* had been greeted by adoring crowds; after losing the World Cup final they had to be diverted to the northern town of Tata to avoid street demonstrations. Puskás was barracked at league games, Sebes's son was beaten up at school, and the goalkeeper, Gyula Grosics, was arrested. Through 1955, the management team Sebes had constructed was dismantled and, following a 4–3 defeat to Belgium the following year, he was replaced by a five-man committee headed by Bukovi. Amid the chaos of the uprising and the subsequent defections of several players, though, his task was an impossible one. Sebes, meanwhile, lingered a while in sports administration as the deputy head of the National Physical Education and Sports Committee, before taking on a string of coaching positions, eventually retiring in 1970. "When I was a kid, Sebes lived in the same area of Budapest as me," remembers the great Ferencváros forward of the seventies, Tibor Nyilasi. "He would come down to the square where I played football with my friends, and take us up to his flat, give us sandwiches, and show us Super-8 films of the 6–3 and 7–1 games. It was he who recommended me to Ferencváros. He was like a grandfather. He only lived for football."

Although it was the national team's performances that attracted the most attention at the time, it was probably Sebes's compatriot Béla Guttmann who had a more lasting influence on the game. To claim that he invented Brazilian soccer is stretching things, but that didn't stop him trying. What is beyond dispute is that he represented the final flowering of the great era of central European soccer; he was the last of the coffeehouse coaches, perhaps even the last defender of soccer's innocence.

The two great Hungarian managers of the era could hardly have been more different. Where Sebes was a committed Socialist, happy to spout the party line and play the diplomatic game, Guttmann was a quick-tempered individualist, a man chewed up by circumstance and distrustful and dismissive of authority as a consequence. The end of his international playing career after three full caps was typical. Selected for the 1924 Olympics in Paris, Guttmann was appalled by Hungary's inadequate preparations. There were more officials than players in the squad, and the party accordingly was based in a hotel near Montmartre: ideal for the officials' late-night socializing, less good for players who needed to sleep. In protest Guttmann led a number of his teammates on a rat-catching expedition through the hotel and then tied their prey by the tails to the handles of the officials' room doors. He never played for his country again. Guttmann lived life like the world's rejected guest, always on the lookout for a slight, always ready to flounce, irritating and irritated in equal measure.

Born in Budapest in 1899 to a family of dance instructors, Guttmann qualified as a teacher of classical dance when he was sixteen. It was soccer that really fascinated him, though, and, playing as an old-school attacking center-half—contemporary accounts almost invariably describe him as "graceful"—he impressed enough the first-division side Torekves to earn a move in 1920 to MTK, a club seen as representing Budapest's Jewish middle class and a club still playing in the style Jimmy Hogan had introduced.

At first, Guttmann was cover for Ferenc Nyúl, but he soon left for the Romanian side Hagibor Cluj, leaving the younger man to function as MTK's fulcrum as they won the championship in 1921, the sixth in a run of ten straight titles interrupted only by a three-year hiatus for the war. The following season, though, Nyúl returned and, ousted from the team, Guttmann did what he would go on to do throughout his career: he walked, following the route of many Jews fearing persecution from the Miklós Horthy regime and heading for Vienna. It was the first of twenty-three moves Guttmann would make across national borders.

Anti-Semitism was not exactly unknown in Vienna, but it was there, amid the soccer intellectuals of the coffeehouses, that Guttmann seems to have felt most at home. "Later," the journalist Hardy Grüne wrote in the catalogue of an auction of Guttmann memorabilia held in the German city of Kassel in 2001, "he would often sit in São Paulo, New York or Lisbon and dream of enjoying a *Melange* in a Viennese café and chatting to good friends about football." When, aged seventy-five, Guttmann finally gave up his wandering, it was to Vienna he returned, living in an apartment near the opera house on Walfischgasse.

He joined Hakoah, the great Jewish club of Vienna, late in 1921, and supplemented the small income they were able to provide by setting up a dancing academy. Hakoah also practiced the Scottish passing game, as preached by their coach Billy Hunter, who had played for Bolton Wanderers—alongside Jimmy Hogan—and Millwall. Although central Europe had never embraced the brute physicality of the English approach, Hunter's ideas were to have a lasting impact.

Hakoah turned professional in 1925 and, with Guttmann at center-half, won the inaugural professional Austrian championship the following year. Just as important to the club were the money-making tours they undertook to promote muscular Judaism in general and Zionism in particular. In 1926, billed as the Unbeatable Jews (although they lost two of their thirteen games), Hakoah toured the East Coast of the United States. In terms of money and profile, the tour was a tremendous success and in that lay Hakoah's downfall. The US clubs were richer than Hakoah and, after signing a much-improved contract, Guttmann joined the New York Giants. By the end of the year, half the squad was based in that city.

From a soccer point of view, Guttmann prospered, winning the US Cup in 1929, but, having bought into a speakeasy, he was ruined as the economy disintegrated after the Wall Street crash. "I poked holes in the eyes of Abraham Lincoln on my last five-dollar bill," he said. "I thought then it wouldn't be able to find its way to the door." Always a man with an eye for the finer things in life—at Hakoah he insisted his shirts be made of silk—he seems also to have vowed then that he would never be poor again. He stayed with the Giants until the US league collapsed in 1932, returning to Hakoah to begin a coaching career that would last for forty-one years.

He stayed in Vienna for two seasons and then, on the recommendation of Hugo Meisl, moved on to the Dutch club SC Enschede. He initially signed a three-month contract but, when they came to negotiate a new deal, he insisted upon a huge bonus should Enschede win the league. As the club was struggling to avoid relegation out of the Eastern Division, the directors readily agreed. Their form promptly revived, and, after they had narrowly missed out on the national championship, their chairman admitted that towards the end of the season he had gone to games praying his side would lose: Guttmann's bonus would have bankrupted them.

He would have had little compunction about accepting it. Some managers are empire builders, committed to laying structures that will bring their clubs success long after they have gone; Guttmann was a gun for hire. He bargained hard and brooked no interference. "The third season," he would say later in his career, "is fatal." He rarely lasted that long. After two years in Holland he returned to Hakoah, fleeing to Hungary after the Anschluss.

What happened next is unclear. Whenever he was asked how he survived the war, Guttmann would always reply, "God helped me." His elder brother died in a concentration camp, and it seems probable that contacts from Hakoah helped him escape to Switzerland, where he was interned. It was certainly there that Guttmann met his wife, but he refused always to speak of his wartime experiences, and his autobiography, published in 1964, contains a single paragraph on the subject: "In the last fifteen years countless books have been written about the destructive years of struggle for life and death. It would thus be superfluous to trouble our readers with such details."

By 1945, he was back in Hungary with Vasas, and the following spring he moved on to Romania with Ciocanul, where he insisted on being paid in edible goods so as to circumvent the food shortages and inflation afflicting most of Europe at the time. His departure was characteristic. When a director sought to interfere with team selection, Guttmann apparently turned to him, said, "OK, you run the club; you seem to have the basics," and left.

The following season he won the Hungarian title with Újpest, and then it was on to Kispest, where he replaced Puskás's father as coach. A fight with Puskás, no shrinking violet himself, was inevitable, and it came in a 4–0 defeat to Győr. Guttmann, who was adamant that soccer should be played the "right way," had spent the first half trying to calm the aggressive approach of the fullback Mihály Patyi. Furious with him, Guttmann instructed Patyi not to go out for the second half, even though that would leave Kispest down to ten men. Puskás told the defender to stay on. Patyi vacillated and eventually ignored his manager, at which Guttmann retired to the stands for the second half, most of which he spent reading a racing paper, then took a tram home and never returned.

On he wandered: to Triestina and Padova in Italy, to Boca Juniors and Quilmes in Argentina, to Apoel in Cyprus, and then, midway through the 1953–1954 season, to AC Milan. He lifted them to third in that first season and had them top of the table when he was dismissed nineteen games into 1954–1955 following a series of disputes with the board. "I have been sacked," he told a stunned press conference convened to announce his departure, "even though I am neither a criminal nor a homosexual. Goodbye." From then on he insisted on a clause in his contracts stipulating he couldn't be dismissed while his team was at the top of the league.

He moved to Vicenza but left twenty-eight games into the season and was without a job for most of 1956, before the Budapest Uprising provided him with an opportunity. When Honvéd (as Kispest had become known after being taken over by the army), seeking to keep their players away from the fighting, accepted a long-standing invitation to tour Brazil and Venezuela, Guttmann, by this time reconciled with Puskás, was placed in charge. Finding himself in demand in South America, he decided to stay on, accepting a contract with São Paulo. And so it was, Guttmann claimed, that the Hungarian 4–2–4 was exported to Brazil—although actually the adoption of the W-M and subsequent developments in South America owe more to two other Jewish Hungarians who had fled in the 1930s: Imre Hirschl and Dori Kürschner.

Guttmann led São Paulo to a Paulista title in 1957 but was quickly off, returning to Europe with Porto. A coach, he said, is like a lion tamer. "He dominates the animals, in whose cage he performs his show, as long as he deals with them with self-confidence and without fear. But the moment he becomes unsure of his hypnotic energy, and the first hint of fear appears in his eyes, he is lost." Guttmann never stayed long enough for that hint of fear to materialize.

He helped Porto overhaul a five-point deficit to squeak by Benfica to the title, at which Benfica promptly hired him themselves. He sacked twenty players on his arrival but, promoting youth players, won the league in 1960 and 1961. Even more significantly, Benfica's free-flowing soccer saw off Barcelona 3–2 in the European Cup final in 1961, ending Real Madrid's five-year monopoly.

But that wasn't enough for Guttmann. A week after the final in Berne, he gave a debut to the player who would become the greatest in the club's history: Eusébio. The Mozambican would probably have joined Sporting had Guttmann not bumped into Carlos Bauer, who had played for him in São Paulo, in a Lisbon barber's shop. Bauer was leading a Brazilian side on a five-week tour of Africa, and Guttmann asked him to keep an eye out for fresh talent. Five weeks later, they met again in the same barber's shop. Bauer spoke of a forward with Sporting's feeder club in Lourenço Marques (as Maputo was then called), whom he wanted to sign but couldn't afford and who was, in any event, destined for Sporting. Guttmann phoned the Mozambican club, hijacked the deal, and had Eusébio's signature two days later. "By signing Eusébio," Guttmann said, "I was able to play Mario Coluna deeper, more as a wing-half than an inside-forward. He did not like it at first because he did not score so many goals, but he became my best player." He became, in other words, Benfica's Hidegkuti.

Benfica finished third that season, conceding more goals than Sporting and Porto—the two teams who had finished above them—put together. Perhaps that was a sign that Guttmann's attacking approach had had its day—"I never minded if the opposition scored, because I always thought we could score another," he said—but few thought that as Benfica came from 2–0 and 3–2 down to beat Real Madrid 5–3 in the European Cup final in Amsterdam.

Puskás, having scored a hat trick in a losing cause, sought out Eusébio at the final whistle and handed him his shirt, a gesture widely interpreted as a symbolic passing of the mantle of Europe's greatest player. Benfica, similarly, seemed to have supplanted Madrid as Europe's greatest team and, with Eusébio only twenty, there was little reason to believe that the club would not go on to dominate the sixties as surely as Real Madrid had the fifties. Had, that is, Guttmann stayed.

He did not. After the final, Guttmann approached Benfica's directors and asked whether he might not be due some kind of bonus. There was, the directors replied, no such provision in his contract. "I got $4,000 less for winning the European Cup than the Portuguese championship," Guttmann said. "No attempt was made by the directors to change the situation, so I began to think about moving on."

Two months later, he did, ignoring the overtures of Third Division Port Vale to return to South America with the Uruguayan side Peñarol. There he constructed a side that would go on to win the Copa Libertadores, although he left before the final to take charge of the Austria national team. Driven out by anti-Semitism after five games, he wandered on to Benfica—briefly—and then to Servette of Geneva, Panathinakos, and Porto before a final return to the city he adored with Austria Vienna. He was never, though, quite the same after Benfica, and neither was the club. The story has developed that he cursed them, vowing they would never win another European trophy until he was paid what he was due; nonsense, of course, but Benfica have been in seven European finals since and lost them all.

In truth, soccer has never been quite the same. Guttmann, more than anybody since Chapman, defined the cult of the manager; the man who would take on his mantle was Helenio Herrera, whose conception of the game could hardly have been more different. Out went all romantic notions of scoring one more than the opposition, and in came cynicism and *catenaccio* and the theory of conceding one fewer.

7

HARNESSING THE CARNIVAL

The Brazil in which Béla Guttmann and Honvéd arrived in 1956 was far from the tactical wilderness he liked to portray. Individual technique and improvisation were prized, certainly, but having come to the W-M late, the 4–2–4 was already well developed—perhaps because the rigidity of the W-M, with its tight marking structure, did not sit easily with local demands for flair and self-expression.

If Brazilian soccer's foundation myth is to be believed, and there seems little reason to doubt its fundamentals, the sport arrived in Brazil with Charles Miller. The son of an English father and a Brazilian mother, members of the coffee and commerce elite of São Paulo, he was sent back to England to be educated. While there he learned the game at school, going on to represent Hampshire and play a handful of games for St. Mary's, the forerunner of Southampton. When he returned to São Paulo in 1894, he brought two soccer balls with him. The legend has him disembarking with a ball in each hand.

"What are those, Charles?" his father is supposed to have asked.

"My degree," he replied. "Your son has graduated in football."

The specifics of the story are almost certainly untrue, but it is not hard to see why it would gain currency. Here, from its origins, was Brazilian soccer as happy, smiling, impertinent, and disrespectful of authority.

The sport spread quickly, both among the Anglo elite and the indigenous population. By 1902 there was a thriving league program in São Paulo, while the game had been imported to Rio de Janeiro by another Anglo-Brazilian, Oscar Cox, who had picked up the game during his schooling in Switzerland. He founded Fluminense with some friends, and, like the early Dutch and Danish clubs, it seems to have become almost a parody of Englishness, all hats and moustaches, hurrahs and manliness.

Miller, equally, was an old-school advocate of dribbling, and there is no reason to believe the game among the expat community was any different in style from the game in Britain at the time. Among the Anglo-Brazilian clubs, as elsewhere, dribbling soon began to give way to passing. Jock Hamilton, one of the many Scottish coaches employed by Harry Bradshaw at Fulham—a first, albeit tenuous, link between Jimmy Hogan and Brazil—was hired at CA Paulistano, and pronounced himself "surprised to find the game so advanced . . . their combination is really clever." It got more clever thanks to the influence of the Scottish Wanderers, a team of Scottish expats formed in São Paulo in 1912.

They practiced the pattern-weaving approach, which, confusingly, became known as the *systema ingleza*—"the English system." Wanderers' most noted player was Archie McLean, a left-winger who had spent two seasons with Ayr United in the Scottish Second Division. He "was an artist, a worthy exponent of the Scottish school," wrote Tomas Mazzoni in his 1950 history of soccer in Brazil. "His scientific football became more prominent when he formed a partnership on the left wing with another of his compatriots Hopkins." The pair later moved to São Bento, where their trick of rapidly exchanging short passes became known as the *tabelinha* (literally, "little chart").

As Aidan Hamilton details in *An Entirely Different Game*, the British influence remained strong in Brazil far longer than it had in Uruguay or Argentina. Mazzoni speaks of Harry Welfare, a center-forward who had played for Liverpool before accepting the offer of a teaching role in Rio de Janeiro, "adapting" to "our style of play" after joining Fluminense but also disseminating his own ideas. Max Valentim, in *On Football and Its Technique*, says that Welfare taught the inside-forwards at the club how to play the through ball and describes two of his dribbling techniques: "This break or feint of the body which the English call 'swerving' and the jump to one side while running with the ball."

The real divergence from the old model, though, began when locals got involved. Barred from Fluminense, they watched the Anglo-Brazilians from nearby rooftops and saw a sport that was both far easier to comprehend and far easier to replicate than cricket. In the informal kickabouts in the streets, often using balls made of rags, a wholly different conception of the game developed. It was based on the unorthodox and individual skills required to thrive in such conditions and—crucially—was uninhibited by any proscriptions against showing off. McLean was not impressed. "There were great players there," he said of soccer in São Paulo, "but they were terribly undisciplined. Their antics would not have been tolerated in Scotland."

Various parallels have been drawn between Brazilian soccer and samba—Brazilian fans at the 1958 World Cup chanted "samba, samba" as they celebrated their country's first win in the tournament—although Simon Kuper in *Football Against the Enemy* compares Pelé to a *capoerista*, an exponent of a martial art invented by Angolan slaves that was disguised as a dance to fool their masters.

The anthropologist Robert DaMatta came up with the theory of *jeitinho*—literally, "the small way"—to explain the creativity on which Brazilians so pride themselves, positing that because the laws and codes of behavior in Brazil, even after the abolition of slavery in 1888, were designed to protect the rich and powerful, individuals had to find imaginative ways of getting round them. *Jeitinho*, he wrote in *What Makes Brazil, Brazil*,

> is a personal mediation between the law, the situation in which it should apply and the persons involved in such a way that nothing really changes, apart from a considerable demoralisation of the law itself. . . . In the USA, France and England, for example, the rules are either obeyed or do not exist. In these societies, it is well known that there is no desire to establish new laws that are not in line with the common good or with the other laws of society, so creating room for bureaucratic corruption and diminishing the trust in the public institutions. . . . So . . . the Americans, the French and the British stop in front of a "Stop" sign, which seems to us a logical and social absurdity.

Brazilians, by contrast, find a way around such restrictions; they come to rely on themselves rather than on external structures. It is not hard to see the imaginativeness that has historically characterized Brazilian soccer as a particular expression of that trait. Individuals find their own way to master situations, and that means both high levels of creativity and a distrust of teamwork. Much of DaMatta's work develops the thinking of Gilberto Freyre, a sociologist who began writing in the late thirties. Freyre was among the first to promote Brazil's racial diversity as a benefit, celebrating the Carioca figure of the *malandro*, typically a mixed-race trickster or con man, who used his wits to best those who in theory had authority over him. "Our style of playing football," Freyre wrote in 1938, "contrasts with the Europeans because of a combination of the qualities of surprise, malice, astuteness and agility, and at the same time brilliance and individual spontaneity. . . . Our passes . . . our dummies, our flourishes with the ball, the touch of dance and subversiveness that marks the Brazilian style . . . seem to show psychologists and sociologists in a very interesting way the roguery and flamboyance of the mulatto that today is every true affirmation of what is Brazilian."

For writers of the time, the *malandro* spirit found its personification in two of the greatest Brazilian players of the thirties, the center-forward Leônidas and the defender Domingos da Guia, both of whom were black. Domingos openly acknowledged that his creative abilities, the technical skills that allowed him to carry the ball out from the back, were rooted initially in the need for self-preservation. "When I was still a kid I was scared to play football," he said, "because I often saw black players . . . get whacked on the pitch, just because they made a foul or sometimes for less than that. . . . My elder brother used to tell me: the cat always falls on his feet. Aren't you good at dancing? I was and this helped my football. I swung my hips a lot. That short dribble I invented imitating the *miudinho*, that type of samba."

However it came about, by 1919 there was a discernibly Brazilian style of play, as was outlined that November in an article headlined "Brazilian Innovation" in the first issue of the São Paulo magazine *Sports*.

> As opposed to the British school, which dictates that the ball be taken by the forwards right up to the opposition's goal and put in from the closest possible range, the Brazilian school states that shots be taken from any distance, the precision of the shot being worth more than the fact that it is made close to the target. And it further states that the collective advance of the whole forward line is not necessary; it's enough for two or three players to break away with the ball, which, by its devastating speed, completely unexpected, disorientates the entire rival defence.

The perception that British soccer was insufficiently direct in front of the goal rings strangely, given how critical British commentators would become of the overelaboration of central European sides. Perhaps it is simply that all things are relative, perhaps the Scottish expats who made up the Wanderers did overpass and that colored the judgment, or perhaps the British game at the time, six years before the change in the offside law, was more intricate than it became. Whatever the truth, it is clear that the Brazilian game was focused more on self-expression than on team play.

Soccer in Brazil, though, was nowhere near as developed at that stage as it was on the River Plate. Their first ten internationals—all against Argentina, Uruguay, or Chile—brought just three victories, and in the 1917 Copa América they conceded four against both Argentina and Uruguay. In 1919, though, they fared rather better, winning the tournament thanks largely to the ploy of having one of the full-backs retain a purely defensive role, while the other was given license to join the attack. It was far from sophisticated, but it was the first time the Brazil national team acknowledged the need for some sort of structure of defense.

That success, though, was far from the start of any continental domination. Brazil won just six of the twenty matches they played against Argentina before 1940, and five of thirteen against Uruguay. They won the

Copa again in 1922, but it would be 1949 before they won it for a third time (astonishingly, it wasn't until 1997 and their fifth success that Brazil won the competition on foreign soil). Internal disputes within the federation meant that Brazil were represented only by Carioca players at the 1930 World Cup. They lost their opening game 2–1 against Yugoslavia—"Brazil were individually cleverer, collectively inferior," Glanville wrote—and were eliminated despite a subsequent 4–0 victory over Bolivia.

Professionalism was formally sanctioned in 1933, which at least helped persuade Brazilian players on tours of Europe with their clubs to return home, but it would take time before it had an impact either on the results of the national side or on their style.

Having been knocked out of the 1934 World Cup after one game, beaten 3–1 by Spain, Brazil traveled on to Belgrade for a friendly against Yugoslavia, who had failed to qualify for the World Cup, and were hammered 8–4. This was a side featuring such talents as Domingos, Leônidas, and Waldemar de Brito, but tactically they were humiliatingly exposed, even more so than they had been in Montevideo four years earlier. "There was a lot of space between the lines," the soccer historian Ivan Soter explained. "The Yugoslavs were able to exploit that, showing up the faults of the old-fashioned system." Something, evidently, had to change.

———

The first attempt to import the W-M to Brazil was made by Gentil Cardoso, but he was beset by two major difficulties: he had next to no background as a player, and he was black. He had been a shoeshine, a waiter, a tram driver, and a baker and had then joined the merchant navy. That entailed frequent voyages to Europe, and while there he seems to have spent most of his free time watching soccer. He became a particular fan of the English game and later claimed to have watched firsthand Herbert Chapman's development of the W-M formation at Arsenal. "He was a larger than life character," said Soter, "somebody who loved telling tales of his travels." Often they were embellished, but what is undeniable is his capacity for tactical analysis. He saw the W-M, recognized its possibilities, and realized that this, vastly different as it was from Brazilian soccer, was the future.

Cardoso was given his chance to coach in the thirties, when he divided his time between soccer and the sea. He implemented the W-M at the small Carioca side Sírio Libanês, where he oversaw the emergence of Leônidas. "He was a thoroughly Brazilian player," the playwright Nélson Rodrigues wrote of the forward. "Full of the fantasy, improvisation, childishness and sensuality that have marked out all the Brazilian greats." He was not, in other words, much like the center-forwards the English preferred to employ in the W-M. Shape could be copied; style, it seems, was rather harder to implement.

Sírio Libanês was too small a club for Cardoso's innovation really to reverberate, and even after he'd moved to Bonsucesso, a slightly larger club, taking Leônidas with him, he found it hard to find an audience for his ideas. He became noted for quoting Socrates, Cicero, and Gandhi in team talks and enhanced Brazil's soccer vocabulary—*snake* to mean "good player," for instance, or *zebra* for a "shock result"—but, as a tactician, as Soter said, "People just didn't take him seriously." It took a European, Dori Kürschner, to implant the W-M firmly in Brazil, although he died before his ideas really took hold. "When Kruschner [*sic*] arrived in Brazil, Gentil was talking a lot about the W-M," Flávio Costa, Kürschner's predecessor and successor at Flamengo, said in an interview with Hamilton, "but he never had the prestige to apply it. Kruschner was the one who tried to apply *futebol sistema*."

Kürschner has become a mythic figure in Brazil, a wise man from a distant land who brought great knowledge and, like all true prophets, went unheralded in his own lifetime. He is portrayed as an evangelist without a history, a man from nowhere. "We don't even know if he was Hungarian, Czech, Bohemian," said Roberto Assaf, the television pundit and great chronicler of Flamengo. The confusion is understandable. At some stage, the *r* and the *u* became transposed, and so in Brazil Kürschner's name is spelled and pronounced *Kruschner*; anyone looking up *Kruschner*, of course, finds that the record is blank. As Alex Bellos notes in his introduction to *Futebol*, "Brazil is not big on facts. . . . It is a country built of stories, myths and Chinese whispers."

That explains Kürschner's aura of mystery, but it does not explain why the Flamengo president Jose Bastos Padilha settled upon him as the man to further his plans for Carioca domination, which had already included funding the construction of a new stadium. Whatever his intentions, what he got when he hired him was somebody with a fine pedigree in Danubian soccer and somebody, moreover, who provided a direct link to Jimmy Hogan. Hogan is regularly hailed as the father of Hungarian, Austrian, and German soccer; what is talked about rather less is that he was also the grandfather of the Brazilian game.

Kürschner was born in Budapest and as a player enjoyed success with MTK, winning the Hungarian title in 1904 and 1908 and earning a handful of international call-ups. A left-half who occasionally operated in the center, he was known for his unfussy acuity in possession and was particularly noted for his heading ability. In his later days, he was coached by Hogan, and he succeeded him as MTK coach in 1918. Kürschner won a title there, but within a year he had left for Germany.

There he had minor success with Stuttgarter Kickers, won a national German title with Nürnberg, and, after a brief stint with Bayern Munich, was their coach again as they shared the title in 1922 after the so-called eternal final against Hamburg. In his early career, Kürschner seems, like Guttmann, never to have been able to settle, and he moved on to Eintracht Frankfurt and then to Switzerland with Nordstern Basel, where he won promotion at the first attempt. He promptly left and joined up with Hogan and the nominal head coach Teddy Duckworth, another Englishman, to prepare the Switzerland national side for the Paris Olympics. There, they achieved the greatest success in the history of Swiss soccer, reaching the final where they were beaten by the defending champions, Uruguay.

Kürschner moved back to Germany with Schwarz-Weiss Essen then, in 1925, he joined Grasshoppers in Zurich. He spent the next nine years there, winning three league titles and four cups, before being replaced by Karl Rappan. Had he stayed in Germany or gone back to Hungary, where the classic Danubian 2–3–5 still held sway (although even there the center-half was just beginning to retreat, moving to a position akin to that he occupied in Pozzo's *metodo*), things might have been different, but it seems that in Switzerland Kürschner became convinced of the merits of the W-M, or at least a variant of it. So when Padilha approached him in 1937, he took with him to Rio de Janeiro the formation that would kick-start the Brazilian revolution.

Perhaps it is most charitably described as a slow burner, for in its own way Brazilian soccer was just as conservative as the English game. Flamengo's center-half when Kürschner arrived was Fausto dos Santos, the Black Wonder, an elegant stylist who was used to dominating games. There was a clear hierarchy of positions in Brazilian soccer, with center-half at the top and the full-backs at the bottom, and there was no way, he told Kürschner, that he was going to drop back and become a defensive player. Fans and journalists were divided on the issue, which was only resolved when Padilha intervened, fined Fausto, and told him to get on with doing what he was paid to do. That, at least, is the legend, which paints Kürschner as an unyielding modernizer, deaf to both the appeals of tradition and to the individual characteristics and concerns of his players.

It is not, though, quite as simple as that. Ideas rarely spring fully formed from the minds of their creators, and here too circumstance seems to have played its part. According to Assaf, Kürschner was appalled by the medical facilities he found at the club, and his first significant decision, far from being an act of tactical fundamentalism, was to send his players to see a doctor. Fausto, it transpired, was suffering from the early stages of the tuberculosis that would kill him two years later, and the decision to push him into a deeper role seems to have been taken as much with his declining health in mind as for reasons of ideology. Whether, had Fausto been well, Kürschner would have retained the old 2–3–5 or whether he might have used him as a half-back and deployed another player as a defensive center-half in a W-M, it is impossible to say.

Kürschner's notion of the W-M seems to have been rather different from that common in Britain. As a Danubian, even one schooled in Swiss soccer, it is improbable he would have countenanced a Herbie Roberts–style stopper, either at center-half or anywhere else on the field. And even if he had, Fausto dos Santos was absolutely not the right man to replicate that style. What Kürschner and the Brazilians call a W-M, it seems likely, is actually rather closer to the *metodo*, more of a W-W shape, with the center-half playing behind his half-backs but in advance of the two full-backs. As Soter acknowledges, although the system seemed shockingly defensive in the context of Brazilian soccer of the time, it was nowhere near as negative or as rigid as the British model.

Although his background is not as obscure as is made out, what certainly is true is that Kürschner disappeared into nothing. Flávio Costa, the former Flamengo player he had replaced as coach, remained as his assistant and, taking advantage of the fact that Kürschner had no Portuguese, undermined him at every opportunity, pouring scorn on the W-M and backing Fausto during the dispute. Results were disappointing. Despite scoring eighty-three goals in twenty-two games, Flamengo finished second in the Carioca championship behind their arch-rivals Fluminense, and Kürschner found himself and his methods widely derided in the local press. The first game of the 1938 campaign was also the inaugural game at the Estadio da Gavea, and when Flamengo lost 2–0 to Vasco da Gama, Kürschner was sacked—and replaced by Costa.

Widely misunderstood and far from popular, Kürschner might have been expected to return to Europe but, presumably fearing anti-Semitism back in Budapest where Miklós Horthy's regime had declared a formal alliance with Nazi Germany, he stayed in Rio. He was made coach of Botafogo in 1939 but left the following year and died of a mysterious virus in 1941.

For all the suspicion with which he was treated, Kürschner was asked to work as an advisor to the national coach, Adhemar Pimenta, at the 1938 World Cup in France. Before the tournament began, Tomas Mazzoni, then working as a newspaper reporter, went to watch a friendly between France and England at the Stade de Colombes in Paris. England were comfortably superior, winning 4–2, and yet, Mazzoni wrote in shocked tones, they retained three defenders throughout. This, he concluded, would never catch on in Brazil.

Things were changing, though, and while Brazil at that tournament used Martim Silveira as an attacking center-half, the two inside-forwards,

Romeu and José Perácio, were withdrawn into what became known as the *ponta da lança* position (literally, the point of the lance), formalizing a process that had been going on for some time. By the late thirties, even those nations who ostensibly practiced the 2–3–5 had found five forwards strung out in a row too much. Matthias Sindelar dropped off the front line to give the Austrians flexibility, while in Argentina and Uruguay it was common for the inside-forwards to probe from deep. Silveira was a far more attack-minded player than Luisito Monti, but, that aside, Brazil's formation in 1938 was little different from the *metodo* of Pozzo's Italy.

It evidently helped as Brazil reached the semifinals. In a later study of the tournament, though, João Saldanha, the journalist who became national coach in 1969, was critical, concluding they would have gone further with a third back. They did, after all, let in ten goals in their five games, three of them from penalties, which he took as an indication of an over-manned defense panicking under pressure.

––––––––––

Back at Flamengo, Flávio Costa did not, as it had been assumed he would after Kürschner's dismissal, revert to a 2–3–5 but rather tweaked the W-M, creating what he termed the *diagonal*. Essentially all he did was to nudge the square that lay at the center of the W-M so it became a parallelogram. Crucially, it retained three defenders—which had been the bone of contention with Fausto—and three forwards, but rather than simply two half-backs and two inside-forwards, as in the British model, the diagonal featured a deeply-lying half-back—in Flávio Costa's initial conception, which had crystalized by 1941, the right-half, Volante—with a more advanced player to his left—Jayme. The right of the two inside-forwards—Zizinho—then played slightly deeper so as not to leave too large a space behind him, with the inside-left—José Perácio—more advanced in the classic *ponta da lança* role.

The formation could just as well be flipped, so that the right side was more attacking. Ondino Viera, later Uruguay's manager at the 1966 World Cup, for instance, employed the diagonal at Fluminense, but with Spinelli, the left-half, operating defensively, and Romeu providing the *ponta da lança*. How new the diagonal was is debatable. According to the author and former Portugal coach Candido de Oliveira in his book *The W-M System*, when Flávio Costa was later taken to Europe by a director of Vasco da Gama to explain his formation, it was laughed off as a cheap imitation of the W-M. Perhaps the truth is rather that Flávio Costa formalized an unspoken process that was inherent in the W-M. One inside-forward would always be more creative than the other; one half-back more defensive. At Arsenal in the thirties, as Bernard Joy explains in *Soccer Tactics*, the left-half

The Diagonal (Pela Direita): Flamengo 1941

The Diagonal (Pela Esqueroa): Fluminense 1941

Wilf Copping played deep, with the right-half Jack Crayston given more freedom. When the Wolves and England captain of the late forties and early fifties, Billy Wright, who could play as a center-half, played as a half-back, did he not play deeper than Billy Crook or Jimmy Dickinson? As Richard Williams points out in *The Perfect 10*, it was usual—perhaps giving credence to theories linking left-sidedness with creativity—for the inside-left to be more attacking than the inside-right, which is why the number 10 rather than the number 8 became lionized as the playmaker.

It is easy, as for instance the Paulista commentator Alberto Helena Junior is, to be cynical about Flávio Costa, suggesting he was doing nothing more than repackaging Kürschner because, having been so critical of him, he could not simply reuse his methods, but the effect was of huge significance. Flávio Costa's tinkering made apparent that the W-M was no more inviolable than the pyramid had been. Once the square has become a parallelogram, it doesn't take much more of a nudge for it to become a diamond, and when that has happened, what is left is 4–2–4. Before that could take place and be widely accepted, though, Brazil had first to go through the agonies of 1950.

Brazil are almost universally recognized as having been the best side at the World Cup finals they hosted, but they did not win it. Rather they suffered a defeat in their final game so stunning that Nélson Rodrigues wrote of it as "our catastrophe, our Hiroshima." The diagonal imposed by Flávio Costa had undergone a minor modification, with Ademir, really an inside-forward, acting as the center-forward, Jair, the inside-left, as the *ponta da lança*, and Zizinho the deeper-lying inside-forward. The result was an enhanced fluidity and flowing triangles of passes. Brazil swept to victory in the 1949 Copa América, scoring thirty-nine goals in seven games before a playoff, in which they demolished Manuel Fleitas Solich's Paraguay 7–0.

Zizinho was injured for the start of the World Cup, but Brazil were still the overwhelming favorites and lived up to that billing in their opening match, hitting the post five times on their way to a 4–0 win over Mexico in the inaugural game at the Maracanã. Their problems began when they left Rio for their second match, against Switzerland in São Paulo. As was common at the time, Flávio Costa made several changes, bringing in three Paulista midfielders to appease local fans. Perhaps that disrupted the side, perhaps it was the 1–3–3–3 *verrou* system favored by Switzerland, but Brazil were nowhere near their usual fluency and, despite twice taking the lead, could only draw 2–2, meaning they had to beat Yugoslavia in their last group game to qualify for the final group.

Fit again, Zizinho returned in place of the robust center-forward Baltazar, allowing Ademir to resume his role as a mobile number 9. That would have allowed a return to the side that had won the Copa so impressively the previous year, but the draw against Switzerland seems to have caused Flávio Costa to lose faith with the diagonal and switch to a more orthodox W-M, perhaps reasoning that, with such an adventurous and fluid central attacking three, his two half-backs, Danilo and Carlos Bauer, could both play deeper and offer additional defensive solidity.

Initially, the change worked. Yugoslavia began with ten men as Rajko Mitić received treatment after gashing his head on an exposed girder shortly before kickoff, and, by the time he had made it onto the field, Ademir had given Brazil the lead. Zizinho sealed an otherwise tight game in the second half. Yugoslavia were physically tough, technically adept opponents and, having seen them off, Brazil's confidence appears to have been restored. In the opening two games of the final group, Brazil were sensational. As they hammered Sweden 7–1 and Spain 6–1, Brian Glanville wrote of them playing "the football of the future . . . tactically unexceptional but technically superb."

They may have been unexceptional tactically, but they were far more advanced than Uruguay, who were still playing a version of Pozzo's *metodo*, with a ball-playing center-half in Obdulio Varela. They had equalized late to draw 2–2 with Spain in their opening game of the final stage and had required two goals in the final quarter hour to beat Sweden 3–2 in their second. Brazil needed only a draw in the final match to be champions, but nobody in Rio expected anything other than victory. The early editions of *O Mundo* on the day of the final even carried a team photograph of the Brazil side under the headline "These Are the World Champions." Varela, Teixeira Heizer recounts in *The Tough Game of the World Cups*, saw the newspaper on display at the newsstand in his hotel on the morning of the final and was so enraged that he bought every copy they had, took them back to his room, laid them out on his bathroom floor, and encouraged his teammates to urinate on them.

Before the game, Angelo Mendes de Moraes, the state governor, gave an address in which he hailed, "You Brazilians, whom I consider victors of the tournament. . . . You players who in less than a few hours will be acclaimed champions by millions of your compatriots. . . . You who have no equals in the terrestrial hemisphere. . . . You who are so superior to every other competitor. . . . You whom I already salute as conquerors."

Only Flávio Costa seemed at all concerned by the possibility of defeat. "The Uruguayan team has always disturbed the slumbers of Brazilian footballers," he warned. "I am afraid that my players will take to the field on Sunday as though they already had the Championship shield sewn on their jerseys. It isn't an exhibition game. It is a match like any other, only harder than the others."

What made it particularly hard was the acuity of Varela, the Uruguay captain. The war in Europe had meant an end to the tours, so, playing largely South American opposition, the *rioplatense* school had had little chance to witness tactical developments elsewhere. Varela, though, had learned about new ways of defending from his coach at Peñarol, Imre Hirschl, the Hungarian who had had such an effect in Argentina. Drawing inspiration from how Switzerland had unnerved Brazil, Valera instructed the full-back Matias González to stay deep, almost as a sweeper, which meant that Eusebio Tejera, the other full-back, became effectively a center-back. The two wing-halves, Schubert Gambetta and Victor Andrade, were set to man-mark the Brazilian wingers, Chico and Albino Friaça, while Varela and the two inside-forwards played deeper than usual in a system approaching Rappan's 1–3–3–3.

Officially there were 173,850 at the Maracaná that day; in reality there were probably more than 200,000. So overcome by nerves was Julio Pérez, Uruguay's inside-right—or right-half, in the revised formation—that he wet himself during the anthems. Gradually, though, the pressure shifted. Brazil controlled the early stages—Uruguay's tactics perhaps subdued the hosts, but they did not neutralize them—but the opening goal would not come. Jair hit the post, Roque Maspoli, in Glanville's words, "performed acrobatic prodigies in goal," but at half-time it was still goalless. Home nerves were mounting.

Hindsight suggests the turning point came after twenty-eight minutes, when Varela punched Bigode, Brazil's left-back. Both players agree it was barely more than a tap, but in the mythology of the game it was at that moment that the fear enveloped Bigode, at that moment that he became "a coward," the taunt that would pursue him for the rest of his life.

Two minutes after half-time, a reverse ball from Ademir laid in Friaça. He held off Andrade and, with a slightly scuffed cross-shot, gave Brazil the lead. In the first half, it might have been devastating, but having held out for so long, Uruguay knew they could live with Brazil, that they would not be overwhelmed. Whether it was a deliberate policy is difficult to say, but Uruguay seemed to prefer to attack down their right. That was the side that, when Brazil played the diagonal, had been the more vulnerable, with Danilo the more advanced of the two half-backs. In a W-M, he couldn't help himself but push forward, which created a fatal space, because Bigode was now operating as an orthodox left-back rather than in the slightly advanced role he would usually have adopted. Alcides Ghiggia, Uruguay's frail, hunched right-winger, could hardly have dreamed he would have been granted so much room.

Brazil were twenty-four minutes from victory when the first blow fell. Varela, who was becoming increasingly influential, advanced and spread the

Brazil 1 Uruguay 2, World Cup final pool, Maracanã, Rio de Janeiro, 16 July 1950

ball right to Ghiggia. He had space to accelerate, checked as Bigode moved to close him down, then surged by him, crossing low for Juan Schiaffino to sweep the ball in at the near post. "Silence in the Maracanã," said Flávio Costa, "which terrified our players." As blame was apportioned after the game, even the crowd did not escape. "When the players needed the Maracanã the most, the Maracanã was silent," the musician Chico Buarque observed. "You can't entrust yourself to a football stadium."

A draw would still have been enough for Brazil, but the momentum had swung inexorably against them. Thirteen minutes later, Ghiggia again picked up the ball on the Uruguayan right. This time Bigode was closer to him, but isolated, so Ghiggia laid it back to Pérez. Nerves forgotten, he held off Jair and slipped a return ball in behind Bigode. Ghiggia ran on, and with Moacyr Barbosa, the Brazilian goalkeeper, anticipating a cross, struck a bobbling shot in at the near post. The unthinkable had happened, and Uruguay, not Brazil, were world champions.

Since becoming a republic in 1889, Brazil has never been in a war. When Rodrigues spoke of the 1950 World Cup final as his country's Hiroshima, he meant it was the greatest single catastrophe to have befallen Brazil. Paulo Perdigão expresses the same point less outrageously in *Anatomy of a Defeat*, his remarkable meditation on the final, in which he reprints the entire radio commentary of the match, using it as the basis for his analysis of the game almost as though he were delivering exegesis upon a biblical text. "Of all the historical examples of national crises," he wrote, "the World Cup of 1950 is the most beautiful and most glorified. It is a Waterloo of the tropics and its history our *Götterdämmerung*. The defeat transformed a normal fact into an exceptional narrative: it is a fabulous myth that has been preserved and even grown in the public imagination."

Bigode, Barbosa, and Juvenal—probably not by coincidence Brazil's three black players—were held responsible. In 1963, Barbosa, in an effort to exorcise his demons, even invited friends to a barbecue at which he ceremonially burned the Maracanã goalposts, but he could not escape the opprobrium. The story is told of how, twenty years after the final, he was in a shop when a woman pointed at him. "Look at him," she said to her young son. "He's the man who made all of Brazil cry."

"In Brazil," he said shortly before his death in 2000, "the maximum sentence is thirty years, but I have served fifty." Yes, it was a mistake, but if a reason is to be found for the defeat, Zizinho insists, it is the use of the W-M. "The last four games of the World Cup were the first time in my life I played W-M," he explained in an interview with Bellos. "Spain played W-M, Sweden played W-M, Yugoslavia played W-M. The three that played W-M we beat. But Uruguay didn't play W-M. Uruguay played with one deep back and the other in front." They played, in other words, a system with the same defensive base Brazil used to win the Copa América in 1919.

Just as England reacts to any setback by lamenting technical inadequacy, so Brazil blames defensive frailties. Perdigão's reference to *Götterdämmerung*, of course, echoes the *Mirror*'s "Twilight of the Gods" headline after England's 6–3 defeat to Hungary, and that is not coincidence. The plaintiveness comes from the same source—a railing against habitual failings, an angry realization that the traditional way of playing is not innately superior. The irony is that Brazil's traditions and England's could hardly be more different. There is no right way of playing; at some point every soccer culture doubts its own strengths and looks wistfully to the greener grass abroad.

No matter that twenty-two goals had been scored in six games; what was important was those two that had been conceded at the last. Clearly, Brazil's pundits decided, the defense needed bolstering. By the time of the 1954 World Cup, the attack-minded Flávio Costa had been supplanted by the more cautious Zézé Moreira. It was, a French journalist said, like replacing an Argentinian dancer with an English clergyman.

The great trio of inside-forwards was gone, and a stopper center-half was introduced in Pinheiro, a far more defensive player than Juvenal. Brazil swatted Mexico aside but then drew with Yugoslavia before going out to Hungary in a vicious quarterfinal, beaten 4–2 in the so-called Battle of Berne. In his official report on the tournament, the head of the Brazilian delegation, João Lyra Filho, concluded that "flashy trim lends artistic expression to the match, to the detriment of yield and results," something he blamed largely on black players. He was, fortunately, ignored, and the consensus agreed with Garrincha's complaint—or at least that ghosted for him in Stratton Smith's collection *The Brazil Book of Football*—that "Brazil planned to win the World Cup by burying the individual in a general team plan. So they went to Europe to play like Europeans. . . . What counted in Brazilian football was the ability of our players to improvise."

Garrincha was never a player for tactical discipline but improvisation couldn't be allowed to run anarchically unchecked. What was needed was a structure in which improvisation could flourish, without leaving the defense as exposed as poor Bigode had been. The answer, strangely, had been practiced in Brazil almost since the beginning of the decade.

Just who invented the 4–2–4 is a matter of some debate: as Assaf says, "it has many fathers." Some credit Zézé Moreira, some Manuel Fleitas Solich, some Martim Francisco; there are even some who say it didn't emerge in its true form until Lula applied it at Santos. If Axel Vartanyan is right, it is possible that it is not even a Brazilian invention but one of a number of variations employed by Boris Arkadiev at Dinamo Moscow. The truth is that Brazil, with the diagonal, and Hungary, with their withdrawn center-forward (and correspondingly withdrawn left-half), had independently moved to a position from which the 4–2–4 was an inevitable development.

The Paraguayan coach Manuel Fleitas Solich certainly had a key role in promoting the 4–2–4, winning three Carioca titles in a row with it at Flamengo between 1953 and 1955, but the first man consciously to employ the system seems to have been Martim Francisco. He was coach of Vila Nova, a club from Nova Lima, a town about twenty miles from Belo Horizonte. He pushed his left-half, Lito, back to play as the *quarto zagueiro*—the "fourth defender"—the term that is still used today in Brazil for the defender whose job it is to step up and join the midfield. Right from the start, though, that was recognized as inadequate to prevent a two-man midfield being swamped, and so one of the front four also had a brief to drop back. In Francisco's team, it was Osorio, the right-winger. In practice, the 4–2–4 almost never appeared in that form. In possession, while attacking, it would be a 3–3–4; out of possession, a 4–3–3. The system was widely adopted and soon developed two further modifications.

The first was a system of zonal marking, introduced by Zézé Moreira at Fluminense, which obviated the need for the strict man-to-man marking of the W-M—the aspect that had failed so disastrously in 1950—and also permitted a greater fluidity. When Arsenal toured Brazil in 1949, they had been struck by the willingness of Brazilian sides to attack from all positions, something they seem both to have feared and regarded as a weakness, a sign of tactical indiscipline. "Suddenly, a bloke comes dashing through and he's had a shot at goal and the ball went wide," said the full-back Laurie Scott, describing Arsenal's 5–1 win over Fluminense to Aidan Hamilton. "And we started looking around to see who we'd got to blame for this. We couldn't find it. We found out it was their full-back. See, they didn't care. I never went up there like that."

Attacking full-backs would become an increasingly important part of the Brazilian game. Given the space in front of the full-backs, 4–2–4 was a system that encouraged them to advance, while at the same time providing immediate cover. Once marking had ceased to be man to man, it became a simple process for the "fourth defender" to react to the forward movement of the full-back by not pushing out himself, leaving his side still with the three-man defensive cover they would have had in the W-M.

The second was the reintroduction of the *ponta da lança*, one of the two central forwards dropping slightly deeper than his partner, providing a natural link with the midfield. This was nothing particularly new—it was no different to the attacking inside-forward role in the diagonal, and Puskás had been performing a similar function for years in the Hungarian system—but it was a position that seems to have been naturally suited to

The 4–2–4: Vila Nova 1951

the temperament of the Brazilian game. It soon found its apogee in a scrawny teenager from Três Corações. Pelé was sixteen when Lula gave him his debut at Santos; within a year he was inspiring his national side to their first World Cup.

For all Guttmann's claims, when he arrived with Honvéd in November 1956, their system caused few surprises. If anything, Brazil were further down the road to 4–2–4 than the Hungarians, although the similarity of shape was obvious. "Basically, the only difference between Brazil's interpretation of the system and that of Hungary was in the number worn by the forward who withdrew into midfield," said Nándor Hidegkuti. "In 1958, the Brazilians opted for inside-right Didi, while for Hungary it was the centre-forward who fell back. In both teams the withdrawn forward operated in what we might call left midfield, and again in both teams the left-half fell back to play a more defensive role, while the right-half maintained the balance in midfield by playing a more open attacking game."

Guttmann's impact had less to do with system than with style, and this is where the orthodoxy—or at least the British orthodoxy—about the great Hungary side requires a gloss. English observers tended to be overwhelmed by the *Aranycsapat*'s technical ability and the fluidity facilitated by the withdrawn center-forward. Perhaps they differed marginally in degree, but, had that been all they were about, they would not have been substantially different from the Austrian *Wunderteam*. Hungary, though, also had a briskness about them, a sense of purpose: their artistry was directed towards the end of winning, and in that they were very much Jimmy Hogan's heirs. Geoffrey Green perhaps flattered England when he spoke of the Hungary of 1953 as having hit a midpoint between British directness and continental elaboration, but the general point was sound. English advocates of the long-ball game would later see validation for their methods in the fact that, so often in that game at Wembley, Hungary transformed defense into attack with a counter of two or three passes. It was not 4–2–4 itself that Guttmann brought to Brazil but that sense of purpose.

The difference in approach was perhaps best summed up by Nélson Rodrigues, who often wrote brief dramatic scenes featuring real-life personalities—effectively imaginary interviews. He responded to Honvéd's tour with a piece featuring Ferenc Puskás and Zizinho, still Brazil's great hero, ending by asking each what was the most magical thing for them to do during a game. Zizinho answered that it was setting up a teammate to score a goal, although for Puskás it was, not surprisingly, scoring a goal. The example may be whimsical, but it does give an indication of Brazilian football's lack of pragmatism at the time.

São Paulo had had a poor season in 1956, finishing second in the Paulista championship, seven points behind Santos, and they did not begin 1957 well, lying fifth after the first half of the championship, seven points behind the leaders Corinthians. Gradually, though, Guttmann's methods began to take effect.

He had a grid painted on a wall at the training ground and in practice sessions would roll the ball to his forwards, shouting to them which square he wanted them to hit. He worked on long balls aimed at the center-forward to flick on for the wingers. He discouraged dallying on the ball, drilling his players in rapid passing to such an extent that his calls of "tat-tat-tat" and "ping-pang-pong" became catchphrases. Everything was about moving the ball at speed, about getting his side playing by instinct.

Perhaps most crucially, he signed Zizinho, then thirty-four, from the Rio club Bangu, and—in a foreshadowing of what he would later do with Mario Coluna at Benfica—installed him as the more creative of the midfield two, with Dino Sani, who had been the playmaker, dropping into the more defensive midfield role. "It was only then," Zizinho said, "that I really began to play."

São Paulo won the Paulista championship that year, at which Guttmann decamped for Europe. His influence, though, was carried on by Vicente Feola. Little more than an average player, Feola had led São Paulo to the Paulista championship in 1949 and had stayed on at the club after standing down as coach, serving as Guttmann's assistant. When he was hired as national coach for the 1958 World Cup, it came as something of a surprise. Osvaldo Brandão had been forced to quit after Brazil finished third in the Copa América in 1957 and neither Silvio Pirilo nor Pedrinho, his two immediate successors, really impressed. There was a movement to recruit Solich, but the fact he was Paraguayan counted against him, and so the Brazilian federation turned to Feola as a safe, uncontroversial choice. He was a bon vivant so relaxed, rumor said, that he was prone to catnapping on the bench during training, although it is doubtful how true that is. Ruy Castro argues in his biography of Garrincha that Feola suffered coronary problems brought on by his excessive weight and would occasionally feel a stabbing pain in his chest. The best way to deal with it, he had learned, was to close his eyes, lower his head and wait for the spasm to pass, which a hysterical press supported by paparazzi photographs interpreted as sleeping.

Antonio Rattín, the Argentinian center-half who played under Feola during his brief spell at Boca Juniors, though, insists that, on at least one occasion, he did drift off. "Every training session we ended with a game," he said. "One day, a very hot day, we started playing, and kept playing, and kept playing. We were waiting for him to blow the whistle for half-time, but he just sat there. We kept looking at him, waiting for him to do something. So eventually I went over to him, and he was snoring. He'd been asleep all the time."

Yet although Feola may have been a jovial fat man who enjoyed playing up to the stereotype, he was not the pushover the federation had imagined him to be. With funding from the Juscelino Kubitschek government, the squad for the 1958 World Cup was the best prepared in Brazil's history. Officials visited twenty-five different locations in Sweden before selecting a training base and then had all twenty-five female staff at that hotel replaced with men to minimize potential distractions. They even campaigned, without success, to have a local nudist camp closed for the duration of the tournament.

The backroom staff included a doctor, a dentist, a trainer, a treasurer, a psychologist, and, in the former Fluminense coach Ernesto Santos, a spy, employed to gather information on opponents. After initial medical tests, the doctor prescribed the majority of the squad medication to tackle intestinal parasites, while one player had to be treated for syphilis. The dentist was just as busy, extracting a total of 470 teeth from the thirty-three players in the provisional squad. Feola was happy enough to go along with those measures, but he was openly dismissive of the psychologist Dr. João Carvalhães.

Carvalhães, who usually assessed the psychological suitability of those applying to be bus drivers, had performed a series of tests on the squad, the most derided of which involved asking them to draw a picture of a man. The results were intriguing—the more instinctive the player, apparently, the more likely he was to draw a stick figure or something representational rather than attempting mimetic detail—but his conclusions were laughable. Pelé, he said, was "obviously infantile" and did "not possess the sense of responsibility necessary for a team game." As Garrincha had scored just 38 out of a possible 123 on his test—lower than the minimum required to drive a bus in São Paulo—Carvalhães suggested he was unsuited to high-pressure games. Feola ignored him and insisted both should be in his squad.

Neither, though, played in Brazil's opening game, an unexceptional 3–0 win over Austria. Pelé was injured, while Garrincha had fallen out of favor for showboating in a warm-up friendly against Fiorentina (having rounded the goalkeeper he decided not to roll the ball into an empty net, but to wait for him to recover, upon which he beat him again before walking the ball over the line). Yet Feola it seems would have played him had Santos not warned about the strength of the four midfielders in Austria's W-M. Feola could rely on Mario Zagallo to track back on the left—he, in effect, fulfilled the Osorio role—but that was not Garrincha's natural game, and so he turned instead to the more disciplined Joel of Flamengo.

They were also omitted against England, who were themselves experimenting with backroom staff—an indication of the growing professionalism of the game across the world. The Tottenham manager Bill Nicholson was sent to scout Brazil, and he concluded the way to stop Brazil was to stop Didí. On his suggestion, the England manager Walter Winterbottom—in a move almost without precedent—made tactical changes to counter Brazil's threat. The lanky Don Howe, a full-back at West Bromwich Albion, was brought in to play as a second center-half alongside Billy Wright, with Thomas Banks and Eddie Clamp, a right-half at Wolves, operating as attacking full-backs on either side of them and Bill Slater deputed to sit tight on Didí. Vavá hit the bar, Clamp cleared one off the line and Colin McDonald twice produced fine saves to keep out headers from José Altafini (who was still going by the nickname of Mazzola), but the system dulled Brazil, and England got away with a goalless draw.

That left Brazil needing to beat the USSR in their final group game to be sure of progression to the last eight. Carvalhães conducted further tests, asking the players to draw the first thing that came into their heads. Garrincha produced a circle with a few spokes radiating from it. It looked vaguely like a sun, but when Carvalhães asked what it was supposed to be, Garrincha replied that it was the head of Quarentinha, a teammate at Botafogo. Carvalhães promptly ruled him out. In total, of the eleven who would eventually start against the USSR, he judged nine unsuitable for such a high-pressure game. Fortunately Feola trusted his own judgment and selected both Pelé and Garrincha.

"You may be right," Pelé recalls him saying to Carvalhães. "But the thing is, you don't know anything about football."

Feola was concerned by reports of the Soviets' supreme fitness and decided that his side had to intimidate them with Brazilian skill from the start. "Remember," he said to Didí just before he left the dressing room, "the first pass goes to Garrincha." It took a little under twenty seconds for the ball to reach the winger. Boris Kuznetsov, the experienced Soviet left-back, moved to close him down. Garrincha feinted left and went right; Kuznetsov was left on the ground. Garrincha paused and beat him again.

And again. And then once again put him on the ground. Garrincha advanced, leaving Yuri Voinov on his backside. He darted into the box and fired a shot from a narrow angle that smacked against the post. Within a minute Pelé had hit the bar, and a minute after that Vavá gave Brazil the lead from Didí's through ball. Gabriel Hanot called them the greatest three minutes of soccer ever played.

Brazil won only 2–0, but the performance was every bit as special as the demolitions of Spain and Sweden had been eight years earlier. Wales offered surprising resistance in the quarterfinal, even without the imposing presence of the injured John Charles, and lost only 1–0, but this Brazil side could not be denied. France, hampered by an injury to Bob Jonquet, were brushed aside 5–2 in the semifinal, and Sweden went down by the same score in the final. "There was no doubt this time," Glanville wrote, "that the best, immeasurably the finest, team had won."

It was, Feola said, Zagallo's role, balancing the anarchic brilliance of Garrincha, that had proved key. Initially an inside-forward, Zagallo had converted himself into a winger because he realized that was his only chance of getting into the national side and so was ideally suited to the role of tracking back and forth on the left flank. By the 1962 World Cup, he had taken to playing so deep that the system began to be referred to as a 4–3–3. "The age factor, in Chile, was one we had always to take into consideration," explained Aimoré Moreira, who replaced Feola as his health deteriorated but picked a similar squad for the following World Cup.

That was responsible for our tactics being less flexible than some, remembering the team's sparkle in Sweden, expected. In Chile we had

Brazil, 1958 World Cup

Brazil, 1962 World Cup

strictly to employ each player in accordance with what we knew about the yield of the whole team. For example, Didí was more and more a player good at waiting in midfield, and blocking the centre to the opponents. . . . Zito, quicker, more dynamic, was able to shuttle backwards and forwards, and could last out a full ninety minutes while doing this. This meant, because of the need carefully to relate the role of one to the other, the elasticity of attacks was limited—with this one great compensation, that every player was free and had the ability to use his own initiative, and make variations.

The greatest compensation of all was Garrincha. Opponents regularly set two or even three men to mark him, and he simply bypassed them. Pelé played only the opening two matches in Chile before injury ended his involvement, but Garrincha was enough. He missed a penalty but scored twice as England were seen off 3–1 in the quarterfinal, and scored two more and was sent off in a 4–2 victory over Chile in the semi. Reprieved for the final, he was relatively subdued, but it didn't matter: 1962 had been his tournament, the final triumph of the winger before the culls of the midsixties.

In a piece in *A Gazeta* in 1949, Mazzoni wrote that

For the Englishman, football is an athletic exercise; for the Brazilian it's a game.

The Englishman considers a player that dribbles three times in succession is a nuisance; the Brazilian considers him a virtuoso.

English football, well played, is like a symphonic orchestra; well played, Brazilian football is like an extremely hot jazz band.

English football requires that the ball moves faster than the player; Brazilian football requires that the player be faster than the ball.

The English player thinks; the Brazilian improvises.

There was nobody who exemplified the difference more than Garrincha. At São Paulo, Guttmann had had a left-winger called Canhoteiro, who was regarded as the left-footed Garrincha (the name translates as "left-footed"). "Tactics," Guttmann once said after seeing Canhoteiro ignore him brilliantly once again, "are for everybody, but they are not valid for him." The beauty of playing four at the back was that, although it wasn't predicated on such players—as Viktor Maslov and Alf Ramsey would prove—it provided an environment in which they could thrive. The world soon got the message, and by the time of the 1966 World Cup, the W-M had all but passed into history.

8

THE ENGLISH PRAGMATISM (1)

"You in England," Helenio Herrera announced at an impromptu press conference at Birmingham Airport in March 1960, "are playing in the style we continentals used so many years ago, with much physical strength, but no method, no technique." No one who had seen his Barcelona side deconstruct Wolverhampton Wanderers, the English champions, the night before could have been in much doubt that he was right. Barcelona, already 4–0 up from the first leg, had dazzled in the second, completing a 9–2 aggregate victory. The days of the floodlit friendlies, in which Wolves had beaten the likes of Honvéd and Spartak Moscow, seemed an awfully long time ago.

Wolves, in fairness, were more direct than most, but Herrera believed the fact they had been so dominant domestically was evidence of a more general weakness in the English game. "When it came to modern football, the Britons missed the evolution," he said, mocking their instinctive conservatism. "The English are creatures of habit: tea at five." The irony of that is that Stan Cullis, the Wolves manager, was actually one of England's more progressive thinkers.

The heavy defeats to Hungary had made clear that any notion of English superiority was a myth, and there was at least a recognition that the English style had to change, something demonstrated by the publication of a slew of books lamenting the passing of a golden age. The problem was that nobody seemed too sure how to go about it. The W-M was widely blamed but remained the default. Inasmuch as solutions were suggested, they tended to follow the course prescribed by Willy Meisl in *Soccer Revolution*: go back to the golden age and readopt the 2–3–5; which tended, of course, rather to prove Herrera's point: as the rest of the world became increasingly tactically sophisticated, there were serious and influential soccer writers in Britain advocating a return to a formation that had looked outmoded twenty years earlier.

The option of copying Hungary was something that was only really considered at Manchester City. Johnny Williamson had had success playing as a deep-lying center-forward in the reserve side at the end of the 1953–1954 season and, the following year, the manager Les McDowall had Don Revie play there for the first team.

Revie subsequently devoted twenty pages of his memoir, *Soccer's Happy Wanderer*, to explaining the system. After an uncertain start—they were beaten 5–0 by Preston on the opening day of the season—and some difficult times on the heavy pitches of the winter, City went on to reach the Cup final and finish seventh, while Revie was named Footballer of the Year. That summer, though, Revie took a family holiday in Blackpool against the wishes of the club and, after being suspended for the opening two weeks of the season, remained on the periphery. Injuries restored him to the lineup for the FA Cup final, in which City beat Birmingham, but Revie had become disillusioned and joined Sunderland the following season.

City reverted to more traditional methods, while Revie struggled to settle at Roker Park. Locked in a spiral of reckless spending, Sunderland then tumbled into an illegal payments scandal, found to be offering win bonuses of £10, when the stipulated maximum was £4. Amid the chaos, as their manager Bill Murray was replaced by Alan Brown, Sunderland were relegated. Revie, regardless, may not have adapted. "There was only one way he could play," said Sunderland's inside-right Charlie Fleming. "He did a lot of things foreign to us. . . . Don's system was alright in Manchester, but everybody knew about it when he came to Sunderland and how to play against it. Don couldn't change." Or perhaps it was that British players couldn't change. Either way, Revie soon departed for Leeds, where he was used as an inside-forward, and the momentum of his experiment was lost.

Even those British teams who enjoyed success in the early European Cup tended simply to prosper not through innovation but because they were very good at applying the old model. Hibernian, for instance, semi-finalists in the first European Cup, were renowned for their Famous Five front line of Gordon Smith, Bobby Johnstone, Lawrie Reilly, Eddie Turnbull, and Willie Ormond. The Manchester United of Bobby Charlton, Dennis Viollet, and Duncan Edwards, for all their youth and vibrancy, were a side rooted in the W-M. "By a combination of short and long passes," Geoffrey Green wrote, they "have discarded a static conventional forward shape and, with the basic essential of a well-ordered defence, have found success by the sudden switching and masking of the final attacking thrust by their fluid approach. This aims at producing a spare man—or 'man over'—at the height of the attack." Matt Busby's United may have been fluid in British terms, and their brilliance is not in doubt, but they were still orthodox by European standards.

The most successful radicalism came at Tottenham Hotspur who, in 1912, hired Peter McWilliam as their manager. He is an oddly neglected figure now, but his influence was extraordinarily wide-ranging. He had learned the Scottish passing game from Bob McColl, a signing from Queen's Park, while operating as a cultured wing-half at Newcastle, and he soon imposed its principles on his new side. Perhaps even more significantly, McWilliam came to recognize the importance of youth development to school players in the close passing game and established the Kent League side Northfleet United as effectively a feeder club for Spurs, a move that, if not unprecedented, was extremely rare. "We train the players to have only good habits," he explained. "I always tell them to treat the ball as their best friend and always to pass it with care and consideration. Belting the ball . . . has no place in the Tottenham way of doing things."

His ideas may have been progressive, but in other ways McWilliam was very traditional in approach. "Peter McWilliam never minced his words with anyone," said the wing-half Ron Burgess. "He believed in calling a spade a spade in his broad Scottish brogue, and if a player displeased him, he was not backward in telling him so. I shall never forget the way he called everyone 'Boy,' nor the way some of the younger players tried to look the other way as he walked into the dressing-room after we had lost a match which he thought we should have won."

In his autobiography, Burgess recalled playing in a reserve game at Coventry, dashing forward from right-half and being battered in "a hard and gruelling game." As he took his uniform off in the locker room afterwards, McWilliam looked his bruised body up and down. "Serves ye right, boy!" he said. "Perrrhaps that'll teach ye not to hang on to the ba'!" Unsympathetic McWilliam may have been, but Burgess concluded he was right. "It *was* my own fault for hanging on to the ball unnecessarily and trying to force my way through solid defenders, but it did me good. It taught me a painful lesson, for those bruises were as sore as they were highly coloured, and for that reason alone it was well that it happened."

McWilliam left Spurs for Middlesbrough in 1927, tempted by a salary of £1500 a year, but he seems never to have felt entirely comfortable back in the northeast and returned to London in 1934 as chief scout of Arsenal before, in 1938, being rehired as manager at White Hart Lane. In his team in those final years before the Second World War were three men who would go on to have a huge impact as managers; two of them, Arthur Rowe and Bill Nicholson at Tottenham, the other, Vic Buckingham, at Ajax and Barcelona.

Rowe had played as a deep-lying center-half for Spurs but had been a far more rounded player than Herbie Roberts and his many imitators, preferring to hold possession and delay until he could make accurate passes rather than simply hoofing it forward without design. Encouraged by McWilliam, Rowe had always been a thoughtful player, and he was eager to put some of his ideas into practice. He undertook a lecture tour in Hungary in 1939 and made such an impression that he was asked to prepare the national side for the 1940 Olympic Games in Helsinki while acting as a mentor for Hungarian coaches. The journalist László Feleki of *Nemzeti Sport* magazine, apparently acting as an intermediary for the Hungarian federation, wrote to the FA saying the plan was for Rowe to "lay down new foundations for Hungarian football with English help." Given how Hungarian soccer was progressing without English help, that is revealing. Perhaps there was still a residual sense of respect for the country of Jimmy Hogan, but Rowe's ideas clearly chimed with those already current in the coffeehouses, and it's fair to assume there was a certain amount of cross-pollination.

War prevented Rowe from taking up the Hungarian offer, and he returned home to coach the army side. He won a league title with Chelmsford City and, in 1949, was hired by Tottenham, in the Second Division at the time, to replace Joe Hulme. He soon explained his theory of how the game should be played. "Soon after we reported for training," Burgess, by then Tottenham's captain, wrote in his autobiography, Rowe "introduced us to his new playing scheme. At first the whole project was discussed in the dressing room and as we listened to Arthur's rather revolutionary ideas, I saw expressions of doubt on the faces of some of the lads." After two weeks of training, though, Burgess said he "couldn't wait" to try out the new style of play in a competitive environment.

Although Burgess is clear on what the new style was, he is less certain as to how new it was—understandably, because Rowe, emboldened by what he had seen in Budapest, had essentially taken to extremes what McWilliam had been doing before the war. On the one hand Burgess called the tactics "revolutionary" but on the other admitted "there was nothing exactly original about them." He wrote, "Our style was merely the adaption of the modern continental style. It was based on the short pass of fifteen to twenty yards, the ball never being held longer than was absolutely necessary by any player."

Rowe's vision led him to make Alf Ramsey, then an attacking right-back at Southampton, his first signing. In *And the Spurs Go Marching On*, Rowe explained how he admired Ramsey's willingness to attack but encouraged him not to rely so heavily on long forward passes. "Had he [Ramsey] ever thought how much more accuracy was guaranteed, how much more progress could be made if he pumped 15- or 20-yard passes to a withdrawn [outside-right Sonny] Walters?" he asked him. "The opposing left-back would hesitate to follow Walters back into the Spurs half, which was definitely no man's land to the full-back then, thus giving Walters the vital gift of space. And Sonny could now make an inside pass if Alf followed up and made himself available."

Almost uniquely in Britain, Spurs began building from the back, with Ramsey given license to push on. "There is no limit to where even a defender will go to attack," he said. "Maybe you have noticed how often I go upfield to cross a ball or even have a shot at goal. That a defender should not attempt to score a goal is something to which I can never subscribe." He could only do that, though, because his center-half, Bill Nicholson, was prepared to sit in and provide cover.

This was the style that would become known as push and run, but it wasn't quite as simple as that. "The wingers had to play further back than in the normal long-kicking tactics, and were thus brought more into the game, for their inter-changing with inside-forwards was another essential of this scheme," Burgess explained. His role, as a half-back, changed to accommodate that. "I could no longer consider myself an attacking half-back," he said, "for both Bill Nicholson and I had to be in position to take the short ball from the full-backs ready for pushing it on to the inside or wing-man."

This wasn't so much about finding men in space as about the creation and manipulation of space. "We changed things," the inside-forward Eddie Baily, later Bill Nicholson's assistant, told Phil Soar in his 1982 history of the club. "We gave the ball to the man who was marked. But other players slipped into support positions to give the man with the ball more options. That in turn depended on how the ball had been given and we had to guarantee that our man received it." It didn't matter if a player had a defender tight on his back if all he was doing was bouncing the ball off, changing the angle of attack. "A good player runs to the ball," Rowe said. "A bad player runs after it."

Spurs cruised to promotion in 1949–1950 and thrashed Sunderland, at the time third in the First Division table, 5–1 in the fourth round of the FA Cup. Defeat to Everton in the fifth round, though, prompted questions about whether Spurs would have to change their style to compete in the top flight. Rowe was adamant that they didn't.

Since the old offside law changed [in 1925] and since the Arsenal introduced their system of play, very successfully it must be admitted, football, to my mind, has been of a negative type. There is nothing wrong with the Arsenal style, but to work it successfully you have to have a certain number of typed players. If you haven't got these types, your system won't be successfully exploited. Many clubs have tried to copy the Arsenal style without having the men to do it properly. The result has been stalemate. Our method is better—to obtain an appreciation of the fact that the team is more important than the individual. I feel that the individual gets more benefit, too.

At times during that 1950–1951 season, their first back in the top flight, Spurs were magnificent. After a 7–0 win over Newcastle in November, for instance, the *Telegraph* was moved to write that

Tottenham's method is simple. Briefly, the Spurs principle is to hold the ball a minimum amount of time, keep it on the ground and put it ahead into an open space where a colleague will be a second or two later. The result is their attacks are carried on right through the side with each man taking the ball in his stride at top pace, for all the world like a wave gathering momentum as it races to the far distant shore. It is all worked out in triangles and squares and when the mechanism of it clicks at speed, as it did on Saturday, with every pass placed to the last refined inch on a drenched surface, there is simply no defence against it.

They won the title by four points, becoming only the third side to win the Second and First Division titles in successive seasons, an indication of how revolutionary their style was, according to the correspondent of the *Tottenham Weekly Herald*, Concord. "Spurs have proved beyond all doubt the vast superiority of their new-style soccer," he wrote.

Successful application of this style will, I predict, create a revolution in British soccer. Just as clubs found it necessary to discover an answer to the third-back game, so they will have to remould their ideas to counter Spurs' system. . . . Credit for this immensely encouraging development goes to Spurs' manager Arthur Rowe. . . . In his short period with the club he has produced results whose effect will be felt wherever first-class football is played. He has recognised and applied a fundamental truth, that soccer is a team game and that teamwork alone can bring success.

They were second the following year, but, as Rowe perhaps remained loyal to aging players for too long, Spurs' form disintegrated. Rowe struggled to cope. In January 1954, he suffered a nervous breakdown. He returned to work in the summer but defeat to York City in the fifth round of the cup proved too much. He was readmitted to a hospital in April 1955 and resigned in July. He never returned to White Hart Lane. Jimmy Adamson, who had been his assistant, took over as manager, with Bill Nicholson becoming his assistant. The foundations of the Spurs style were assured, and it was playing push-and-run soccer that they clinched the double under Nicholson in 1961.

Tottenham Hotspur 2 Leicester City 0, FA Cup final, Wembley, London, 6 May 1961

Such progressiveness was rare in England, though, and Spurs were regarded with suspicion, despite their success. As the rest of the world developed technically and worked out increasingly sophisticated defensive patterns or means of structuring fluidity, British soccer ploughed its own, less subtle, furrow. In its own way, it was just as rooted in fear—or, to its apologists, pragmatism—as the *catenaccio* Herrera would eventually adopt, but this was a very British insecurity. Skill, or anything that required thinking too much, was not to be trusted, while physical toughness remained the ultimate virtue. It is no coincidence that, the World Cup triumph of 1966 aside, the iconic image of English soccer remains a blood-soaked Terry Butcher, bandaged but unbowed after inspiring England to the goalless draw against Sweden that ensured qualification for the 1990 World Cup. Even the manner of that stalemate was characteristic. Italy might have set out to kill the game, passing the ball at deathly pace around midfield, wasting time, breaking the rhythm—as England in fact did in a scarcely credible role reversal against Italy in Rome in 1997. In Stockholm in 1989, though, England simply sat back, defended deep, and relied on courage under fire: what Simon Kuper has called the urge to re-create Dunkirk at every opportunity.

To blame Cullis for a trait that has run through English soccer from its earliest origins would be nonsensical, just as it was for writers in the fifties to blame Chapman (or even, as Willy Meisl did, on the basis of a hint supposedly dropped in a conversation with his brother, to persist in the wishful thinking that, had Chapman not died when he did, he would have reverted to a more classical system). Besides, if results rather than aesthetics are the goal, there is nothing necessarily wrong with functional physicality; thirteen years after the Hungary debacle, it would, after all, win England a World Cup. What are important are the method and the thought behind it.

Cullis's side might have been overwhelmed by Herrera's Barcelona, but they had achieved notable results against elite sides only a few years earlier. Floodlights were installed at Molineux in the summer of 1953 and officially turned on for a game against a South Africa national side that September. Racing Club of Buenos Aires were beaten 3–1, a game in which "Wolverhampton Wanderers efficiently demonstrated that English soccer played with speed and spirit is still world class," according to the ever-opinionated Desmond Hackett in the *Express*. Wolves then beat Dinamo Moscow 2–1 and Spartak 4–0, but the most memorable match, without question, was the meeting with the Honvéd of Puskás, Czibor, Bozsik, and Kocsis on December 14, 1954. After the two humiliations Hungary had inflicted on England, this was a chance for revenge.

On the morning of the game, Cullis, remembering how Hungary had struggled in the mud in the World Cup final against West Germany that

Wolves 3 Honvéd 2, friendly, Molineux, Wolverhampton, 13 December 1954

summer, sent out three apprentices—one of them a sixteen-year-old Ron Atkinson—to water the field. "We thought he was out of his mind," Atkinson said in an interview quoted in Jim Holden's biography of Cullis. "It was December and it had been raining incessantly for four days."

Honvéd struck twice in the opening quarter hour, but the conditions soon began to take their toll. "Honvéd gradually got bogged down," Atkinson went on. "Their tricks got stuck in the mud." Cullis determined to bring the mud into play as little as possible and at half-time ordered his players to hit more long passes, to get the ball forward quickly to try to catch out the Honvéd full-backs, who he believed were playing too square. Four minutes into the second half, Wolves got the lifeline they needed as Johnny Hancocks converted a penalty. "Bit by bit Wolves began to tighten the screws . . . ," wrote Geoffrey Green. "They seemed to double in number and swarm everywhere. The pitch, more and more churned up, resembled thick glue. And the Molineux crowd surged, tossed and roared like a hurricane at sea, and called for the kill." With fourteen minutes remaining, Dennis Wilshaw, who had almost been ruled out through injury after crashing his bike on the way to the game, crossed for Roy Swinbourne to head an equalizer. Within ninety seconds the same pair combined for the winner.

After a year of misery, English soccer reveled in the victory. "I may never live to see a greater thriller than this," wrote Peter Wilson in the *Daily Mirror*. "And if I see many more as thrilling I may not live much longer anyway." Charlie Buchan, in his column in the *News Chronicle*, saluted the affirmation of the English style. The *Daily Mail* captured the sense of ecstasy as it ran the headline "Hail Wolves, 'Champions of the World.'" It was a proclamation that so riled Gabriel Hanot he was inspired to institute the European Cup to disprove it.

Only Willy Meisl remained aloof, pointing out that only a few days earlier Honvéd had also lost to Crvena Zvezda, who at the time were seventh in the Yugoslav league, well behind the leaders, Partizan. "No one called Partizan champions of the world," he said. "Dare I also remark in passing that quagmires are not usually considered the best pitches on which world championships ought to be decided, not even neutral quagmires." When it came to a battle of physique against technique, England could still mix it with the best of them, and yet the emptiness of such consolation was exposed in the years that followed. Wolves went on—admittedly in the void left by the Munich plane crash—to win the league in 1958 and 1959 and the FA Cup in 1960, but the impression they made in formalized European competition, which began in 1955, was all but nil. Herrera's jibe stung because it was so accurate.

Like so many managers, Cullis's style as a coach bore little relation to the player he had been. He was generally regarded as a cultured, attack-minded center-half. Even Puskás spoke of his reputation as "the most classical centre-half of his time." His leadership skills became apparent early, and he captained Wolves at nineteen and England at twenty-two. So, too, did his meticulousness, as he kept a book in which he recorded his impressions of the center-forwards against whom he played. Tommy Lawton said that to beat Cullis a forward needed "the penetrative powers of a tank and the pace of a racing whippet." Cullis also developed a reputation for scrupulous fairness, famously deciding against hacking down Albert Stubbins when the forward got behind him to score for Liverpool in a title decider against Wolves. John Arlott referred to him as "the passionate puritan."

Cullis had the advantage, in his coaching education, of playing under the eccentric Major Frank Buckley, one of the more adventurous managers of the thirties. In the locker room at Molineux, Buckley installed a therapeutic diathermy machine, a universal machine for galvanism, sumsoidal and paradic treatments, and a machine that gave out ultraviolet rays for irradiation. He also, notoriously, ahead of the 1939 FA Cup final had his players injected with "animal secretions," supposedly taken from monkey's glands, although Cullis believed they were placebos designed more to enhance self-belief than muscle mass.

Encouraged to question the orthodoxy, Cullis went back to the basics. "There is no substitute for hard work," he always insisted, and he was one of the first coaches in England to take fitness training seriously. He would have his players go on preseason stamina-building runs across Cannock Chase and employed Frank Morris, a former international runner, as a fitness coach. His players, he said, "must have tremendous team spirit, they must be superbly fit, and they must use the correct tactics on the field." Those tactics mainly involved a W-M in which every effort was taken to play the ball forward quickly. Wolves, Cullis insisted, as countless managers of similar philosophy would, did not hit aimless long balls but rather attempted to transfer the ball swiftly to the two wingers, Jimmy Mullen and Johnny Hancocks. "Some ill-advised critics called it kick and rush," the center-half and captain Billy Wright said. "Nothing could be further from the truth. Every phase is strictly logical and, although placing unselfish coordination before individualism, Cullis has never scorned ball players."

While he accommodated such gifted players as Peter Broadbent, Jimmy Murray, and Bobby Mason in his side, skill, for Cullis, was to be harnessed for the ends of the team and was certainly not an end in itself. Although he believed devoutly in the importance of fairness, notions of there being a "right way" to play meant nothing to Cullis; for him the game was about winning. "Because we insist that every player in possession of the ball makes rapid progress towards the business of launching an attack," he said, "our forwards are not encouraged to parade their abilities in ostentatious fashion, which might please a small section of the crowd at the cost of reducing the efficiency of movement."

Where others praised Hungary's 6–3 victory at Wembley as a festival of passing and individual skill, Cullis instead saw a vindication of his own beliefs. The goalkeeper, Gyula Grosics, he pointed out, had a tendency to clear the ball long. Only one of Hungary's goals, he noted, came from a move begun in their own half of the field: three resulted from moves of one pass, one from a move of two passes and one from a free kick. The pass-and-move soccer that was so admired, he said, came only in the second half when Hungary were keeping possession from England. "The number of scoring chances which will arrive during the course of a match is in direct proportion to the amount of time the ball spends in front of goal," he explained. "If the defenders in the Wolves team delay their clearances, the ball will be in front of our goal for too long a period and the scoring chances will go to the other side. If too much time is spent in building up our own attacks, the ball will spend less of the game in the other team's penalty area and, of course, we shall score fewer goals."

In that, Cullis found an ally in Wing-Commander Charles Reep, an RAF officer stationed at nearby Bridgnorth. Reep had been based at Bushy Park in southwest London in the thirties and had become fascinated by the style of Herbert Chapman's Arsenal after attending two three-hour lectures given by their right-half, Charles Jones, in 1933. In them, Jones emphasized the need for the rapid transfer of ball from back to front and explained Chapman's concept of the functional winger.

Reep was stationed in Germany at the end of the war and, on his return in 1947, was disappointed to find that although the W-M shape had been adopted, Chapman's other ideas had not. The play, he believed, was too slow, while the winger had again become a figure who performed his tricks almost in isolation before sending over crosses that rarely produced goals. Reep became increasingly frustrated, until, as he wrote in an autobiographical article for the Scottish fanzine the *Punter* in 1989, he finally lost patience during a Swindon Town match at the County Ground on March 19, 1950.

There was no game on March 19, 1950, which is troubling given Reep's concern for statistical accuracy (although he may, in fairness, have been let down by a subbing error), but Swindon did beat Bristol Rovers 1–0 at home in Division Three (South) on March 18, so it seems probable that that is the game to which he refers. After a first half in which he saw attack after attack come to nothing, Reep decided to record them in the second. Swindon, his notes showed, had 147 attacks in the second half. Reep, extrapolating this, and assuming 280 attacks per game and an average of two goals scored, realized this equated to a failure rate of 99.29 percent, which meant that an improvement of only 0.71 percent was necessary for a side to average three goals a game. That, he saw, would almost certainly guarantee promotion.

Reep made his analysis more sophisticated and began recording attacking moves for both sides. "Back in 1950," he wrote, "these findings were by no means firmly established, but time was to prove them correct. . . . Only two goals out of nine came from moves which included more than three received passes." He also observed that a long pass from inside a team's own half appeared to make a move more effective, that possession regained either inside or just outside the opponents' box was the most effective way of scoring, and that it took roughly eight attempts on goal to produce a goal. At the time, Reep was stationed at Yatesbury, and he began working with the RAF team there. He developed a theory about how wingers should play, and although no contemporary record survives, Øyvind Larson, in an essay on Reep's influence on Norwegian soccer, discusses a report Reep sent to the then–Norway manager Egil Olsen in the nineties. It was initially produced for Walter Winterbottom (although there is no evidence Winterbottom ever read it), ahead of England's friendly against Uruguay in 1954 and was based on his observations of Uruguay's 7–0 victory over Scotland in the World Cup earlier that year. In it he argued that wingers should remain as high up the field as they could while remaining onside, almost on the touchline, waiting for long balls out of defense; that in possession they should head always for the near post and then either shoot or cross; and that when out of possession they should make for the far post (in relation to the ball) in order to support their center-forward. That, loosely, was how Chapman's wingers behaved, and if it was how Yatesbury's were performing, it brought them success, as they won the Army Southern Command's knockout cup in 1950.

Reep was redeployed back to Bushy Park in 1950. While there, his theorizing caught the attention of Jackie Gibbons, the manager of Brentford, and, from February 1951, Reep was employed on a part-time basis by the club. When he arrived, with fourteen games of the season remaining, they were in danger of relegation, but with Reep advising, their goals per game ratio went up from 1.5 to 3, and they took twenty of twenty-eight possible points to stay up comfortably. Later that year, though, Reep was transferred back to Bridgnorth.

Between 1953 and 1967, he and Bernard Benjamin, the head of the Royal Statistical Society, studied 578 games—including three World Cups, but mainly English league matches—and discovered that only 5 percent of all moves consist of four or more received passes and only 1 percent of six or more. "The reason for this is clear," Ken Bray, a visiting fellow in the Sport and Exercise Science group at the University of Bath, wrote in his book *How to Score*. "Long chains of passes require repeated accuracy, very difficult to sustain as defenders move in to close down space—man-mark the targets as the sequence stretches out." Reep's conclusion was that possession soccer was counterproductive, and, at a low level, such as an RAF side or Brentford, there is probably a large element of truth to that. Reep never differentiated, but Bray is strangely uncritical of either him or Charles Hughes, the FA technical director who developed similar theories in the eighties. Just because long passing moves were rare in the English game of the fifties does not mean they were not desirable. Common does not necessarily equal good. From Chapman's time players had been encouraged to hit the ball long and early, and given the mud baths that passed for fields for the middle portion of the season, with good reason. As long chains of passes were rare, it is hardly surprising so few goals resulted from them.

There is a startlingly obvious flaw in the arguments of those who would use Reep's analysis to argue that direct soccer is more effective. His figures show that 91.5 percent of moves in the games he studied consisted of three received passes or fewer. If the number of passes in a chain before a goal made no difference, then logically the percentage of goals resulting from moves of three or fewer received passes would also be 91.5 percent. If direct soccer were more effective, this figure should be higher. Yet Bray concludes from Reep's figures that "around 80 percent of all goals resulted from moves of three passes or fewer." As has already been noted, Reep himself claimed that "only two goals out of nine came from moves which included more than three received passes" (so seven out of nine, 77.8 percent, came from moves of three or fewer). Admittedly, Watford in 1981–1982 scored 93.4 percent of their goals from moves of three received passes or fewer, but, then, only 72 of 106 goals at the 1982 World Cup (67.9 percent) resulted from moves of three passes or fewer.

If, as those figures suggest, roughly 80 percent of goals result from moves of three received passes or fewer, but 91.5 percent of moves consist of three received passes or fewer, then it surely follows—even within the unsubtle parameters Reep sets out—that moves of three passes or fewer are *less* effective than those of four or more. And these figures do not even take into account the goals scored when long chains of passes have led to a dead ball or a breakdown. Nor do they even consider the fact that a side holding possession and making their opponents chase is likely to tire less quickly and so will be able to pick off exhausted opponents late on. It is, frankly, horrifying that a philosophy founded on such a basic misinterpretation of figures could have been allowed to become a cornerstone of English coaching. Anti-intellectualism is one thing, but faith in wrongheaded pseudointellectualism is far worse.

One significant statistic does emerge from the article Reep published in the *Journal of the Royal Statistical Society*, although, as it runs counter to his thesis, it goes unremarked. At the 1958 World Cup, 1.3 percent of all moves comprised seven or more passes, as opposed to 0.7 percent in his selection of English league games (across all divisions) for 1957–1958. At the 1962 World Cup, it was 2.3 percent compared to 1.3 percent in league games the previous season, and in 1966, 2.6 percent compared to 1.2 percent. That would seem to lead to two conclusions (inasmuch as any meaningful conclusions can be drawn from such a small sample). First, that long chains of passes became increasingly common between 1958 and 1962 and, second, that international soccer—at the time surely still the pinnacle of the game—was roughly twice as likely to produce long chains of passes as club soccer. If long, direct play really were superior, surely there would be more of it the higher the level?

That is not to say that direct soccer is wrong at all times, merely that fundamentalism in tactics tends to be as misguided as in any sphere. Tactics must rather be conditioned by circumstances and the players available. Reep's apologists misinterpret the figures, but even if they had not, his method is so general as to be all but meaningless. Why would it follow that an approach suited to a Third Division match in Rotherham in December would be equally applicable to a World Cup game in Guadalajara in July? Part of the genius of the great tacticians is their ability to apply the right system at the right time. Even Alf Ramsey, adopting a more possession-based approach for the Mexico World Cup of 1970, acknowledged that.

Still, Reep's statistics supported Cullis's instincts, and—in the English league at least—the two enjoyed a fruitful working relationship. "It helped me modify and improve points of tactics which were either costing us goals or reducing our scoring potential," Cullis said. He was also much taken by Reep's isolation of the Position of Maximum Opportunity (POMO), an area a short distance from goal towards the back post from which a striking percentage of goals was scored and into which Reep encouraged wingers to run. "Reep's recordings of the Hungary match showed in exact detail the principles which I believed to be true," Cullis said. "He was able to establish in black and white the facts for which I was forced to trust my memory where, inevitably, some would become lost or confused."

Just as convinced that the 6–3 defeat to Hungary was illusory was Alf Ramsey, who played at right-back in that game and scored England's third goal from the penalty spot. He too noted how many of Hungary's goals had come from long passes and suggested, in a veiled criticism of Gil Merrick, the England goalkeeper, that they'd just had one of those days when every shot they took flew in. That is disingenuous, ignoring the fact that Hungary had thirty-five shots to England's five and the almost embarrassing ease with which Hungary kept possession from England in the second half, but it is intriguing. Perhaps it was simply a function of Ramsey's blinkeredness when it came to foreigners (this, after all, was a man who once turned down the chance of watching *Sleeping Beauty* at the Bolshoi so as not to miss a screening of an Alf Garnett film at the British Embassy Club in Moscow). Perhaps, having developed as a player at a club whose style was not too far removed from that of the Hungarians, a side moreover in which forward players were encouraged to drop off to create space, he was simply not so awestruck as others by the technical and tactical mastery of his opponents. Ramsey, certainly, was not a man to be blinded by beauty.

Given that he led England to their only success, it seems bizarre that the general assessment of him should be so ambivalent. While there are those who look back on 1966—as others before them had looked back to Chapman, or to the 2–3–5—and see it as the blueprint for all football to come, and there are those who seem somehow to blame Ramsey for having such devotees, as if it were his fault that, having been successful, others without the wit to evolve should seek to copy him. Even as England won the World Cup, respect for him was grudging. "His detractors would point to his dissection of the game as though it were a laboratory animal, arguing that it robbed football of its poetry, reduced it to a science," as his biographer Dave Bowler put it. "It's an assessment he would not disagree with, one which he might well take as a compliment. For he saw football as a tactical exercise, a mental as much as a physical sport." Not that he cared, but it did not help Ramsey's reputation that he could be so willfully cussed.

Ramsey was, at heart, a realist. That was apparent as soon as he took charge of Ipswich in August 1955. He may have approved of Rowe's methods with Spurs, but he soon realized that push and run had no place at a Third Division South team of whom little was expected. He began with the simple things, and although his first game in charge was lost 2–0 to Torquay United, the reporter for the *East Anglian Daily Times* admitted he was impressed by the range of corners on display.

Results soon picked up, but it wasn't until December that Ramsey made the switch that would set in motion a decade of evolution that ended in the World Cup. Jimmy Leadbetter was an inside-forward, a skillful, intelligent player whose major failing was his lack of pace. He had been signed in the summer by Ramsey's predecessor Scott Duncan and, having played just once in Ramsey's first four months in charge, was concerned for his future. Then, just before the new year, Ramsey asked Leadbetter to play on the left-wing. Leadbetter was worried he wasn't fast enough, but Ramsey's concern was more his use of the ball.

"I was supposed to be the left-winger, but I wasn't playing that game," Leadbetter said. "I was pulled back, collecting balls from defence—the other full-backs wouldn't come that far out of defence to mark me, so I had space to move in. As I went further forward, I could draw the full-back out of position. He wouldn't stay in the middle of the field marking nobody; he felt he had to come with me. That left a big gap on the left-hand side of the field. That was where [the centre-forward] Ted Phillips played. He needed space, but if you could give him that and the ball, it was in the back of the net."

Promotion was won in 1957, and as the center-forward Ray Crawford was signed from Portsmouth and the orthodox right-winger Roy Stephenson from Leicester City, Ramsey's plan took shape. This was 4–2–4, but, like the formation with which Brazil won the World Cup, it was 4–2–4 with a twist. Where Brazil had Mario Zagallo shuttling deep from a high position, Ipswich had Leadbetter, whose lack of pace meant he sat deep naturally. If anything, it resembled in shape more the skewed 4–3–3 Brazil would adopt in 1962 than the 4–2–4 of 1958, although the style was very different.

"We believe in striking quickly from defence," Ramsey said. "A team is most vulnerable when it has just failed in attack. If I had to suggest an ideal number of passes, I would say three." Three, perhaps not coincidentally, was also Reep's magic number, although there is no suggestion that the two ever met. "Alf's idea was the less number of passes you take, the less chance there is of making a bad pass," Leadbetter said. "It's better to make three, good, simple ones, because if you try to make ten, as sure as anything you'll make a mess of one of them. You should be in a position to shoot with the third one. You could do that then because of the way teams played."

The great weakness of the W-M was the pivot necessitated by the fact that there were only three defenders. If an attack came down the attacking side's left, the right-back would move to close the winger down, with the center-half picking up the center-forward and the left-back tucking behind him to cover—and, if playing against a 4–2–4 or another system with two central strikers, picking up the other center-forward. "That was the only cover you got, so if you beat your full-back, your forwards had a good chance," Leadbetter explained.

Ipswich went up again in 1961 and, to the bewilderment of many, went on to win the title the following year, despite having spent only £30,000 assembling their squad, less than a third of what Tottenham paid to bring Jimmy Greaves back from Italy. Ipswich, the *Times* said "defy explanation—they do the simple things accurately and quickly; there are no frills about their play and no posing. They are not exciting; they do not make the pulses race. . . . Maybe, after all, there is a virtue in the honest labourer."

With little or no television coverage to expose the tactic, even the best defenders found it difficult to cope. "Leadbetter laid so deep, I didn't know who the hell I was supposed to be marking," said the Fulham and England full-back George Cohen. "He pulled me out of position and started pumping the ball over me to Crawford and Phillips and they had two goals before we knew where we were. . . . Substitute Phillips and Crawford for Hurst and Hunt and you have the England set-up."

The next season, though, teams knew what to expect. Ipswich lost the Charity Shield 5–1 to Spurs as Bill Nicholson had his full-backs come inside to pick up the two center-forwards, leaving the half-backs to deal with Leadbetter and Stephenson. Other teams did similarly and, by the end of October 1962, when Ramsey was appointed England manager, Ipswich had won just two of fifteen games.

Ramsey's predecessor in the national job, Walter Winterbottom, had been hamstrung by having his team selected by a committee of which he was only part; Ramsey demanded absolute control. Without that, tactical experimentation was impossible. If a group of men was simply voting for the best player to fill each position, the positions had to be laid out in advance, without much regard for balance or the interaction between players. In the past that had meant unthinking faith in the merits of the W-M. "People say Matthews, Finney, Carter and so on, they never needed a plan," Ramsey protested. "Well, I played with many of these players and I would say England's team was good then, but it would have been many times better if we had also had a rigid plan."

Outright control, though, was only granted from the following May, so Ramsey faced two games in which he worked with the committee. In the first, they selected a W-M, and England lost 5–2 to France in Paris. That persuaded the committee to follow Ramsey's wishes and switch to a 4–2–4, and although that brought a 2–1 home defeat to Scotland, he stuck with the formation for most of his early reign.

It was May 1964 and a postseason tour of South America was to prove key to Ramsey's tactical development. England had hammered the United States 10–0 in New York—some revenge for Ramsey, having played in the side beaten 1–0 by them in Belo Horizonte in 1950—but, exhausted by the effects of travel and scheduled to play Brazil just three days later, they were thrashed 5–1 in their first game of a four-team tournament. A draw against Portugal followed, but it was the third game, against Argentina, that was crucial. Argentina knew a draw would be enough for them to win the competition and so, the days of *la nuestra* a distant memory, sat men behind the ball, content to spoil, hold possession, and see out time. England, like "a bunch of yokels trying to puzzle their way out of a maze," as Desmond

Hackett put it in the *Daily Express*, were nonplussed. They dominated the play but never looked like scoring and, caught on the break, lost 1–0. "We played 4–2–4 with Roberto Telch coming back, like Zagallo in 1962," said the Argentina captain José Ramos Delgado. "England had a great team with Moore, Charlton and Thompson, but we played intelligently. It's true that England had much more possession, but only because we gave up a midfielder so he could defend against certain players."

As far as some players were concerned, Hackett went on, "the triple lion badge of England could be three old tabby cats." His reaction was typical: England may have been outwitted by disciplined opponents sticking to an intelligent plan, but the assumption was—as it so often had been, and would continue to be—that they hadn't tried hard enough, that they hadn't shown enough pride in the uniform. Brian James in the *Daily Mail*, while no less angry, came rather closer to a realistic assessment. "If you do not give a damn about the game, and are prepared to leave entertainment to music halls you can win anything," he wrote. "Argentina have simply taken logic and pushed it to the limit. Their policy lays down that, 'if they do not score, we do not lose.' . . . Only in their wildest moments of heady recklessness were they prepared to open out." Ramsey, of course, would rather have admitted to a love of Tchaikovsky than to having been influenced by Argentina, but he did acknowledge the "tremendous gap" between the two South American giants and England. Significantly, the FA's report on the triumph of 1966 made a point of noting how important the experience gained on that tour had been.

Over that summer, Ramsey rethought his strategy: system, he seems to have decided, was more important than personnel. His taciturn nature makes it hard to be sure, but it is not implausible to suggest that the two years that followed represent a carefully controlled evolution towards winning the World Cup. The players he had been playing wide in a 4–2–4, Bobby Charlton and Peter Thompson, weren't the kind to track back, and neither could Jimmy Greaves or Johnny Byrne, the two center-forwards, realistically have been asked to drop in. George Eastham, who commonly played as one of the central midfielders, was a converted inside-forward, and his partner Gordon Milne was no spoiler either. Ramsey realized that although 4–2–4 was a fine formation for beating lesser sides, it was unsuitable for playing stronger opponents and could leave even a markedly better team vulnerable if it had an off day. In short, the problem came down to the fact that while 4–2–4 was potent when you had possession, it didn't help you get the ball in the first place.

It is unclear when Ramsey's thoughts first turned to Nobby Stiles, the combative Manchester United anchor, but what was apparent as soon as he selected him was that Stiles could not play in a 4–2–4. Do that, and it placed an undue creative burden, the entire task of maneuvering the ball from back to front, on one man. The victim of that realization was Thompson, even though he had probably been England's best player in Brazil, being dubbed the White Pelé by the local press. To Ramsey's new way of thinking, the Liverpool winger was too much of an entertainer and, as he turned to the likes of John Connelly, Ian Callaghan, and Terry Paine, Thompson slowly drifted out of the setup.

England's first game of the new season was a Home International away to Northern Ireland the following October. Ramsey again picked a 4–2–4, but with Bobby Charlton moving back into Eastham's role in midfield and Paine selected on the right and encouraged to drop deep in the manner of Zagallo or Leadbetter. England were up 4–0 by half-time but ended up winning only 4–3. The *Mail*, speaking of "ninety minutes of shambles," called for Ramsey's head, but, while he was furious at his side's sloppiness, he was not a man to allow adverse media reaction to divert him from his plan.

An unconvincing 2–2 draw against Belgium followed, but the real breakthrough came in a get-together in February 1965. Six players, including Gordon Banks, Bobby Charlton, and Peter Thompson, withdrew because of FA Cup commitments, but Ramsey persisted in his program, sending out a senior side for a practice game against the Under-23s in a 4–3–3 formation. He was delighted by the result. "I played what amounted to a rather cruel trick on the younger players, in that I gave them no advance warning of the tactics the seniors were about to employ," he said. "The seniors, with three recognised outstanding footballers in midfield— Bryan Douglas on the right, Johnny Byrne in the middle and George Eastham on the left—ran riot with the young lads." The "Wingless Wonders" had been born. "To have two players stuck out wide on the flanks," Ramsey said, "is a luxury which can virtually leave a side with nine men when the game is going against them."

For Dave Bowen, the Wales manager between 1964 and 1974, Ramsey's genius had been to recognize earlier than anyone else in Britain that if sides played four at the back, the traditional winger was dead. "With three defenders it was different," he explained. "The back on the far side was covering behind the centre-half so the winger always had space from the cross-field pass. With four defenders the backs can play tight on the winger and he's lost his acceleration space. Without that, the winger's finished."

The formation clear, Ramsey then set about finding the best players to deploy within it. In April, Stiles and Jack Charlton made their debuts in a 2–2 draw against Scotland, and the following month Alan Ball came in for a 1–1 draw against Yugoslavia. It was only later that month, though, in a friendly against West Germany in Nuremberg, that Ramsey unveiled his

4–3–3 in public. Ron Flowers of Wolves replaced Stiles, with Ball in midfield, Leeds United's Mick Jones and Eastham up front and Paine and Everton's Derek Temple, in his only appearance for his country, alternating between the wing and offering support to the midfield. England won the game 1–0 then beat Sweden 2–1, with Stiles back in the side, leaving Ramsey convinced the switch to 4–3–3 was right. The key to the system was probably Ball, whose tremendous energy meant he could operate both as a winger and as an auxiliary midfielder—just as Zagallo had for Brazil in 1962.

Early performances in 1965–1966 were less impressive, but, in December, England, with Stiles, Ball, and Bobby Charlton in midfield and Roger Hunt, Eastham, and Joe Baker up front, beat Spain 2–0 in a performance of overwhelming quality. Ramsey, realizing just how effective his system was, immediately decided to keep it under wraps. "I think it would be quite wrong to let the rest of the world, our rivals, see what we are doing," he told Brian James of the *Mail*. "I think it is my duty to protect certain players until the time we need them most. This was a step and a very big one in our education as a football party. My job will be to produce the right team at the right time and that does not always mean pressing ahead with a particular combination just because it has been successful."

Ramsey went back to a 4–2–4 for a friendly draw against Poland and a 1–0 win over West Germany. Geoff Hurst made his debut that day and immediately struck up an understanding with Hunt. A subsequent 4–3 victory over Scotland pleased the fans and the media, but it confirmed in Ramsey's mind what he already knew: that defensively the 4–2–4 was inadequate. And then, in a 2–0 win over Yugoslavia at Wembley in May 1966, Ramsey introduced the final piece of the jigsaw: the undemonstrative West Ham midfielder Martin Peters. Although Ramsey's designation of him as being "ten years ahead of his time" would become a burden, Peters was, like Ball and Hurst, a modern multifunctional soccer player, capable both of creativity and of doing his share of defensive legwork.

In a friendly away to Finland, Ramsey played 4–3–3, with Ball, Peters, and Charlton in midfield and Callaghan as the sole winger. England won that game 3–0, and three days later they beat Norway 6–1 in Oslo, this time with two wingers: Connelly in orthodox mode and Paine dropping deeper in the Leadbetter role. Peters was still not considered a first choice—or not by the media anyway—but he was recalled for England's final warm-up game, against Poland in Katowice. This, at last, was the formation to which Ramsey had been building, a fact acknowledged as he read out the lineup to the press, pausing with an uncharacteristic sense of drama before revealing that he had given the No. 11 shirt to Peters.

England 4 West Germany 2, World Cup final, Wembley, London, 30 July 1966

This was a side with no wingers, orthodox or otherwise. Although it continued to be referred to as 4–3–3, it was really, as Nobby Stiles pointed out in his autobiography, a 4–1–3–2, with him as the anchor and Peters, Charlton, and Ball ahead of him, all given license to break forward and support the front two of Hunt and, it seemed probable at the time, Greaves. England won 1–0, through a Hunt goal; it was then, Ray Wilson said, that he began to accept that Ramsey might have been right when, three years earlier, he had insisted England would win the World Cup.

Yet against Uruguay in the first game in the World Cup, Ramsey opted for Connelly ahead of Peters and went back to the lopsided 4–3–3. Perhaps he was still playing his cards close to his chest; perhaps he believed a winger still had a role to play in overcoming a weaker side that was sure to pack its defense. Either way, it didn't really work, and, as the midfield struggled to get forward to support the front three, Uruguay held out for a 0–0 draw.

Peters came in for the injured Ball in the second game, against Mexico, with Paine replacing Connelly. That reversed the skew, so the winger was on the right rather than the left, but the essentials were the same, Ramsey again using a winger against opposition he expected to beat. They did so, not exhilaratingly but well enough, winning 2–0. Callaghan was selected against France in the third group game, and England again won 2–0, although the match was more notable for a dreadful tackle by Stiles on Jacky Simon. FIFA warned him as to his future conduct, at which Ramsey received a message from the FA asking whether it was really necessary to carry on fielding Stiles. Ramsey, maybe partly on principle, but surely mainly because he knew how vital his midfielder spoiler was, threatened to resign.

At last, against Argentina in the quarterfinal, he turned again to 4–1–3–2. Perhaps the tactical switch would have been enough, but Ramsey was aided by an injury to Greaves. That allowed him to include Hurst—a less spectacular forward but one capable of winning the ball in the air and holding it—without fear of the reaction if he dropped the darling of the press. The game was grim and violent—"not so much a football match as an international incident," as Hugh McIlvanney put it—but England were resolute, and, after Antonio Rattín, the Argentina captain, had been sent off, a headed goal from Hurst gave them a 1–0 win. It had been no exhibition, but as far as Ramsey was concerned, the lessons of England's defeat in the Maracaná two years earlier had been learned. Stiles, unusually, had been asked to man-mark Ermindo Onega and had done so with discipline, while Ball, playing high on the right, was superb, not merely troubling Argentina offensively but preventing their full-back, Silvio Marzolini, from advancing.

Stiles's role was again crucial against Portugal in the semifinal, as he neutralized Eusébio in a 2–1 win. Bobby Charlton scored both that day, and the efficacy of the system in allowing the three attacking midfielders to break was seen once more in the final, as Peters got England's first and then as Ball, tireless on the right, sent in the cross from which Hurst—controversially—made it 3–2 in extra time. The decisive fourth, belted in by Hurst in the dying seconds after a long pass from Bobby Moore, was, as Leadbetter later noted, just the kind of goal Ramsey had delighted in at Ipswich: no fuss, just a simple ball and an emphatic finish. Perhaps that was fitting, but it was also a touch misleading, because England, as they would show even more conclusively in Mexico four years later, were perfectly capable of holding possession.

Nonetheless, as time went by, Ramsey's pragmatism became increasingly wearing. McIlvanney spoke for many when he noted caustically, after the 3–1 defeat at home to West Germany in 1972, that "cautious, joyless football was scarcely bearable even while it was bringing victories. When it brings defeat there can only be one reaction." As England, thanks to Jan Tomaszewski's heroics for Poland at Wembley, failed to qualify for the 1974 World Cup, Ramsey was sacked.

For all the terseness of his dealings with the media, the antipathy towards Ramsey was a recasting of the old tension between aesthetics and results. There was no question on which side Ramsey lay. He despised Argentina's approach, and his sides were certainly not guilty of the excesses of *antifútbol*, but he would have agreed with Osvaldo Zubeldía's thoughts on the role of a manager. "I'm employed to win football matches," Ramsey said. "That's all."

9

THE BIRTH OF THE NEW

Perhaps all soccer pundits are condemned to reiterate the fears of their forbears. Take the following two examples: "Speed was made a fetish. Quick was equal to good—no, better"; "hurried clearances . . . the panicky power game . . . the terror of failure, the inability to keep the ball and stay calm, the howling from without that freezes the blood and saps all creativity." The first is Willy Meisl writing in 1957, the second Martin Samuel in the *Times* two days after the 3–2 defeat to Croatia in 2007 that confirmed England would not qualify for the European Championship in 2008. Both, of course, are right in highlighting the principal failing of the English game, a failing the likes of A. C. Jephcott and Jocky Simpson had lamented in 1914: if something goes wrong for England, it tends to be rooted in a mistrust of technique, and that was as true a century ago as it is today and at all points in between.

And yet complaints about speed are relative. If the English game in the midfifties was too quick for Meisl's tastes, what on earth would he have made of the Premier League? To look at videos from the years immediately following the Second World War is to see a sport played almost in slow motion by modern standards—and it is getting quicker. Watch the Hungarians of the fifties or the Brazilians of the sixties, and what is noticeable to the modern eye is how long players have on the ball—and not just because their technical ability gave them instant control. It is simply that nobody closes them down. A player receiving the ball had time to assess his options. The dribbling technique of Garrincha or Stanley Matthews doesn't exist in today's game not because the skills have been lost but because no side would ever give them the three or four yards of acceleration room they needed before their feints became effective. Would they have been great players today? Probably, but not by dribbling like that.

It is that diminution of space, that compression of the game—pressing, in other words—that marks out modern soccer from old. It is such a simple idea that once one side started doing it, and had success by doing so, it is baffling that everybody did not follow them, and yet the spread of pressing is curiously patchy.

It arrived in Germany only in the nineties. When Arrigo Sacchi imposed it on AC Milan in the late eighties, it was hailed as groundbreaking, yet Rinus Michels's Ajax and Valeriy Lobanovskyi's Dynamo Kyiv—even Graham Taylor's Watford—had been using it for years. It was central, too, to the success of the Argentinian side Estudiantes de la Plata under Osvaldo Zubeldía in the late sixties. It was invented, though, by a Russian working in Ukraine, by a coach virtually unknown today outside the former Soviet bloc. The game's evolution, of course, is not linear, and there are others who have had significant roles to play, but if there is a single man who can claim to be the father of modern soccer, it is Viktor Maslov.

He was an unlikely revolutionary, noted at the time less for his vision or any kind of explosive leadership than for his warmth. "It always intrigued me that he was known as Grandad," said Mykhaylo Koman, probably Dynamo's best forward of the fifties. "The players who played under him could have been his sons, but he was far too young for them to have been his grandsons. It seems the nickname had stuck before he arrived in Kyiv, and that it had nothing to do with his age. Maybe the way he looked contributed to his grandfatherly image: he was of plump constitution, had a bald head, and thick, bushy eyebrows. Still, the main reason for the name was his colossal wisdom, humanity and kindness."

Born in Moscow in 1910, Maslov had been one of the leading players of the early years of the Soviet league, a robust and authoritative half capable of a wide range of passing. He was on the Torpedo side that finished second in the Moscow championship in 1934 and 1935, and then he captained the club from 1936 to 1939, leading them to victory in an international tournament in France in 1938. After ending his playing career in 1942, he took over as coach of Torpedo and had four stints in charge of them before leaving for Rostov-na-Donu in 1962. The last of those, beginning in 1957, was by far the most successful, as Maslov led Torpedo twice to second place in the Soviet league and, in 1960, to their first championship. It was after arriving at Dynamo Kyiv in 1964, though, that he really began to give free rein to his ideas, as he shifted the center of Soviet soccer from Moscow to the Ukrainian capital.

Avuncular he may have been, but a feat like that was not achieved without a certain toughness and an ability to play the political game. He, for instance, made the most of the love Volodymyr Shcherbytskyi, who ran the Ukrainian Communist Party central committee's ideological department, had for football (Lobanovskyi maintained the strong relations after Shcherbytskyi had become head of the party in Ukraine). Dynamo had always been able to recruit from across the republic—their side in the fifties, for instance, included several players from Zakarpattya—but under Maslov almost all the best Ukrainian players gravitated to Dynamo, attracted by apartments in Kyiv and other benefits that could be conferred by the Party leadership.

At the same time, though, he was strong enough to maintain his independence. On one occasion, Kyiv legend has it, the assistant of a senior party official came to berate the team at half-time of a game in which they were playing badly. "Tomorrow I have a free day," Maslov is supposed to have said as he shepherded him to the door. "I'll come and see your boss then and answer all his questions. As for today . . . could you close the door on your way out?" The tale may be apocryphal—there is no agreement as to the game at which the incident happened or which functionary was involved—but the fact that it is widely repeated suggests a basic truth behind it.

"We appreciated Grandad first for his human qualities and only second as a coach," said Andriy Biba, Dynamo's captain between 1964 and 1967. "And for his part, he looked at us first of all as people with all our positives and negatives, and only after that as footballers. He managed his relations with the players in such a manner, and was so sincere with us that it was impossible to have any bad feelings against him. He trusted us and we responded in the same way."

Perhaps that was true for those who were members of the inner circle, but Eduard Streltsov, the great star of Maslov's Torpedo side before his imprisonment in 1958 on a—possibly trumped up—charge of rape, remembers a different side to him. "If Maslov disliked any of his players," he said, "he could never hide his antipathy."

Either way, there is no doubt that to those with whom he did get along, Maslov was an inspirational figure. "His pre-match instructions lasted no more than five minutes," Biba went on. "He could never remember things properly, and he distorted the names of opposing players hopelessly, but he was always precise in telling us how to counteract their strengths. He would always finish with an aphorism to touch our hearts: 'Today you must be strong like lions, fast like stags, agile like panthers!' And we would always do our best."

Certainly there was in him none of the authoritarianism that would later characterize Lobanovskyi, his greatest disciple. Rather, he was willing to discuss and compromise and on occasions even seemingly to be overruled by his players, as Arkady Galinsky, one of the most popular soccer journalists of the sixties and seventies, recalled. "At one of Torpedo's league matches I was sitting close to the pitch and the reserve bench," he wrote.

The team wasn't doing well and the coach decided to substitute one of his players. . . . The substitute took off his coat and tracksuit and after a short warm-up, he went to the half-way line, waiting to replace one of his team-mates the next time the referee stopped the game.

It was just as usually happens in football. But what happened next I found extremely interesting. The Torpedo captain, the well-known forward [Valentin] Ivanov, came running over to this player after the referee had whistled and told him the team needed no substitute. After spending some time in confusion, the reserve player returned to the bench. I glanced at the coach: how would he react? But he simply shrugged his shoulders, looking indifferent to what had happened.

I supposed this to be an attempt to motivate the player who was to be substituted, pre-conceived by the coach and the captain, but it appeared after the match that the team had simply rejected the substitution proposed by the coach. I have never seen anything like this in football before. A few years later I witnessed the same episode once again. The match was played at the same stadium—the Central Lenin Stadium [now the Luzhniki] in Moscow—the coach was the same, only the team was different: Dynamo Kyiv. Once again Maslov expressed no emotion.

During his time as the Kyiv correspondent of *Sovetsky Sport*, Galinsky became noted for his pro-Moscow sympathies. He was critical of Dynamo's use of a zonal marking system and seems to have had various personal spats with Maslov, who, however Biba saw it, had a tendency to be at times rather more "sincere" than tactful. Galinksy's conclusion, though, was that the two incidents were indicative not of any weakness on Maslov's part but rather of his strength. "He understood that the players rejected the substitution not to undermine his authority," he wrote, "but for the benefit of the affair. Dynamo players—like the Torpedo ones formerly—were telling their coach: don't worry, everything is OK, we'll soon turn the game in our favour. And that was what happened in both cases."

Consultation was a key part of the Maslov method. The evening before games he would gather his squad together—or the senior players at least—to talk through the next day's match, canvassing their thoughts before drawing up his final game plan. It was that level of trust and mutual understanding that allowed Maslov to implement his more radical tactical innovations. And they were radical, almost incomprehensibly so in the context of the times. In the early sixties, the USSR, like most of the world, had begun to turn to the 4–2–4, a process pioneered by the national coach Gavriil Kachalin. He had led the USSR to victory at the 1956 Olympics and in the inaugural European Championship with a W-M, but he had seen in Brazil's performances in the 1958 World Cup the way soccer was headed. Several club coaches followed his lead, and, for once, the habitually conservative Soviet establishment supported his experiments. The change, or at least the pace with which it had been imposed, was widely blamed for the USSR's disjointed showing at the 1962 World Cup, when they beat Yugoslavia and Uruguay but went out in the quarterfinal against Chile, but the Brazilian method was so in vogue that Konstantin Beskov, Kachalin's successor, continued to insist he was using a 4–2–4 when he had actually reverted to a W-M for his eighteen months in the job.

Maslov was rather more astute than Beskov. Like Alf Ramsey, he recognized how important Zagallo had been to Brazil's success, tracking back to become a third midfielder. Maslov went one further and pulled back his right-winger as well. Ramsey is regularly given the credit (or the blame) for abolishing the winger and, given the lack of communication between the USSR and the West in those days, there is no suggestion he did not come up with the idea independently, but the 4–4–2 was first invented by Maslov. Like Ramsey, though, and unlike so many who followed, Maslov withdrew his wingers in such a way that it did not impinge upon his side's creative capacity. The likes of Andriy Biba, Viktor Serebryanykov and Josef Szabo all began their careers as forwards before being converted into midfielders by Maslov, and they and more orthodox halves such as Volodymyr Muntyan and Fedir Medvid retained a creative brief, functioning almost as a second line of attack. There were, though, casualties. Maslov may have coached by consensus, but he could be ruthless when he saw a player who did not fit his system. Former stars such as Viktor Kanevskyi and Oleh Bazylevych were swiftly dispensed with and so, too, most controversially, was Lobanovskyi.

Exactly why Maslov and Lobanovskyi fell out—if indeed they did—remains unclear. Their conceptions of soccer were very different, but, if Galinsky is to be believed, there was also a personal antagonism. Then again, it should be borne in mind that Galinsky was one of the prime movers in attempting to lure Lobanovskyi away from Ukraine to Moscow, so his evidence may not be entirely objective. According to his version of events, the problems flared after a training camp on the Caucasian Black Sea coast ahead of the 1964 season.

"Everything seemed to be going well," Galinsky wrote. "The players seemed to be fond of their new coach, the team had worked well, and Maslov seemed pleased with Lobanovskyi." On the flight home, though, bad weather forced Dynamo's airplane to land at Symferopol. Their departure was repeatedly postponed; eventually Maslov ordered lunch. To the amazement of the players, he also ordered them each a glass of *horilka*—Ukrainian vodka.

"They couldn't believe their eyes," Galinsky. "Nothing like this had been seen before at Dynamo. Maslov proposed a toast to good luck in the coming season. Everybody drank to it, apart from Lobanovskyi, who didn't even touch his glass. Seeing this, Maslov asked him to drink to the team's success. When Lobanovskyi again refused to do so, Maslov cursed him. Lobanovskyi swore back at him." From then on, Galinsky claimed, there was bad blood between them.

Kanevskyi, though, insists Galinsky has exaggerated the episode. He was at the meal and agrees there was *horilka* and that everybody apart from the fastidious Lobanovskyi drank the toast, but he also maintains that Lobanovskyi's strict self-discipline was well known, even admired, and that Maslov was unconcerned by his abstinence. "Maslov said nothing to him," he recalled, "and certainly he didn't use any insulting words."

Others believe their relationship broke down during a game in Moscow against Spartak on April 27, 1964. Lobanovskyi had given Dynamo the lead, and they were still 1–0 up when he was substituted—for the first time in his career—with twenty minutes to go. Spartak then equalized and the game ended in a draw, leading to speculation that Maslov had arranged the result in advance with the Spartak coach Nikita Simonyan and that Lobanovskyi was taken off because he had refused to go along with their agreement. True or not, the next game, away to Shinnik in Yaroslavl, was Lobanovskyi's last for the club.

Then again, it may be that there was no falling out. Maslov was just as swift to get rid of Mikhail Gershkovich, David Pays, and Grigory Yanets—all leading players—when he returned to Torpedo in 1971, apparently for no other reason than that they did not fit his system, and it is easy to see why Lobanovskyi would not have suited Maslov's plans, whatever Galinsky may say. Nicknamed Cord in the Moscow press because of the way the ball at times appeared to be tied to his boot laces, Lobanovskyi was a genuine star, talented and popular with the crowd. On his death in 2002, several messages of condolence from fans recalled how they had gone to Dynamo games in the early sixties excited by the prospect of watching him take corners packed with backspin so they dropped almost vertically in the box—a variant of the "falling leaf" free-kicks devised by Didí a few years earlier. The problem was that he was a left-winger, and wingers had no place in Maslov's plan.

"I'd not call what happened between Maslov and Lobanovskyi a conflict," Biba explained. "It was just that Valeriy often opposed the coach's directions. Maslov was seeking new forms of football and footballers who held on to the ball for too long didn't suit him. Even the 'banana shot' invented by Lobanovskyi couldn't persuade him. But then, after becoming a coach, Valeriy acknowledged that Lobanovskyi the player could not have played in his team." This was the debate raised by Mikhail Yakushin's preference for the collective over the individualism of a Stanley Matthews taken to its logical extreme. No matter how talented the individual, if he did not function as part of the collective, he had no place within it.

That is not to say that Maslov was opposed to great individuals per se. On the contrary, Biba was one of the most gifted midfielders Ukraine has ever produced, functioning in Maslov's system as Bobby Charlton did in Ramsey's England side. "When he gets the ball, he knows in advance what his team-mates and his opponents are going to do," said Iosif Betsa, who was part of the USSR team that won gold at the 1956 Olympics and who went on to become a respected coach. "He has a plan of his next actions and with his first touch puts the ball in a comfortable position to execute it quickly. And if the opponent has guessed his intentions, he changes the direction of the attack immediately. At the same time, Biba possesses a magnificent long shot and can finish off attacks arriving in the right place at just the right time."

Biba reached his peak in 1966. In the spring he beat Lev Yashin with a forty-yard drive in a game against Dinamo Moscow; he was superb in the crucial 4–0 victory over CSKA in the autumn, setting up two of Dynamo's goals; and he rounded off the year with the decisive goal in the Cup final victory over Torpedo as Dynamo won the double. He was the creative hub of the team, and, to widespread agreement, he was named Soviet Player of the Year.

Soviet soccer seems to have become obsessed by Didí after the 1958 World Cup and, more particularly, by the lack of such playmakers in their own game. In the sixties there were only two: Biba and Gennady Gusarov of Dinamo Moscow. Crucially, Maslov was able to develop on his side an understanding of how best to make use of a playmaker, something that wasn't always clear. Galinsky, for instance, recalls Beskov in 1968 responding to Gusarov's retirement by attempting to retrain the forward Yuri Avrutsky as a playmaker: "He treated the role quite seriously," Galinsky wrote.

He was always finding space, offering himself to his team-mates, moving, and when he got the ball, executing good passes, but when he found space again he almost never got the ball back. I don't know whether the players didn't follow Beskov's directions or whether they weren't clear enough, but often when Avrutsky was free of his marker the other players preferred to dribble with the ball or pass it forwards themselves. But in such a situation a playmaker is pointless. Even worse, he becomes a burden for his team because he isn't marking any specific opponent while they are attacking.

It remains a common complaint, and the distrust of "luxury players" is still widespread, at least in northern Europe. Galinksy was scathing of the special treatment granted them, but in his mockery he happened upon the truth. "Some coaches in football," he wrote, "interpret the playmaker to be something like a patient at a health resort. It might be all right to release one or two forwards from their defensive obligations, but to do the same with a midfielder? Is he Charlton or Didi?"

Maslov's solution was exactly that which had allowed Didi such freedom. It was the forgotten innovation, the one devised by Zezé Moreira and used by Brazil for the first time at the World Cup in 1954: zonal marking. It was the theory that had prepared the ground for Brazil's blossoming in 1958 and 1962, but it didn't find immediate favor in the USSR. The difficulty with zonal marking is that it requires organization and understanding between defenders. It is not quite so easy as a defender merely picking up any player in his area. Two forwards could come into his zone, or overmanning in another zone could require him to track a forward outside his zone, which then requires another defender to pick up anybody coming into the zone the original defender has just vacated, and that is not something that can simply be improvised.

An attempt by Nikolai Morozov to introduce zonal marking with the national team ahead of the 1966 World Cup was a failure. After six goals were conceded over the course of pre–World Cup friendlies against France and CSKA, Morozov became so paranoid that he ended up fielding five defenders, with a sweeper picking up the pieces behind the other four and the midfielders encouraged to drop deep whenever possession was lost, attacking only on the counter. The USSR reached the semifinal of that tournament—their best placing in a World Cup—but the ultradefensive approach, which mimicked that of Helenio Herrera's Internazionale, was never seen as anything other than a one-off solution to a particular problem.

Maslov, though, remained convinced zonal marking was the right way to proceed, something that seems almost to have been for him an ethical principle. "Man-marking," he once said, "humiliates, insults and even morally oppresses the players who resort to it." Biba didn't pick up any specific opponent, but then neither did any other Dynamo midfielder. "Only Biba retains full rights of democracy," Maslov said. "He is a very clever and honest player, who would never allow himself any excess and never abuses his skills. Andriy will do exactly what is necessary. He has the right to construct the game as though he were the coach himself during the match, making decisions as to how to shape it. The others then grasp his ideas and develop them as far as they can."

Maslov believed that through good organization it was possible to over-man in every part of the pitch, an idea the journalist Georgiy Kuzmin suggested in *Kiyevskiye Vedomosti* that he took from basketball. With Biba in a free role, though, to do that he needed a fixed defensive point in his midfield to allow the full-backs to step up from the back-four as required. That was provided by the veteran defender Vasyl Turyanchyk, who was deployed in front of the back-four, becoming the first holding midfielder in Soviet soccer. His job, as Maslov put it, was to "break the waves," presenting the first line of resistance to opposing forwards, while also initiating Dynamo's attacks. In other words, he played almost as József Zakariás had for Hungary. In that context, it helped that he had begun his career as a forward, but it is perhaps just as significant that, like Szabo and Medvid, he came from Zakarpattya, where the Hungarian influence was strong.

Most crucially of all, though, Turyanchyk was instrumental in the application of the pressing game. Would Maslov have tried it—would he even have thought of it—if he hadn't had a player as commanding and with such a fine grasp of the geometry of the game? Given the absence of a diary or journals, it is impossible to say. As in his use of Biba, his genius was, having spotted the possibilities offered by Turyanchyk's ability to step out from the back, to teach the rest of the team how best to make use of it. By the time Dynamo won their first title under Maslov in 1966, their midfield was hunting in packs, closing down opponents and seizing the initiative in previously unexpected areas of the field. The Moscow press was appalled, one newspaper printing a photograph of four Dynamo players converging on an opponent with the ball with the caption "We don't need this kind of football."

Demanding as it did almost constant movement from the midfielders, pressing required supreme physical fitness, which may explain why it had not emerged earlier. Full-time professionalism was a prerequisite, as was a relatively sophisticated understanding of nutrition and condition. Dynamo had been noted for their physical fitness when they won the title for the first time under Vyacheslav Solovyov in 1961, but Maslov took things to a new level. "He was the first Dynamo coach really to put an emphasis on the physical preparation of players," the midfielder Volodymyr Muntyan said. "Not Lobanovskyi as is often thought, but Maslov, although he did what felt right, whereas Lobanovskyi was acting on a scientific basis."

The statistics are telling. When Dynamo won the title in 1961, they conceded twenty-eight goals in thirty games, so they had a history of defensive soundness. The following season, when they were fifth, they let in forty-eight in forty-two, and in 1963, as they slipped to ninth, forty-eight in thirty-eight. Maslov arrived the following season, and twenty-nine goals were conceded in thirty-two games as Dynamo came sixth. They were runners-up in 1965, letting in twenty-two in thirty-two, and it got better in their three championship seasons: seventeen in thirty-six games in 1966, a staggering eleven in thirty-six in 1967, and twenty-five in thirty-eight in 1968. Not surprisingly, the debate over Maslov's tactics soon abated. In his review of the 1967 season, Martin Merzhanov, the doyen of Soviet soccer journalism and the founder of *Futbol* magazine, wrote that "zonal defence, when defenders base their play on mutual understanding and mutual securing, and are dealing with not one concrete opponent but whoever comes into their zone, has proved far more efficient [than man-marking]."

It was not foolproof, however, and Dynamo's 2–1 defeat to Shakhtar Donetsk in 1967 hinted at things to come. After leaving Dynamo, Lobanovskyi spent two seasons with Chornomorets Odessa before moving east to Donetsk. In that time, his tactical thinking had evolved and, with the coach Oleg Oshenkov, he came up with a plan to combat Dynamo's system. Where most sides sought to do no more than contain the champions, Lobanovskyi insisted Shakhtar should attack them, and so they adopted a 4–2–4, but with their two midfielders man-marking Muntyan and Szabo. That left Medvid, a less creative player, free, but that didn't bother Lobanovskyi: although he wanted to blunt Dynamo's cutting edge as far as possible, his greater concern was to overwhelm their defense by weight of numbers. The pattern was repeated in the European Cup that year when Dynamo, having beaten the holders Celtic in the first round, lost 3–2 on aggregate to the Polish champions Górnik Zabrze in the second, undone by the pace and mobility of Włodzimierz Lubański and Zygfryd Szołtysik.

Still, those were rare examples, and Dynamo, regularly changing their approach according to the opposition—something extremely rare at the time—proved adept at dealing with the many stylistic variations presented by the Soviet league. "This team has something like two different squads," Galinsky wrote. "One is fighting, engaging in a frank power struggle if that is offered by the opponent, while the other plays in the 'southern' technical, combinational style, at an arrhythmic tempo. But the transformation from one squad to the other happens very simply at Dynamo. One or two changes before the match and sometimes even one substitution in the course of it is enough. They can go straight from the southern style to a much more simple game with runs down the flanks, crosses, shots and long aerial balls."

Maslov would have gone further. Having instigated the move to just two forwards, he speculated that a time would come when sides only used

Dynamo Kyiv 1 Celtic 1, European Cup first round, second leg, Olympskyi, Kyiv, 4 October 1967

one up front. "Football," he explained, "is like an aeroplane. As velocities increase, so does air resistance, and so you have to make the head more streamlined." In terms of range, novelty, and success, his work is extraordinary enough as it is, but there was one more step he wanted to take. His conception would be realized soon enough by Dynamo and by Ajax, but it never quite came to fruition under his management, although by instituting zonal marking and pressing he had laid the groundwork.

In October 1981, Lobanovskyi's Dynamo beat Zenit Leningrad 3–0 to win the Soviet title for the tenth time. A piece in *Sportyvna Hazeta* eulogizing their fluidity of movement in that game and over that season makes the progression clear: "Viktor Maslov dreamt once of creating a team that could attack with different groups of players. For instance [Anatoliy] Byshovets and [Vitaliy] Khmelnytskyi would start the match battering the opposition defence, but then at some point they could drop back into midfield and their places could be taken by, say, Muntyan and Serebryanykov. But at that time such a way of playing didn't come together. It is an achievement of the present day."

And yet every now and again Maslov's players did, by chance or by instinct, switch positions. "The 4–4–2 system introduced by Grandad was only a formal order; in the course of the game there was complete interchangeability," Szabo said. "For example, any defender could press forward without fear because he knew that a team-mate would cover him if he were unable to return in time. Midfielders and forwards could allow themselves a much wider variety of actions than before. This team played the prototype of Total Football. People think it was developed in Holland, but that is just because in Western Europe they didn't see Maslov's Dynamo."

Maslov was eventually sacked in 1970 as Dynamo slipped to seventh in the table. In 1966, with several members of the squad away at the World Cup, he had managed to maintain Dynamo's league form because of the emergence of a number of players from the youth team. In 1970, he found no such reserves. "Any coach's fate depends on results," said the defender Viktor Matviyenko.

After the spring half of the season we were second in the table, and I'm sure Grandad would have kept his job if we'd have maintained that position to the end. He just needed to repeat the experience of 1966 when the outstanding youth players kept the players who had come back from England out of the squad. It was a similar situation in 1970. The Dynamo players who were at the World Cup in Mexico were absent for a month and a half, and played only a couple of games. They lost more there than they gained simply because they had no match practice. But Grandad didn't take it into account and brought straight back players who had lost their sharpness, and so we began to fall in the standings.

Perhaps that was understandable. Maslov had, after all, been at the club for seven years, and the feeling was that he had perhaps gone stale. The manner of his dismissal, though, leaves a sour taste; Koman called it "the most disgraceful episode in Dynamo's history."

It was decided that it was more politically expedient to dismiss him away from Kyiv, and so when, towards the end of the 1970 season, Dynamo traveled to Moscow for a game against CSKA, they were joined by Mizyak, the deputy head of the Ukrainian SSR State Sport Committee. He usually had responsibility for winter sports, but in the Hotel Russia before the game, he made the official announcement that Maslov had been removed from his position. With Maslov sitting in the stand and no replacement appointed, Dynamo lost 1–0. After the game, as the team bus carried the players to the airport for the flight back to Kyiv, they stopped at the Yugo-Zapadnaya metro station and dropped Maslov off. As he walked away, he looked back over his shoulder and slowly raised a hand in farewell. "If I hadn't seen it myself," Koman said, "I'd never have believed a giant like Maslov could have wept."

Maslov returned to Torpedo and won the cup with them and then had a season in Armenia with Ararat Yerevan, where he again won the cup, but he never had the resources—or perhaps the energy—to repeat the successes of Dynamo. By the time he died at age sixty-seven in May 1977, Lobanovskyi, the player he had exiled, was ensuring his legacy lived on. His impact was perhaps less direct than that of Jimmy Hogan, but no coach since has been so influential.

Jimmy Hogan, the father of central European football, demonstrating heading technique to the RAF in France, 1940

Vittorio Pozzo looks on nervously as Italy beat Czechoslovakia in the 1934 World Cup final

Herbert Chapman, the inventor of the W-M (all pics © *Getty Images*)

Boris Arkadiev outlines his theory of organized disorder to his CDKA players
(*Pavel Eriklinstev*)

Matthias Sindelar, the withdrawn center-forward, whose genius lay at the heart of the Austrian *Wunderteam*

Sándor Kocsis beats Gil Merrick to the ball in Hungary's 6-3 victory over England at Wembley in 1953 (both pics © *PA Photos*)

Alcides Ghiggia beats Moacyr Barbosa at his near post to win the 1950 World Cup for Uruguay (*PA Photos*)

Jules Rimet hands over the trophy to Uruguay's captain, Obdulio Varela (*Getty Images*)

Three men who brought tactics to Brazil: Martim Francisco (top), Gentil Cardoso (bottom left) and Fleitas Solich (bottom right) (all pics © *Arquiro/Agência O Globo*)

Béla Guttmann, the wandering Hungarian, during his time as coach of Benfica (*PA Photos*)

Vicente Feola, the Brazil coach who introduced 4–2–4 to the world (*Getty Images*)

Garrincha, the winger whose anarchic style flourished in the 4–2–4 (*Getty Images*)

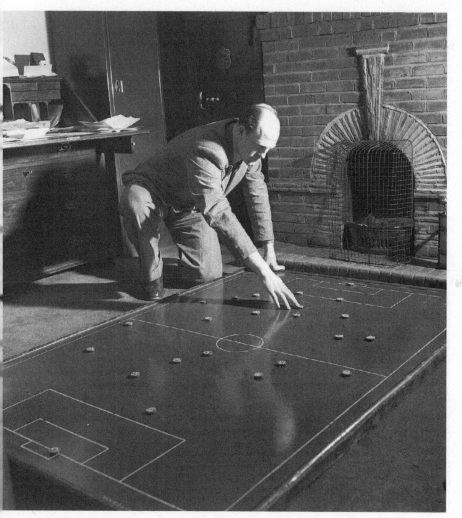

Stan Cullis devises another tactical masterplan for Wolves (*Getty Images*)

Viktor Maslov talks his Torpedo players through his latest stratagem (*Pavel Eriklinstev*)

10

CATENACCIO

There is no tactical system so notorious as *catenaccio*. To generations, the word—which means "chain," in the sense of a chain on the door of a house—summons up Italian soccer at its most paranoid, negative, and brutal. So reviled was it in Britain that when Jock Stein's Celtic beat Helenio Herrera's Internazionale, its prime exponents in the European Cup final of 1967, the Liverpool manager Bill Shankly congratulated him by insisting the victory had made him "immortal." It later emerged that he had instructed two Celtic coaches to attend the postmatch banquet and abuse Herrera throughout. Herrera would always insist he was misunderstood, that his system, like Herbert Chapman's, had acquired an unfavorable reputation only because other, lesser sides that attempted to copy his team's style implemented it so badly. That remains debatable but, sinister as *catenaccio* became, its origins were homely.

It began in Switzerland with Karl Rappan. Soft spoken, understated, and noted for his gentle dignity, Rappan was born in Vienna in 1905, his professional career as a forward or attack-minded half coinciding with the golden age of Viennese soccer in the mid- to late twenties. So rooted was he in coffeehouse society that later in life he ran the Café de la Bourse in Geneva. He was capped for Austria and won the league with Rapid Vienna in 1930, after which he moved to Switzerland to become player-coach at Servette.

His players there were semiprofessional and so, according to Walter Lutz, the doyen of Swiss sportswriting, Rappan set about devising a way of compensating for the fact that they could not match fully professional teams for physical fitness. "With the Swiss team tactics play an important role," Rappan said in a rare interview with *World Soccer* magazine shortly before the World Cup in 1962.

The Swiss is not a natural footballer, but he is usually sober in his approach to things. He can be persuaded to think ahead and to calculate ahead.

A team can be chosen according to two points of view. Either you have eleven individuals, who owing to sheer class and natural ability are enabled to beat their opponents—Brazil would be an example of that—or you have eleven average footballers, who have to be integrated into a particular conception, a plan. This plan aims at getting the best out of each individual for the benefit of the team. The difficult thing is to enforce absolute tactical discipline without taking away the players' freedom of thinking and acting.

His solution, which was given the name *verrou*—"bolt"—by a Swiss journalist, is best understood as a development from the old 2–3–5—which had remained the default formation in Vienna long after Chapman's W-M had first emerged in England. Rather than the center-half dropping in between the two full-backs, as in the W-M, the two wing-halves fell back to flank them. They retained an attacking role, but their primary function was to combat the opposition wingers. The two full-backs then became in effect central defenders, playing initially almost alongside each other, although in practice, if the opposition attacked down their right, the left of the two would move towards the ball, with the right covering just behind, and vice versa. In theory, that always left them with a spare man— the *verouller* as the Swiss press of the time called him or the *libero* as he would become—at the back.

The system's main shortcoming was that it placed huge demands on the center-half. Although on paper the formation—with four defenders, a center-half playing behind two withdrawn inside-forwards, and a string of three across the front—looks similar to the modern 4–3–3 as practiced by, say, Chelsea in José Mourinho's first two seasons at the club, the big difference is how advanced the wingers were. They operated as pure forwards, staying high up the field at all times rather than dropping back to help the midfield when possession was lost. That meant that when the *verrou* faced a W-M, the front three matched up in the usual way against the defensive three and inside-forwards took the opposition's wing-halves, leaving the center-half to deal with two inside-forwards. This was the problem sides playing a *libero* always faced: by creating a spare man in one part of the pitch, it necessarily meant a shortfall elsewhere.

Against a 2–3–5, the situation was even worse. The side playing the *verrou* had a man over at both ends of the field, but that meant the center-half was trying to cope not only with the opposing inside-forwards but also the other center-half. That was all but impossible, so Rappan's team tended

Rappan's *Verrou*, 1938

to drop deep, cede the midfield to their opponents, and, by tight marking, present a solid front to frustrate them so they ended up passing the ball fruitlessly sideways. As the system developed, the burden was taken off the center-half as an inside-forward gradually fell back to play alongside him, but the more striking change was that made to the defensive line as one of the two full-backs (that is, the de facto center-backs) dropped behind the other as an orthodox sweeper.

Rappan won two league titles with Servette and five more with Grasshoppers, whom he joined in 1935, but it was his successes with the Swiss national side that really demonstrated the efficacy of his system. Rappan became national coach in 1937, with a brief to lead Switzerland into the 1938 World Cup. At the time, Switzerland were regarded as the weakest of the central European nations, and their record in the Dr. Gerö Cup was correspondingly poor: played thirty-two, won four, drawn three, lost twenty-five. Using the *verrou*, though, they beat England 2–1 in a pre–World Cup friendly and then beat Germany—by then encompassing Austria—in the first round of the tournament itself, before going down 2–0 to Hungary.

That was an honorable exit—far more than Switzerland had achieved previously, but the *verrou* was considered little more than a curiosity, a means for lesser teams to frustrate their betters, maybe, but no more.

————————

Perhaps not surprisingly given the rethink of defensive tactics necessitated by Boris Arkadiev's organized disorder, a similar system sprang up, seemingly independently, a few years later in Russia. Krylya Sovetov Kuybyshev (the city is now Samara), a team backed by the Soviet Air Force, were founded in 1943, winning promotion to the Supreme League in 1945. They soon became noted for their defensive approach, specifically a tactic known as the *Volzhskaya Zashchepka*—the "Volga Clip." It may not have been so flexible as the *verrou*, and it was a development of the W-M rather than the 2–3–5, but the basic principle was the same, with one of the half-backs dropping deep, allowing the defensive center-half to sweep behind his full-backs.

Its architect was Krylya's coach, Alexander Kuzmich Abramov. "Some people were amazed because he wasn't a football professional in the usual sense of the term," the former Krylya captain Viktor Karpov said.

> He came from the world of gymnastics, so maybe because of that he wasn't directed by dogma, but had his own opinions on everything. He paid a lot of attention to gymnastic exercises, using training sessions to improve our coordination. An hour could go by and you wouldn't touch the ball, yet somehow it helped us to be more skilful. Kuzmich made us think on the pitch. Before each game he would gather the team together and we would discuss the plan for the match. As far as I'm aware, other coaches didn't do this.
>
> How we played depended on our opponents. If we were playing Dinamo, for instance, and their forward line was Trofimov, Kartsev, Beskov, Soloviov, Ilyin, then of course you had to take measures to counter such a star quintet. At that time most teams played with three defenders, but our half-backs would help them out more. Usually that meant me and [the left-half] Nikolai Pozdyanakov.
>
> We didn't man-mark as such. We tried to play flexibly, and the system meant that the range of action of each player became broader. Sometimes a reserve player would come in and he would try to chase his opponent all over the pitch—his man would go and have a drink and our novice would follow him. We would laugh at players like that, because we regulars had been taught that we should act according to the circumstances.

As when Nikolai Starostin first had his brother operate as a third back, there were those who protested at Abramov's innovation, seeing it as a betrayal of the ideals of Russian soccer. But gradually the system became accepted, as Lev Filatov puts it in *About Everything in an Orderly Manner*, as "the right of the weak." The forward Viktor Voroshilov, who also captained the side under Abramov, was scathing of the system's critics. "Let's say we were playing against CDKA," he said. "In attack they had Grinin, Nikolaev, Fedotov, Bobrov and Doymin. So we're supposed to venture upfield? That's why we played closer to our own goal. Once against Dinamo Moscow we opened up, [their coach] Mikhey Yakushin outwitted us and we lost 5–0."

The Volga Clip's success as a spoiling tactic could hardly be faulted. After winning just three of twenty-two games in 1946 and finishing tenth of the twelve top-flight sides, Krylya climbed to seventh of thirteen in 1947, recording a famous win over Dinamo Moscow. They beat them again in 1948 and, in 1949, they won 1–0 both home and away against CDKA. "Their famous opponents tried to make it a game," Filatov wrote. "They combined in passing moves, won corners and free-kicks, but every time they were denied and the ball flew into the sky or on to the running track that ran round the pitch. Eventually their spirits dropped, because they realised they were banging their heads against a wall."

Essentially, though, the clip was seen as a small team's tactic, a means of countering superior sides rather than a proactive strategy in its own right. Krylya finished fourth in 1951 and got to the Soviet Cup final two years later, and Karpov recalled man-marking the giant Hungarian forward Gyula Szilagyi as the USSR employed the clip to win a B-international 3–0 in Budapest in 1954, but it largely remained confined to Krylya. The bolt had to move to Italy before it became mainstream.

———

The fishing fleet lies dark against the sun-washed sea. Along the Tyrrhenian waterfront, a stressed soccer manager, unable to sleep, takes an early morning walk. Oblivious to the shrieking of the gulls and the haggling of the dockside mongers, he strides on, asking himself again and again how he can get the best out of his side, pondering how he can strengthen a defense that, for all his best efforts, remains damagingly porous. As he paces the harbor, churning the problem in his head, a boat catches his eye. The fishermen haul in one net, swollen with fish, and then behind it, another: the reserve net. This is his eureka moment. Some fish inevitably slip the first net, but they are caught by the second; he realizes that what his side needs is a reserve defender operating behind the main defense to catch those forwards who slip through. That manager was Gipo Viani, his team was Salernitana, and his invention was *catenaccio*.

That, at least, is the story Viani told—and with its vaguely biblical overtones it is an attractive one—but it is, at the very least, overromanticized. Nonetheless, among the many theories of how *catenaccio* developed in Italy, Viani's claim to be the originator seems strongest. Perhaps others did use it before him, but he was the first to employ the system on a regular basis and with a level of success. Again, it seems to have grown up independently of Rappan, although the historical influence of Switzerland on Italian soccer is significant. Vittorio Pozzo, for instance, spent two years playing for the reserve team of the Zurich club Grasshoppers, while Franz Cali, the first captain of Italy, was educated in Lausanne. Between the wars, it would have been unusual to find a leading northern Italian side without at least one Swiss expat, their presence being felt particularly strongly at Genoa, Torino, and Internazionale.

Whether it was inspired by a dawn walk by the sea or not, it seems that Viani, recognizing the limited resources at his disposal, decided the most fruitful policy was to try to stop the opposition playing—to exercise "the right of the weak." One of the notional half-backs, Alberto Piccinini, who went on to win two *scudetti* with Juventus, dropped in to mark the opposing center-forward, with the central of the three defenders in the W-M, which had come by then to supplant Pozzo's *metodo* as the default formation in Italy, falling back as the sweeper. Viani had his team sit deep, drawing out the opposition, leading them to commit extra men to the attack and so rendering them vulnerable to the counter. The shape may have been different, but the thinking behind his innovation was no different to Herbert Chapman's at Northampton in 1907.

Salernitana's use of what became known as the *vianema*, though, was not *catenaccio*'s breakthrough. They were a small side and although the system helped them to promotion in 1947—when they had the best defensive record of any team in the three parallel second divisions—they failed to win an away game in their one season in Serie A and were immediately relegated. Viani's relative success at Salernitana made *catenaccio* fashionable, and it began to spring up in varying guises across the country. "Smaller teams began realising that they stood no chance if they turned the game into a series of individual battles," explained Lodovico Maradei, the former chief soccer writer of the *Gazzetta dello Sport*.

> And so, while maintaining the W-M, many made small adjustments so they could have a spare man at the back. Usually this was done by pushing one of the wingers back and letting the full-back slide across behind the defence. Still, this was not something that was done system-

atically, but was rather extemporaneous. Many would disagree, but the reason I say this is that, because it was smaller teams doing this, most of the time they were pegged back anyway and, therefore, even if the full-back wanted to slide across, often you wouldn't even notice it, since the whole side was further back defending.

The most striking exponent of the new style was Nereo Rocco, who rapidly transformed Triestina. He would go on to lead AC Milan to two European Cups, but it was his unfashionable hometown club that formed him and his way of thinking about the game. He had worked in his grandfather's butcher's shop before Triestina offered him a contract and, after pursuing a modest playing career that took him to Padova and Napoli—and, crucially, earned him the international cap necessary at the time in Italy to become a manager—he returned home to the city he loved. Aside from television appearances, when he affected something more neutral, he spoke always with a strong Trieste accent and became a Christian Democrat councilor there in 1948. It was his achievements with the local soccer club, though, that cemented his place in local folklore.

When Rocco was appointed in 1947, Triestina were in a mess. They had just finished bottom of Serie A, avoiding relegation only through an exemption granted because, with British and US troops still occupying the city, they were unable to play any matches at home. Few saw much reason to believe things would have been much better had they not always been forced to travel. In Rocco's first season, though, they remained unbeaten at home and finished tied for second. That was as good as it got, but successive eighth-place finishes in the following two seasons were still respectable for a club of Triestina's limited means, and when Rocco then left following a disagreement with the club's board and was replaced by Béla Guttmann, they slumped immediately to fifteenth.

Still, *catenaccio* was seen as "the right of the weak," and it was only when Internazionale adopted it under Alfredo Foni that it began to be seen as a system with which big clubs could win trophies. He had Gino Armano, the right-winger, drop back to mark the opposing left-winger, allowing Ivano Blason, the right-back, to shift across as a sweeper. Armano was the first of what are known in Italy as *tornanti*—"returners"—wingers who track back and help with the defense.

Blason, meanwhile, became lionized as the first great *libero*. When he had joined the club from Triestina in 1950, he had been a clumsy full-back, but in his new role he became noted for his long clearances and his uncompromising nature. Legend has it that before kickoff he would scratch a line on the pitch and tell opposing forwards they were not allowed beyond it, chopping them down if they tried. "Blason was not the elegant *libero* some may imagine," Maradei said. "He was basically a hacker who just belted the ball into touch whenever he could. That's why the *libero* was originally known as *battitore libero*—'free hitter'—because more often than not he would simply hit the ball into touch."

In 1952–1953, Inter scored just forty-six goals in thirty-four games, twenty-seven fewer than Juventus, yet still edged past them to the *scudetto* by virtue of having conceded only twenty-four (to put that in context, Juventus had won the league the previous season scoring ninety-eight and conceding thirty-four). Describing their style, Gianni Brera said Inter would defend, then "suddenly, Blason fired off a mortar shot: seventy metres away there were not many players around and a lot of empty space that Inter's individual players could exploit." Eight times that season they won 1–0, four times drew 0–0. "They were harshly criticised by the press at the time because their football was generally very defensive and lacklustre, despite a stellar frontline which included Benito Lorenzi, Nacka Skoglund and Istvan Nyers," Maradei said. "It was quite revolutionary: you have to remember that, at the time, the *scudetto* winners regularly scored around a hundred goals."

Variations on the theme sprung up. Fiorentina, for instance, won the title in 1956 under Fulvio Bernardini, the center-half discarded by Pozzo, using a variant of *catenaccio* in which the left-half, Armando Segato, played as the *libero*. Maurilio Prini, the left-winger, retreated as a *tornante*, with the added twist that the inside-left, Miguel Angel Montuori, would push on into the position vacated by Prini, effectively becoming a spare center-forward. Unpopular it may have been, but the template for Italian soccer had been set.

———

Inter went on to become the most noted practitioners, but it was the red half of Milan that first showed the rest of Europe how potent *catenaccio* could be, thanks to the genius of Rocco. Square-faced and plump with short legs, he cut a vaguely comical figure, but he dominated his players almost absolutely, even having them watched after they'd left the training ground so he could be sure their private lives would not interfere with their soccer. So controlling was he that, at Torino in the midsixties, the forward Gigi Meroni went through a period of pretending his girlfriend was his sister to deflect Rocco's attentions. He was ebullient and charismatic, quick-tempered and charming, an enthusiastic drinker who would use a local restaurant as his office. Once, in a fury, he kicked out at what he thought was a bag full of spare shirts lying on the locker-room floor, discovering too late that it was actually a tool kit. Players who were there remember staring desperately at the ground, terrified to laugh until he was out of earshot.

At Torino, Rocco would often drop into the bar at the training ground, have a couple of drinks, and then sleep them off on top of the lockers in the locker room. He liked nothing better than sitting up late into the night downing bottle after bottle of wine with the journalist Gianni Brera, another northern Italian who shared his views on the how the game should be played. "The perfect game," Brera once wrote, "would finish 0–0." Rocco perhaps did not go quite that far, but he did have a fanatical aversion to the ball being lost in midfield with meaningless sideways passes, and he insisted that all his players should track back, even the forwards. The idea was not always well received. The Brazilian forward José Altafini (or Mazzola, as he was known during his early career in Brazil), for instance, although he had a fruitful time at Milan, struggled to accept it, although it was one of the major sources of Jimmy Greaves's dissatisfaction with life in Italy. It is often forgotten that Greaves, who returned home after just five months in Serie A in 1961–1962, scored nine goals in the ten games he played for Milan, but for Rocco that was not enough. "Those two," he said, "need to understand that during a football match you get kicked, not just well paid."

After a brief spell with Treviso, Rocco returned to Triestina, but it was only when he moved to Padova in 1953 that the success of his methods became apparent again. They were far from being giants, but between 1956–1957 and 1959–1960, they finished third, seventh, fifth, and sixth, by some distance the best run in the club's history. And then came Rocco's big chance, as he was called upon to take over at AC Milan after Viani—who had won the *scudetto* in 1959—suffered a heart attack. Viani stayed on as sporting director and later claimed it was then that he persuaded Rocco of the merits of the sweeper. Perhaps there were some discussions over the finer details of the system, but Rocco had, without question, been using a form of *catenaccio* since he first took over at Triestina.

His form of it, though, was far removed from the negative stereotype. In winning the *scudetto* in 1961–1962, for instance, Milan scored eighty-three goals in thirty-four games, twenty-two more than Roma, the next most prolific side. Although Cesare Maldini, who was also born in Trieste and began his career with Triestina, was as resolute a defender as there has been, he was not the bogeyman the sweeper became in the popular imagination. Rather when he left for Torino in 1966 after twelve years of service, he left behind, in the words of the club's official history, "the memory of a gentleman footballer, a player with a clean game, with a sense of style, who nevertheless always observed his defensive duties."

Rocco was also able to accommodate such a languid creative presence as Gianni Rivera, compared by Richard Williams in *The Perfect 10* to "Camus's existential stranger, palely loitering on the fringe of life." On the subject of Rivera, Brera could never agree, calling the issue the "Stalingrad" in his relationship with Rocco. A fundamentalist for what he liked to term "defensivist" soccer, Brera saw Rivera as a luxury, dismissing him as *l'abatino*—"the monk"—a term that hinted at a lack of courage. Yet Rivera's importance to Rocco's side can be seen from their two European Cup final successes. Twice in the space of eight second-half minutes, he laid on goals for Altafini as Milan came from behind to beat Benfica in 1963, and he set up another two in Milan's 4–1 victory over Ajax in the 1969 final.

Rocco's *catenaccio* may not have been as defensive as some suggested, but it was still a very different game to that practiced by Guttmann's Benfica. They shared a cantankerous disposition, but Guttmann's notion of soccer remained essentially romantic; Rocco simply wanted to win. Ahead of an Intercontinental Cup game against the notorious Argentinian side Estudiantes de la Plata in 1969, Rocco is supposed to have issued the instruction "kick anything that moves; if it's the ball, so much the better." The story may be apocryphal, but it was not uncharacteristic. When Ipswich Town were beaten by Milan in the second round of the European Cup in 1962–1963, their captain Andy Nelson was left complaining that Rocco's side "were up to all the cynical stuff—pulling your hair, spitting, treading on your toes." In the final, the winger Paolo Barison, despite having scored freely throughout the tournament, was dropped. With Bruno Mora switching from the right to the left flank, he was replaced by Gino Pivatelli, who was given a specific brief to nullify Benfica's majestic inside-forward, Mario Coluna. Perhaps it was bad luck or mistiming, but when Coluna was left hobbling following a heavy challenge by Pivatelli a minute after Altafini had equalized, nobody was too surprised.

———————

Whatever the excesses of Rocco's team, they were nothing compared to those perpetrated by their city rivals. La grande Inter, the side created by Helenio Herrera, were hugely gifted, undeniably successful, and thoroughly ruthless. They were the supreme exponents of *catenaccio* and came, in the popular imagination, to embody all that was seen as wrong with soccer. It was hard to deny them respect, but equally it would be hard to deny that that respect—in Britain most particularly—was grudging.

Herrera claimed to have invented the sweeper independently of Rappan during a game in France in "around 1945." He was playing at left-back in a W-M, and his side led 1–0 with fifteen minutes remaining. Realizing they were coming under increasing pressure, Herrera instructed the left-half to drop back into his position, while he moved infield to cover behind the defensive center-half. "Already when I was a player, I thought like that," he said. "And we won, and when I became manager I remembered that." That may or may not be true—and Herrera was certainly not averse to polishing his own myth—but what is beyond dispute is that he became the godfather of the system, and it brought him two European Cups. Rocco, with his rotund stature and his love of wine, always seemed at odds with the ethos of his system; Herrera, erect, cadaverous, and rigorously disciplined, was its personification, even if his hair always "seemed a bit too black" as the journalist Camilla Cederna put it.

Herrera was born in Buenos Aires, although exactly when remains unclear. It is said that his father, a Spanish migrant, falsified his date of birth to avoid a fine for late registration of his son's arrival in the world, while Herrera, at least according to his wife, later altered the date on his birth certificate, changing 1910 to read 1916. His father was a carpenter—"like Jesus," he said in his autobiography—and an anarchist trade unionist, while his mother, whom he described as "illiterate but with extraordinary intelligence," worked as a cleaner.

At the age of four, perhaps fleeing the authorities, the family moved to Morocco where Herrera only just survived a bout of diphtheria. Later, shortly before becoming manager of Barcelona, he narrowly avoided death in a plane crash. The escapes seem to have convinced him of his own specialness, his status as a chosen one, a leader with a mission. That manifested itself in the asceticism of his life: the only adornment in his room at Inter's training camp was a crucifix. Having recovered from diphtheria, he gained in strength sufficiently that by his teens he was recognized as a physically imposing full-back. "From fourteen or fifteen years old, I played with the Arabs, Jews, with the French, with Spaniards," he told Simon Kuper in an interview given five years before death finally caught up with him in 1997. "That is the school of life."

He began his formal playing career with Racing Casablanca but, discovered by "scouts looking under the rocks in poor countries," as he put it, soon moved to Paris. There he played for Red Star 93 and Racing Club and won two caps for France at full-back. His career had never threatened to be much more than average, and it was brought to an end at the age of twenty-five after he suffered a serious knee injury. Typically, given his acute sense of his own destiny, Herrera later in life drew a positive from the setback. "As a player I was a very sad thing," he said. "My advantage is that big-star players are monuments of presumptuousness when they become managers. They do not know how to teach someone what they naturally did with so much grace. Not in my case."

As the Second World War came to an end, Herrera was hired as coach of the amateur side Puteaux and, after impressing there, he moved to Stade Français while working part time with the national team as an assistant to Gaston Barreau. It was there that he first acquired the nickname Le Sorcier

("The Wizard"—it was later translated to become Il Mago in Italy). Herrera hated the title, believing it detracted from his achievements. "The word wizard doesn't belong to football," he said. "'Passion' and 'strength' are football words. The greatest compliment I've ever had was someone saying I worked thirty hours a day." He was similarly dismissive of the concept of luck in football. "I hate it when they ask about being fortunate," he said towards the end of his career, with sixteen major titles to his name. "I don't believe in good luck. When someone has won so much in twenty years, can it be fortune? Modestly, I've won more than any other manager in the world. My case is unprecedented." For him, everything was controllable, everything could be made better. In that regard he was the first modern manager. Guttmann might have followed Chapman in establishing the cult of the manager, but it was Herrera who defined his role, who showed just what an effect a manager could have. "When I started, managers carried the teams' bags," he said. "I put them in the place they deserved to be, earning what they should earn."

Herrera was not just a fine tactician, he was a perfectionist, involving himself in all aspects of team affairs. He would control his players' diets, developed the system of the *ritiro*, by which players would be confined to the team's training base the evening before games, and was a pioneer of sports psychology. Every morning he would rise before seven to practice yoga, reciting to himself the phrase, "I am strong, I am calm, I fear nothing, I am beautiful." He would pin motivational notices to the locker-room walls: "Fighting or playing? Fighting and playing," read one; another insisted: "He who plays for himself plays for the opposition. He who plays for the team, plays for himself." He encouraged his players to sleep twelve hours a day and rarely stayed up later than nine o'clock himself. He was, Brera said, "a clown and a genius, vulgar and ascetic, voracious and a good father, sultan and believer . . . boorish and competent, megalomaniac and health freak."

When Stade Français's president sold the club's franchise in 1949, Herrera moved to Spain, becoming manager of Atlético Madrid after a brief spell with Real Valladolid. He won two championships there and continued through Malaga, Deportivo la Coruña, Sevilla, and the Portuguese side Belenenses before arriving at Barcelona, where he enjoyed his first European success. It was his predecessor, Domènec Balmanya, who took them to the final of the Fairs Cup, even overseeing the first leg, a 2–2 draw at Stamford Bridge against a London XI, but he was sacked as Barcelona's league form faltered, allowing Herrera to arrive, inspire a 6–0 win in the second leg, and take the glory.

Herrera acknowledged he had inherited an "extraordinary group of players." "All one could do was win every competition in which the team participated," he said. "Until now the triumphs achieved by Real Madrid at home and abroad have intimidated the team." And so he set about bolstering their self-belief, not only with motivational slogans, but with a series of rituals that played on his exotic heritage. "Too many managers," he said, "limit their role to little taps on the players' shoulders as they are about to go on to the pitch, or making the occasional patriotic speech, which, while maybe warming up the hearts of some players, only serves to cool the muscles of the whole team."

Players were given herbal tea before kickoff, supposedly a magic potion of South American or Arab origin. Herrera would gather his team in a circle before they went on the field and throw them each the ball in turn, staring into their eyes and asking: "How are we going to play? Why are we going to win?" When he had been round every player, they would link arms over each other's shoulders and affirm, "We are going to win! We are going to do this together!" The midfielder Luis Suárez had a belief that if wine was spilled during a meal, he would score in his next game; Herrera made a point before key games of knocking over his glass during the team meal, at which Suárez would damp his finger on the wine-soaked tablecloth, before touching it to his forehead and his foot.

By the time he got to Inter, the rituals had become even more complex, as he sought to improve what he saw as the cold atmosphere surrounding the club. There, before the game, Herrera would hold a ball in the center of the circle, and the players would reach towards it, calling out: "I must have it! I must have it!" "It is important to touch the ball before the match," he explained. "The players are nervous. It is a big match, a big crowd, but the ball: that is their life. Then I made the players hug each other. Not kiss, just hug! And I told them, 'We are all in the same boat!' . . . Then they would get changed and I would say, 'Speak to each other! Defence, speak among yourselves!' *Une équipe, une famille.*"

Herrera's style at Barcelona spoke of his great self-confidence, as he deployed inside-forwards in the wing-half positions, giving them creativity throughout the midfield square. They scored ninety-six goals in thirty games in winning the league by four points in 1958–1959, and eighty-six goals in 1959–1960 as they edged out Real Madrid on goal difference. Herrera, though, was sacked before the end of that season after a 6–2 aggregate defeat to Real Madrid in the European Cup semifinal. He departed, as he had arrived, between the two legs of a Fairs Cup final in which Barça overcame English opposition. Fans had attacked him at his hotel after the European Cup defeat, but after his sacking they carried him on their shoulders down the Ramblas. By then, only Guttmann could challenge him as the most wanted coach in Europe.

After receiving a number of offers, Herrera opted for the most lucrative and moved to Milan with Inter. Their president, Angelo Moratti, had sacked twelve coaches in the previous five years. Herrera promised he would provide the success Moratti so desperately sought but demanded a then-record annual salary of £35,000. "Sometimes an expensive choice can be a cheap one, a cheap one very expensive," he said and was vindicated as ticket sales went up fivefold in his first season at the club.

A few weeks after his arrival he met the players' wives and explained to them the importance of nutrition and the routines he wanted his players to follow. Herrera wanted his control to be all-encompassing, even if his implementation of the *ritiro*, confining players to their Appiano Gentile headquarters before games, was far from popular. "The idea was that we would focus on the upcoming match and nothing else," said the defender Tarcisio Burgnich. "During the retreat, you couldn't leave; you would just train, eat and sleep. When we did get a free moment, there was nothing to do beyond playing cards. So you ended up doing nothing but thinking about the next game. The problem with such retreats is that they're OK once in a while, but if you do them too often it's really tough on the players."

Everything, from sleep to training to diet to the courses of oxygen players were given the night before each game, was strictly regulated. The English forward Gerry Hitchens described leaving Herrera's Inter as being "like coming out of the bloody army" and told the story of how he, Suárez, and Mario Corso were once left behind at the training ground by the team bus after lagging on a cross-country run and had to make the six-mile journey back into town themselves. Even Sandro Mazzola, the great star of the side, admitted there were times when Herrera's obsession with preparation became too much. "After beating Vasas in the European Cup," in 1966–1967, he said, "we were in the showers chatting about the chance of a couple of days off because we literally lived in our camp. Unfortunately he was listening. He said to me: 'No matter how successful you think you are, you always have to keep your feet on the ground.' Nobody said a thing and we all returned to the Appiano Gentile."

Discipline was absolute, and any challenge to his authority was pitilessly suppressed. At Barcelona, Herrera described the Hungarian forward László Kubala as "the greatest player I have ever known" but ostracized him because, he said, his bouts of heavy drinking were undermining his form and destabilizing the team. Kubala's apologists suggest Herrera was rather trying to break the cult of *kubalismo* that had given him disproportionate influence at the club. Similarly, when he arrived at Inter, Herrera jettisoned the Argentinian forward Antonio Angelillo, who had scored thirty-three goals in thirty-three games in the 1958–1959 season, because of his turbulent social life. Even Armando Picchi, the renowned *libero*, wasn't safe, being sold on to Varese in 1967 after questioning Herrera's judgment. "I've been accused of being tyrannical and completely ruthless with my players,"

Herrera said, "but I merely implemented things that were later copied by every single club: hard work, perfectionism, physical training, diets and three days of concentration before every game."

That preparation extended to maintaining dossiers on the opposition. Players came to know their opponents so well that it was said they could recognize them from Herrera's descriptions without recourse to photographs. Suárez, who became the world's most expensive player when he joined Inter from Barça in 1961, regarded Herrera's approach as unprecedented. "His emphasis on fitness and psychology had never been seen before. Until then, the manager was unimportant. He virtually slapped the best players, making them believe they weren't good enough, and praised the others. They were all fired up—to prove him right or wrong."

Inter hammered Atalanta 5–1 in Bergamo in Herrera's first game in charge, won their next away game 6–0 at Udinese, then put five past Vicenza. They ended up third in the table but scored seventy-three goals in thirty-four games—more than anybody but the champions Juventus. They were second the following year, but that was not enough for Moratti. That summer, the president even invited Edmondo Fabbri to the Appiano Gentile to offer him Herrera's job, only to have second thoughts at the last minute and send him home, telling Herrera he had one more season to deliver the success he had promised. It was then that Herrera decided he had to change. "I took out a midfielder and put him sweeping behind the main defenders, liberating the left-back to attack," he said. "In attack, all the players knew what I wanted: vertical football at great speed, with no more than three passes to get to the opponents' box. If you lose the ball playing vertically, it's not a problem—but lose it laterally and you pay with a goal."

Picchi, who scored just once in his Serie A career, proved a diligent sweeper, described by Brera as "a defensive director . . . his passes were never random, his vision was superb." Aristide Guarneri operated as a stopper center-back, with Burgnich, the right-back, sitting alongside him. "By this point," said Maradei, "many teams were employing a *tornante*, usually the right-winger, which meant that effectively the left-winger was the more attacking, often cutting inside to shoot on goal. Many great Italian forwards— most notably Gigi Riva and Pierino Prati—started like that."

That gave the left-back Giacinto Facchetti, who had arrived at the club as a forward, greater license to push forward, because the man he was marking tended to sit deeper. "Jair was in front of Burgnich," Maradei went on.

> He was not a great defender, but dropped deep because he was the kind of player who liked to run at people and needed space in front of him. On the left, in front of Facchetti, you had Corso, a very creative player, not the quickest or the most attacking, but a man capable of unlocking

opposing defences. He was the link man with the front guys. Carlo Tagnin and, later, Gianfranco Bedin, sat in front of the defence and did most of the running and defending. Alongside him was Suárez who had great vision and the ability to hit very accurate long passes. That was the typical way Inter restarted after winning possession. They would either get the ball to Jair, who would run into space, or leave it for Suárez, who would hit it from deep over the midfield for Mazzola or the centre-forward—Beniamino Di Giacomo or Aurelio Milani, neither of whom was particularly gifted—or Jair cutting in from the right to run on to.

Facchetti was the key, and it was he who gave Herrera his best defense against the accusations of negativity. "I invented *catenaccio*," Herrera said. "The problem is that most of the ones who copied me copied me wrongly. They forgot to include the attacking principles that my *catenaccio* included. I had Picchi as sweeper, yes, but I also had Facchetti, the first full-back to score as many goals as a forward." That is a slight exaggeration—Facchetti only once got into double figures in the league—but his thrusts down the left give the lie to those who suggest Herrera habitually set up his team with a *libero* and four defensive markers.

The effectiveness of Herrera's system could hardly be questioned. They won Serie A in 1963, 1965, and 1966—missing out in 1964 only after losing a playoff to Bologna—were European champions in 1964 and 1965, and reached the final again in 1967. Success alone, though, does not explain why Shankly so hated Herrera and *catenaccio*, even allowing for their perceived defensiveness. The problem was the skullduggery that went along with it.

Even at Barcelona there had been dark rumors. Local journalists who felt aggrieved by Herrera's abrasive manner began referring to him as "the pharmacy cup coach" and, although players of the time deny the allegations, they are given credence by what followed. "He was serious at his job, but had a good sense of humour, and knew how to get the best out of his players," said the Spain midfielder Fuste, who came through Barcelona's youth ranks during Herrera's reign. "All that stuff about him giving us all drugs is all lies. What he was, was a good psychologist."

That he certainly was, but the suggestion he was also a decent pharmacologist never went away. Most notorious were the claims made in his autobiography by Ferruccio Mazzola, Sandro's younger and less talented brother. "I've seen with my eyes how players were treated," he said. "I saw Helenio Herrera providing pills that were to be placed under our tongues. He used to experiment on us reserve players before giving them to the first-team players. Some of us would eventually spit them out. It was my brother Sandro that suggested that if I had no intention of taking them, to just run to the toilet and spit them out. Eventually Herrera found out and decided to dilute them in coffee. From that day on '*Il Caffè Herrera*' became a habit at Inter." Sandro vehemently denied the allegations and was so angered by them he subsequently broke off relations with his brother, but the rumors were widespread. Even if they were not true, their proliferation further sullied the image of the club, and the fact that they were so widely believed is indicative of how far people thought Herrera would go in his pursuit of victory.

At Inter, tactics, psychology, and ethos became commingled. Herrera might have had a case when he argued that his side's tactical approach was not necessarily defensive, but it can hardly be denied that there was a negativity about their mentality. In *The Italian Job*, Gianluca Vialli and Gabriele Marcotti speak at length of the insecurity that pervades Italian soccer; in Herrera's Inter it revealed itself as paranoia and a willingness to adopt means that would have appalled Chapman, never mind an idealist like Hugo Meisl. Brera, eccentrically, always maintained that Italians had to play defensive soccer because they lacked physical strength.

Gamesmanship became a way of life. Ahead of the 1967 European Cup final against Celtic, for instance, Herrera arrived in Glasgow by private jet to watch Celtic play Rangers at Ibrox. Before leaving Italy, he had offered to give Jock Stein a lift back so he could see Inter's match against Juventus. Stein, wisely, did not cancel the tickets he had booked on a scheduled flight, and his caution was justified when Herrera withdrew the invitation on arrival in Glasgow, saying the plane was too small for a man of Stein's girth. The taxi and tickets Inter had promised in Turin similarly failed to materialize, and Stein ended up seeing the game only because a journalist persuaded ticket takers to admit him with a press card.

They were minor examples, but even leaving aside the accusations of drug taking and match fixing, there were times Herrera appeared monstrously heartless. When Guarneri's father died the night before a match against AC Milan, for instance, Herrera kept the news from him until after the game. In 1969, when he had left Inter and become coach of Roma, the forward Giulano Taccola died under Herrera's care. He had been ill for some time, and, after an operation to remove his tonsils brought no relief, further medical examination revealed he had a heart murmur. Herrera played Taccola in a Serie A game at Sampdoria, but he lasted just forty-five minutes before having to be taken off. Two weeks later Herrera had him travel with the squad to Sardinia for an away game against Cagliari. He had no intention of playing him, but on the morning of the game, he made Taccola train on the beach with the rest of the squad, despite a cold and gusting wind. Taccola watched the match from the stands, collapsed in the dressing room after the game, and died a few hours later.

Then there were the allegations that Herrera habitually rigged games. The suggestions Inter manipulated referees first surfaced—at international level at least—after their European Cup semifinal against Borussia Dortmund in 1964. They had drawn the first leg in Germany 2–2 and won the return at the San Siro 2–0, a game in which they were significantly helped by an early injury to Dortmund's Dutch right-half Hoppy Kurrat, caused by a kick from Suárez. The Yugoslav referee Branko Tesanić took no action. That might have passed without notice, but then a Yugoslav tourist met Tesanić on holiday that summer and claimed the official had told him that his trip had been paid for by Inter.

In the final in Vienna, Inter faced Real Madrid. Tagnin was detailed to man-mark Alfredo di Stéfano, Guarneri neutralized Puskás, and two Mazzola goals gave them a 3–1 win. The Monaco forward Yvon Douis had criticized Inter's approach earlier in the tournament, and Madrid's Lucien Muller echoed his complaints after the final. Herrera simply pointed to the trophy. They were more attacking in Serie A the following season, scoring sixty-eight goals, but they had lost none of their defensive resolve. Leading

3–1 from the first leg of their quarterfinal against Rangers, they conceded after seven minutes at Ibrox but held out superbly. That was the legitimate side of *catenaccio*; what followed in the semifinal against Liverpool was rather less admirable.

Liverpool took the first leg at Anfield 3–1, after which, Shankly claimed that an Italian journalist told him, "You will never be allowed to win." They weren't. They were kept awake the night before the game by rowdy local fans surrounding their hotel—a complaint that would become common in European soccer—but it was when the game started that it became apparent something was seriously wrong. Eight minutes in, Corso struck an indirect free kick straight past the Liverpool goalkeeper Tommy Lawrence, and José María Ortiz de Mendíbil, the Spanish referee, allowed the goal to stand. Two minutes later Joaquin Peiro pinched the ball from Lawrence as he bounced it in preparation for a kick downfield, and again Ortiz de Mendíbil gave the goal. Facchetti sealed the win with a brilliant third.

Ortiz de Mendíbil was later implicated in the match-fixing scandal uncovered by Brian Glanville and reported in the *Sunday Times* in 1974, in which Dezso Solti, a Hungarian, was proven to have offered $5,000 and a car to the Portuguese referee Francisco Lobo to help Juventus through the second leg of their European Cup semifinal against Derby County in 1973. Glanville believes he was in the pay of Juventus's club secretary, Italo Allodi, who had previously worked at Inter. He showed that the games of Italian clubs in Europe tended to be overseen by a small pool of officials, and that, when they were, those Italian clubs were disproportionately successful. In so doing, Glanville simply proved what anecdotal evidence had suggested all along: referees were being paid off. It was that that Shankly could not forgive.

The 1965 final against Benfica—played, controversially, at the San Siro—was almost a case study in the classic Herrera match. Inter took the lead three minutes before half-time as Jair's shot skidded through Costa Pereira in the Benfica goal, but even after he had been injured, leaving his side down to ten men and with Germano, a defender, in goal, even though they were effectively playing at home, Inter continued to defend, happy to protect their lead. Was it pragmatism, or was it that, for all Herrera's efforts at building self-confidence, they didn't quite have faith in their own ability? Was it even that they had come to rely not just on their own efforts but on those of the referee?

Benfica, losing their second final in three years, blamed the curse of Guttmann, but the truth was that their attacking approach had become outmoded; at club level at least, *catenaccio*—by means both justified and illegitimate—had superseded the remnants of the classic Danubian style that still lingered in their 4–2–4. When all else was equal, though—when referees had not been bought off—*catenaccio* could still come unstuck against talented attacking opposition. Inter won the *scudetto* again in 1965–1966, but were beaten by Real Madrid in the semifinal of the European Cup. The referee for the second leg of that tie was the Hungarian György Vadas. He officiated with scrupulous fairness as Madrid secured a 1–1 draw that took them through by a 2–1 aggregate, but years later he revealed to the Hungarian journalist Peter Borenich that he too had been approached by Solti. He, unlike an unknown number of others, turned Inter down.

It was the following year, though, that Herrera's Inter disintegrated, and yet the season had begun superbly, with a record-breaking run of seven straight victories. By mid-April they were four points clear of Juventus at the top of Serie A and in Europe had had their revenge on Real Madrid, beating them 3–0 on aggregate in the quarterfinals. And then something went horribly wrong. Two 1–1 draws against CSKA Sofia in the semifinal forced them to a play-off—handily held in Bologna after they promised the Bulgarians a three-quarter share of the ticket receipts—and although they won that 1–0, it was as though all the insecurities, all the doubts, had rushed suddenly to the surface. They drew against Lazio and Cagliari and lost 1–0 to Juventus, reducing their lead at the top to two points. They drew against Napoli, but Juve were held at Mantova. They drew again, at home to Fiorentina, and this time Juve closed the gap, beating Lanerossi Vicenza. With two matches of their season remaining—the European Cup final against Celtic in Lisbon and a league match away to Mantova—two wins would have completed another double, but the momentum was against them.

Herrera was said to have fallen out with Allodi and was being courted by Real Madrid; Suárez was reported also to be considering a return to Spain, his fiancée's homeland, and Moratti was believed to be eager to give up the presidency to devote more time to his business interests. Worse, Suárez was ruled out of the final with what was variously described as a thigh strain or cartilage damage, while Mazzola suffered flu in the days leading up to the game.

Celtic had dabbled with a defensive system, away to Dukla Prague in the semifinal, but although they got away with a goalless draw, that game had made clear that their strength was attacking. Their basic system was the 4–2–4 that had spread after the 1958 World Cup, but the two center-forwards, Stevie Chalmers and Willie Wallace, took turns dropping deep, trying to draw out Inter's central defensive markers. The two wingers, Jimmy Johnstone and Bobby Lennox, were encouraged to drift inside, creating space for the two attacking full-backs, Jim Craig and Tommy Gemmell. If Inter were going to defend, the logic seemed to be, Celtic were going to attack with everything in their power.

And Inter were set on defending, particularly after Mazzola gave them a seventh-minute lead from the penalty spot. They had done it against Benfica in 1965, and they tried to do it again, but this was not the Inter of old. Doubts had come to gnaw at them, and as Celtic swarmed over them their neuroses intensified. "We just knew, even after fifteen minutes, that we were not going to keep them out," Burgnich said. "They were first to every ball; they just hammered us in every area of the pitch. It was a miracle that we were still 1–0 up at half-time. Sometimes in those situations with each minute that passes your confidence increases and you start to believe. Not on that day. Even in the dressing room at half-time we looked at each other and we knew that we were doomed."

For Burgnich, the *ritiro* had become by then counterproductive, serving only to magnify the doubts and the negativity. "I think I saw my family three times during that last month," he said. "That's why I used to joke that Giacinto Facchetti, my room-mate, and I were like a married couple. I certainly spent far more time with him than my wife. The pressure just kept building up; there was no escape, nowhere to turn. I think that certainly played a big part in our collapse, both in the league and in the final."

On arriving in Portugal, Herrera had taken his side to a hotel on the seashore, half an hour's drive from Lisbon. As usual, Inter booked the whole place. "There was nobody there, except for the players and the coaches, even the club officials stayed elsewhere," Burgnich said.

I'm not joking, from the minute our bus drove through the gates of the hotel to the moment we left for the stadium three days later we did not see a single human being apart from the coaches and the hotel staff. A normal person would have gone crazy in those circumstances. After many years we were somewhat used to it, but by that stage, even we had reached our breaking point. We felt the weight of the world on our shoulders and there was no outlet. None of us could sleep. I was lucky if I got three hours a night. All we did was obsess over the match and the Celtic players. Facchetti and I, late at night, would stay up and listen to our skipper, Armando Picchi, vomiting from the tension in the next room. In fact, four guys threw up the morning of the game and another four in the dressing room before going out on the pitch. In that sense we had brought it upon ourselves.

Celtic, by contrast, made great play of being relaxed, which only made Inter feel worse. In terms of mentality, it was *catenaccio*'s reductio ad absurdum, the point beyond which the negativity couldn't go. They had created the monster, and it ended up turning on its maker. Celtic weren't being stifled, and the chances kept coming. Bertie Auld hit the bar, the goalkeeper

Internazionale 1 Celtic 2, European Cup final, Estadio Nacional, Lisbon, 25 May 1967

Giuliano Sarti saved brilliantly from Gemmell, and then, seventeen minutes into the second half, the equalizer arrived. It came thanks to the two full-backs who, as Stein had hoped, repeatedly outflanked Inter's marking. Bobby Murdoch found Craig on the right, and he advanced before cutting a cross back for Gemmell to crash a right-foot shot into the top corner. It was not, it turned out, possible to mark everybody, particularly not those arriving from deep positions.

The onslaught continued. "I remember, at one point, Picchi turned to the goalkeeper and said, 'Giuliano, let it go, just let it go. It's pointless, sooner or later they'll get the winner,'" Burgnich said. "I never thought I would hear those words, I never imagined my captain would tell our keeper to throw in the towel. But that only shows how destroyed we were at that point. It's as if we did not want to prolong the agony."

Inter, exhausted, could do no more than launch long balls aimlessly forward, and they succumbed with five minutes remaining. Again a full-back was instrumental, Gemmell laying the ball on for Murdoch, whose mishit shot was diverted past Sarti by Chalmers. Celtic became the first non-Latin side to lift the European Cup, and Inter were finished.

Worse followed at Mantova. As Juventus beat Lazio, Sarti allowed a shot from Di Giacomo—the former Inter forward—to slip under his body, and the *scudetto* was lost. "We just shut down mentally, physically and emotionally," said Burgnich. Herrera blamed his defenders. Guarneri was sold to Bologna and Picchi to Varese. "When things go right," the sweeper said, "it's because of Herrera's brilliant planning. When things go wrong, it's always the players who are to blame."

As more and more teams copied *catenaccio*, its weaknesses became increasingly apparent. The problem Rappan had discovered—that the midfield could be swamped—had not been solved. The *tornante* could alleviate that problem, but only by diminishing the attack. "Inter got away with it because they had Jair and Corso in wide positions and both were gifted," Maradei explained. "And, also, they had Suárez who could hit those long balls. But for most teams it became a serious problem. And so, what happened is that rather than converting full-backs into *liberi*, they turned inside-forwards into *liberi*. This allowed you, when you won possession, to push him up into midfield and effectively have an extra passer in the middle of the park. This was the evolution from *catenaccio* to what we call '*il gioco all'Italiana*'—'the Italian game.'"

In 1967–1968, morale and confidence shot, Inter finished only fifth, thirteen points behind the champions Milan, and Herrera left for Roma. *Catenaccio* didn't die with la grande Inter, but the myth of its invincibility did. Celtic had proved attacking soccer had a future, and it wasn't just Shankly who was grateful for that.

11

AFTER THE ANGELS

The World Cup in 1958 was, in a very different way, just as significant in shaping the direction of Argentinian soccer as it had been for Brazilian. Where for Brazil success and the performances of bright young things such as Pelé and Garrincha confirmed them in their individualist attacking ways, for Argentina a shocking failure left them questioning the fundamentals that had underpinned their conception of the game for at least three decades. Tactical shifts tend to be gradual, but in this case it can be pinpointed to one game: the era of *la nuestra* ended with Argentina's 6–1 defeat to Czechoslovakia in Helsingborg on June 15, 1958.

The change in the offside law in 1925 had made little tactical difference in Argentina, where idealistic belief in attacking soccer prevailed. Essentially most teams played with a 2–3–5, although increasingly the inside-forwards were withdrawn, creating the W-shaped forward line that was so common in Europe. There was, though, an intriguing variation, perhaps best seen at Independiente with the front five of Zoilo Canavery, Alberto Lalín, Luis Ravaschino, Manuel Seoane, and Raimundo Orsi, in which the wingers were the most advanced players, the inside-forwards slightly withdrawn from them, and the center-forward was a *conductor* (the team that prompted the discussion in Ernesto Sabato's *On Heroes and Tombs*). Nolo Ferreira, similarly, played as a deep-lying *conductor* at Estudiantes, but there was a swing towards more English-style center-forwards, all pace and muscle, after the success of the explosive Bernabé Ferreyra at River Plate that led to many *conductors* being redeployed as inside-forwards.

Argentina, though, also had its mysterious stranger arriving from overseas to impart a mysterious wisdom. Like Kürschner and Guttmann, Imre Hirschl was Hungarian and Jewish. He had played for Ferencváros on their 1922 tour of Argentina and returned ten years later to take charge at Gimnasia La Plata, becoming the first foreign manager in the Argentinian league.

Hirschl led Gimnasia to fifth in 1933 and so attracted the attention of River Plate, who had begun to invest heavily after the arrival of professionalism at the start of the decade. He was appointed there in 1935 and, he said, slowly began to implement the M-shaped defense—although his version of it seems to have been the less defensive Danubian version favored by Kürschner; certainly his philosophy was an attacking one, as a record 106 goals in thirty-four games in the double championship-winning year of 1937 indicates. The Argentinian soccer establishment and media generally ignored the new possibility until the national team faced Brazil in the Copa Julio Roca in January 1939. Argentina won the first of four scheduled games 5–1 but were beaten 3–2 in the second fixture a week later after Brazil changed defensive shape, adopting the M by importing wholesale a Botafogo defense that had learned the system from Kürschner.

That game led to a reassessment of defensive structure, and it was in light of that that River turned in 1940 to another Hungarian, the former Barcelona goalkeeper and coach Ferenc Plattkó. He tried to introduce the M-defense, but results were disastrous, and he was dismissed in July 1940 after less than half a season in charge. "His failure," said Carlos Peucelle, the great right-winger of the 1930s who became River's technical director, "was due more than anything to an ignorance of the sporting environment."

Yet Plattkó's role was vital. "He couldn't make it work but he left the seed of change," Peucelle said, although it would probably be more accurate to say he began the process of nurturing the seed that had been sown five years earlier by Hirschl. It was brought into full flower by Renato Cesarini, who had been a part of Hirschl's double-winning side. His education in the possibilities of the M-defense, though, had begun earlier than that.

Cesarini was one of the original *oriundi*, who left Argentina for Italy in the late 1920s. He had been born in Senigallia, Italy, in 1906, but his family immigrated to Argentina when he was a few months old. He began his playing career with Chacarita Juniors, but, in 1929, Juventus enticed him back to the land of his birth. He was spectacularly successful there, winning five consecutive Serie A titles and developing such a knack of scoring crucial late goals that, even now in Italy, last-minute winners are said to have been scored in the *zona cesarini*.

Juve developed the *metodo*, the system of playing with withdrawn inside-forwards while retraining a creative center-half, at roughly the same time as the national coach Vittorio Pozzo, but Cesarini had a very specific role in it, often man-marking the opponents' most creative player. Not surprisingly, when he returned to Argentina in 1935—initially as a player with Chacarita and then with River—he brought those ideas with him. What Cesarini nurtured at River was less the W-M than the *metodo*, as he deployed Bruno Rodolfi as a forward-thinking center-half, slightly deeper than the wing-halves, in the manner of Luis Monti (himself, of course, an *oriundo*). After Cesarini had been succeeded by José María Minelli, who had played under him, Rodolfi was replaced by Néstor Rossi. Although Rossi had to provide defensive cover, the Howler of the Americas—as fans dubbed him for the ferocity of his organizational shouting—was also expected to initiate attacks. "Rossi was my idol," said the great holding midfielder Antonio Rattín, who was Argentina's captain at the 1966 World Cup. "I tried to do everything Rossi did. Not just the way he played, but the way he yelled, the way he moved, the way he did everything. My first game for Boca Juniors was against River. I was nineteen, he was thirty-one. The first thing I did after that first match, which we won 2–1, was to get a picture with him."

That defensive shape provided the platform for a forward line that was extremely fluent and adventurous even by the standards of Argentina at the time. The front five of—reading from right to left—Juan Carlos Muñoz, José Moreno, Adolfo Pedernera, Ángel Labruna, and Félix Loustau became fabled (although they only played as a quintet eighteen times over a five-year period). Rather than the two inside-forwards withdrawing, it was Moreno and Pedernera who dropped off into the space in front of the half line. Loustau, meanwhile, patrolled the whole of the left flank, becoming known as a *ventilador-wing*: "fan-wing" (*puntero-ventilador* is used, but the half-English term seems more common)—because he was a winger who gave air to the midfield by doing some of their running for them.

Loustau's running meant that the left-half could shuffle across, which in turn meant the center-half—first Rodolfi and then Rossi—moving right, allowing Norberto Yácono, the nominal right-half, a more defensive brief. He became known as the Stamp for the way he would stick to the player he was marking (everybody and everything at the time, it seems, had nicknames, an indication perhaps of how central soccer was to popular culture and everyday conversation in Argentina at the time). Hirschl, taking over at San Lorenzo in 1941, imposed a similar system, although there it was the left-half who dropped back as a marker. As other teams replicated Yácono's role, Argentinian soccer gradually developed what was effectively a third back, but rather than it being the center-half, the number 5, dropping in between the two full-backs (numbers 2 and 3), it was the right-half, the number 4, operating to the right of them. When 4–2–4 was adopted in the aftermath of 1958, it was—as elsewhere—the left-half, the number 6, who moved back into a central defensive position, alongside the number 2 and with the number 3 to his left, while the center-half, the number 5, remained as a holding midfielder. (Even today in Argentina, positions tend to be known by their numbers, so Rattín, for instance, was a 5, while Osvaldo

Ardiles was an 8.) So, where a typical English back-four would read, from right to left, 2, 5, 6, 3, an Argentinian one would read 4, 2, 6, 3.

In Uruguay, meanwhile, there was no corresponding movement of the right-half backwards and so no consequent shuffle of the two full-backs to the left. When the 2–3–5 (or the *metodo*) became 4–2–4, the two wing-halves simply dropped straight in as wide defenders (what would in Britain today be called full-backs), and a back-four there would read, 4, 2, 3, 6, although the 2 would often—as Matias González had in the 1950 World Cup final—play behind the other three defenders as a sweeper, thus replicating the numbering system in the Swiss *verrou*.

Cesarini's River side, la Máquina, became the most revered exponents of *la nuestra*. "You play against *la Máquina* with the intention of winning," said Ernesto Lazzatti, the Boca Juniors number 5, "but as an admirer of football sometimes I'd rather stay in the stands and watch them play." As befits the self-conscious romanticism of the Argentinian game at the time, though, River were not relentless winners. Although they were, by general

Numbering in the 4–2–4

consent, the best side in the country, between 1941 and 1945 River won just three titles, twice finishing second to Boca, who adopted the M-defense under Alfredo Garasini in 1943. "They called us the 'Knights of Anguish' because we didn't look for the goal," said Muñoz. "We never thought we couldn't score against our rivals. We went out on the pitch and played our way: take the ball, give it to me, a *gambeta*, this, that and the goal came by itself. Generally it took a long time for the goal to come and the anguish was because games were not settled quickly. Inside the box, of course, we wanted to score, but in the midfield we had fun. There was no rush. It was instinctive." La Máquina was a very different machine from Herbert Chapman's Arsenal. As such, they were the perfect representatives of the Argentinian golden age, when soccer came as close as it ever would to Danny Blanchflower's ideal of the glory game. Isolation—brought about by war and Perónist foreign policy—meant there were no defeats to international sides to provoke a rethink, and so Argentinian soccer went ever further down the road of aestheticism.

It may have been insular, but that is not to say that the impression of superiority was necessarily illusory. On the odd occasion when foreign opposition was met, it tended to be beaten. Over the winter of 1946–1947, for instance, San Lorenzo toured the Iberian Peninsula playing eight games in Spain and two in Portugal. They won five, lost just once, and scored forty-seven goals. "What would have happened if Argentina had played in the World Cup at that time?" asked the forward René Pontoni. "I feel like I have a thorn stuck in my side that has not gone away over the years. I don't want to be presumptuous, but I believe that if we'd been able to take part, we'd have taken the laurels."

Victory in the representative game over England in 1953 seemed only to confirm what everybody in Argentina had suspected: that their form of the game was the best in the world and that they were the best exponents of it. Who, after all, was leading Real Madrid's domination of the European Cup but Alfredo di Stéfano, brought up in the best traditions of *la nuestra* at River and operating in the best traditions of the *conductor*? That conclusion was corroborated as Argentina won the Copa América in 1955 and retained it in Peru two years later.

That 1957 side bubbled with young talent, the forward-line of Omar Oreste Corbatta, Humberto Maschio, Antonio Angelillo, Omar Sívori, and Osvaldo Cruz playing with a mischievous verve that earned them the nickname the Angels with Dirty Faces. They scored eight against Colombia, three against Ecuador, four against Uruguay, six against Chile, and three against Brazil. They lost their final game to the hosts, but by then the title was won and Argentina's isolation emphatically over. They weren't just back: they were the best side in South America—and possibly the world.

By the time of the 1958 World Cup, though, Maschio, Angelillo, and Sívori had moved to Serie A, and all three ended up playing international soccer for Italy. Di Stéfano, similarly, had thrown in his lot with Spain. Come Sweden, Argentina were so desperate for forwards that for cover they were forced to turn to Labruna, who was by then approaching his fortieth birthday. A 3–1 defeat to the defending champions West Germany was no disgrace, but it did suggest Argentina weren't quite as good as they had believed themselves to be. "We went in wearing a blindfold," Rossi admitted.

Still, self-confidence was restored as they came from behind to beat Northern Ireland 3–1 in their second game. They ended with party pieces—"taking the mickey" said the Northern Ireland midfielder Jimmy McIlroy—but the warning signs were there. Northern Ireland had been told of Argentina's great tradition, of the skill and the pace and the power of their forward play, but what they found, McIlroy said, was "a lot of little fat men with stomachs, smiling at us and pointing and waving at girls in the crowd."

That win left Argentina needing a draw in their final group game against Czechoslovakia to progress. Czechoslovakia didn't even make it to the quarterfinals, losing in a play-off to Northern Ireland, but they blew Argentina away. "We were used to playing really slowly, and they were fast," said José Ramos Delgado, who was on the squad for the tournament but didn't play. "We hadn't played international football for a long time, so when we went out there we thought we were really talented, but we found we hadn't followed the pace of the rest of the world. We had been left behind. The European teams played simply. They were precise. Argentina were good on the ball, but we didn't go forwards."

Milan Dvorák put Czechoslovakia ahead after eight minutes with an angled drive, and by half-time Argentina were three down as individual errors handed two goals to Zdeněk Zikán. Omar Oreste Corbatta pulled one back from the penalty spot, but Jiří Feureisl had restored the three-goal margin within four minutes, before two late strikes from Václav Hovorka completed a 6–1 humiliation.

"If I had to look for an explanation to explain such a bad performance, I would sum it up with one word: disorganisation," said the goalkeeper Amadeo Carrizo.

We travelled to Sweden on a flight that took something like forty hours. It was not the best way to start. Compare that to Brazil, who went in a private plane and after making a tour in which the team adapted their tactics. The football was disorganised as well. We didn't know anything about our rivals. The Czechs scored four goals past me that were identical. They pulled a cross back and it was a goal. They pulled another cross back and it was another goal. They grew tired of scoring in that way. We stepped off the plane thinking it would all be easy for us. We came back having made it all easy for everybody else.

The reaction was furious. Players were pelted with coins and vegetables when they landed back at Ezeiza and the coach, Guillermo Stábile, who had been in charge since 1941, was dismissed. "He didn't know about tactics," said the historian Juan Presta. "He just picked the best players and told them to play. He was a romantic."

"It was terrible," Ramos Delgado recalled. "In every stadium, we were abused by everyone; even those of us who had not played. The national team had to be modified. A different kind of player was looked for, players who were more about sacrifice than play. Football became less of an art after that."

The reaction against *la nuestra* was brutal. There was a realization that the *metodo* was outdated, but the backlash went far further than a simple switch to a 4–2–4. Crowds for league matches fell sharply, partly because of a sense of disillusionment, and partly because the growing middle class began watching games on television rather than at the stadiums. Clubs, which had enjoyed state support under Perón, lost their subsidies. Many turned to foreign talent in an attempt to woo back spectators with exoticism, further diluting the culture of *la nuestra*, but, most crucially of all, the ethos changed. With the financial stakes raised, soccer became less about the spectacle than about winning, or at least, not losing. As in Italy in the late twenties, the result was that tactics became increasingly negative.

"It was then that European discipline appeared," said the philosopher Tomás Abraham. "That was the way that modernity, which implies discipline, physical training, hygiene, health, professionalism, sacrifice, all the Fordism entered Argentinian football. There came these methods for physical preparation that gave importance to defence—and who had cared about defence before? It's a strange thing that it should come then, in parallel with the Brazilian triumph, which really should be an argument for our own local football."

Boca, at least, did try to repeat the Brazilian success, appointing Vicente Feola, although he lasted only a season before being replaced by José D'Amico. Feola brought with him two Peruvians and six Brazilians, the most significant of whom was probably Orlando, his World Cup–winning central defender from 1958. "It was Orlando who introduced us to the idea of a caged No. 6, sitting in defence rather than in midfield," said Rattín. "Feola was unlucky. Under him we kept hitting the post or missing penalties, and then D'Amico won the championship with the same team."

The triumph of 1962—sealed with a 1–0 victory over River as Antonio Roma saved a late penalty—was achieved with a 4–3–3, but with Alberto González operating as a *ventilador* (or *tornante*, as the Italians would have called him), tracking back to become a fourth midfielder and add solidity. That defensive resolve reached its apogee two years later as, under Pedernera, Boca won the title again, conceding just fifteen goals in thirty games—only six in their final twenty-five—and scoring a mere thirty-five. Pedernera may have been a member of la Máquina, but he was unapologetic about his side's approach. "The Bohemian from before doesn't exist anymore," he said. "Today the message is clear: if you win, you are useful, if you lose, you are not." Significantly, Boca proved just as useful in Europe, going unbeaten through an eight-game tour of Europe in 1963.

The Independiente coach Manuel Giúdice, who led his side to the league title in 1960 and 1963, and then to successive Libertadores triumphs, was more of a traditionalist, but even his side were known for their *garra*—their "claw," forcefulness, or fighting spirit. "Independiente and Boca in the early sixties were very strong marking sides and played a lot on the counter-attack," said Ramos Delgado. "There's a first modernity there," said Abraham. "For many years this would divide Argentinian football between those who want to keep the tradition and those who insist that we've been left behind." That would find its most famous manifestation in the disputes between Carlos Bilardo and César Luis Menotti, but it existed earlier, most notably in the tension between Labruna, who coached at River and Rosario Central, and Juan Carlos Lorenzo, who led the Spanish side Real Mallorca to successive promotions and then interspersed spells with San Lorenzo with several years in Italy. He was unequivocal about his methods. "How do you beat a team that has a great forward?" Lorenzo asked. "Very simple. If you don't want somebody to eat, you have to stop the food coming out of the kitchen. I don't send somebody to mark the waiter; I have to worry about the chef."

When Lorenzo was appointed as national coach ahead of the 1962 World Cup, the soccer federation was explicitly seeking a European approach. He tried to install a *catenaccio* system—even having the *libero* wear a different colored shirt in training so the players could better see his role—but found he had too little time to implement something wholly alien and returned to a 4–2–4 for the tournament itself.

He was reappointed in 1966 and during the tournament instituted for the first time what would become the classic Argentinian formation: the 4–3–1–2, essentially a midfield diamond, with Rattín at its base, Jorge Solari and Alberto González, the *ventilador* of Boca, shuttling up and down on either side of him as what were known as *carrileros*, and Ermindo Onega given the playmaking brief at the diamond's point. Width was provided by

Argentina 1966

forward surges from the two full-backs, Roberto Ferreiro and Silvio Marzolini. Once it became apparent that there was no need for out-and-out touchline-hugging wingers, the midfield four became far more flexible. England's shape was essentially similar, the major difference being that where England had a designated defensive midfielder in Nobby Stiles, Argentina had a designated attacking midfielder in Onega. English and Argentinian sources agree on little about their quarterfinal meeting in that tournament, but both accept that the major reasons for England's victory—once the refereeing conspiracies and FIFA's supposed financial need for the home team to reach the final in the days before satellite television are set aside—were that Stiles silenced Onega and that Alan Ball, attacking from the right side of midfield, prevented Marzolini getting forward.

The major change in the Argentinian game in the years following 1958, though, was less the system than the style. Their soccer became increasingly violent, as Celtic discovered against Racing Club in the Intercontinental Cup final of 1967. Celtic won the first tie in Glasgow 1–0 but then walked into a storm in Buenos Aires. As far as Argentinian soccer was concerned, there was a score to be settled after the national side's controversial defeat to England in the World Cup quarterfinal a year earlier, and distinctions among the component parts of Great Britain meant little.

Celtic took to the field amid a hail of missiles. Ronnie Simpson, their goalkeeper, was struck on the head by a stone during the warm-up and had to be replaced. An intimidated referee denied them a clear penalty before he finally did award one and, although that was converted by Tommy Gemmell, Norberto Raffo leveled for Racing before half-time with a header from what Celtic claimed was an offside position. Celtic were further unsettled when they returned to their dressing room at half-time to find there was no water. It got worse in the second half. Juan Carlos Cárdenas scored early to give Racing the lead, after which they set about wasting time, with the crowd hanging onto the ball for long periods.

A win apiece meant a playoff in Montevideo, and this time Celtic decided to fight back. "The time for politeness is over," said Jock Stein. "We can be hard if necessary and we will not stand the shocking conduct of Racing." This game was even more brutal than the first. It was settled by another Cárdenas goal, but the result hardly mattered amid the violence. Celtic had three men sent off and Racing two, but it could easily have been many more. Celtic fined their players, Racing bought theirs new cars: victory was everything.

Racing may have been representative of the way things had gone in Argentina, but they certainly weren't the worst exponents of the win-at-all-costs mentality. That prize, without question, went to the Estudiantes de la Plata of Osvaldo Zubeldía.

In a sense, it was logical that Zubeldía should become the pioneer of the new style of soccer, given he had grown up in the Vélez Sarsfield team of Victorio Spinetto, a hugely influential coach who had stood apart from *la nuestra* long before 1958. In fact, Spinetto was one of a triumvirate of coaches Argentina turned to in the aftermath of Helsingborg to see them through the 1959 Copa América, along with José Della Torre and José Barreiro. Perhaps it would be unfair to say Spinetto was not a romantic but his romanticism took a very different form from that of most of his contemporaries. His passion was not to create a spectacle or to prove his sides more capable of artistry than others; what he cared about was his Vélez, and about winning.

Spinetto was born on June 3, 1910 in the barrio of Flores. He lived there for the first years of his life and studied at El Nacional de Buenos

Aires, a renowned school, until the third year. "I was a boy from a good family, posh," he recalled in an interview with Osvaldo Ardizzone in *El Gráfico* in 1971. "My grandparents had money, but my father liked living as well, and he spent the money that would have been my inheritance. I remember that when I was thirteen or fourteen years old we all went to live in my grandmother's house in the Barrancas de Belgrano—a big house, like they used to build."

He was far from a diligent student, preferring sports to books, which didn't just mean soccer. "I was well developed for my age, and I liked displays in which strength and boldness mattered," he said.

> A boys' thing, you see? Every afternoon I got locked in fights typical of boys of that age. It was about struggling, not about punches . . . a vain contest to see who was the strongest. But I liked football, do you understand? And that was not the preferred sport of the *barra*, so I went every afternoon to the car park that is still in front of Belgrano station. And at about four or five in the afternoon, all the boys who were awaiting the arrival of the newspapers met up . . . the newsboys. . . . I was the posh boy that they let join in the kick-abouts maybe because I was capable of giving a kick and because I never refused an invitation to a fight.

Spinetto's family moved to Quilmes, where he joined a formal club for the first time, Honor y Patria of Bernal, who played in Primer División B, the second division. There his toughness found a more practical purpose. "What a struggle!" he said. "Today you see the protection that stadiums offer. But then those little fields offered no defence. You got out on foot, without buses, without anything . . . and the rows of opposing fans."

He left there when his family returned to the west of Buenos Aires. "This time we went to live in La Paternal," he said. "And so I went to play for a team that was also called La Paternal and was also in the second division." A year after the coming of professionalism, as a highly promising center-half, Spinetto joined Platense. They already had two fine central midfielders, though, in Roberto Devoto and the Paraguayan Manuel Fleitas Solich. Finding first-team opportunities limited, Spinetto's six months there were frustrating, and he soon accepted an offer from Vélez. "Vélez Sarsfield was the club that became my life," he said. "There is always *one* club in the career of a player even if he changes jersey only by chance, as happened to me."

In Liniers, Spinetto soon became known for his spirit and his ability to score goals. He was the center-half as *caudillo*, a term that could translate as "leader" or "governor" but is often used of warlords and encapsulates the Argentinian ideal of the number 5: a tough, ruthless figure and yet rather more than a brute—somebody with both ability and an uncompromising outlook. "I was a centre-half who ran at everybody—I didn't go easy on anyone," he said in an interview with *Súper Fútbol* in 1988.

> I never liked losing and I never gave up a game as lost before the ninety minutes were up. I always gave my all, for the people, for the club and for my team-mates. And I played hard, yes, but I was not alone. I was always open and loyal and I respected all my opponents. But do not think these things are easy. Before things were not as they are today, when all the kicks given and received during the game are lost to the memory. In my era, if you played dirty, the matter did not end with the whistle of the referee; they came to search for you at your house. . . . You had to be honest with your use of force, because if not. . . .

Spinetto spent six seasons with Vélez, went to Independiente and returned after a season. They were relegated in 1940—for the only time in their history—after Atlanta beat Independiente 6–4 on the final day of the season. Spinetto was devastated and effectively retired, aged thirty, although he did play a handful of times for Acassuso in the second division in 1942. "I remember Victorio on the day that Vélez were relegated in 1940," said Pablo Policastro, a *socio vitalicio* of Vélez, at a conference on Vélez's history in 2006. "I was eight years old and it still makes me emotional. I saw him walking on calle Escalada and I realised that he was crying."

It was a blow Spinetto had to rectify, and in 1942 he was given his opportunity as he was hired as coach. "They told me that I was stuck with what I had, that I had to cope with the players and the money that was there," Spinetto said. "It was a conversation similar to that of 1932, when they came to sign me as a player. This time they sold me the future and this time they sold it more easily, because I was already a *socio protector* of the club, and I could not let them down."

Spinetto immediately began promoting young players. The likes of Miguel Rugilo, Armando Ovide, Juan José Ferraro, and Alfredo Bermúdez all came through in Spinetto's first full season as coach as Vélez won promotion back to the Primera. Many years later, Policastro went to watch Spinetto laying a plaque at Floresta station to mark the site where Vélez was founded. "I saw you relegated with Vélez in 1940," Policastro said nervously to him. A "half-angry" Spinetto replied, "and they were promoted with me in 1943."

Vélez established themselves again as a top-flight club, and, in 1953, they finished as runners-up behind River Plate, becoming the first side from outside the traditional Big Five (Boca Juniors, River Plate, San Lorenzo, Independiente, and Racing) to break into the top two (Huracán had finished level with River in second in 1939, but the second leg of their play-off for silver never took place). Spinetto's reign, though, was less about league position than about style. He gave Vélez a sense of self-esteem that would ultimately make them a club of similar stature to Racing and San Lorenzo and imbued them with *garra*—that semimythical combination of spirit, toughness, and street smarts so prized in *platense* soccer.

Spinetto became famous for the way he lived the game on the touchline, in a way no coach had previously in Argentina. In his first years as a manager he wore a tracksuit, a towel draped over his shoulder; later he graduated to a blue jacket, with a T—for *técnico*—marked on the pocket in adhesive tape. Always he would stand with his right foot raised, his right elbow resting on his knee and chin supported on his right palm. He would rage in his booming, hoarse voice, attacking his players, the opposition, and the referee, frequently being sent from the touchline because of it. "The players loved him very much, but they were killed by him," said Adolfo Mogilevsky, who worked with Spinetto at Atlanta and then with the national team. "He had a reputation for being hard, but he was always warm and would stress human values."

There are countless anecdotes about Spinetto's toughness. He would motivate his players at half-time by asking what their mothers would think of them if they lost. "A player who doesn't go on to the field to defend his position fearing disgrace shouldn't be on the field," he would say. "Football is a game for men."

At the 2006 conference, Antonio Settino, another *socio vitalicio*, recalled a game at Lanús in which Vélez trailed 2–0 at half-time:

> Don José Amalfitani [the club's principal director and the man after whom their stadium is named] went to the dressing-room and said to the players, "Boys, look after your legs, a player is worth a lot," he said. He wanted them to take it easy. Barely had Don José gone when Spinetto shouted, "Queers! We have to win this game!" And Vélez won, and the players had to wait until about 10pm to leave the ground because the fans wanted to beat them up. Don Victorio won this game, and that demonstrated the toughness and the passion for Vélez he had.

Spinetto hated the focus on tricks of *la nuestra*. "Of course it matters whether a player is technically gifted or not," he said, "but if he doesn't have *fibra* [toughness, stamina, determination], he cannot become a great. Take the case of Carlos Bianchi [a forward who would become a highly successful coach himself]. He was a man since he was a kid . . . and that's why he gives his all on the field. You know which are the most generous players on the pitch? Those who are men in the full sense of sacrifice. Together with their talent they give everything that they have inside. . . . Because they have shame and they don't like to leave the field defeated."

Spinetto's players remember him as a great motivator. "He was a man who worked a lot with the players on psychology, because a player has to be a little bit aggressive," said the attacking midfielder Norberto Conde. "If he's cold, if he's slow, or if he doesn't give everything, he doesn't have the purpose that others have." He delighted in being unpredictable. "More than once when I'd played badly," remembered the forward Ernesto Sansone, "he'd applaud me as if I'd done very well, but when I had played well, and I knew I'd played well, he'd hammer me as if I'd played badly."

Perhaps his greatest gift was his ability to lift his side if they trailed at half-time. There was a game against River in which Vélez trailed 3–0 at half-time, with the goalkeeper Miguel Rugilo having been responsible for two of the goals. At half-time, he lay exhausted in the bath, so Spinetto took Huss, Ángel Allegri, and Armando Ovide to one side. "Look at how Miguel is," he said. "If you are his friends you have to play for him." Vélez were level within twenty minutes, and the center-forward Osvaldo Bottini even missed a fine chance to win the game at the end.

Spinetto's principal legacy, though, was not what he did for Vélez but the foundations he laid for *antifútbol*; the sense he left that soccer was as much about motivation and toughness as it was about skill. To call him a tactical revolutionary is perhaps too strong, for his ideas look basic by comparison with what was going on in Europe or in Brazil at the same time, and yet the very fact he thought so deeply about tactics and the style of the game made him a radical in the Argentina of the late forties. Spinetto never played for Cesarini, but he was open in his praise for him, admiring the way he challenged prevailing assumptions.

Spinetto was equally prepared to amend the traditional roles, eschewing the tradition of neat technical moves threaded down the center of the field, using the inside-forwards as creative fulcrums. "I demand teams with *fibra*," he said.

> Defenders who defend, forwards who attack . . . but you know for me what is a team? It's the sum of players who hand out work and those who get down and look for it. And you have to attack on the wings . . . always on the wings. . . . Do you know what attacking is for me? To get behind the defenders. A forward must look to get behind his marker and at the same time his team-mate must try to give him the pass to hit the space behind the defender. And that must be done through the wings.

Where Argentinian forwards traditionally confined themselves to attacking, Spinetto encouraged them to play a more all-round role. His most conspicuous success was with Zubeldía, a player with a notably enquiring mind. He was nominally a number 10, an attacking inside-left, but in that 1953 season, when Vélez finished as runners-up, Spinetto had him tracking back, working the length of the pitch like a modern midfielder. Whether that was Spinetto's idea or Zubeldía's it's impossible at this remove to know: better perhaps to see it as a symbiosis between the intelligence of the player and the willingness of the coach to try something different.

Spinetto also coached Carlos Griguol, who won Nacional championships with Rosario Central and Ferril Carro Oeste (twice) and a Copa Interamericana with River Plate, and Bianchi, who with Vélez won three championships, the Libertadores, the Copa Interamericana, and the Intercontinental Cup and then went to Boca and had even greater success, claiming four championships, three Libertadores, and two Intercontinental titles. Griguol and Bianchi's teams were never as overtly cynical as those of Zubeldía, but both played an aggressive, disciplined game, one that favored pragmatism over beauty.

More recently, Spinetto coached Diego Simeone in the Vélez youth team, bestowing upon him the nickname "Cholo" after a former player who shared his surname. Then, of course, there are the disciples of Spinetto's disciples. Griguol begat Héctor Cúper and Mario Gómez, Bianchi begat Diego Cagna and Omar Asad, and Zubeldía begat Eduardo Manera and, most famously, Carlos Bilardo. Bilardo himself now has followers—the likes of Miguel Ángel Russo, who won the *clausura* with Vélez in 2005 and the Libertadores with Boca in 2007, and Alejandro Sabella, who led Estudiantes to the Libertadores in 2009 and the Apertura title in 2010 before becoming national coach. His name, meanwhile, has become synonymous with the whole philosophy of *antifútbol*.

It was Zubeldía who took *antifútbol* into the mainstream. Juan Carlos Onganía seized power in a coup in June 1966 and, realizing the influence of sports, made money available to the clubs to clear their debts. In return, the championship was revised, split into two—the Metropolitano and the Nacional—the aim being to encourage the development of sides from outside Buenos Aires. The stranglehold of the big five was broken and, in 1967, Estudiantes became the first Metropolitano champions.

When Zubeldía arrived at Estudiantes in 1965, having been dismissed from the national side, his initial target had simply been avoiding relegation. As a midfielder or forward with Boca Juniors, Vélez, Atalanta, and Banfield, he had been noted for his intelligence and his positional sense, and that awareness of shape and space was the cornerstone of his management. "He was a right-half, so he played just alongside me at Boca," said Rattín. "Even as a player he was a real studier of the game. He would look at the law and he would stand right there on the border of it."

Zubeldía led Atalanta to two respectable finishes but found things rather more difficult with Argentina, perhaps because, as Valeriy Lobanovskyi later discovered with the USSR, it is a much harder thing to impose a vision on a team at national level, where the time available to work with players is so brief, than it is at club level where the involvement is day to day.

"He came to the club a month before starting," said Juan Ramón Verón, who is generally acknowledged to have been the most naturally gifted player in that Estudiantes side. "He looked at the first team and he looked at the third team and he saw the third team was playing better, and asked himself what was the point of keeping the old players."

He retained only four of them, preferring to try to mold young minds. "Zubeldía was a very simple man, and work was his goal," Verón went on.

> He was very fond of teaching, of spending time with and working with the players. He came here with another trainer, Argentino Geronazzo, who was a very crazy guy, who was never at any club for long because he was always falling out with people. But when they got here they had a plan and they already knew what they wanted to do. We had a pre-season, which had not happened before. Coaches started to get heavily involved in daily training, which before then had not been usual. When Zubeldía came here, we started going into concentration the day before the game. We lived at the training ground. We learnt tactics on a blackboard and then practised them on the pitch.

No club from outside the capital had ever won the title before, so there were no expectations, no demand for instant success. "The fans here were more patient, so Zubeldía could work here for three years without having to win championships, which he would not have been able to do at, for instance, Boca," Verón said. "We were really young and didn't really notice what was happening. Things just started growing, and we realised one day that we had a great team."

In *El Gráfico*, the journalist Jorge Ventura wrote of their style as "a football that is designed over a hard week of laboratory work, and explodes on the seventh day with an effectiveness that consecrates the tale of positions. Because Estudiantes continue to manufacture points just as they manufacture football: with more work than talent . . . Estudiantes keep winning."

They trained harder and more meticulously that any Argentinian side ever had before. "All the possibilities afforded by the game were foreseen and practised," Bilardo said. "Corners, free-kicks, throw-ins were used to our best advantage and we also had secret signs and language which we used to make our opponents fall into the trap."

Estudiantes finished second in Group A of the Metropolitano championship in 1967, qualifying for the last four. That in itself was some achievement, but they went on to come from 3–0 down to beat Platense 4–3 in the semifinal before a comfortable 3–0 win over Racing in the final. "Their victory has been a triumph for the new mentality, so many times proclaimed from Sweden until now, but rarely established in facts," the columnist Juvenal wrote in *El Gráfico*. "A new mentality served by young, strong, disciplined, dynamic, vigorous, spiritual and physically upright people. It is clear that Estudiantes didn't invent anything. They followed the path already traced by Racing the previous year. . . . Estudiantes won after the thirty-six-year 'ban' of championships for ambitious 'small' teams. Estudiantes defeated their convictions and their limitations as an ultra-defensive-destructive-biting team. Estudiantes defeated the intoxication of a unique week in their club history, claiming the most exemplary of their attributes in the hour of victory: humility."

Just as Pozzo's Italy side had been hailed as representing the militaristic side of fascism, so too Estudiantes became poster boys for Onganía's new Argentina. Juvenal made the point even more clearly in January 1969, by which time Estudiantes were on their way to a third successive Copa Libertadores success. He praised their "defensive structures, dynamics, temperament, sacrifice, aggression in defence, fighting spirit, team thinking, organisation. We eliminate improvisation. We improve and evolve into what had caused our inferiority according to some critics." They were, in other words, being praised very specifically for what they did differently from *la nuestra*; moreover, they were hailed for defying the European stereotype of South Americans as stylish but indolent.

Estudiantes may have been following Racing in their style and their absolutist rejection of the tenets of *la nuestra*, but in certain key regards what they were doing was new. The shape was the 4–3–3 that was gaining in popularity across the continent, but what they did with it was unique not only in Argentina but in South America as a whole: they pressed and played an aggressive offside trap. "It was something unknown in Argentina," said Verón, "and it was that that allowed a humble team like Estudiantes to have such success."

The question then is where the idea came from. Zubeldía was noted for his curiosity and his study of coaching practices from around the world, and most of his squad seems to agree that pressing was something he picked up from, as Verón put it, "some European team." Others go further and insist it was an Eastern European side, but none can remember which one. As far as they were concerned, at least when the idea was introduced, it was just another one of Zubeldía's schemes, just another video he was showing them. It is tempting to believe that Zubeldía was influenced by Viktor Maslov—and given that at that stage his Dynamo Kyiv were the only side really proficient at pressing it is even probable—but there is no direct evidence. Even so, if it were some other Eastern European side from which Zubeldía picked up pressing, they must themselves have picked it up from Maslov. Maslov's influence was global.

Pressing and the high offside line were Zubeldía's legitimate innovations, but there was also a more sinister side. It was the violence of Estudiantes that shocked Europeans, but, according to Presta, in that they were no different to any other Argentinian side of the time. Where they stood out was in their use of dirty tricks. "You don't," Zubeldía said, "arrive at glory through a path of roses." It is difficult now to separate fact from fiction, but the story has grown up that Bilardo would carry pins with him on the field to jab into opponents. "A myth," Verón said, but Rattín insisted it was true, although he admitted he had not seen it himself. Bilardo seemed to admit it was true in an advertising campaign in 2011. "Bilardo was sneaky," Rattín said. "He was always up to something. Tricky: he'd pull your shirt, pretend to be hit, anything."

Although he was reluctant to go into specifics, Verón acknowledges that Estudiantes "tried to find out everything possible about our rivals individually, their habits, their characters, their weaknesses, and even about their private lives so we could goad them on the field, get them to react and risk being sent off."

"They used psychology in the worst possible way," said Presta. "There was a player from Independiente who had accidentally killed a friend on a hunting trip—when he played Estudiantes, all game long they chanted 'murderer' at him. Or there was a goalkeeper for Racing who had a really close relationship with his mother. She didn't want him to marry, but eventually he did, and six months later his mother died. Bilardo walked up to him and said, 'Congratulations, finally you've killed your mother.'"

It has even been alleged that Bilardo, who was a qualified doctor, drew on his contacts in the medical profession. The Racing midfielder Roberto Perfumo, for instance, was sent off for kicking Bilardo in the stomach, supposedly because Bilardo had taunted him about a cyst his wife had recently had removed.

Unpalatable their methods may have been, but Estudiantes were undeniably effective and, at least at first, that was enough for commentators to overlook their excesses. There was, after all, more to them than thuggishness. "They were really well constructed," said Delgado, who played against them after his move to Santos. "Aside from marking, they knew how to play. Verón was the key player. He gave them a flow. The two central midfielders—[Carlos] Pachamé and Bilardo—were not really talented. Pachamé was really defensive, and Bilardo was not talented but really really smart. Bilardo was the least talented of them all."

Estudiantes won the Libertadores in 1968, beating Racing in a brutal three-game semifinal and then opening up to beat Palmeiras of Brazil in a final that also went to a third-game play-off. It was during that run that the term *antifútbol* was coined to describe their methods, but *El Gráfico* remained supportive, although acknowledging that their style was "more solid than beautiful."

Later in the year they faced Manchester United in the final of the Intercontinental Cup over two games of predicable violence. In the first leg in Buenos Aires, Denis Law complained of having his hair pulled, George Best was punched in the stomach, and Bobby Charlton was left requiring stitches following a foul by Bilardo. Nobby Stiles received a cut eye from a head butt and then, having been goaded all game, was sent off late on for flicking a V-sign at a linesman. Amid it all, Marcos Conigliaro headed in a Verón corner to give Estudiantes the win. It was a similar story back in Manchester, where Law needed four stitches in a leg wound and Best and José Hugo Medina were sent off after throwing punches at each other. Willie Morgan canceled out a Verón header late on, but a 1–1 draw gave the title to Estudiantes.

"That was the high point," said Verón, but others were less convinced. The United midfielder Paddy Crerand called Estudiantes "the dirtiest team I've played against," and the press reaction was just as bitter. "The night they spat on sportsmanship," read the *Daily Mirror*'s headline after the first leg, although Brian Glanville in the *Sunday Times* was despairing. "Some of their tactics," he wrote, " . . . draw us again to question how football, at the highest level, can survive as a sport. Tactical fouls as practised tonight by Estudiantes, by Racing last year and by Argentina in 1966 at Wembley, simply make it impossible to practise the game."

In *El Gráfico*, Ardizzone defended Estudiantes after that victory— explaining it away as a natural product of England's World Cup quarterfinal win over Argentina, but by the time Estudiantes had won a second Libertadores, beating Nacional of Uruguay in both legs of the final, he was beginning to sound doubtful. "Estudiantes go out to destroy, to dirty, to irritate, to deny the show, to use all the illegal subterfuges in football . . . ," he wrote. "If it is good to win, it must be good."

The tide was turning and not merely against Estudiantes. There were insurrections against the military regime in Córdoba and Rosario in 1969, suggesting that tolerance for an ends-justifies-the-means philosophy was diminishing. There were also, though, simple soccer reasons for the backlash against Estudiantes. Verón speaks of how delight in the triumph of a "humble" team soon developed into resentment among clubs and press from the capital, although defeats away to Bolivia and Peru in the middle of 1969 effectively eliminated Argentina from the 1970 World Cup.

Besides, that July there was a new underdog to cheer as Chacarita Juniors, a team from San Martín, a poor suburb of Buenos Aires, beat River Plate 4–1 in the Metropolitano final. In *El Gráfico*, Juvenal's position had clearly changed. "Chacarita's victory validates the values that made Argentinian football great . . . ," he wrote. "Those values seemed to have been forgotten by many teams, players and coaches. . . . Because Chacarita is not an 'enlarged small' team that enjoys its greatest historical victories by running and playing roughly, by biting and fighting, by sweating and continuous rough play. Chacarita run, bite, sweat, give, sacrifice, but they also play football. Rather: they want to play, taking care of the ball throughout the park, and they also fight."

It was the failure to qualify for the World Cup in Mexico, though, that really focused minds. An editorial in *El Gráfico* proclaimed "the school of Argentinian football" as a "great victim" of the revolution that followed the embarrassment of 1958. "The desire to erase the memory of those six Czechoslovakian goals propelled us towards a more defensive game, towards the eternal fear of losing, making us forget the necessity and pleasure of scoring more goals than our opponents to win," it said. "The desire to overcome our lack of speed and physical power before the Europeans induced in us an indiscriminate imitation, a contempt for ability and intelligence."

Estudiantes soon gave their critics further ammunition. In September 1969, they lost the first leg of the Intercontinental final 3–0 away to AC Milan, which raised doubts about the efficacy of their style, but it was the return in the Bombonera that really hardened opinion against them. Estudiantes won 2–1, but far more significant was the violence of the game. Aguirre Suárez elbowed Néstor Combin, breaking his cheekbone, and the goalkeeper Alberto Poletti punched Gianni Rivera, an assault Eduardo Manera followed up by kicking him to the ground.

A wave of revulsion was unleashed. "Television took the deformed image of a match and transformed it into urban guerrilla warfare all over the world," said the match report in *El Gráfico*, and the watching president was just as unimpressed. "Such shameful behaviour has compromised and sullied Argentina's international reputation and provoked the revulsion of a nation," Onganía said. All three were sentenced to thirty days in jail for disgracing a public spectacle.

Zubeldía was vilified, which immediately led his defenders to claim that he sanctioned only the system, not the gamesmanship. A more credible argument in mitigation might be that his side weren't that much worse than anyone else in Argentina at the time, merely more effective. "Those who attribute a dimension of Mephistophelean leadership in regards to the roguery," Walter Vargas wrote in *Football Delivery*,

> should know that on the sadly famous night in 1969, at the Bombonera against Milan, he went on to the pitch himself to try to stop the violent incidents and, once they had been committed, he condemned them and cautioned his players. Does that mean that 100 percent of the sins attributed to Estudiantes are purely myths? Of course not. But the one suffered by Rivera, Combin and co. was the most unjustifiable stain, the one that is impossible to expunge. Then, as is well known, [Juan] José [Pizzuti]'s Racing, the Independiente of 68, Rattín's Boca and the rest were not exactly a monastery of Trappist monks.

Although Estudiantes went on to win the Libertadores the following year, losing to Feyenoord in the Intercontinental final, the mood was set against them. "The Estudiantes that we admired, applauded and defended, were a very different thing," another editorial in *El Gráfico* proclaimed. "When they won their first finals, their play was not *anti-fútbol*, but authentic football suffused with effort, vitality and sacrifice." Perhaps, like Herrera's Inter, they pursued their idiosyncrasies so far that they ended up becoming a parody of themselves.

12

TOTAL FOOTBALL

Sometimes the world is simply ripe for innovation. Just as Newton and Leibniz happened upon calculus independently and roughly simultaneously, so, on opposite sides of Europe, Rinus Michels and Valeriy Lobanovskyi each came to the same realization about how soccer should be played. The game, as they saw it, was about space and how you controlled it: make the field big when you have the ball and it is easy to retain it; make it small when you do not and it becomes far more difficult for the opposition to keep it.

Both encouraged their players to interchange positions, both relied on teammates being able to cover, and both produced sides that were capable of exhilarating soccer. In that, they were the logical next step from the *passovotchka* of the forties or the Hungarian style of the fifties—certainly it was to the latter that the Dutch were frequently compared—but what allowed Ajax and Dynamo to do that was their implementation of an aggressive offside trap. Pressing was the key, but it was probably only in the mid- to late sixties that it became viable.

In an amateur context, pressing is all but impossible. It is hugely demanding physically, requiring almost constant motion and thus supreme levels of fitness. By the time of Michels and Lobanovskyi, the shortages of the war years were over, nutrition was good, and sports science (both legal and illicit) had advanced sufficiently that players could keep running for ninety minutes. This was a stage of soccer's development that stemmed as much from enhanced physical possibility as from advances of theory.

———

It is difficult now, given its modern reputation for liberalism and excess, to imagine how Amsterdam must have been in the years immediately following the war. There has been an undeniable commodification of its bohemian nature, but it is still readily comprehensible that the city should nurture revolutionary ideas. Back in the fifties, it was not. In *The Fall*, which was published in 1955, Albert Camus writes of how bored he was by Amsterdam, a city where "for centuries, pipe smokers have been watching the same rain falling on the same canal."

Dutch soccer was similarly staid. The moustaches and the Victorian stylings of the early Anglophile clubs may have been gone by the fifties, but the style was still backward looking, and the result was a national side that was barely even a joke. Between a 4–1 win over Finland in June 1949 and a 1–0 win over Belgium in April 1955, Holland played twenty-seven internationals, winning just two, and twice losing to Norway. When England hammered Holland 8–2 at Huddersfield in 1948, the Dutch, long after the W-M had become the default across Europe, were still using a classic 2–3–5 formation, leading the English center-forward Tommy Lawton, who scored four that day, to marvel that he'd "never had so much room."

The coming of a limited form of professionalism in 1954 was the main stimulus for the rise of Dutch soccer in the sixties, but it does not explain why the upsurge took the form it did. It helped that the Netherlands all but skipped the W-M phase of evolution, meaning that the notion of rigid one-to-one marking never became instilled, and they were fortunate also that their earliest teachers themselves seemed to flourish outside the pressures of the league structure. It may strike modern readers as eccentric when Brian Glanville writes of the "incubus of the league," but it does explain why so many European nations found their soccer development enhanced by enlightened British coaches. Perhaps it was not so much that they themselves were forward thinkers—although the fact they were prepared to emigrate in itself suggests a level of open-mindedness—but that the new environments in which they found themselves allowed them to pursue experiments that back home would have been dismissed as hopelessly idealistic.

Dutch soccer's founding father was Jack Reynolds. Although he had once been a second-string player at Manchester City, he, like so many influential coaches, pursued a far from stellar playing career, moving from Grimsby Town to Sheffield Wednesday and then Watford. In 1912, Reynolds went to Switzerland to become manager of St. Gallen, and he was set to take up a position in Germany when war broke out in 1914. He sought refuge in the Netherlands and was appointed manager of Ajax—for the first time—in 1915. Over the following thirty-two years, he would spend twenty-five years at the club in three separate stints. His first departure was caused by an argument with the directors; his second by the Second World War, during which he was interned in the Tost detention center in Upper Silesia, a former lunatic asylum. There he was held with P. G. Wodehouse, who had been picked up in the French resort of Le Touquet. "An Associated

Press man, who came down to interview me later," Wodehouse said, "wrote in his piece that Tost Lunatic Asylum was no Blandings Castle. Well, it wasn't of course, but still it was roomy. If you had had a cat, and wished to swing it, you could have done so quite easily."

When Reynolds returned to Amsterdam in 1945, Michels came under his tutelage, and the similarities in their styles of management are obvious. Reynolds was a strict disciplinarian and believed in the primacy of technique, encouraging his players to work with a ball in training. He also laid the foundations of the Ajax youth system, commonly working a fourteen-hour day to ensure that teams at each level played the same style of soccer. He transformed what had been a minor team into one of national importance, while maintaining an attacking ethos. "For me," he said in an interview in 1946, "attack is and remains the best form of defence." Ajax's philosophy was encapsulated by a couplet of the thirties: "Open game, open game / You can't afford to neglect the wing."

Those were the seeds, but it wasn't until Vic Buckingham arrived in 1959 that they began to sprout. He had played in the same Tottenham Hotspur side as Arthur Rowe and had inherited from Peter McWilliam similar ideas about the value of pass-and-move soccer, retaining possession rather than endlessly lumping it long. "Possession football is the thing, not kick and rush," he said in a 1993 interview with David Winner quoted in *Brilliant Orange*. "Long-ball football is too risky. Most of the time what pays off is educated skills. If you've got the ball, keep it. The other side can't score." This is the fundamental of passing soccer, from the Queen's Park of the 1870s through McWilliam's Tottenham to the Barcelona of Pep Guardiola.

His own beliefs, he discovered, gelled with what he found at Ajax. "Dutch football was good," he said.

> It wasn't a rough-tough, got-to-win-things mentality. Their skills were different, their intellect was different and they played proper football. They didn't get this from me; it was there waiting to be stirred up . . . it was just a case of telling them to keep more possession. I've always thought possession is nine-tenths of the game and Ajax played possession football. . . . I influenced them, but they went on and did things above that which delighted me. For instance, two of them would go down the left side of the field passing to each other—just boom-boom-boom—and they'd go thirty yards and two men would have cut out three defenders and created a vast acreage of space.

Buckingham was a devotee of W-M, and it was with that formation—albeit a far more fluid version of it than would have been found in Britain at the time—that Ajax won the Dutch league title in 1960, playing an attacking style that brought them an average of 3.2 goals per game. Buckingham left after two seasons to join Sheffield Wednesday, and, when he returned in 1964, he struggled to replicate his earlier success. By January 1965, Ajax were in trouble near the relegation zone, and Buckingham was sacked.

He was replaced by Michels who, after retiring as a player in 1958, had studied at the Amsterdam sports academy and taught gymnastics at a local school before becoming coach of the amateur side JOS. Like Lobanovskyi, by the time he returned to the club at which he had spent the bulk of his playing career, his outlook had undergone a radical overhaul. Michels the player, Winner says, had been "an easy-going artist on the pitch with a taste for practical jokes off it." As a coach, he was completely different, as the long-time Ajax assistant coach Bobby Haarms recalls. "The main thing with him was now discipline," he said. "Fantastic discipline. Even with the assistant coaches he was like an animal trainer."

Michels kept Ajax up in his first season; the next, they won the league. Although they played attractive and fluent soccer, there was no talk of Total Football at that stage, and certainly Michels did not turn up clutching a blueprint of how he believed soccer should be played. "In starting," he said, "you have no exact idea about the aims for which you are going to strive." His immediate task was to avoid relegation. "To do that I especially needed to change the team spirit and I had to change the team tactically," he explained. "Of course, the team-spirit development, the team's tactical development, that just went on."

He altered the nature of training, prioritizing ball work even more than Reynolds had and so putting in place the structures that would produce the technical proficiency that became such a key feature of the Ajax style. Crucially, he modernized the management of the club so that by the end of his second full season every player in his squad was wholly professional and could commit absolutely to his training schedule. Tactically, his first change was to abandon the W-M for a 4–2–4, with Piet Keizer, Johan Cruyff, Sjaak Swart, and Henk Groot up front and the combative Bennie Muller alongside the more technical Klaas Nuninga in midfield.

That in itself was not especially radical—rather, it was part of a wider trend that swept Europe in the years that followed the 1958 World Cup— but there was a radicalism in the air. Amsterdam in the sixties was, as the British anarchist Charles Radcliffe said, "the capital of the youth rebellion." The establishment after the war of the welfare state and the growing prosperity of Europe had led, as elsewhere, to a blurring of society's traditional divisions. Art and culture became increasingly avant-garde and, in December 1962, Amsterdam witnessed its first "happening" with the poet Simon Vinkenoog's "Open the Grave" event, which insisted that "the victory over old ways begins in Magic Centre Amsterdam."

By the middle of the decade, the whole atmosphere of Amsterdam was surreal and anarchic, with the Provos, dressed all in white, holding regular anticonsumerist demonstrations. Most significant was their reaction in 1966 to the wedding of Princess Beatrix to Claus von Amsberg, a German aristocrat who had served in the Wehrmacht. They announced they would attempt to disrupt the ceremony and encouraged the circulation of rumors listing a series of ingenious ways by which they would do so. It was said that LSD would be introduced to the water supply, that lion dung would be spread on the streets to spook the horses pulling the wedding-carriages, and that laughing gas would be pumped into the church through the organ pipes. In the end, the protest amounted to nothing more than setting off smoke bombs on the Raadhuisstraad, but that was enough. The police panicked and, overreacting as they had repeatedly through the Provos's campaign, set upon protestors with batons. Similar incidents had happened before, but never on this scale—and never live on national television. Viewers were horrified and, when a strike over holiday pay three months later led to further rioting, public attitudes were set on the way to change.

An inquiry into the riots led to the dismissals of the mayor and the chief of police, and the authorities decided that the best way to deal with the youth rebellion was simply to tolerate it. Within a couple of years Dam Square had become a camp for foreign hippies, and the Amsterdam police had a reputation as the most easygoing in Europe. It is no coincidence that it was in the Amsterdam Hilton in 1969 that John Lennon and Yoko Ono celebrated their marriage with a weeklong "bed-in."

Most of Michels's Ajax side are dismissive of the links between the cultural and soccer revolutions, but it is difficult to disagree with Winner when he concludes that they are there, even if they extend no further than a self-confidence that was prepared to question the orthodoxy. Structures and traditions were not to be accepted but to be challenged.

At the center of that lay Cruyff, even at that stage very obviously the leader of the team. Young, iconoclastic, and unselfconscious about ensuring he was paid what he was worth—itself a product of the new classlessness—he became an icon of the burgeoning Dutch youth movement of the time, the equivalent, the former Ajax youth coach Karel Gabler said, of Lennon in Britain. In 1997, in a piece in *Hard Gras* magazine marking Cruyff's fiftieth birthday, the journalist Hubert Smeets wrote that "Cruyff was the first player who understood that he was an artist, and the first who was able and willing to collectivise the art of sports."

Cruyff was not a Provo—his conservatism in such matters as family values was diametrically opposed to their beliefs—and yet he shared with them an awkwardness, an anarchic attitude, and a love of provoking the establishment. Most famously, he refused to wear the three Adidas stripes on his shirt during the 1974 World Cup, honoring his contract with Puma by insisting on wearing only two. "The Dutch," Smeets went on, "are at their best when they can combine the system with individual creativity. Johan Cruyff is the main representative of that. He made this country after the war. I think he was the only one who understood the sixties."

The notion of individuality within a system, Winner argues, is characteristic of the Netherlands at the time. The structuralist architect Aldo van Eyck, for instance, wrote that "all systems should be familiarised, one with the other, in such a way that their combined impact and interaction can be appreciated as a single complex system." He was speaking specifically of architecture, but he could just have well have been describing the soccer of Michel's Ajax.

The term *totaalvoetbal* itself appeared only in response to performances of the national side in the 1974 World Cup, but the prefix *totaal* was used across a range of disciplines. Another architect, J. B. Bakema, who wrote for the influential *Forum* magazine, spoke of "Total Urbanisation," "Total Environment," and "Total Energy." "To understand things," he said in a lecture given in 1974, "you have to understand the relationship between things. . . . Once the highest image of interrelationship in society was indicated by the word 'God' and man was allowed to use earth and universal space under condition that he should care for what he used. But we have to actualise this kind of care and respect since man came by his awareness nearer the phenomenon of interrelationship called the relation of atoms. Man became aware of his being part of a total energy system." As in architecture, as across a range of disciplines at the time—the literary theory and semiology of Roland Barthes, the anthropological theory of Claude Levi-Strauss, the psychoanalytic theory of Jacques Lacan—so in soccer. Within the Ajax model, players derived their meaning, their significance, from their interrelationship with other players. To suggest that could not have occurred without a decline in faith is probably a theoretical leap too far, but again, it is hard not to see a link between Dutch soccer and the intellectual spirit of the time—and it is a beguiling coincidence that the two greatest exponents of system as an attacking force, Ajax and Dynamo Kyiv, sprang up in the Netherlands and the USSR, arguably the two most secular societies in Europe at the time.

The first signs that something special was brewing at Ajax came in 1966, when Liverpool were hammered 5–1 at De Meer in the second round of the European Cup. The result came as such a surprise that Bill Shankly's boast that Liverpool would win 7–0 at Anfield was taken seriously, but two Cruyff goals helped Ajax to a comfortable 2–2 draw in the second leg. In the quarterfinal against Dukla Prague, though, their weaknesses were exposed as a 1–1 draw at De Meer, followed by a 2–1 defeat in Czechoslovakia. It was then that Michels showed his ruthlessness for the first time. Tonny Pronk, who had conceded a penalty in the away leg, was moved from defense into midfield, while Ajax's captain and center-back, Frits Soetekouw, having scored an own goal, was traded to PSV Eindhoven.

Although Ajax eventually became renowned for their attacking flair, Michels began his construction from the back, bringing in the experienced sweeper Velibor Vasović from Partizan Belgrade to replace Soetekouw alongside Hulshoff. Ajax won the league four times between 1966 and 1970—and also lost in the final of the European Cup to AC Milan in 1969. It was that achievement that captured the imagination of the Dutch public, with more than forty thousand traveling to Paris to watch a play-off against Benfica after Ajax had overcome a 3–1 deficit from the home leg to draw 4–4 on aggregate in the quarterfinal.

The system at that stage was still a modified 4–2–4, but with Vasović both dropping behind the other defenders and then stepping out to provide a third man in midfield. They still, though, could be overmanned in midfield. Bertie Mee, after seeing his Arsenal side beat Ajax 3–0 at Highbury in the semifinal of the Fairs Cup in 1970, described Ajax as "amateurish"; there was an idealism about them that bordered on naivety. Later that month Ajax drew 3–3 against Feyenoord, at which Michels came to the conclusion Brazil had reached eight years earlier and Viktor Maslov and Alf Ramsey a little later: playing four forwards could make it very hard for a team to regain possession.

Feyenoord themselves were on their way to a European Cup, under Ernst Happel, who had been part of the Austria side that had finished third in the 1954 World Cup. That side had been the last to use an attacking center-half to any level of success, but Happel was no nostalgist and had already made the move to 4–3–3. Rinus Israel was a ferocious sweeper, while the creative duties in midfield fell to Wim van Hanegem. He was flanked by the Austrian Frank Hasil and Wim Jansen, with the rapid Coen Moulijn providing attacking thrust from the left wing. "Michels was an expert in planning the tactics before the match and preparing players physically and mentally, but Happel was a fine dissector of the game," explained Theo van Duivenbode, who had played at left-back for Ajax when they lost the 1969 European Cup final to AC Milan, before being traded to Feyenoord because Michels judged him too flimsy. "He saw things so quickly that he would make changes from the bench after only a few minutes' play. Happel did not have at Feyenoord the outstanding individual players that Michels had at Ajax, so he went into greater tactical detail and produced more of a cooperative team. Not so much flair, perhaps, but very thorough teamwork."

That makes them sound stodgy, which they were not—merely less fluent than Ajax. Nonetheless, that draw convinced Michels, and Ajax's 4–2–4 became 4–3–3, with Vasović pushing up whenever possible to make a 3–4–3, which still left two markers to deal with the two opposing center-forwards, plus a spare man as cover. "I played the last man in defence, the *libero*," said Vasović. "Michels made this plan to play very offensive football. We discussed it. I was the architect, together with Michels, of the aggressive way of defending."

Vasović was never a man to hide his light under a bushel, and his claims should be treated with a degree of skepticism, but he was certainly pioneering as a defender who advanced up from the back line to become an additional midfielder, an idea that has remained constant in Dutch soccer through such sweepers as Horst Blankenburg, Arie Haan (in his later days), and Danny Blind. It was the combination of that with pressing that made it such an effective weapon.

Pressing for Ajax stemmed largely from Johan Neeskens's aggression. He was usually deputed to pick up the opposing playmaker, and Haarms described him as being "like a kamikaze pilot" as he pursued him, often deep into opposition territory. At first other Ajax players hung back, but by the early seventies they had become used to following him. That meant they were playing a very high defensive line, squeezing the space in which the opposition had to play. That was risky, but Vasović was adept at stepping out to catch opposing forwards offside.

That required a particular skill. Captaining Brazil in their 2–0 defeat to Holland in the 1974 World Cup, the center-back Marinho Peres had seen firsthand just how devastating the Dutch way could be, but he nonetheless found it hard to adjust after his 1974 move to Barcelona, who were by then under Michels's management and had acquired Cruyff and Neeskens. "Defenders in Brazil would never be able to push up like that," he said. "When I went to Barcelona, Michels wanted the centre-backs to push out to make the offside line. In Brazil this was known as the donkey line: people thought it was stupid. The theory was that if you passed one defender, you passed all the others." This had been a constant in Brazilian soccer since the full-backs were first split for the 1919 Copa América and remained in the concept of the *quarto zagueiro* as developed by Lito at Vila Nova: as one defender went to the ball, another dropped off to provide cover. "What Cruyff said to me was that Holland could not play Brazilians or Argentinians, who were very skilful, on a huge pitch," Marinho went on. "The Dutch players wanted to reduce the space and put everybody in a thin band. The whole logic of the offside trap comes from squeezing the game. This was a brand new thing for me. In Brazil, people thought you could chip the ball over and somebody could run through and beat the off-side trap, but it's not like that because you don't have time."

The pressing had a dual function, though; it wasn't just about frustrating the opposition. "In one training session," Marinho recalled,

> I pushed up and we caught four or five players offside. I was pleased, because it was still new to me and I was finding it difficult, but Michels came and shouted at me. What he wanted was for us then to charge the guy with the ball with the players we had spare because they had men out of the game in offside positions. That's how offside becomes an offensive game. If when we got the ball like this, we couldn't create a chance, the defenders dropped back and made the pitch bigger. It was all about space.

The theory Winner sets out in *Brilliant Orange*—that the Dutch are particularly adept at the manipulation of space because of the way their flat, frequently flooded landscape forces them to manipulate space in everyday life—is persuasive (and just as the Viennese coffeehouse writers saw a connection between Sindelar's genius and their own literary output, it doesn't seem a huge leap to see a relationship between the precise, glacial brilliance of Dennis Bergkamp and that of, say, Piet Mondriaan), but that is not to say Total Football was thought out in advance.

Buckingham spoke of how even in his day Ajax players were capable of what he called "habit football": "They could find each other by instinct. They'd have a rhythm; go from the left side of the field to the right but make progress of 30 or 40 or 50 yards as well." The eventual flowering of Dutch soccer, first with Ajax and then with the national side, seems to have been less the result of any plan than the harnessing of a process that occurred naturally among a group of intelligent players who played with each other often enough for long enough that they were capable of "habit football." "When I saw Suurbier going forward, I knew I had to go back," Swart said. "I didn't have to be told. And after two years everybody knew what to do."

To call it serendipitous would be to downplay the roles of Cruyff and Michels unfairly, but they were reacting to circumstance rather than, as Lobanovskyi did, imposing a vision. Even the rapid interchanging of positions, which became the defining feature of Ajax's play, had developed initially as a measure to overcome the packed defenses with which opponents attempted to combat their attacking style. This, in a sense, was the lesson learned from Celtic's victory in the 1967 European Cup final: massed defenses were best overcome by massed attacks, which meant defenders advancing to provide attacking options from deep. "In the fourth or fifth year," Michels said,

I tried to find guidelines that meant we could surprise a little those walls. I had to let midfield players and defensive players participate in the building up and in the attacking. It's easy to say, but it's a long way to go because the most difficult thing is not to teach a full-back to participate in attacking—because he likes that—but to find somebody else who is covering up. In the end, when you see they have the mobility, the positional game of such a team makes everyone think "I can participate too. It's very easy." And then you have reached the top, the paramount of the development.

The move to 4–3–3 made that switching of positions rather easier to structure, because it tended to happen either down one flank or down the middle. So Suurbier, Haan, and Swart interchanged on the right; Vasović (or Blankenburg or Hulshoff), Neeskens, and Cruyff down the middle; and Ruud Krol, Gerrie Mühren, and Keizer on the left. "People couldn't see that sometimes we just did things automatically," said Hulshoff. "It comes from playing a long time together. Football is best when it's instinctive. This way of playing, we grew into it. Total Football means that a player in attack can play in defence—only that he can do this, that is all. You make space, you come into space. And if the ball doesn't come, you leave this space and another player will come into it."

What was revolutionary was that the interchanging of positions was longitudinal rather than lateral. In Boris Arkadiev's Dinamo Moscow side, wingers had moved into the center, and inside-forwards had played on the wing, but the three lines of defense, midfield, and attack had, broadly speaking, remained constant. The great Hungarians, by withdrawing their center-forward and sitting the left-half so deep, had blurred the lines, and with 4–2–4 came attacking full-backs, but Michels's Ajax were the first to encourage such whole-scale interchanges, and what allowed them to do so was pressing. Suddenly it didn't matter if there was forty yards of space behind the deepest outfield player because, if an opponent received the ball, he would be hounded so quickly it would be almost impossible for him to craft an accurate pass.

"We could play sixty minutes of pressing," Swart said. "I've never seen any other club anywhere who could do that." Within a few years, Lobanovskyi's Dynamo certainly could, but there was no one else, which raises the question of how they were able to maintain that intensity for so long. Both Ajax and Dynamo invested significantly in the science of preparation, working on nutrition and training schema, but both also looked to pharmaceutical means. In an interview he gave to the magazine *Vrij Nederland* in 1973, Hulshoff spoke of having been given drugs ahead of a match against Real Madrid six years earlier: "We took the pills in combination with what we always called chocolate sprinkles," he said. "What it was I don't know, but you felt as strong as iron and suffered no breathlessness. One disadvantage was you lost all saliva, so after thirty-five minutes of the game I was retching." Salo Müller, who was Ajax's masseur between 1959 and 1972, admitted as much in his autobiography, published in 2006, and revealed that Hulshoff and Johnny Rep had both come to him with concerns over pills given them by John Rollink, the club doctor.

Over time, Müller collected pills Rollink had distributed from other athletes and had them analyzed. "The results were not a surprise to me," he wrote. "They ranged from painkillers, muscle relaxants and tranquilising pills to amphetamine capsules." Even before joining Ajax, Rollink had form. The first drug scandal to hit Dutch sports came at the 1960 Rome Olympics, when a female swimmer took two prescriptions from a teammate's bag and gave them to the press. A doctor said one was indicative of doping, pure and simple, and that the other was likely to be part of a program of drug use: Rollink's signature was on one of the prescriptions. He later left the Dutch Cycling Union when doping controls were instituted and said that Ajax would have refused to comply had doping controls been brought in to Dutch soccer. He even admitted to taking amphetamines himself if he was working late. It may have been the systematic drug programs of the Soviet bloc that attracted the greatest attention, but they were certainly not the only ones doing it.

———————

Michels was the father of Total Football, and he continued it at Barcelona, but it was only after he had left Amsterdam that Ajax reached their peak. Ajax, it is said, responded to his departure by drawing up a short list of fifteen names to replace him. They ended up with the cheapest, Ştefan Kovács, a Romanian of Hungarian ethnicity who had led Steaua Bucharest to a league title and three Romanian Cups in the previous four years. He had had a brief spell with the Belgian side Charleroi during his playing career, but he was far from well known in the Netherlands, and most greeted the arrival of the squat, gray-haired raconteur with a mixture of bewilderment and skepticism. He even, it is said, bought a return ticket to Amsterdam from Romania because he couldn't quite believe himself that his stay would be a long one. "How do you like the length of our hair?" one player is supposed to have asked at Kovács's first training session, seeing a soft target after the stringent days of Michels. "I've been employed as a coach, not a hair-dresser," Kovács replied. A few minutes later, as he stood on the touchline, a ball fizzed towards him at knee height. In one movement, he trapped and returned it. The test was passed, but the questions about his temperament would never go away.

"Kovács was a good coach," Gerrie Mühren said, "but he was too nice. Michels was more professional. He was very strict, with everyone on the same level. In the first year with Kovács we played even better because we were good players who had been given freedom. But after that the discipline went and it was all over. We didn't have the same spirit. We could have been champions of Europe for ever if we'd stayed together."

Well, perhaps. Or perhaps the side's eventual disintegration was simply built into its emotional makeup. It is easy to see familiarity breeding discontent, particularly given the unusually confrontational atmosphere of the Ajax locker room. Others, however, believed the slackening of the reins was necessary after Michels's rigors. "The players were fed up with the hardness and discipline of Michels," Rep insisted. Liverpool, similarly, blossomed after the avuncular Bob Paisley had succeeded Bill Shankly and his more abrasive approach.

Certainly it was in 1971–1972 that Ajax were at their most fluent, as Kovács replaced Vasović with Blankenburg and encouraged him, Suurbier, and Krol to advance, safe in the knowledge that Neeskens, Haan, and Mühren could drop in to cover. Vasović himself always insisted Kovács's impact was minimal. "Those who say Total Football started with Kovács are wrong," he said shortly before his death in 2002. "Kovács had nothing to do with it. He simply took over a very good team, the champions of Europe, and let them continue the way they had already been playing." As Kovács's supporters point out, though, sometimes the hardest thing for a manager to do is to sit back and do nothing.

Doubts always pursued Kovács. His record was extraordinary—two European Cups, an Intercontinental Cup, two European Super Cups, two Dutch championships, and a Dutch Cup in two seasons—and yet there was always a sense that he was only a caretaker. In April 1972, shortly after a goalless draw away to Benfica had confirmed their progress to a second successive European Cup final, Ajax's board members held an emergency meeting and decided to fire him. At the time, Ajax were five points clear in the league, had just hammered Feyenoord 5–1 in Rotterdam, and had reached the Dutch Cup final. The sense, though, was that beating the Portuguese champions 1–0 over two legs was somehow not worthy of Ajax, and there were continual rumors of poor discipline, with the assistant coach Han Grijzenhout and Rollink suggesting to the board that Kovács had lost control of his squad.

If he had, though, the players evidently enjoyed the freedom. They rebelled, and Kovács stayed. "The results show that Kovács was not wrong,"

Cruyff said. "Our team was ready to take part in making decisions." They may not have impressed in the semifinal against Benfica, but the 2–0 victory over Internazionale in the final, with Cruyff getting both goals, confirmed the superiority of their method and hammered yet another nail into the coffin of old-school *catenaccio*. "Ajax proved that creative attack is the real lifeblood of the game," the report in the *Times* read the following morning; "that blanket defence can be outwitted and outmanoeuvred, and by doing so they made the outlines of the night a little sharper and the shadows a little brighter."

The following year, by winning the European Cup again, Ajax became the first side since Real Madrid to complete a hat trick of titles. Appropriately, having hammered Bayern Munich 4–0 in the first leg of the quarterfinal, it was Real Madrid whom Ajax beat in the semi. The aggregate score of 3–1 barely does justice to their superiority, and the tie is better remembered for Mühren's keepie-ups in the second leg at the Bernabéu, a moment of arrogance, and joie de vivre that encapsulated the ethos of Kovács's Ajax. "I knew I was going to give the ball to Krol, but I needed some time until he reached me," Mühren recalls. "So I juggled until he arrived. You can't plan to do something like that. You don't think about that. You just do it. It was the moment when Ajax and Real Madrid changed positions. Before then it was always the big Real Madrid and the little Ajax. When they saw me doing that, the balance changed. The Real Madrid players were looking. They nearly applauded. The stadium was standing up. It was the moment Ajax took over."

In Belgrade in the final, they beat Juventus 1–0, but it was as emphatic as a one-goal victory can be as, having taken a fourth-minute lead, Ajax taunted the Italians with long strings of passes. A year later, Holland tried something similar in the World Cup final after going ahead in the first minute and were beaten by West Germany.

Winner claims that that Ajax side was "probably as close as anyone has ever come to running a major football team like a workers' cooperative," although there is no doubt that there was one major figure within that. "Cruyff was a big influence," Haarms said, "especially as he grew older and talked more and more about tactics with other players." Kovács was close to Cruyff, but he wasn't entirely cowed by him. On one occasion, it is said, when Cruyff complained of pains in his knee before a game, Kovács, knowing his captain's reputation for loving money, took a 1,000-guilder note and rubbed the afflicted area. With a smile Cruyff agreed he was feeling better, and played without any ill effect. He was not, though, tough enough. Where a ruthlessness lay beneath Paisley's shabby cardigan, it seems probable that Kovács was too nice, lacking the steel to rein Cruyff in as he took on an increasing prominence in that second season. Rep accuses Kovács of

Ajax 1 Juventus 0, European Cup final, Marakana, Belgrade, 30 May 1973

"not having the guts" to promote him in place of Swart until Cruyff gave his approbation, and the players in time came to resent Cruyff's influence.

Kovács left after that second European Cup success to become manager of France, and when his replacement, George Knobel, held a vote for club captain in the 1973–1974 season, Cruyff was deposed in favor of Piet Keizer. Cruyff played only two more games for Ajax before joining Barcelona. The team rapidly disintegrated, and Knobel was fired in 1974, shortly after a newspaper interview in which he accused his players of drinking and womanizing—what many saw as the license of the Kovács days taken too far.

Kovács's subsequent career never approached the same heights. He managed just one win in the qualifying competition for the 1976 European championship and was replaced by Michel Hidalgo, and although a subsequent spell with Romania saw him take them to the brink of qualification for the 1982 World Cup, it ended shamefully as the Communist authorities—ludicrously—accused him of throwing a game against Hungary. "We must accept," the veteran Romanian coach Florin Halagian said, "that Ajax was his opera. It was one of the greatest football has known." The paradox was that by giving that squad the freedom to reach its peak, Kovács also paved the way for its destruction. Total Football itself, meanwhile, lived on under Michels at Barcelona.

13

SCIENCE AND SINCERITY

Valeriy Lobanovskyi was a twenty-two-year-old winger when, in 1961, Dynamo Kyiv won the Soviet Supreme title for the first time. They had come so close so often that their fans had begun to despair of it ever happening, and the joy at Dynamo's victory was heightened by relief. Amid the jubilation, though, Lobanovskyi wasn't happy, as he made clear on what was supposed to be a celebratory visit to the Science and Research Institute of the Construction Industry with his teammates Oleh Bazylevych and Vladimir Levchenko. "'Yes, we have won the league,'" Volodymyr Sabaldyr, a Kyivan scientist and longtime amateur soccer player, remembers him saying in the face of excited congratulations. "'But so what? Sometimes we played badly. We just got more points than other teams who played worse than us. I can't accept your praise as there are no grounds for it.'"

Sabaldyr asked him how it felt to have achieved something that had been a dream for Kyivans for decades. "A realised dream ceases to be a dream," Lobanovskyi replied. "What is your dream as a scientist? Your degree? Your doctorate? Your post-doctoral thesis?"

"Maybe," Sabaldyr replied. "But a real scientist dreams about making a contribution to scientific development, about leaving his mark on it."

"And there you have your answer."

Lobanovskyi the player was dilettantish and opposed to Viktor Maslov's strictures, and yet the perfectionist rationalism, the ambitious and analytic intelligence, was there from the start.

Perhaps that is no great surprise. He was, after all, gifted enough as a mathematician to win a gold medal when he graduated from high school, while the era in which he grew up was obsessed with scientific progress. Born in 1939, Lobanovskyi was a teenager as the USSR opened its first nuclear power plant and sent Sputnik into space, while Kyiv itself was the center of the Soviet computer industry. The first cybernetic institute in the USSR was opened there in 1957 and quickly became a world leader in automated control systems, artificial intelligence, and mathematical modeling. It was there in 1963 that an early prototype of the modern PC was developed. At the time Lobanovskyi was studying heating engineering at the Kyivan Polytechnic Institute, the potential of computers and their possible applications in almost all spheres was just becoming apparent. It was exciting, it was new, and it is no great surprise that Lobanovskyi should have been carried along by the wave of technological optimism.

In him was acted out the great struggle between individuality and system: the player in him wanted to dribble, to invent tricks, and to embarrass his opponents, and yet, as he later admitted, his training at the Polytechnic Institute drove him to a systematic approach, to break down soccer into its component tasks. Soccer, he explained, eventually became for him a system of twenty-two elements—two subsystems of eleven elements—moving within a defined area (the field) and subject to a series of restrictions (the laws of the game). If the two subsystems were equal, the outcome would be a draw. If one was stronger, it would win.

So much is obvious, even if the manner of addressing it is not. But the aspect that Lobanovskyi found truly fascinating is that the subsystems were subject to a peculiarity: the efficiency of the subsystem is greater than the sum of the efficiencies of the elements that compose it. This, as Lobanovskyi saw it, meant that soccer was ripe for the application of the cybernetic techniques being taught at the Polytechnic Institute. Soccer, he concluded, was less about individuals than about coalitions and the connections among them. "All life," as he later said, "is a number."

It took time for Lobanovskyi, though, to come to that conclusion. As Maslov's Dynamo wrapped up a third straight title in 1968, the Shakhtar side for whom he was playing finished a poor fourteenth. Thoroughly disillusioned, he decided to give up soccer altogether. His frustration, though, had less to do with their poor form than the reasons for it. As he saw it, they played "antifootball"—although that had nothing to do with the term *antifútbol* as applied to Zubeldía's Estudiantes. "It's impossible to play as we do," he wrote in his autobiography, *Endless Match*. "It is impossible to rely on luck or on accidents in modern football. It is necessary to create the ensemble, a collective of believers who subordinate themselves to the common playing idea."

Lobanovskyi contemplated a move back into plumbing, but he found himself unable to turn down Dnipro Dnipropetrovsk, then in one of the four parallel second divisions, when they offered him the position of coach in 1969. There, he set about applying the scientific methods he had become convinced represented the future. "If you want to be a good coach, you must forget the player you were," he said. "My relationship with Maslov didn't turn out well, but that's not important. He was a great tactician who taught his players how to play football." By that stage, if he had a disagreement with Maslov's philosophy, it was purely methodological. Maslov had worked by his instincts; Lobanovskyi wanted proof.

In his third season with Dnipro, Lobanovskyi led them to promotion. The following season they finished sixth in the Supreme League, just a point behind Dynamo. 1972 was more significant, though, as the year in which Lobanovskyi met Anatoliy Zelentsov. Lobanovskyi had for some time been frustrated by the difficulties of evaluating the physical condition of his players and the strains placed on them by his attempts to institute a system of pressing. Zelentsov, a specialist in bioenergetics, he realized, was the solution.

"Lobanovskyi and I became really inseparable," Zelentsov said. "He once told me in public at a party: 'You know, if not for you, I might not have come off as a coach. I owe you my formation, my knowledge, skills, understanding and realisation of football.'" The two of them would meet regularly with Bazylevych, who had become manager of Shakhtar. "We would analyse in detail our new training regimes," Lobanovskyi said. "It seemed to us that we were taking the process of training to a completely new level. In the course of one of these heated debates (Bazylevych and I were always questioning Zelentsov's statements, believing them to be only theories) somebody suddenly exclaimed, 'Wouldn't it be great to do this at a higher level than Shakhtar or Dnipro?'"

They soon got their chance. After Maslov's dismissal in 1970, Dynamo turned to Alexander Sevidov, who had served a long apprenticeship with Dinamo Minsk before leading the Kazakh side Kairat Almaty to promotion. He won the title in his first full season in Kyiv, but his style was very different from Maslov's, as he abandoned both pressing and zonal marking. "The team played some really bright football that season," Oleh Blokhin, who was just beginning to emerge from the youth ranks, wrote in *Full-Life Football*. "Synchronisation of the actions and thoughts of players, arrhythmia (a combination of fluent play with sudden bursts into the box), and an intensity of attacking action—they were the main principles of Dynamo in 1971. The team stopped physical pressing almost completely, and also aerial balls into the box. We strove for sharp combinations, and the creation of unexpected chances."

In contrast with the frank and emotional Maslov, Sevidov was always calm and business-like, even in defeat. A devotee of high culture, he preferred his players to continue their education, whereas Maslov had been committed to soccer and soccer alone. He was no great evangelist for his style of play, though, and admitted freely that part of the reason for Dynamo's success was that their opponents expected them to play in a quite different way. "We need two or three years of planned work to consolidate our grip on first place," he said at the ceremony at which Dynamo were presented with the trophy. "We'll have to spend time coming up with new combinations that our opponents aren't used to. But that's the law of any sport: to defend and counterattack is easier than to attack."

Over the next two seasons, Sevidov could not reproduce the same success, and Dynamo finished as runners-up each year. As early as the end of 1972, it seems, the party hierarchy had lost faith in him, and Lobanovskyi was offered the Dynamo job. The problem was probably less Dynamo's second-place finish than the identity of the team who finished first. Zorya, from the eastern Ukrainian city of Luhansk (or Voroshylovhrad, as it then was called), had never threatened to win the title before—and never would again—but, as Volodymyr Shevchenko, the first secretary of the regional Communist Party, encouraged the local mines to back the club financially, they finished five points clear of Dynamo. That was a huge embarrassment to Volodymyr Shcherbytskyi, and Shevchenko was soon fired, narrowly escaping prosecution for alleged financial malpractice. Zorya immediately fell away and finished in the bottom half of the table the following season.

Lobanovskyi turned the job down then, but Sevidov was fired with three games of the 1973 season remaining. Exactly why he was dismissed at that particular moment remains unclear. Dynamo finished second behind Ararat Yerevan—another provincial side with no great history of success—but that was largely because they dropped three points in those final three matches. The official reason was that Sevidov had been removed "because of a collapse of pedagogical work in the team," but no details were given. Arkady Galinsky claims that Shcherbytskyi had been persuaded by an administrator at Dnipro that the calm and reliable Lobanovskyi was just the man to help his son, Valeriy, a huge soccer fan, get over his problems with drug abuse. That sounds outlandish, but even if there is some truth to the theory, it does not adequately explain why Sevidov was dismissed just then, when a far smoother handover could have been enacted a couple of weeks later.

Whatever the reason, Lobanovskyi returned to Kyiv late in 1973 to become Dynamo's first Kyivan manager since Viktor Shylovskyi had been replaced by Vyacheslav Solovyov in 1958. By that stage, he saw a soccer team as a dynamic system, in which the aim was to produce the optimal level of energy in the optimal pattern. He had come to the conclusion that, to win titles, what happened off the field in terms of physical preparation and, particularly, rehabilitation was just as important as what happened on it.

Lobanovskyi arrived at Dynamo as part of a team of four. He had specific responsibility for modeling playing systems; Zelentsov was in charge of the individual preparation of players; Bazylevych, having been prised from Shakhtar, took care of the actual coaching; while Mykhaylo Os-hemkov dealt with what was known as "informational support"—that is, the collation of statistical data from games.

Everything was meticulously planned, with the team's preparation divided into three levels. Players were to have individual technical coaching to equip them better to fulfill the tasks Lobanovskyi assigned them during a game, specific tactics and tasks for each player were drawn up according to the opponents, and a strategy was devised for a competition as a whole, placing each game in context by acknowledging that it is impossible for a side to maintain maximal levels over a protracted period. Dynamo, accordingly, would regularly lose late-season games with the title already won and habitually killed games away from home, looking only for a draw while attempting to conserve their energy. "When we are talking about tactical evolution," Lobanovskyi and Zelentsov wrote in their book, *The Methodological Basis of the Development of Training Models*,

> the first thing we have in mind is to strive for new courses of action that will not allow the opponent to adapt to our style of play. If an opponent has adjusted himself to our style of play and found a counterplay, then we need to find a new strategy. That is the dialectic of the game. You have to go forward in such a way and with such a range of attacking options that it will force the opponent to make a mistake. In other words, it's necessary to force the opponent into the condition you want them to be in. One of the most important means of doing that is to vary the size of the playing area.

Like Michels's Ajax, Lobanovskyi's Dynamo could press, seeking to pen in their opponents and win the ball high up the field, but they were equally capable of sitting deep and striking on the counterattack. As Lobanovskyi was always at pains to make clear, it all depended on circumstance. One thing remained central: keep the preferred playing area as large as possible while in possession and as small as possible while the opponent had the ball. "Sometimes people say that football's meaning is only in attack," Lobanovskyi and Zelentsov went on. "But it is nearer the truth to say that when we possess the ball, we are attacking; when our opponents possess the ball, we are defending. From this fundamental, football strategy is derived: how, where and when to attack or defend." Possession was everything; their approach could hardly have been more different from that preached by the likes of Charles Hughes and Egil Olsen.

On the wall at Dynamo's training camp were hung lists of the demands Lobanovskyi placed on players. Significantly, of the fourteen defensive tasks, four concerned the distribution of the ball and the establishment of attacking positions once the ball had been won. There was no notion of simply getting the ball clear, for that would have been to surrender possession and thus place their side back on the defensive. The thirteen demands on forwards, as well as including a line about pressing and attempting to regain possession high up the field, are also dominated by calls for movement and the search for ways to shift the ball away from areas in which the opponent has a high concentration of players.

Perhaps nobody had compiled such lists before, but their content, even if the emphasis on possession was extreme, was far from revolutionary. Far more radical was the list of twenty items concerning what Lobanovskyi and Zelentsov called "coalition actions." These concerned both defensive applications, such as the setting of an offside trap, and attacking, such as the creation of overlaps. "To attack," Lobanovskyi said, "it is necessary to deprive the opponent of the ball. When is it easier to do that—with five players or with all eleven? The most important thing in football is what a player is doing on a pitch when he's not in possession of the ball, not when he has it. So when we say that we have an excellent player that comes from the following principle: one percent talent and 99 percent hard work."

Lobanovskyi's goal was what he termed "universality." He wanted his forwards to defend and his backs to attack, and he saw no contradiction in the instruction because, to him, attacking and defending were related not to position on the field but to possession. "No other coach ever demanded that I should chase opponents even back into my own penalty box," said the former Russia forward Serhiy Yuran, who began his career at Dynamo under Lobanovskyi. "For example, Oleg Romantsev, both with the national team and Spartak Moscow, told me to work hard, but only in the opponents' half. He told me to do everything in my area, but not to intervene where others should be playing."

Set moves were practiced, to be used, Zelentsov said, not robotically but like a chess player adapting gambits according to circumstance. These were the key to their conception of soccer, and it was through their models of training to develop among players a better understanding of the structures of the game that they carried soccer forward. The classic example of such principles in action, perhaps, came in the Cup-Winners' Cup final of 1986, with Dynamo's second goal in their 3–0 win over Atlético Madrid. Vasyl Rats advanced down the left, drew two men, and played the ball inside to Ihor Belanov. He then took two touches, and, as the center-back moved across to close him down, he, without so much as a glance, laid the ball right for Vadym Yevtushenko. He took one step forward, forcing the opposing left-back inside to close him down, then instinctively flicked the ball right for the overlapping Oleh Blokhin, who ran onto his pass and lifted his finish over the goalkeeper. It was a move so quick and instinctive as to be

Lobanovskyi's three great teams
3–0 v Ferencváros, Cup-Winners' Cup final, St. Jakob Stadium, Basle, 14 May 1975

3–0 v Atlético Madrid, Cup-Winners' Cup final, Stade Gerland, Lyon, 2 May 1986

3–3 v Bayern Munich, Champions League semifinal, first leg, Olympyskyi, Kyiv, 7 April 1999

virtually unstoppable, resembling less soccer than a rugby team working the ball along a line of backs until the overlap is created.

Critics often suggest that Lobanovskyi stifled individuality, but the truth is rather that he made his players aware that they were not individuals, that individual skill was of use only within the context of the system. "The tactics are not chosen to suit the best players," Lobanovskyi explained. "They must fit our play. Everybody must fulfil the coach's demands first and only then perform his individual mastery."

In *Methodological Basis*, Lobanovskyi and Zelentsov give as an example of their preparation for a specific game—the European Cup semifinal against Bayern Munich in 1977. "The play," they wrote, "was constructed on attacking actions, with the obligatory neutralisation of the opponent's players, the intention being to deprive him playing space and to defend against the attacks from wide at which Bayern were so strong. The objective was a draw, but we ended up losing 1–0. In the match in Kyiv, we chose a playing model based on squeezing the play and fighting for the ball in our opponents' half of the pitch, trying to create a numerical advantage in various areas. Eventually we won 2–0."

Their other great advance was to work out a far more sophisticated method of recording and analyzing games than the shorthand of Charles Reep. Each element of the game was broken down and targets set according to the style Lobanovskyi had adopted (see table on page 227). The day after matches, the statistical breakdown of the game would be posted on the bulletin boards at the training ground, an innovation that gave Lobanovskyi great power. "When I was a player," he said, "it was difficult to evaluate players. The coach could say that a player wasn't in the right place at the right moment, and the player could simply disagree. There were no videos, no real methods of analysis, but today the players cannot object. They know that the morning after the game the sheet of paper will be pinned up showing all the figures characterising his play. If a midfielder has fulfilled sixty technical and tactical actions in the course of the match, then he has not pulled his weight. He is obliged to do a hundred or more."

The attitude, inevitably, led to conflict and, although most players seem to have respected Lobanovskyi—most notably Andriy Shevchenko, who insisted "he made me as a player"—he inspired little warmth. "My relationship with Lobanovskyi wasn't hostile, but it wasn't friendly either," said Belanov. "It was simply professional. But he did a lot for me. He invited me to Dynamo and persuaded me to play his way. We had quarrels, but we were aware that we were doing a great thing." As if to prove there were no hard feelings, Belanov named his son Valeriy.

Oleksandr Khapsalys, who played for Dynamo in the late seventies and early eighties, recalled how Lobanovskyi would simply shout down any

Action	Target actions per game		
	Squeezing (pressing only in opponent's half)	Counterattacking (pressing only in own half of pitch)	Combination of both models
Short passes:			
Forwards	130	80	30–130
Sideways	100	60	40–100
Backwards	70	40	20–70
Medium passes:			
Forwards	60	80	40–90
Sideways	50	25	30–80
Backwards	25	15	10–30
Long passes:			
Forwards	30	50	15–40
Sideways	20	30	10–30
Backwards	0	0	0
Headed passes	20–40	20–40	15–70
Runs with the ball	140	80	70–150
Beating the opponent	70	50	20–70
Interceptions	80	110	70–140
Tackles	50	70	30–80
Shots on goal	10–20	15–35	10–35
Headers on goal	10–15	5–10	5–15
Returning the ball to play	10–30	10–30	10–40
Error percentage	20–35	15–30	25

perceived criticism. "It was better not to joke with Lobanovskyi," he said. "If he gave an instruction, and the player said: 'But I think . . .' Lobanovskyi would look at him and scream: 'Don't think! I do the thinking for you. Play!'" With Dynamo, he was hugely successful, winning eight Soviet titles, six Soviet Cups, five Ukrainian titles, three Ukrainian Cups, and two European Cup-Winners' Cups and defining Ukrainian soccer. In his various stints with the USSR, though, Lobanovskyi was less successful. Twice in 1975—against Turkey and the Republic of Ireland—his demand for "a star-team" rather than "a team of stars" led him to field a national team made up entirely of Dynamo players, and the squad he took to the 1976 Olympics in Montreal was similarly Dynamo dominated.

They had won successive league titles and were undoubtedly one of the best teams in Europe, but Lobanovskyi still wasn't satisfied and increased their training schedule even further. The players were appalled, and many complained that they were too exhausted to perform to the full extent of their abilities. Matters came to a head in the semifinal as the Soviets played sluggishly in losing to East Germany. The players blamed Lobanovskyi and went on strike. The incident was hushed up and agreement eventually reached as Lobanovskyi resigned from the national job. "The problem was that we were applying scientific methods to players who were semi-amateurs, and that led to conflict," explained Zelentsov.

The dispute made Lobanovskyi aware that more training did not necessarily produce fitter players, and that was where Zelentsov made his great breakthrough. He constructed a training program that managed to balance the twin but conflicting needs for speed and stamina; Zelentsov claims that Italy borrowed the model when they won the 1982 World Cup. Increasingly, he used computers in analyzing games and it was through that development that they were able to revolutionize the game.

"In my laboratory, we evaluate the functional readiness of players and how their potential can best be realised," Zelentsov explained. "And we influence players in a natural way—we form them following scientific recommendations. With the help of modelling we assemble the bricks and create the skeleton of the team. It is true that not every player will fit the Dynamo system, but we don't just give a coach advice, we justify it with numbers. We recommend how to compose the training programmes, how to evaluate them, how to understand the actions of players on the field—all from a scientific point of view, no emotions."

Lobanovksyi's conception became the default Soviet style, partly because it was successful, partly because of Lobanovskyi's domineering personality, and partly because it felt ideologically right. For all that players of the time protest against the stereotype, the philosophy was rooted in the team: perhaps there is no such thing as the "socialist football" to which Gusztav Sebes glibly referred, but the style of Lobanovskyi's teams was nonetheless a development of the "collective play" of which Mikhail Yakushin had spoken during Dinamo Moscow's tour of Britain in 1945. Yet there was an internal opposition and for a few years in the early eighties: Soviet soccer was torn between two radically different philosophies of how the game should be played.

Where Lobanovskyi was taciturn and analytical, his outbursts rooted in his desire to make his players conform to his system, Eduard Malofeev was loquacious and ebullient, frighteningly so. "There is no one in Belarus with his energy or optimism," said Gennadiy Abramovich, who played with Malofeev at Dinamo Minsk and then worked alongside him as an assistant coach. In the late nineties, Malofeev appeared on what Abramovich described dismissively as "a women's programme" on television. Asked what he did each morning, he replied that first he thanked God he was alive, then he got out of bed and jumped up and down to celebrate the fact. His soccer, in conception at least, was similarly joyous.

Malofeev became a respected forward in twelve seasons with Dinamo Minsk, winning forty caps for the USSR, playing in the 1966 World Cup, and topping the scoring charts in the Soviet League in 1971. A cartilage injury brought his career to a close and, after a brief spell working in youth soccer, he graduated as a coach in 1975, being appointed manager of Dinamo Minsk in 1978. He led them to promotion in his first season, and they were sixth in his second. Even more remarkable, it was all achieved playing what Malofeev termed "sincere football." "It was honest football," explained Abramovich. "No causing injuries, no bumping, no barging: just kicking the ball. No paying money to referees outside the ground. And attacking, pure football. Football of the heart, not of the head."

Malofeev's other great strength was his ability to handle players and get the best out of them. It is an oversimplification to say Lobanovskyi saw his players as tools to be deployed, but not much of one; Malofeev, though, was concerned with individuality and self-expression. "The main thing about Malofeev was his psychology," explained Mikhail Vergeenko, Dinamo Minsk's goalkeeper in the early eighties. "We would have a team-talk three hours before each game. He would gather everyone together and read out the team. He looked into the players' eyes, at each one, eye to eye. He was always looking, searching to discover something. He was like a doctor. He analysed players and he knew straightaway their strong points and their weak points. He was a person who could get to your heart, your soul. He knew how to talk to people."

Malofeev's failure at Hearts in 2006—statistically, he is their worst ever manager, taking two points from his four games in charge—Vergeenko attributed to the absence of a good translator. It didn't take long for comparisons to be made with what was going on 270 miles to the southeast. "The rivalry between Minsk and Kyiv was the rivalry between two minds," Vergeenko explained. "Lobanovskyi was a coach by mathematics; Malofeev was more romantic. The main thing he wanted from the players was that they should express themselves on the pitch. If you give your all, he said, the fans will love you."

The player the fans loved most was a man whose lifestyle would have disbarred him from getting anywhere near a Lobanovksyi side: Alexander

Prokopenko. He was a heartbreak of a midfielder, a genius whose talent was as unbridled as his capacity for alcohol. A painfully shy man, he was so tormented by a speech impediment that he refused ever to be interviewed. It didn't matter: Dinamo fans knew what he thought because he drank with them. More than that, he was one of them, just another worker from Minsk who happened to be a superb instinctive soccer player and an industrious one at that. "The tribune knew he would go for ninety minutes," the journalist Vasily Sarychev wrote in *The Moment and the Destiny*, his book celebrating Belarus's top sportsmen. "He would sooner die than cease his motion on the pitch through tiredness or laziness."

After the USSR team of which he had been a part finished third in the 1980 Olympics, his drinking led him to miss the end of the season, but he returned in glory and scored the iconic goal of the 1982 campaign, a backheel against Dynamo Kyiv. As Dinamo's form slid in the mideighties, his alcoholism got worse, and he was forced to spend time at the LTP, a state-sponsored rehab clinic. The club, acting under the instructions of the local Communist Party, refused to take him back, but Abramovich, whom he came to refer to as a second father, persuaded the second division side Dnepr Mogilev to take him on. After a season there he moved to Azerbaijan with Neftchi Baku, playing against Dinamo Minsk and scoring against Spartak.

It was only a brief respite, though, and he began drinking heavily again. He was readmitted to the LTP in 1989 but died two months later, aged just thirty-five. "He was followed by the smell of grass and of skin, by the joy of his goals and by empty cans," Sarychev wrote. "When the need for football went, the urge died in him, the urge he was born to fulfil." Brilliant but unpredictable, his demons masked by the charm of his play, Prokopenko was the model of a Malofeev soccer player.

Lobanovskyi, predictably, was scathing of Malofeev's idealism. As he pointed out, for all Dinamo Minsk fans raved about the Prokopenko backheel, the match had ended in a draw and a valuable away point for Dynamo. "When somebody mentioned it," Abramovich recalled, "he slapped his hand to his head and said, 'In my life I have seen many things, but never *sincere* football.'" Nonetheless, at least for one glorious season, it worked. "What happened with Dinamo in 1982 was about the harmony of youth and experience," the midfielder Sergei Aleinikov wrote in his autobiography. "Everybody, whether they were veterans or novices, played every game like it was the last of their career. But the main thing was that Malofeev was the head of the team, the unique and only one. That was his victory, the triumph of his principles and his understanding of football."

That year, every ploy Malofeev initiated paid off. Vergeenko remembered in particular the game away to Pakhtakor Tashkent, who went on to

Dinamo Minsk 1982

finish sixth that season. "It was forty degrees [104 degrees Fahrenheit] plus in the shade," he said.

> The game was at 6 p.m., but at noon, Malofeev said, "OK, let's go and train." Everybody was stunned. Even in the hotel it was over thirty-five at night, no air-conditioning. Imagine: we were just thinking how to escape the heat; then Malofeev says we're training at noon. "But afterwards," he said, "you will see—just thirty minutes, you will sweat, but you will be OK." We had thirty minutes training. The workers in the ground were shocked. They were sitting there out of the heat drinking water, and Malofeev brings his team for training. But that evening, we knew we could deal with the heat and we won 3–0, and they were a good team at that time.

Malofeev's team talks were equally eccentric. Dinamo went into their final league game away to Spartak Moscow needing a win to clinch the title. Twenty-nine years earlier, it was widely believed in Belarus, Spartak had cheated Dinamo Minsk out of second place in the league with a bout of late-season match fixing, and the fear was they would do something similar to hand the title to Dynamo. Malofeev knew he had to break down his side's cynicism, to persuade them that defeat was not inevitable, and so he came up with something that sounds like the rejected draft of a Just So story. "'Imagine there is a troop of monkeys crossing a field,'" Vergeenko remembers him telling a hushed dressing room. "'On the other side of the field is a group of lions. Many different things could happen. Maybe the lions will tear the monkeys to pieces. Or maybe one of the monkeys will go first, and will distract the lions, and will sacrifice himself so the other monkeys will live. Today, as monkeys, we must sacrifice ourselves for the victory.'"

"I thought: I am the goalkeeper, maybe I will be injured, but the main thing is that the team will win." And they did, by the typically Malofeevan score of 4–3. "When the team got back from Moscow to Minsk, it was amazing," Vergeenko went on. "There were people with flowers and kisses and love: nothing organised, just love."

Malofeev promptly left for Moscow to take charge of the USSR Olympic side, leaving him ideally placed to step in when Lobanovskyi's second stint in charge of the main national team came to an end. All seemed to be progressing well for him, particularly after a 5–0 demolition of Portugal in Moscow in qualifying for Euro 84. Away in Lisbon, though, Lobanovskyi—as he always did in tough away games—set out for the draw, only to be undone by a penalty awarded for a foul that clearly took place outside the box. Portugal won 1–0, the USSR failed to qualify, and Lobanovskyi, condemned for his pragmatism, was dismissed.

Lobanovskyi's star had never been lower, and only the personal intervention of Shcherbytskyi saw him reinstated at Dynamo. Even that looked like an error when Dynamo finished that 1984 season tenth. Lobanovskyi, though, stuck to his guns. "A path always remains a path," he said. "It's a path during the day, it's a path during the night and it's a path during the dawn." The next season, Dynamo did the double before adding the Cup-Winners' Cup. Malofeev, meanwhile, was faltering. The USSR won just one of their opening five qualifiers for the Mexico World Cup but salvaged a place in the finals by winning their last three games.

"Malofeev became very nervous, and there was no clear pattern to our football, but Mexico was waiting," Aleinikov wrote in his autobiography. "The media was attacking both the players and the coaches. The final straw was the grey 0–0 draw against Finland [in a friendly] at the Luzhniki Stadium. It was rumoured that Malofeev might be replaced, and Lobanovskyi had just won the Cup-Winners' Cup, but I didn't believe it would come to reality before the start of the World Cup."

Nonetheless, it did, as Malofeev was called away from the Novogorsk training camp and didn't return. "There was a strange atmosphere in the squad," Aleinikov went on.

> The Kyiv boys liked the decision, as you can imagine, because most of them were not in favour of Malofeev's ideas. On the other hand, there were the boys who understood there were no positions for them in the

squad under Lobanovskyi. They were prepared for Mexico, but they knew they would not be going.

Lobanovskyi made us train harder. To say it was difficult would be an understatement. In the evening I was just looking to get to bed as soon as possible. For Lobanovskyi the game was about the result, not about fun. Football had to be rational. For him, 1–0 was better than 5–4.

For all the doubts, Lobanovskyi received immediate vindication as his side hammered the much-admired Hungary 6–0. In the second round, though, the USSR, let down by poor refereeing and a catastrophic performance from defender Andriy Bal, were beaten 4–3 by Belgium in one of the greatest games the World Cup has known. "As a coach you can't account for individual errors and you certainly can't account for refereeing blunders," said Lobanovskyi—an acknowledgment that there were factors beyond the control of even a system as scientific as his.

Two years later at the European Championship in West Germany, the USSR came as close to glory as they ever would under Lobanovskyi. They beat Holland and England in the group stage and then outplayed Italy in the semifinal. So impressed was the former Italian coach Enzo Bearzot by the USSR's 2–0 win that he sought out Lobanovskyi after the final whistle. "I realised once again that you are a great team," he told him. "You play modern football at 100km/h. The pressing you showed today is the sign of great ability, and the physical shape of the Soviet players is clearly the result of great self-sacrifice and professionalism."

The only flaw in an otherwise awesome performance was the booking collected by the sweeper Oleh Kuznetsov, which ruled him out of the final against Holland. "Have you seen how bees fly?" asked Zelentsov. "A hive is in the air, and there is a leader. The leader turns right and all the hive turn right. It turns left and all the hive turn left. It is the same in football. There is a leader who takes a decision to move, say, here. The rest need to correct their motion to follow the leader. Every team has players who link coalitions; every team has players who destroy them. The first are called on to create on the field, the latter to destroy the team actions of the opponent." Without their leader, the USSR missed a penalty, suffered Marco van Basten's preposterous volley, and lost 2–0.

After a disappointing World Cup in 1990, Lobanovskyi left the USSR for the Middle East, but he was persuaded back to Dynamo in 1996, partly by the riches promised by new investors but mainly by the potential of the generation of Shevchenko, Oleh Luzhny, Serhiy Rebrov, and Vyacheslav Vashchuk. He inspired them to a Champions League semifinal in 1999—his third great team—but, by the time of his death from a stroke in 2002, the suspicion was that he was struggling as, having had to trade the majority of his better players, he was forced to turn to imports. According to Serhiy Polkhovskyi, the Dynamo vice president, it became apparent in his final months that he was having difficulty dealing even with local players who had not been brought up under Communism. "He had internal torments," Polkhovskyi said. "Previously a word, a glance, was enough to assert his authority and explain what he wanted. Maybe it was typical of the Communist system, but now players have a greater freedom and an individuality."

Still, his legacy is secure. As Marcello Lippi, who coached Juventus to the Champions League and Italy to the World Cup, said, "Everybody plays a pressing game now."

14

FLY ME TO THE MOON

The 1970 Mexico World Cup now stands, mythically and perhaps in fact, as the apogee of soccer. In the popular consciousness, it was a festival of attacking soccer, and the Brazil side that won the tournament—Pelé, Tostão, Gérson, Rivellino, and all—is regarded as some unmatchable paradigm, the greatest side the world has known and probably will ever know. And yet there is also an acceptance that their style of play would be impossible today; their achievement was an achievement of the old soccer, before system had taken charge.

As part of their buildup for the tournament, Brazil's squad underwent a NASA training program, the metaphorical significance of which seems to have been lost on nobody. The *Jornal do Brazil* is usually an austere newspaper, but on June 22, 1970, it made an observation that was startling in its boldness. "Brazil's victory with the ball," it said, "compares with the conquest of the moon by the Americans."

At first the comparison seems ludicrous, and yet there is something there, some grain of truth. To begin with, there is the use of abstract terms: "victory with the ball . . . conquest of the moon." The Americans beat the Soviets in the space race, and Brazil beat Italy in the World Cup final, yet neither opponent is mentioned. Rather, the triumphs, which happened less than a year apart, come to be regarded as a greater endeavor, a victory attained less against corporeal rivals than over external, nonhuman elements, as though to play soccer of that majesty were somehow a victory for all of humanity.

It is surely significant that all the most memorable moments of the 1970 tournament are essentially noncompetitive: Pelé's lob from the halfway line against Czechoslovakia did not go in; having extravagantly dummied the Uruguay goalkeeper Ladislao Mazurkiewicz in the semifinal, he then missed an open goal. Even Carlos Alberto Torres's famous goal in the final came with four minutes to go when the outcome was already decided.

This was *futebol d'arte* in a very literal sense: celebrating not events that determined the result but passages of play that transcended the immediate context of the matches of which they were part—although, that said, had Brazil not won the tournament, they may be remembered not with the fondness that they are but as counterproductive extravagances.

Whether the moon landing was the supreme technological achievement of the twentieth century, whether Brazil's 1970 World Cup success was the supreme sporting achievement is debatable, but what is sure is that no other event in either sphere had such an immediacy of impact, such a universal symbolic importance. The reason for that is simple: television. Instantly, to a viewing audience of millions across the world, Neil Armstrong's one small step and Carlos Alberto's thunderous strike became icons, destined from the moment of their happening to be reproduced again and again in a multiplicity of forms. These were the first two great global events of the telecultural age. As if to seal the symbolic link, the second moon landing happened on the same day that Pelé converted a penalty for Santos against Vasco da Gama to reach one thousand career goals.

It helped that Brazil played in vibrant yellow with shorts of cobalt blue: they were perfect for the new age of color television. Under the iridescent heat of the Mexican sun, it seemed as though this was the future: bright and brilliant. Brazil kept just one clean sheet in the tournament, but it didn't matter. Fallibility was part of their charm: there was a naivety about them that gave them a universal appeal—except, perhaps, in Argentina. "Those last minutes," Hugh McIlvanney wrote in his match report of the final,

> contained a distillation of their football, its beauty and élan and almost undiluted joy. Other teams thrill us and make us respect them. The Brazilians at their finest gave us pleasure so natural and deep as to be a vivid physical experience . . . the qualities that make football the most graceful and electric and moving of team sports were being laid before us. Brazil are proud of their own unique abilities but it was not hard to believe they were anxious to say something about the game as well as themselves. You cannot be the best in the world at a game without loving it and all of us who sat, flushed with excitement, in the stands of the Azteca sensed that we were seeing some kind of tribute.

The moon landing was the culmination of a project in which the United States had concentrated their scientific, technological, financial, and emotional resources. Once Kennedy had acknowledged the start of the space race in 1962, conquering the moon became the United States' great goal. In 1962, Brazil won their second World Cup and set about directing their resources into winning a third. By 1970, as the military government became involved in soccer, players underwent preparatory programs of previously unimaginable sophistication. "We knew we needed to do something to improve our physical condition," Gérson said, noting that was where the European nations had progressed. "In 1966 we were in good physical condition, but not as good as theirs." Each Brazilian player went to Mexico with pairs of individually fitted handmade cleats, while two weeks before departure they began living on Mexican time with a strictly controlled program of diet and sleep. Even their uniform was redesigned so as not to become weighed down by sweat. Brazil's triumph was one of imagination and spontaneity, but it was backed up by science and preparation—and by economic circumstance.

The long economic boom that lasted from the end of the Korean War in 1953 to the oil shocks of 1973—and so effectively funded the space program in the United States—created a wider market for Brazil's raw materials, leading to increased employment and wages through the fifties. That prompted a rise in consumption among the working classes and the creation of an urban middle class, but the gap between city and country widened, leading to an influx of migration and the escalating growth of favelas. Put bluntly, the conditions were perfect for soccer. As David Goldblatt notes in *The Ball Is Round*, "Too little wealth and the football infrastructure cannot be maintained. Too much wealth and the social production line of *malandros* and *pibes* cannot be maintained."

An aging side was found out at the 1966 World Cup in England, their cause not helped by lax refereeing that allowed Pelé effectively to be kicked out of games. Hugely frustrated, he retired from international soccer, only returning to the national side two years later. "I had found the violence and the lack of sportsmanship as dispiriting as the weak refereeing that had allowed it to go unchecked for so long," he explained in his autobiography. Even in Brazil, though, soccer had become increasingly violent, mirroring the trend in a society in which guerrilla groups regularly launched attacks against the military regime and met with savage reprisals in their turn.

When General Emílio Médici, the most authoritarian of Brazil's military rulers, replaced Marshal Artur da Costa e Silva as president in October 1969, soccer had an advocate in power. Dissent had been quelled, and the general, a staunch Flamengo fan, quickly realized that soccer could give him the popular legitimacy he desired. That was good news for Brazilian soccer generally, in that it ensured there would be significant investment in the 1970 campaign, but it was bad news for the national coach João Saldanha. He had been a member of the Communist Party in his youth and, with his habitual candor, he made little secret of his ideological opposition to the regime.

Saldanha had played for Botafogo and became a journalist after his playing career had come to an end. He gained the nickname *João sem Medo*— "Fearless João"—for his outspoken style, and, after regularly criticizing his former side, he was appointed their manager in 1957. He promptly led them to the Carioca championship, and although his subsequent lack of sustained success meant a return to journalism, he was given the national job in 1969. He was, Pelé said, "smart and sharp-tongued and he brought a new directness to the job of national coach." There, the refusal to play the diplomatic game that had made him so popular as a columnist proved his undoing. His demise, though, was precipitated by a tactical issue.

Saldanha's side had cruised through World Cup qualifying, totaling twenty-three goals in winning six games out of six against Colombia, Venezuela, and Paraguay in 1969. In those days he would proudly announce, "What I want is goals," but he went on a scouting trip to Europe that October and was troubled by the muscular, defensive soccer, the "brutal play and lenient referees," he saw there. "The finals," he announced, after the draw had grouped Brazil with England, Czechoslovakia, and Romania, "will develop into a brawl if we are not vigilant and the European teams with the best boxers and wrestlers will win it."

Although emotionally opposed to negativity, Saldanha recognized that a naive faith in improvisational soccer had led to Brazil's underperformances in the thirties, and he was terrified of making the same mistake again. On his return, he tried to set Brazil up to deal with increasingly physical opponents, changing personnel so as to raise the average mass of his defense by five pounds and their average height by three inches. His modifications, though, led only to confusion. "He couldn't take criticism and the relationship between him and his former colleagues in the press deteriorated," Pelé said. "He liked a drink and started to behave erratically."

Matters came to a head in March 1970 as Brazil faced back-to-back warm-up games against Argentina. He dropped Dario, a forward whose move from Atlético Mineiro to Flamengo had been engineered by Médici. That probably would not have mattered had a journalist not asked whether he were aware that Dario was a favorite of the general. "I don't choose the president's ministry," Saldanha said, "and he doesn't choose my forward line." Médici had already been offended by Saldanha's refusal to adjust his training schedule to allow the players to attend a banquet at the presidential palace, and from that moment the coach was living on borrowed time.

Defeat at home to Argentina, who had failed to qualify for the World Cup, pushed him closer to the edge, particularly when the Argentina defender Roberto Perfumo described Saldanha's side as "the poorest Brazil team I have played against." Wilson Piazza and Gérson had been swamped in the middle of the midfield, something for which Saldanha blamed Pelé, accusing him of failing to follow his orders to track back and help. This was seen as insanity: criticizing Pelé at all was bad enough, but to tell him to defend was heretical.

Saldanha's temper only made things worse. In 1967 he had twice fired a gun into the air after a confrontation with Manga, a Bangu goalkeeper he had accused of match fixing, and he reacted similarly when Yustrich, the Flamengo coach, called him a coward during a radio interview, storming into the lobby of the Rio hotel in which Yustrich was staying and brandishing a loaded handgun. Yustrich, fortunately, had gone out.

Yet somehow, amid the madness, Saldanha pulled a masterstroke in the second game, as he brought on the nineteen-year-old Clodoaldo of Santos for Piazza. He immediately gave the midfield added zest and resolve, and Pelé scored a late winner. Still, though, Saldanha thought Pelé was not doing sufficient defensive work and publicly admitted he was considering dropping him. He was promptly sacked amid accusations of emotional instability. Public sympathy was limited, and the little that remained was lost as he responded with a bizarre outburst in which he claimed that Gérson had mental problems, Pelé was too short-sighted to play, and that Emerson Leão, the reserve keeper, had short arms.

After Dino Sani and Otto Glória had both turned down the job, Mario Zagallo, the shuttling left-winger of 1958 and 1962, was hired as his replacement. He had been Saldanha's protégé at Botafogo, but, more importantly, he was seen as a safe pair of hands, unencumbered by any dangerously left-wing political beliefs. When the military government installed Captain Cláudio Coutinho to work as his fitness coach—it was he who went on the fact-finding mission to NASA—and added Admiral Jerônimo Bastos to the touring party, he raised no fuss. He did not, though, pick Dario.

In fact, Zagallo was faced with only two significant selection decisions. By the time he arrived, Pelé said, "the team was more or less chosen but there were a few changes to be made." Saldanha had based his squad around Santos and Botafogo, working on the same logic as Vittorio Pozzo and Gusztáv Sebes: players who play together on a regular basis will have a greater mutual understanding than those who don't. Zagallo, though, brought in Roberto Rivellino from Corinthians and confirmed the importance of Cruzeiro's Tostão. When critics suggested they were too similar to Gérson and Pelé, Zagallo replied, "What this team needs is great players, players who are intelligent. Let's go with that and see where it takes us."

It took them to heights that perhaps remain unsurpassed. "Our team was the best," said Gérson. "Those who saw it, saw it. Those who didn't will never see it again." The final against Italy was billed as a battle for soccer's soul, between the *futebol d'arte* of the Brazilians and the *futebol de resultados*—as the Brazilians had it—of the Italians. Art won, but never again would a side enjoy such success simply by throwing their best players on the field and asking them to play.

It was not, of course, quite as simple as that, although it is difficult to know just how central Zagallo was. Gérson, Pelé, and Carlos Alberto formed a subcommittee of senior players—the *cobras*, as they became known—and they suggested the lineup to Zagallo after a warm-up game against Atlético Mineiro had ended with them being booed off following an uninspiring 3–1 win. The back-four was relatively straightforward, with Piazza being used as the *quarto zagueiro*. So, too, was the selection of Gérson, the elegant, deep-lying playmaker—playing as what the Italians would call a *regista*. He needed protection, so Clodoaldo, untouchable after that second Argentina game, operated alongside him, a more physical, defensive presence—he may be best remembered for his part in Brazil's final goal in the final, dribbling nonchalantly through three Italians in his own half, but that was utterly uncharacteristic.

But what then? Could Pelé and Tostáo really play together? "Tostáo was not a typical centre-forward," said the historian Ivan Soter. "He was a *ponta da lança* like Pelé. So he would drop off and Pelé would become the centre-forward. It was very fluid." The danger then was that there would be nobody in the box to take advantage of their attractive approach play, but that was alleviated by Jairzinho, a rapid right-winger (he more than lived up to his nickname of *Furacáo*—"the Hurricane") with an eye for goal. His strike against England, hurtling late into the box to hammer an angled finish across Gordon Banks after Pelé had held up and then laid off Tostáo's cross was typical, and he finished the tournament as the only man to score in every game in the finals. In training, Gérson spent hours practicing clipping diagonal balls for Jairzinho to run onto, in effect calibrating his left foot, making adjustments for the thinness of the Mexican air. Jairzinho's forward surges left space behind him, but that was no problem because Carlos Alberto was an attacking right-back in the spirit of Nílton Santos. He advanced and the defense shuffled over.

That still left two major issues: who to play on the left, and where to fit Rivellino. He was another who favored the *ponta da lança* role, and there were questions about his fitness. Everaldo was a far more defensively minded full-back, which balanced the back-four, but that meant that if a flying left-winger—like Edu of Santos—was selected, damaging space could appear on that flank: just the sort of weakness Alcides Ghiggia had exploited in the 1950 final. Two problems became one solution, as Rivellino was stationed vaguely on the left, although he often drifted infield,

Brazil 4 Italy 1, World Cup final, Azteca, Mexico City, 21 June 1970

asked to provide some sort of balancing counterweight to Jairzinho's surges and encouraged to unleash his left foot whenever possible. Was it 4–4–2, was it 4–3–3, was it 4–2–4, was it even 4–5–1? It was all of them and none of them: it was just players on a field who complemented each other perfectly. In modern parlance, it would probably have been described as a 4–2–3–1, but such subtleties meant nothing then.

Italy's coach, Ferruccio Valcareggi, meanwhile, dared not play both his great playmakers, Sandro Mazzola and Gianni Rivera, at the same time and so came up with the unhappy compromise of the *staffetta*—the relay— whereby one played the first half, and the other the second. The contrast could hardly have been more pronounced.

Fittingly, Brazil even completed their victory with a goal of supreme quality. No thought from them of sitting on a 3–1 lead, no question of running the clock down. Rather, they simply kept playing and produced a goal still regularly voted the greatest ever scored, a wonderful parting gift from a wonderful team at a wonderful tournament.

It began with Clodoaldo and his unlikely dribble inside his own half, the thoughtless backheel that, forty-nine minutes earlier, had presented an equalizer to Italy apparently banished from his mind. He fed Jairzinho, now appearing on the left. As Giacinto Facchetti checked his run, the winger turned infield and laid the ball onto Pelé. He waited, and with the same languid precision that had produced goals against England and Uruguay earlier in the competition, he rolled it outside for Carlos Alberto, the full-back and captain, who charged through the space vacated by Jairzinho to flash a first-time shot into the bottom corner.

It was exuberant, it was brilliant, and it wasn't just Brazil that reacted with euphoria, but it marked the end of the age of soccer's innocence. In club soccer, in Europe at least, that era had ended much earlier, but in Mexico, the heat and the altitude combined to make pressing or any kind of systematic closing down of opponents impossible. For the last time in major competition, there was space, and Brazil had a team perfectly equipped to make the best use of it. What had appeared, as satellites beamed it in vibrant Technicolor around the globe, as the beginning of a brave new world, actually signaled the end of the old one. And there, perhaps, is the final parallel with the moon landing: the illusory nature of the bold future it seemed to herald. Just as there are no human settlements in outer space, so soccer has found itself restricted by earthly concerns.

Even Brazil seem to have accepted that 1970 was a zenith never to be repeated. It may have cost him his job, but Saldanha's assessment of how soccer was going turned out to have been broadly right—just about twelve months premature. Although the cerebral and aesthetic qualities of the Dutch sides that dominated soccer in the early seventies were undeniable, they were physically robust and far more conscious of the demands of system than the Brazil of 1970 had been.

———

Sergio Markarián watched the 1974 World Cup on television in Montevideo. He was thirty and was the general manager of a fuel distribution company, having given up his dreams of being a soccer player twelve years earlier. Seeing Uruguay humiliated by Holland, he decided he had to become a coach so his country would never again suffer in the same way. He studied for his badges, got a job as reserve-team coach at Bella Vista, eventually being promoted to oversee the first team. Struggling to make an impression in Uruguayan soccer, he moved to Paraguay in 1983. Markarián won two league championships there with Olimpia, but it was his work with the national team ahead of the 1992 Olympic Games that made him probably the single most important coach in Paraguayan history. He instilled the classic Uruguayan virtues of toughness, defensive resilience, and, vitally, *garra*, making Paraguay regular qualifiers for World Cups.

Markarián's example was extreme but he wasn't the only South American shocked by what the Dutch had done. In Europe, their performances prompted awe; in South America they provoked a desperate sense that their way of playing was no longer relevant. Having overcome Uruguay 2–0 in the first group phase, Holland then passed their way to a 4–0 victory over Argentina and a 2–0 victory over Brazil in the second: the pride of Conmebol cut down in three games by an 8–0 aggregate—not just beaten but outplayed.

Brazil seemed to have anticipated what was coming, the warnings of João Saldanha taken seriously even as he was ousted, the extravagance of the victory in Mexico accepted as a one-off tribute to the style of a decade earlier. Certainly, the Brazil of 1974 were unrecognizable as that of 1970, something for which Zagallo was widely blamed, although he was not helped by withdrawals. Pelé had retired, while Tostão, Gérson, and Clodoaldo were all injured. Still, there was a cynicism to them that had been absent four years earlier, which manifested itself most obviously against Holland. Marinho Peres knocked Johan Neeskens out cold, and Luis Pereira was eventually sent off for a horrible hack on the same player. Holland, who had always had a chip of ice in their hearts, gave as good as they got and were clearly the superior side. Brazil went on to take fourth place, but it was widely perceived that they didn't deserve it.

As Tim Vickery argued in Issue Six of the *Blizzard*, the Brazilian lurch away from *jogo bonito*, the mythical essence of its soccer, was conditioned by two things: that Brazilians, for all the talk of style and spectacle, privilege winning above all else; and the relationship of football to the military government that had come to power after a coup in 1964 and had become increasingly hardline under Médici.

With the possible exception of the Dutch, winning is vital to everybody, of course; Vickery claims, though, that Brazil's economic inequality and the importance of soccer in creating the sense that the social order can be overturned makes it particularly so there. If a skillful player jinks by a defender and leaves him in the dust, it doesn't matter what their backgrounds are or how much they earn; the pawn can become king. That is why tricks are important, why Brazilian soccer is in thrall to the ethos of the *malandro*. But it needs ultimately to be validated by victory, which is why the attendance figures of Brazilian clubs can fluctuate so wildly. "It's as if," Vickery wrote, "the supporter is saying, 'When the team is doing well it is my team. When it's struggling it's not my representative and I refuse to be humiliated by identifying myself with it.'" The way members of the side that had lost the final game to Uruguay in 1950 were ostracized speaks of the same logic. Elsewhere, once the sting of defeat and the embarrassment at their hubris had faded, there would probably have been a recognition that the team had played some extraordinary soccer and that, sometimes, soccer doesn't give the result you want, perhaps even deserve. In Brazil, though, the failure to win was cast as an endless shame, something that even three World Cup successes in the twenty years that followed couldn't entirely erase.

So, how to set about winning? How to respond to the new style of the Dutch? Tactically, what that defeat made obvious was that modern soccer had no place for the old-style midfield creator. In 1950, Brazil had had Danilo Alvim, in 1958 and 1962 Didí, and in 1970 Gérson, players who sat deep and directed the play—*registas*, as they would have been known in Italy. Rivellino, moved in off the left flank, occupied that role in 1974 but found himself hounded by a phalanx of white Dutch shirts every time he got the ball.

In Italy and Spain in the 1930s, in Argentina in the 1960s, right-wing dictatorships led to tough, muscular, pragmatic soccer. So, eventually, it was in Brazil. As Vickery points out, for all the later condemnation of military rule, there was at the time a widespread acceptance that it might be a necessary step for the country's economic development. The historian David Aarão Reis, for instance, even questions the term *military dictatorship*, pointing out that "business, political and religious leaders, entities of civil society such as the lawyers organisation and the council of bishops, the right-wing in general" all supported the coup and suggesting "civil-military dictatorship" would be a more accurate description. The economist Celso Furtado, an opponent of the regime, termed it "military-technocratic," based on alliance between the armed forces and middle-class technical specialists. A fleet of economists were brought in to tackle rising inflation and unemployment while a range of construction projects meant engineers were in demand as well. Soccer, naturally enough, also fell into the hands of the technocrats, specifically those linked to the military.

The national squad, of course, had long dabbled with science, from the dentist and psychologist of 1958 to the NASA training course in 1970, but after Mexico the support staff grew and grew. From 1970, promising goal-keepers were looked after by Raul Carlesso, a teacher of physical education in the army who later wrote a book outlining the twenty-five key attributes needed to be a goalkeeper. By 1978, Brazil were in the hands of Cláudio Coutinho, the army captain who had worked with Zagallo in 1970. He insisted his goal was "polyvalence"—which appears to have been another term for Total Football—and, as he recalled Francisco Marinho, the adventurous left-back, for the qualifying series, there seemed a measure of truth to that. By the training camp ahead of the finals, though, he had fallen back on what he knew best—physical preparation. His side were no more fluent and no less brutal than Zagallo's team of four years earlier: Coutinho's relationship with Zico was fractious, Rivellino was unfit, and they ended up playing Toninho, a right-back, on the right-wing. Somehow they blundered on to finish third.

———

In Argentina, the reaction to the defeat to the Dutch was no less extreme, but it led their soccer down a different course. It had had its great shock six-teen years earlier in Helsingborg, and the counterrevolution to the revolution that had provoked was already in full swing. As physicality and gamesmanship became unfashionable, so there awoke a nostalgia for the lost age of *la nuestra*. Three weeks after the Milan game, *El Gráfico* ran a piece claiming la Máquina would have beaten Estudiantes. A need developed for a side to take on their mantle, to reintroduce the old style. It emerged in Rosario with Newell's Old Boys under the management of Miguel Antonio Juárez. It was his assistant, though, who would become far more acclaimed: César Luis Menotti.

Menotti was an ineffably romantic figure. A pencil-thin chain-smoker with collar-length hair, graying sideburns, and the stare of an eagle, he seemed the embodiment of Argentinian bohemianism. He was left-wing, intellectual, a philosopher, and an artist and, as such, fit perfectly Argentin-ian soccer's tradition of romanticism. Although there certainly was a strand of the Argentinian game that was concerned only with the result and pre-pared to believe that the ends justified the means, there was another that saw soccer as a means of self-expression, a way for a player or a coach to live out their ethical beliefs. "I maintain that a team is above all an idea," Menotti said,

> and more than an idea it is a commitment, and more than a commitment it is the clear convictions that a coach must transmit to his players to defend that idea.
>
> So my concern is that we coaches don't arrogate to ourselves the right to remove from the spectacle the synonym of festival, in favour of a philosophical reading that cannot be sustained, which is to avoid taking risks. And in football there are risks because the only way you can avoid taking risks in any game is by not playing. . . .
>
> And to those who say that all that matters is winning, I want to warn them that someone always wins. Therefore, in a thirty-team championship, there are twenty-nine who must ask themselves: what did I leave at this club, what did I bring to my players, what possibility of growth did I give to my footballers?
>
> I start from the premise that football is efficacy. I play to win, as much or more than any egoist who thinks he's going to win by other means. I want to win the match. But I don't give in to tactical reasoning as the only way to win, rather I believe that efficacy is not divorced from beauty.

Under Menotti, beauty and efficacy went hand in hand. In 1973, he won the Metropolitano title with Huracán, playing glorious attacking soccer. "To watch them play was a delight," an editorial in *Clarín* asserted. "It filled Argentinian fields with football and after forty-five years gave the smile back to a neighbourhood with the cadence of the tango." So beguiling were they, that when they beat Rosario Central 5–0, the opposing fans applauded them. "The team was in tune with the popular taste of Argentinians," said their forward Carlos Babington. "There were *gambetas*, one-touch moves, nutmegs, *sombreros* [a trick involving lifting the ball over the opponent's head], one-twos, overlaps."

After the 1974 World Cup, Menotti was made national coach. For him, as Vickery said, soccer was "the true manifestation of the country's working class." He didn't see what Holland had done as having invalidated the traditional South American approach; it simply meant the tempo had to be raised. "The point of training," he said, "is to increase the speed at which one can be precise."

The irony, of course, was that the great validation of Argentinian soccer's ideological shift was played out in a political environment with which it could hardly have been more at odds. Isabel Perón had been deposed as president in a coup in 1976 and replaced by a right-wing military junta that savagely repressed dissents. Onganía's right-wing dictatorship had led to a ruthlessness in sports and a disregard for the woolly virtues of artistry, but the relationship between soccer and the military government of the late seventies was far more complex. In that Menotti self-consciously harked back to a lost golden age—"our victory is a tribute to the old and glorious Argentinian football," he said after the 1978 World Cup—he appealed to the conservatism of the generals, and that, plus the fact that he was successful, compensated for a worldview wholly opposed to the ideology of the junta.

The way the triumph of 1978 was exploited clearly made Menotti uncomfortable, and he addresses the issue at length in his autobiography, *Football Without Tricks*. What should he have done, he asked, "To coach teams that played badly, that based everything on tricks, that betrayed the feelings of the people? No, of course not." Instead, he argued, his soccer, being free and creative, offered a reminder of the free, creative Argentina that existed before the junta. "We are the people," he is reported to have told his players before the final. "We come from the victimised classes, and we represent the only thing that is legitimate in this country—football. We are not playing for the expensive seats full of military officers. We represent freedom, not the dictatorship."

Yet that is to idealize his side. It is notable that his belief in artistry did not extend so far as including a seventeen-year-old Diego Maradona on his squad, even though he had handed him an international debut almost a year earlier. Perhaps the comparison with Feola and his treatment of Pelé twenty years before is unfair, but it is hard to avoid. It is true that Menotti's aggressive 4–3–3 had its roots in la Máquina, but it was an update that was laced with pragmatism. At the back of midfield, Américo Gallego was a classic Argentinian number 5, while in front of him was the modern incarnation of the W attacking shape that had held sway since the late 1920s. In the front line, Leopoldo Luqué was flanked by Daniel Bertoni and Oscar Ortiz, and linking back to front were the modern incarnations of inside-forwards: to the left the goalscoring Mario Kempes, a direct number 10, and to the right Osvaldo Ardiles, the embodiment of the new style of number 8, technically gifted but inexhaustible, always fetching and carrying. Not that Gallego wore 5 or Ardiles 8; as if in acknowledgment of the modernity of the Dutch, Argentina followed their lead from four years earlier and numbered the squad in alphabetical order.

Argentina's soccer at that tournament was at times thrilling, but it had a muscularity and a directness that set it apart from *la nuestra*. Abraham went so far as to suggest a level of duplicity on the part of Menotti. "He spoke a traditional discourse," he said, "but in 1978 he shut the players in a laboratory for months, without women, eating vitamins . . . [and playing] a pace of game that when they went out on River's pitch, even the

Hungarians said looked desperate." Hungary, beaten 2–1 at El Monumental in Argentina's first game of the tournament, became so frustrated by a series of niggling fouls that Tibor Nyilasi and András Töröcsik were both sent off for retaliation in the final three minutes—almost the only thing that united the two great rivals in their careers. "Menotti prepared the players physically with technical advances," Abraham went on, "but his discourse was this: the important thing is to feel the ball, to pass it, to knead it, to dribble with it."

Given the developments in defensive organization and physiological preparation, perhaps a certain level of compromise between the scientific and the artistic is only realistic, but it can hardly be denied that Argentina's success came with a measure of chicanery. Most notoriously, there was the second-phase game against Peru. Moronic scheduling meant Argentina went into that match knowing that they needed to win by three, while scoring at least four, to make it to the final. They did that, and more, winning 6–0, but the result has always been tainted by suspicion.

In 1986, the *Sunday Times* cited an anonymous civil servant claiming that the Argentinian government shipped thirty-five thousand tons of grain—and possibly some arms—to Peru and that the Argentinian central bank released $50 million of frozen Peruvian assets. But proof is hard to come by, and the fact that the story was published on the day England met Argentina in the World Cup quarterfinal does not suggest meticulously researched, impartial journalism.

It is doubtful that anybody watching the video of the game with no knowledge of context would see anything untoward. Juan José Muñante hit the post for Peru early on, while their goalkeeper, Ramón Quiroga, who was born in Argentina and would later take much of the blame, made a number of scrambling saves. If the game really had been fixed, it looked as though nobody had told Peru until midway through the first half. Certainly Peru wilted after Alberto Tarantini's diving header made it 2–0 just before half-time, but that is hardly surprising. They were already out of the tournament, there were thirty-seven thousand spectators rammed into the Arroyito, creating a fearsome atmosphere, and Argentina's passing was at times sensational. The Kempes volley that made it 3–0 and Luqué's late sixth both followed bursts of magnificent soccer.

Where there was clear malpractice—*viveza*, gamesmanship, cheating, whatever term is used—was ahead of the final against Holland. The bus carrying the Dutch team took a deliberately circuitous route from their hotel to the stadium, and fans were allowed to crowd around it, hammering on the windows, chanting, and generally being intimidating. Argentina then delayed their arrival on the field before kickoff, leaving Holland standing around, exposed to the full fury of the crowd, and when they finally did

Argentina 2 Holland 1, World Cup final, El Monumental, Buenos Aires, 25 June 1978

emerge, they protested about the cast on René van der Kerkhof's arm. Given that he had been wearing it without controversy all tournament, their only purpose could have been to unsettle their opponents. The refereeing of the Italian Sergio Gonella was weak, and Argentina seemed to benefit from a number of decisions, but, after Rob Rensenbrink's last-minute effort had come back off the post, extra-time goals from Kempes and Daniel Bertoni gave them the title.

Victory for Argentina, victory for the junta, victory for Menotti, and, slightly tarnished, slightly modified for the modern age, victory for the ideals of *la nuestra*.

Not until 1982 did Brazil really cut loose again, perhaps significantly amid the atrocious heat of Spain. Falcão only started Brazil's opening game, against the USSR, because Toninho Cerezo was suspended, but he played so well he had to be retained, leaving their coach, Telê Santana, to follow Zagallo's policy from 1970 and just let his players get on with it. With Zico and Socrates also in the side, Brazil had four vastly talented creative midfielders but no wide players apart from Eder. So again a deficiency was made a virtue as Cerezo and Falcão—both *registas*, deep-lying playmakers—sat behind Zico and Socrates—the *trequartistas*—while Eder was deployed as an auxiliary center-forward, playing off the lumbering Serginho, who would surely never have been anywhere near the side had either Reinaldo or Careca been fit.

The formation was thus a 4–2–2–2, with a strong central column flanked by two marauding full-backs in Leandro and Júnior. In a European context, they would have been perceived as lacking width, but this was a team of such fluency and poise in possession that they created width with their movement. It was a system that never spread—the Brazilian coach Vanderlei Luxemburgo's attempts to institute what he called "the magic quadrilateral" at Real Madrid in 2005 failed amid general bewilderment—but it seemed to suit the Brazilian mentality, the two deep-lying midfielders (by 1994, when Dunga and Mauro Silva occupied the positions, they would be bona fide holding players) providing a platform for four out-and-out attacking players—two center-forwards and two *trequartistas*—while still allowing the full-backs to tear up and down the flanks as they had been doing in Brazil since the days of Nílton Santos.

The Brazil of 1982 produced the most exhilarating soccer the World Cup had known since 1970. They beat the USSR 2–1, swatted aside Scotland 4–1, and New Zealand 4–0, playing an effortless, fluid game full of deliciously angled passes and fearsome long-range shooting. In the second

Italy 3 Brazil 2, World Cup second group phase, Sarrià, Barcelona, 5 July 1982

group phase, they comfortably beat the reigning world champions, Argentina, leaving them needing just a draw against Italy to reach the semifinals. It was considered a formality.

Italy were in the phase of *il gioco all'Italiana* rather than out-and-out *catenaccio*, but they were still notably defensive. Just as the game in the Azteca in 1970, their meeting with Brazil in the Estadí de Sarría was seen as an allegory. To try to alleviate the shortfall in midfield caused by Herrera's version of *catenaccio*, Italian soccer had followed the route of Dutch and German soccer, by making the *libero* a far more rounded player—a converted inside-forward such as Pierluigi Cera or Gaetano Scirea rather than a converted full-back like Ivano Blason or Armando Picchi—capable of stepping out from the back and making an extra midfielder when his side had possession.

Italy began the tournament slowly, progressing through the first group—in which they drew all three of their games—only by virtue of having scored one goal more than Cameroon, who also drew all three of their matches. Paolo Rossi, returning after a ban for his involvement in a match-fixing scandal, looked far from his best, but a 2–1 win over Argentina gave them belief and raised doubts among the Brazilians. Waldir Peres, the latest in a long line of hapless Brazilian goalkeepers, admitted before the game that his great fear was that Rossi would suddenly spring into life. He proved a far better mystic than he was goalkeeper.

Was it the greatest World Cup game ever? Probably, although Hungary's 1954 victory over Uruguay will always have its devotees. Certainly it had an epic feel, something enhanced by overcrowding, as far more than the official forty-four thousand squeezed in. Had Brazil scored an early goal, Italy could easily have wilted, their system and their mentality not equipped for chasing a game, but it was the Italians who took a fifth-minute lead, as Bruno Conti, having been allowed to advance almost forty yards down the right, cut infield and released the attacking left-back Antonio Cabrini, who crossed for Rossi to justify the faith of his manager, Enzo Bearzot, with a fine header.

And so was set in motion the pattern for the game: Brazilian attacking and Italian resistance. Within seven minutes, it was level, as Socrates played a one-two with Zico and advanced to drive the ball in at Dino Zoff's near post. Then surely, it seemed, Brazil would kick on to win. Perhaps they would have, had it not been for a dreadful error from Cerezo after twenty-five minutes, casually knocking a square pass in the vague direction of Júnior. Rossi, suddenly a poacher again, stole in and beat Waldir. This time the lead lasted, and Brazil became increasingly edgy. Rossi, with the chance to make it 3–1 midway through the second half, side-footed wide, and when, two minutes later, Brazil equalized through Falcão's ferocious drive, it looked once again as though they would prevail.

Perhaps, needing only a draw to progress, they should have tightened up and held what they had, but that was not the Brazilian way. They kept attacking and paid the price. A Conti corner was half cleared, Marco Tardelli half hit his shot from the edge of the box, and Rossi, played onside by a dozing Júnior, hooked the ball past Waldir. It was, as Glanville said, "the game in which Brazil's glorious midfield, put finally to the test, could not make up for the deficiencies behind and in front of it."

It was a game, moreover, that lay on a fault line of history and, unlike in 1970, soccer followed the victors, in style if not in formation. Zico called it "the day that football died," but that is to percolate everything through the consciousness of a particularly romantic Brazilian. Rather, it was the day that a certain naivety in soccer died; it was the day after which it was no longer possible simply to pick the best players and allow them to get on with it; it was the day that system won. There was still a place for great individual attacking talents, but they had to be incorporated into something knowing; they had to be protected and covered for.

Santana's style lived on to 1986, when Brazil were beaten on penalties after a memorable quarterfinal by a magnificent French team based around their *carré magique* midfield of Luis Fernández, Alain Giresse, Jean Tigana, and Michel Platini. But by 1990, under Sebastião Lazaroni, Brazil had added an extra center-back and played a 3–5–2, a system that suited their wing-backs and pretty much nobody else. Statistics had taken over from the old instincts.

A study carried out by the physical preparation specialist Murici Sant'anna claimed that the ground covered by players doubled between the midseventies and the midnineties. The logic seemed incontrovertible: a Brazilian midfield based on elaboration and passing had been overwhelmed by Dutch pressing in 1974, so two decades later, when pressing was even more ferocious, there was no sense going back. The physical development of players meant there was less time and space and more contact. This, of course, was an age-old complaint, but that didn't invalidate the conclusion: Brazilian players had to be as robust and muscular as Europeans, and if that meant a certain flair and technical finesses was lost, that was a necessary price of progress. In 1958, Brazil had had Didí and Zito in the middle of midfield; by 2010 they had Gilberto Silva and Felipe Melo.

For a time, the theory worked: between 1994 and 2002, Brazil played in three successive World Cup finals, winning two of them, and they won four of the five Copas América held between 1997 and 2007 (all of them on foreign soil—something they'd never previously achieved). But those successes never seemed to prompt quite the same joy or admiration as the victories of 1958 to 1970. Brazilian soccer, Zizinho wrote in his autobiography in 1985, "has given the central midfielder, the man who has 70% of his team's possession in his hands, the specific function of destroying, when it should be to set up the play." The emphasis has swung even more to destructiveness since.

Nereo Rocco, one of the pioneers of
catenaccio (PA Photos)

Helenio Herrera, the grand wizard of
catenaccio (PA Photos)

Ronnie Simpson claims a cross as Celtic beat Inter in the 1967 European Cup final
(Getty Images)

César Luis Menotti, who won the World Cup with his reinterpretation of *la nuestra* . . . (*Getty Images*)

. . . and his ideological opposite, Carlos Bilardo, who won the World Cup after devising 3–5–2 (*PA Photos*)

Rinus Michels on the
Dutch bench at the
1974 World Cup . . .
and Johan Cruyff, with
whom he developed
Total Football (both
pics © *Getty Images*)

The two schools of Soviet football, Eduard Malofeev (left) and Valeriy Lobanovskyi (*Igor Utkin*)

Sacha Prokopenko: playboy and player (both pics © *Dinamo Sports Society*)

Graham Taylor, who introduced pressing to the English game, and Elton John, his chairman at Watford (*Getty Images*)

Arrigo Sacchi makes a point to Marco van Basten (*PA Photos*)

Pelé heads home the opener in the 1970 World Cup final (*Getty Images*)

Mario Zagallo, the coach who oversaw the greatest display of football's pre-systemic age (*Getty Images*)

The last of the old-style play makers, Juan Román Riquelme . . . (*Rex Pictures*)

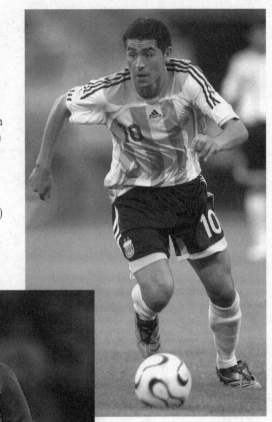

. . . and Luka Modri, the first of the new (*PA Photos*)

15

THE ENGLISH PRAGMATISM (2)

As so often, progress began with defeat. Chris Lawler's goal in a 2–1 loss in the first leg in the Marakana had given Liverpool hope of overcoming Crvena Zvezda of Belgrade in the second leg and reaching the quarterfinal of the 1973–1974 European Cup. But at Anfield, Zvezda, under the guidance of Miljan Miljanić, played a brilliant counterattacking game and struck twice on the break through Vojin Lazarević and Slobodan Janković to complete a 4–2 aggregate win.

The following day, November 7, 1973, in a cramped, windowless room just off the corridor leading to the Anfield locker room, six men set in motion the stylistic shift that led English clubs to dominate Europe in the late seventies and early eighties. The boot-room, as history would know it, was not an obvious place to plot a revolution. It was small and shabbily carpeted, hung on one side with hooks for players' cleats and decorated with team photographs and topless calendars. Joe Fagan, the first-team coach under Bill Shankly, had begun the tradition of postgame discussions there, stocking the room with crates of beer supplied by the chairman of Guinness Exports, whose works team he had once run in nearby Runcorn. Initially he met with only Bob Paisley, in those days the team's physiotherapist, but gradually other members of the club's backroom staff began to drop in. "You got a more wide-ranging discussion in the boot-room than the boardroom," Paisley said. "What went on was kept within those four walls. There was a certain mystique about the place."

Managers of opposing teams willing to offer information and opinions about players were invited, and even Elton John visited during his time as Watford chairman. When offered a drink, Anfield legend has it, he asked for a pink gin; he was given a beer. Gradually the boot-room grew in importance, becoming effectively an archive where coaches could refer to books in which were logged details of training, tactics, and matches. In *Winners and Losers: The Business Strategy of Football*, the economist Stefan Szymanski and the business consultant Tim Kuypers claimed Liverpool's success in the seventies and eighties was a result of their organizational structure, of which the boot-room was a key part. "The boot-room," they wrote, "appears to have been some kind of database for the club, not merely of facts and figures, but a record of the club's spirit, its attitudes and its philosophy."

In November 1973, though, the greater part of that success was still to come, and Liverpool seemed to have reached an impasse. Zvezda, European Cup semifinalists in 1970, were a useful side, of that there was no question, but the manner of their victory seemed to point to a more essential deficiency than the vagaries of form. So a meeting was convened, Shankly, Fagan, and Paisley were joined in the boot-room by Ronnie Moran, the reserve team coach, by Tom Saunders, the head of youth development, and by the chief coach, Reuben Bennett, a dour Scottish disciplinarian famed for his habit of telling injured players to rub away the pain with a wire brush or a kipper.

They weren't crisis talks exactly, but the issues they discussed were fundamental: just why did Liverpool, imperious domestically, look so vulnerable in Europe? Despite the background of English underachievement, it is a mark of Shankly's perfectionism that a flaw was perceived at all. After all, Liverpool had won the UEFA Cup the previous season, beating Borussia Mönchengladbach 3–2 on aggregate in the final. In the years before that success, though, Liverpool had gone out of European competition to the likes of Ferencváros, Athletic of Bilbao, and Vitória de Setúbal—none of them complete minnows, but none of them the cream of Europe, either.

If the UEFA Cup triumph suggested Liverpool had found a solution, the defeat to Zvezda emphatically disabused them. "They are a good side," Shankly said, "even though our fans would not pay to watch the football they play." The way they were prepared to hold possession and frustrate their opponents, though, taught Liverpool an important lesson. "We realised it was no use winning the ball if you finished up on your backside," said Paisley. "The top Europeans showed us how to break out of defence effectively. The pace of their movement was dictated by their first pass. We had to learn how to be patient like that and think about the next two or three moves when we had the ball."

The days of the old-fashioned stopper center-half, the boot-room decided, were over: it was necessary to have defenders who could play. Larry Lloyd, exactly the kind of central defender they had declared extinct (although he would later enjoy an unlikely renaissance at Nottingham Forest), then ruptured a hamstring, and Phil Thompson, originally a midfielder, was pushed back to partner Emlyn Hughes at the heart of the defense. "The Europeans showed that building from the back is the only way to play," Shankly explained.

It started in Europe and we adapted it into our game at Liverpool where our system had always been a collective one. But when Phil Thompson came in to partner Hughes it became more fluid and perhaps not as easy to identify. This set the pattern which was followed by Thompson and [Alan] Hansen in later years.

We realised at Liverpool that you can't score a goal every time you get the ball. And we learned this from Europe, from the Latin people. When they play the ball from the back they play in little groups. The pattern of the opposition changes as they change. This leaves room for players like Ray Kennedy and Terry McDermott, who both played for Liverpool after I left, to sneak in for the final pass. So it's cat and mouse for a while waiting for the opening to appear before the final ball is let loose. It's simple and it's effective. . . . It's also taken the spectators time to adjust to it.

Shankly was no great tactician—he tended to leave that side of the game to Paisley and was so bored when he did attend a weeklong coaching course at Lilleshall that he left on the Tuesday—but from the moment of his arrival at Liverpool, he had a clear sense of the general style he wanted to play. "Shankly," said a piece in the *Liverpool Echo* from December 1959, "is a disciple of the game as it is played by the continentals. The man out of possession, he believes, is just as important as the man with the ball at his feet. Continental football is not the lazy man's way of playing soccer. Shankly will aim at incisive forward moves by which continentals streak through a defence when it is "closed up" by British standards. He will make his players learn to kill a ball and move it all in the same action . . . he will make them practise complete mastery of the ball."

That might have been overstating it, but Shankly certainly had a belief in the value of control almost as profound as Jimmy Hogan's. At the Melwood training ground, he set up four boards to form a square. A player would stand in the middle and would be called upon either to strike first time or to trap balls flung at him from the four corners.

"Above all," Shankly said,

the main aim is that everyone can control a ball and do the basic things in football. It's control and pass . . . control and pass . . . all the time. At the back you're looking for someone who can control the ball instantly and give a forward pass. It gives them more space and time to breathe. If you delay, the opposition have all run back behind the ball. It's a very simplified affair and, of course, very economical.

At Liverpool we don't have anyone running into no man's land, running from their own half with the ball into the opposition half. That's not encouraged at all. That's nonsense. If you get a ball in the Liverpool team you want options, you want choices . . . you want at least two people to pass to, maybe three, maybe more. . . . Get the ball, give an early pass, then it goes from me to someone else and it switches around again. You might not be getting very far, but the pattern of the opposition is changing. Finally, somebody will sneak in.

The side that won the championship in 1964 played an orthodox W-M, but Shankly was prepared to make changes. The following season, Liverpool faced Anderlecht in the second round of the European Cup, shortly after England had played a friendly against a Belgium side featuring seven Anderlecht players. Shankly was at Wembley to see the game and recognized the attacking threat posed by the likes of Paul van Himst and Jef Jurion. It was his decision to switch to red shorts for the game—the first time Liverpool had worn all red—that caught most of the attention, but just as significant was his ploy of withdrawing an inside-forward to use Tommy Smith as an auxiliary central defender; an early example of an English club side using four at the back.

That suggested a flexibility, an awareness that the English way wasn't the only way, but Paisley admitted, "Our approach was a bit frantic. We treated every match like a war. The strength of British football lay in our challenge for the ball, but the continentals took that away from us by learning how to intercept." It was that fault that the November revolution of 1973 corrected, and, after Paisley had replaced Shankly in 1974, Liverpool would come to be defined by their patient passing approach. It took them to four European Cups between 1977 and 1984, and it was with a similar approach that Nottingham Forest under Brian Clough lifted their two European Cups.

Clough had been a prolific striker for Middlesbrough and Sunderland—still the fastest player to 250 goals in the English leagues—but his career was effectively ended by a knee injury sustained on Boxing Day 1962. He drifted towards alcoholism during his convalescence but, after impressing at lowly Hartlepools United, was appointed manager of Derby County, then in the Second Division, in 1967. He and his assistant, Peter Taylor, led them to promotion in his second season and then, astonishingly, to the league title in 1972 and the European Cup semifinal a year later.

A year later, though, they were gone, as Clough, who chafed against authority throughout his career, fell out with the chairman Sam Longson and resigned. He returned at Brighton, then in the Fourth Division, before a disastrous forty-four-day stint replacing his great rival Don Revie at Leeds. Rejected by players he had spent most of his time at Derby abusing, he retreated and stayed out of soccer for more than a year before taking over at Nottingham Forest. Like Derby, Forest was a provincial side in the second

Liverpool 3 Borussia Mönchengladbach 1, Olimpico, Roma, 25 May 1977

Liverpool

Clemence

Neal Smith Hughes Jones

Case McDermott Callaghan R Kennedy

Heighway Keegan

Heynckes Stielike Simonsen

Wittkamp Wimmer Schäffer

Wohlers Vogts Klinkhammer

Bonhof

Borussia Mönchengladbach

Kneib

flight that had never won the league. Clough took them to promotion in his second season and won the league in his third. Even more astonishingly, they won the European Cup the next season and retained it a year after that. Forest remain the only club to have won the European title more often than their domestic league.

Even in the eighties, as the money ran out, Clough kept Forest as one of the top half dozen sides in the country, noted for their neat, patient, passing soccer. "A team," he insisted, "blossoms only when it has the ball. Flowers need the rain—it's a vital ingredient. Common sense tells you that the main ingredient in football is the ball itself." Only when alcoholism, a shadow lurking throughout his managerial career, fully took hold did his gifts leave him. Forest was relegated in his final season in management, the first season of the Premier League, 1992–1993, almost as though the new world had no place for such a maverick.

Clough is one of only four managers to have won the English league title with two different sides (Tom Watson with Sunderland and Liverpool, Herbert Chapman with Huddersfield Town and Arsenal, and Kenny Dalglish with Liverpool and Blackburn Rovers being the others), and it's surely indicative of his genius that those sides were in the second flight when he took them over and have since returned to that level: he made provincial teams champions, at times it seemed, by force of personality alone. He was one of the first managers to recognize the power of the media and to manipulate it accordingly, his Teesside drawl making him a gift for impressionists and satirists. He reveled in the attention, polishing his one-liners and delivering them with devastating timing, always inflating his own greatness. "Rome wasn't built in a day," he once said, "but then I wasn't on that particular job."

He was the first celebrity manager. The public adored the bumptiousness and the wisecracks, but something darker lay behind the mask. In time, as his drinking increased, mask and face fused, and Clough the man became "Clough" the personality, relying on self-caricature to keep the demons at bay. "If you knew him personally as well as professionally, you found a contradictory character," the *Nottingham Evening Post* journalist Duncan Hamilton, who had worked with Clough for several years, wrote in the supplement the newspaper produced on Clough's retirement. "A Chinese box of a man. There was the public persona determined to keep his home life private. The extrovert, with a sense of theatre bordering on pure ham, who basically disliked performing for a crowd. He could be an awkward cuss, curmudgeonly, unforgiving, bombastic, choleric and unnecessarily abrasive. Or he could be compassionate, emollient, charming, over-generous and go out of his way to be no bother to anyone. . . . On occasions he could be all of these within the same hour."

The only constant, at least until the very end, was the brilliance of his soccer mind. Clough was always scornful of what he termed "Subbuteo men being pushed around a felt pitch," but to suggest he ignored tactics completely is ludicrous. Rather, he was a master strategist, highly adept at acquiring players whose abilities complemented each other to the extent that sophisticated individual instruction was unnecessary. Proof of his effectiveness is how many players who looked like world-beaters at Forest only to flop after being traded. Not that Clough would ever have discussed that. Standing firmly in the bluff tradition of English anti-intellectualism—something fueled by his own failure to pass the 11+ exam and so secure a place in the local grammar school—it suited his self-image to scoff at those who sought to explain the game in anything but the simplest terms. Revie, who had been born a few miles from Clough in Middlesbrough nine years earlier, researched opponents rigorously, producing dossiers for his players. To Clough, that was typical of the man: too clever by half, spoiling the simple beauty of the game by his suspicious overcomplications.

His system was simple and barely changed over time. "Telling them how to play," Taylor said of their Derby team, "took no time. To [the target-man center-forward John] O'Hare it was: 'Hold the ball no matter how hard they whack you.' To [the goalscorer Kevin] Hector: 'Watch O'Hare. You've got to be ready when he slips that ball to you.' And to [the winger Alan] Hinton we didn't say any more than: 'Stay wide.'" The midfielder Alan Durban recalled being told he was responsible for his area of the field, advice that, in itself, was enough to make him sit in and protect the right-back rather than charging all over the field looking for glory.

At Forest, John Robertson, a slow but gifted winger Clough had lifted from the scrapheap, took the Hinton role, creating the play from the left flank, with Gary Birtles holding the ball up for Tony Woodcock or Trevor Francis. Robertson's lack of mobility was compensated for by Martin O'Neill on the right of midfield, who tucked in to allow the two central midfielders—typically John McGovern and Ian Bowyer—to shuffle left to cover. Width on the right was then provided by the overlapping full-back, Viv Anderson.

For all he eschewed tactics, Clough when necessary would offer individual instructions to players, as he did for the second leg of the 1978–1979 European Cup first round game away to Liverpool in which Forest protected a 2–0 first-leg lead. "Minutes before we left the visitors' dressing-room at Anfield, the gaffer casually told me that I would be playing as an extra right-back, tucked in just in front of Viv Anderson," Archie Gemmill, another of Clough's midfielders, explained in his autobiography. "The Boss explained quickly that Steve Heighway and Ray Kennedy both saw a lot of the ball and loved attacking down Liverpool's left flank, so he wanted Viv and me to keep a tight grip of things in that area." It was simple and minimalist, rooted in Clough's basic theory that players, having been strategically selected to blend together, should broadly be given responsibility. The basic strategy, though, remained always the same: 4–4–2 with one winger wide and advanced and the other withdrawn and tucked in, with ball retention as the priority.

Although Liverpool and Forest espoused a possession-based passing game, there was at the same time a strand of English soccer that went in the opposite direction, favoring a high-octane style readily dismissed as kick and rush. It was the basis of the rise of Watford and Wimbledon, small clubs who learned to punch above their weight, but, damagingly, it became orthodoxy at the Football Association. When Charles Hughes became technical director of the FA, English soccer was placed into the hands of a fundamentalist, a man who, Brian Glanville claimed, "poisoned the wells of English football."

Hughes still has plenty of apologists, but even if Glanville's assessment is correct, the achievements of Watford and Wimbledon should not be decried—or at least, not on the grounds of directness alone. In English soccer, the seventies is remembered as the age of the mavericks, of the likes of Alan Hudson, Frank Worthington, and Stan Bowles, individuals who did not fit into the increasingly systematized schema that had become the vogue since Ramsey's success in the World Cup. The historically more significant feature of the decade, though, was the introduction of pressing.

It came from a surprising source: a young manager who began his career with Lincoln City and then brought, given the resources available to him, staggering success to Watford: Graham Taylor. England's failure to qualify for the World Cup in 1994 and the vilification that followed has rather sullied his reputation, but in the late seventies he was the most radical coach in the country. There were those who dismissed him as a long-ball merchant, but as he, Stan Cullis, and a host of managers stretching back to Herbert Chapman have pointed out, it is simply impossible for a team to be successful if all they are doing is aimlessly booting the ball forwards. "When," as Taylor asked, "does a long pass become a long ball?"

Many coaches have prospered after less than stellar playing careers—indeed, for the truly revolutionary, it appears almost a prerequisite—but Taylor seems to have known almost from the start that his future lay in the coaching rather than the playing side of the game. "The intention had been to stay on at school, do A-levels and become a teacher," he said. "I left after a year of sixth form to become a footballer but I was still interested enough in my education to do a coaching badge, so I was qualified by the time I was twenty-one. I was always reading and looking for ideas." One of the ideas he seized upon was pressing, the possibilities of which became clear to him after he had read a series of articles about Viktor Maslov in the Football Association's in-house coaching magazine.

Taylor spent four years at Grimsby Town before moving on to Lincoln City. He became a fully qualified FA coach at twenty-seven—the youngest man to do so—and, after a hip injury curtailed his playing career, was twenty-eight when he took over as manager in 1972. Four years later, Taylor led Lincoln to the Fourth Division title, setting new records for most points, most wins, and fewest defeats as he did so.

It was after Elton John appointed him as manager of Watford in 1977, though, that the real breakthrough came. Taylor was offered a five-year contract, but, before agreeing to it, he asked his chairman what he was expected to achieve in that time. "Watford were in the Fourth Division," Taylor said, "and they'd only spent three years in their history in the second flight, so I thought he'd say maybe he wanted Second Division football. He said he wanted us playing in Europe. Here was a singer at the top of his career offering me a five-year contract and asking me to get Watford into Europe—and five years later we were."

Even by the volatile standards of the seventies, Watford's rise was extraordinary. They were promoted in 1978, again in 1979, and then again in 1982. The following season they finished second in the First Division and, the year after that, lost in the FA Cup final. Taylor admits the way his side played had its limitations but makes no apology for it. "Our style was based on pressing the ball wherever it was," he explained.

> So even if the opposition right-back had the ball deep in his own half, we still pressed him. We played high-tempo football, which meant we had to be extremely fit. When the score's 0–0 and there are three or four minutes to go, what do players do? They get the ball forwards. My view is that players then are going looking for the ball. But if they can do that in the last few minutes, why can't they do that from the start? With the very fit side we had, that's what we tried to do. We were always attacking; I knew we couldn't defend our way into Europe.

High-scoring games became the norm: in successive seasons, Watford drew 4–4 at home to Everton and lost to them 5–4. They twice won 5–3 against Notts County and beat Sunderland 8–0. In the 1982–1983 season, they lost 6–1 at Norwich and went down 7–3 in the League Cup to Nottingham Forest. In the last three games of 1984–1985, they beat Tottenham and Manchester United 5–1 then lost 4–3 at Liverpool. It was mad, harum-scarum stuff, but, broadly speaking, it worked. Between 1982–1983 and 1986–1987, after which Taylor left for Aston Villa, Watford

Everton 2 Watford 0, FA Cup final, Wembley, London, 19 May 1984

never finished lower than twelfth, a remarkable achievement for a club of their stature.

The shape mattered less than the method. Although 4–4–2 was the default, with full-backs such as Wilf Rostron and David Bardsley pushing on and with bona fide wingers like Nigel Callaghan and John Barnes playing high up the field, the formation could come to resemble the 4–2–4 of the 1958 Brazilians, and there were times in the 1982–1983 season when they played a 3–4–3. "Because we kept going forwards, the opposition kept going back," Taylor said. "The wide midfielders either had to follow them and get pinned back, or leave them. We kept on posing questions. As you go higher, you keep expecting teams to work out how to cope, but often they didn't."

Aesthetes were appalled, but Taylor attributed much of the outrage to ignorance and snobbery. "A lot of people who complained about long balls just looked at the club and the player," he said. "If Glenn Hoddle played one it was a long pass, but if Ian Bolton did it, it was a long ball because he played for Watford and was a centre-back who sometimes played in midfield who nobody had heard of. Hoddle was a much better player, but for accuracy in his long passing I'd take Bolton every time."

For the purist, things got even worse. Wimbledon's apologists speak of their rise as a fairy tale, but it was one noticeably lacking in magic. Their story, Stephen Crabtree wrote in *The Dons—the Amazing Journey* "would seem far-fetched if it appeared in the pages of *Roy of the Rovers . . .* achieved despite little financial backing, pathetic support, a non-league standard ground and unknown players." Perhaps at first it was far-fetched, as they were elected to the league in 1977 and, under Dario Gradi, who would become renowned for the passing soccer of his Crewe sides, won promotion to the Third Division. They were promptly relegated, Gradi left for Crystal Palace in February 1981, and then, under their new manager Dave Bassett, they were promoted again. And immediately relegated. That next season in the Fourth Division, though, proved a watershed. They started promisingly, but, as results fell away in the November, Bassett changed his approach. "We began the season using a sweeper at the back which worked well," Bassett said that February, "but now we've changed to get the ball up to the front very fast. It suits the team."

Of claims that it was awful to watch, Bassett was dismissive. "It depends on what you mean by attractive," he said. "There is more goalmouth incident for our supporters to enjoy in our games than lots of other teams I've seen this season. Call it what you like. We're here to win games and win promotion."

"Goalmouth incident," it turns out, is the last resort of coaches seeking to excuse mechanically unappealing soccer. If it had just been about uncomplicated forward passing, Wimbledon would have been forgiven, but, right from the start, there was an ugly element to their play. The week after a 3–1 away win at Stockport County, the Stockport program was moved to ask "why they had to resort to some untidy tackling and time-wasting tactics. . . . There seems to be little chance that anyone will stop them from achieving their objective, which appears to be promotion at all costs."

Successful as they were, though, the crowds stayed away. "We have tried everything by serving up good football, but the apathy of Wimbledon and the surrounding area is incredible," said Bassett. But of course they hadn't served up good soccer; they'd served up winning soccer, and the two are not necessarily the same thing. Perhaps his despair was self-justificatory: If fans weren't going to turn up anyway, then why not play grim, flairless antifootball? There may have been goals, but this was emotionally empty soccer stripped of beauty.

It was awful to watch, but Wimbledon soared through the divisions, brushing aside bemused opponents as they did so. "It's like schoolboys all chasing after the ball all at the same time," said the Grimsby Town goalkeeper Nigel Batch after a 1–1 draw at Plough Lane in 1984. It was just like Watford all over again, only worse, as John Vinicombe of the *Brighton Evening Argus* made clear, describing them as "a poor man's Watford when four front men adopt a cavalry charge formation in pursuit of high passes slung from behind."

They finished sixth in the First Division in 1987 and, after Bobby Gould replaced Dave Bassett, won the FA Cup the following year. "Wimbledon don't play," moaned the Coventry City manager, George Curtis. "As soon as they get it they just hit it." That is perhaps a touch unfair, for they were at least hitting balls towards John Fashanu, a brash and ungainly but effective target man, while Dennis Wise, for all his faults, had talent, but they won few admirers. They reveled in their unfashionability, making much of their initiation rites—which consisted largely of destroying suits—and delighting in the brute physicality of their play. A key element in the victory over Liverpool at Wembley in 1988, most of their players claimed, was Vinnie Jones's crunching foul on Steve McMahon in the first minute: after that, Liverpool were intimidated.

Like all bristling outsiders, Wimbledon put their unpopularity down to the "snootiness"—Crabtree uses the word repeatedly—of the establishment, but the attendance figures told their own story. This was soccer nobody wanted to watch. Budget perhaps dictated their style, but it did not excuse the thuggery that lay just below the surface. This wasn't just pragmatic; it was nihilistic.

Taylor, by contrast, was simply being practical. He accepted his system had its limitations and admits that at every stage he expected his side to be found out. When he got to Aston Villa and had a viable budget, although his style remained direct, there was a refinement to it. Tony Daley may have been selected for the Wimbledon side of the time, but it is hard to imagine that a player as cultured as Gordon Cowans would have done so.

It wasn't until his first season of European competition with Watford that Taylor began to find opponents coming up with the sort of solutions to his direct style that he had expected to encounter far earlier. "We were playing sides who were prepared to sit deep, play short passes, hold the ball and pick us off, who had fans who weren't demanding they thump the ball forward," he explained. They overturned a 3–1 first-leg deficit with a 3–0 second-leg victory over Kaiserslautern at Vicarage Road in the first round of the UEFA Cup and edged by Levski Sofia in the second round, but they were comprehensively outplayed by Sparta Prague in the third round, losing 7–2 on aggregate. "It was men against boys," Taylor said. "When you gave the ball away, they didn't give it back to you."

And there, precisely, is the problem with a direct style based on pressing. It's all well and good until you come up against a team good enough technically to be able to keep possession even when under pressure. And, as Taylor points out, when climatic conditions make it impossible to maintain a high tempo and render constant pressing impossible, its deficiencies become even more evident. That, of course, goes some way to explaining England's persistent underachievement in major tournaments, which are almost invariably staged in conditions far hotter than English players are used to at home.

Taylor, in his quest to broaden his knowledge, spoke at length to both Stan Cullis and his captain in the Wolves side of the fifties, Billy Wright. Their influence on his thinking is clear and undisputed, but Taylor also came—inaccurately—to be associated with Charles Hughes. He rejects any notion that he was influenced by Hughes and suggests that if anything the influence, stemming from his brief time as England Under-18 coach while Hughes was director of youth coaching, was the other way round. And this is where the interconnections among Taylor, Hughes, and Charles Reep get complicated.

Hughes's first two books, *Football: Tactics and Teamwork*, published in 1973, and *Soccer Tactics and Skills*, published in 1980, are both practical manuals, giving guidance, for instance, on how to deal with near-post corners or how close a player should get to an opponent he is closing down. They are general works with similar content, although the second is slightly more targeted at the individual. Neither evangelizes a particular philosophy of play: they are perhaps a touch overpragmatic, but they are largely unobjectionable.

And then, in 1981—or possibly 1982—Taylor set up a meeting between Hughes and Reep at his house because, if a letter Reep wrote to the

Norwegian coach Egil Olsen in 1993 is to be believed, Hughes wanted his secretary, Mandy Primus, trained in his shorthand techniques. Reep was initially happy to help, but he became suspicious when Hughes published an article in which he hinted that he and Reep worked together. Worse, Reep claimed in that letter—although it is hard to be sure of the veracity of this claim—that Hughes also set out some of the secrets of Watford's style of play, which neither Reep nor Watford wanted to make public.

There does appear to be evidence of Reep's influence in a series of lectures Hughes gave in 1984. In one of them, Hughes stated, "Over the past two years, the Football Association has been striving to bring the Coaching Scheme into better, more objective and hopefully, more successful lines. To achieve these aims and objectives, the FA has been quite heavily involved in a study of match performance analysis."

That last phrase—"match performance analysis"—was a term Reep had used since the fifties and one that does not appear in either of Hughes's first two books. It is an oddly fussy term—characteristic of Reep—using three words where two would have done, and it seems unlikely Hughes would have happened upon it without having heard of or read Reep. Reep was certainly angered; Hughes turned to the more obvious phrase he could have adopted in the first place and dropped the word *performance*.

Reep's feathers were ruffled further when Richard Bate, chief coach at Notts County, presented what was essentially a review of Reep's theories at the Science and Football forum in Liverpool in 1987 but credited Hughes for his help. In his introduction to *The Winning Formula*, Hughes is keen to stress that he came to his conclusions independently. "My experience of match analysis," he wrote,

> began in January 1964 when I joined the staff of the Football Association. . . . At the FA headquarters at Lancaster Gate was a library of 16mm films of FA Cup finals and international matches. Between 1964 and 1967, I watched all these matches and extracted all the goals. These goals were then analysed more closely to establish what were the key factors in scoring goals and winning matches.
>
> The results of this analysis were used in the playing method of all the international teams I managed between 1964 and 1974—seventy-seven matches in all. The essence of this work was published in 1973 in a book entitled *Tactics and Teamwork* and a series of eleven films under the same title.

Well, maybe the results were, but the work is light on statistics and preaches no unified philosophy. It is hard to be sure either way, but it is easy to see why Reep was suspicious. As the Norwegian academic Øyvind Larson pointed out, "The style of play recommended immediately changed from being general in nature to being penetration-based in particular." Hughes had been an ordinary pragmatic coach; he became, to use the term applied by Howard Wilkinson, his successor as FA technical director, "a zealot."

There were differences in terminology and weighting (Hughes specified five passes or fewer rather than three), but Reep claimed in his letter to Olsen that that was because Hughes was unaware of some of the calculations he was performing. "The work of analysing football matches has continued ever since," Hughes went on. "In the early part of 1982 [Reep says 1981; Taylor can't remember] I had the pleasure of meeting a wonderful man named Charles Reep, who had been analysing football matches for thirty years, successfully advising a number of Football League clubs."

Hughes claims that he then got Primus to begin analyzing games, using her shorthand skills. "The method of analysis itself, which I devised around twenty-five years ago, is actually different from Charles Reep's. . . . Although Charles Reep and I had come by our strategic philosophy by different routes, there was no disagreement on the major conclusion."

There was significant disagreement among the three personalities involved, though: Taylor denied Hughes, who denied Reep, who blamed Hughes. To both Reep and Taylor, Hughes exploited their ideas for his own ends, gaining in reputation and selling his books and videos. Perhaps that is a familiar tale of committee-room back-biting and of the impossibility of copyrighting ideas, but it meant that by the time Taylor was appointed England manager in 1990, his relationship with Hughes was unworkable. It hardly helped either that Hughes was furious at having lost out to Graham Kelly in the battle to succeed Ted Croker as chief executive of the FA in 1989.

Reep wrote to Taylor on August 4, 1980—by which time he was seventy-five—explaining his theory that "all goals come at random within a framework of probability." They met in Exeter later that month for two hours, after which, Reep wrote in a piece in the Scottish soccer magazine the *Punter*, "Any time Graham Taylor wanted to ring me to get further details regarding aspects of the style of play, I would be willing to talk for as long as he wished. We did in fact have several very long indoctrination talks, during which a lot of ground was covered without the need to meet each other again."

Reep did not see Watford play that season, but, he says, he met Taylor again on March 11, 1981, at Reep's house in Plymouth. Receiving reports from Richard Pollard, a Watford fan who had coauthored an early article with him, Reep concluded that, for Watford, "only one goal in five comes from passing moves containing more than three received passes." In other words, Watford's goals fit the pattern Reep had been demonstrating for thirty years—80 percent of goals come from moves of three passes or fewer (which, of course, is still less than the 91.5 percent of moves that, he showed, consist of three passes or fewer).

One of Reep's other constants also remained true: it took roughly nine shots to produce a goal. Convinced of this, he maintained records of how many goals Watford and their (combined) opponents were "in credit" or "overdrawn" (so, if a team had ninety shots, he would expect them to have scored ten goals; if they only managed eight, they were two in credit; if they had had scored twelve, they were two overdrawn). In the first leg of a second round League Cup tie at Southampton, Watford lost 4–0. Reep, noticing ahead of the return leg that Watford were 2.5 goals "in credit" while combined opponents were 4 goals "overdrawn," wrote to Taylor, advising him that this could be evened out in one game and that Watford should therefore pursue an attacking approach.

This, of course, is absurd. Taylor, presumably, would have worked out for himself that to overhaul a four-goal deficit, his side needed to attack. They did, led 5–1 after ninety minutes, and added two more in extra time. "I was enchanted to think," Reep wrote, "that the first time one of my teams had attempted to exploit the calculated situation regarding 'goals in credit' and 'overdrawn,' it had succeeded brilliantly well—always with the admission, of course, that random chance had done us a huge favour. And as might be expected, random chance penalised Watford by awarding us a 1–2 defeat in the next game."

And so the lack of mathematical basis to Reep's research is betrayed. "Random Chance" is not a deity handing out or denying goals to level up some cosmic balance. It is just random. Toss a coin a hundred times, and if the first ninety-nine land heads, the odds of the hundredth landing tails are still one in two. If there really is—and there isn't—a one in nine chance of scoring with any shot regardless of circumstance, it is still one in nine whether a forward has scored with his last ten or missed with his last hundred. That assumes the coin is unbiased, of course. If a coin keeps on landing heads, it is probably because it is weighted; if a striker keeps on missing chances, it's probably because he's not very good.

Nonetheless, ahead of the 1981–1982 season, Taylor decided to employ one of Reep's trainees—an archaeology graduate from the University of Lancaster called Simon Hartley, who had become intrigued by Reep's ideas after seeing him taking notes one day at Plymouth. Reep did not speak to Taylor by telephone that season, but he did write him three letters, one of which dealt with the lack of goals Watford were scoring from the right wing (John Barnes scored thirteen from the left) and hinted at, but did not fully reveal, his plan for how wingers should play. As Watford were promoted that season, 93.4 percent of their goals came from moves of three passes or fewer. Reep noted this was "superb," although if the number of moves consisting of three or fewer passes remained constant at 91.5 percent, of course, it is only just higher than would be expected if the number of passes in a move made no difference. Given Watford were a self-consciously direct side, it is probable that for them a greater proportion of moves consisted of three passes or fewer: even there, in other words, there is still little evidence for the greater efficacy of direct soccer.

Reep claims he and Hartley were both paid a £6,000 bonus but that he then fell out with Taylor over his fee for the following season. Taylor's memory is that they fell out over an obscure statistical point. Reep was obsessed by "reachers"—that is, balls that landed in the final third. Watford averaged 156 a game, although against Chelsea on February 6, 1982, a game they won 1–0, they achieved a record of 202 (this was later taken by John Beck's Cambridge United, with 219). Stan Cullis's Wolves side had managed around 180 a game, and Reep urged Taylor to try to raise Watford's level to match that. Taylor pointed out that his side's main strength was that they regularly won the ball back in the final third, something that did not count as a reacher under Reep's system, and suggested the figures should reflect that. Reep refused to change and although Hartley stayed on for another season, his personal association with Watford came to an end. "With Reep," said Taylor, "it was all or nothing. There was no room for compromise."

Reep may not have liked him, but it was Hughes, as director of education and coaching at the FA between 1983 and 1994, who ensured his principles—or at least Hughes's version of them as set out in *The Winning Formula*—became enshrined at the highest level. That book, in a linkup beyond the dreams of satirists, was sponsored by British Aerospace. "The strategy of direct play," Hughes asserts in his introduction, "is far preferable to that of possession football. The facts are irrefutable and the evidence overwhelming." Some might suggest that the record of an England team largely shaped by that philosophy is in itself a refutation, but then soccer players are fallible: statistics are not.

Noting that the average number of goals per game in World Cup matches fell from 5.4 per game in 1954 to 2.5 per game in 1986, Hughes passed almost immediately to the conclusion that "football is not as good as it was." That a man whose authority came from the supposed application of reason and logic should be allowed to get away with such a leap is staggering. Discerning the quality of soccer is necessarily subjective and, besides, there are bad 4–3 thrillers (excitement and quality are not synonyms) just as there are superb goalless draws. If goals alone were a mark of excellence, there would be thousands lining up to watch primary-school soccer.

The reason for the decline in goals scored, Hughes went on, "lies not in new efficient defensive strategies so much as a misguided attacking strategy, that of possession football." Now, certainly, as Chapman argued and as a glance at the statistics for any given weekend of Premiership soccer will show, there is no necessary correlation between domination of possession and winning games, but neither does that mean that possession is a bad thing. Yet Hughes, deploying that word *overwhelming* again, argued that "the fact is that the longer a team takes to build an attack when it has possession of the ball . . . the more time the defending team has to recover, regroup and reorganise."

In *The Winning Formula*, Hughes used the evidence of 109 matches between 1966 and 1986 in which 202 goals were scored. That, it might be noted, is not a huge sample, particularly not for somebody basing on it the claim that "world soccer has been moving in the wrong strategic direction for the better part of thirty years." It is also tempting to ponder the significance of the fact that although Hughes rails against a World Cup that produced 2.5 goals per game, the matches in his sample produced only 1.85. But still, the results are intriguing, and they have—presumably to head off those, like Taylor, who argue that direct soccer is ineffective at the very highest level—been filtered to include only successful sides: Liverpool, the England Under-16 and Under-21 teams, and World Cup or European Championship matches involving Argentina, Brazil, England, Holland, Italy, and West Germany.

Of those 202 goals, fifty-three came from moves of no received passes, twenty-nine from one pass, thirty-five from two passes, and twenty-six from three passes. In total, 87 percent of the goals came from moves of five passes or fewer, while fewer than 3 percent came from moves of ten or more passes (if Reep's statistic that 91.5 percent of all moves consist of three passes or fewer is correct, of course, that is still no endorsement of direct soccer). Then there is the issue of how many of those goals scored from three passes or fewer are the result of breakdowns brought about by longer moves.

Hughes anticipates the question and presents his figures with a misplaced sense of triumph. Of nineteen no-pass goals (that is, penalties, free-kicks struck directly into the net, or shots fired in from a rebound off the goalkeeper or after a tackle or misplaced pass by the defending team) from sixteen England international matches analyzed by Hughes, only twelve resulted from moves of three passes or fewer—63 percent: far fewer than Reep's benchmark of 91.5. The question then becomes not whether Hughes is right or wrong, but how he got away with it for so long.

Perhaps not surprisingly, Brazil were the side most likely to score after a long string of passes, 32 percent of their goals coming from moves of six passes or more, with West Germany next with 25 percent (given, at the time, they had won between them six of the thirteen World Cups to have been played, that might be taken as an argument in favor of possession soccer). Almost unbelievably, none of the ten Dutch goals under consideration came from moves of six passes or more. And that's when the alarm bells really start to ring: Why are only ten Dutch goals under consideration? They scored fifteen in the 1974 World Cup finals alone. This is not only a small sample, but it is a selective one ("we have extracted 109 games from all those analysed"), and nowhere in *The Winning Formula* is that selection process explained.

Even assuming there is nothing sinister in that, Hughes is, at the very least, guilty of identifying a symptom and not a cause. "The first objective," he stated in his conclusion, "is to get into the attacking third of the field more often than the opponents do, and the final objective is to achieve a minimum of ten shots on target every game. . . . If the strategies we have proposed are adopted and the tactical objectives are achieved, the chances of winning are extremely good—over 85 percent. The chances of not losing are even better. We have *never* recorded a match in which a team achieved ten shots on target and lost." Yes, but are the shots really the reason for that? Or are they simply a natural result of one team dominating? Do teams win games because they're having shots, or do they have shots because they're winning games?

Where Hughes does have a point is in his advocacy of pressing. Chapman and Helenio Herrera had great success by getting their teams to sit deep, but in modern soccer, among the very best teams at least, pressing is almost universal. "If a team can increase the number of times they regain possession in the attacking third," Hughes says, "they will score more goals." His statistics show that 52 percent of goals were scored when possession was gained in the attacking third, as opposed to 18 percent in the defensive third and that moves begun when possession is regained in the attacking third are seven times more likely to produce goals than when possession is regained in the defensive third. Now those figures are skewed, clearly, by occasions when moves break down in the attacking third and the loose ball breaks for the attacking side, but they are a striking vindication of pressing nonetheless. Pressing, of course, has the added advantage of smothering an opposing attack almost before it has begun. This is the basis of Taylor's disagreement with Reep. Pressing is an action that can help a team win a game; getting the ball into dangerous areas is something that happens as a result of those actions.

Hughes went on to argue that a team should shoot whenever it gets the opportunity, noting that "even at the highest level, more than half of all shots miss the target, so players should never shy away from shooting for fear of missing the target." Should a player really shoot even if a teammate is in a markedly better position? Should he always shoot from twenty yards? From thirty? From forty? Hughes argued that even mishit shots can create scoring opportunities, which is true, but why turn the situation into a lottery if a well-placed pass would significantly increase the chances of the initial shot, when taken, being a telling one? It is as though there is a distrust of technique, a fear that by adding an extra element into the move, the chances of it going wrong are increased to a level that makes relying on a lucky bounce or deflection preferable.

Allen Wade, the technical director of the FA from 1963 to 1983, was no aesthete, but he was horrified by his successor's dogma. "This slam-bang-wallop stuff will be the death of football," he said. "Football in which players are controlled by off-pitch Svengalis, backed up by batteries of stat-isticians and analysts, will never hold the magical appeal of what Pelé called the beautiful game."

There is, perhaps, a nod here back to the days of the head-down charging of the Victorians: where Italian paranoia led to *catenaccio* and a faith in strategy over ability, English insecurity led to a style that similarly dis-trusted ability, favoring instead a thoughtless physicality—keep battling, keep running, keep trying. As the German journalist Raphael Honigstein put it sardonically in the title of his work on English soccer, *Harder, Better, Faster, Stronger*. But not more skillful.

Although Hughes advocated increasing shooting practice to improve accuracy—and, supposedly, demonstrated his success in that area with En-gland Under-16s, although his sample included only four matches—this surely is just the kind of argument that had so appalled Jimmy Hogan al-most a century earlier at Fulham: buy enough tickets and you'll win the raffle eventually.

Quite aside from that there is a baffling lack of subtlety to Hughes's work. He claimed that by applying his "formula"—which arguably just comes down to being better than the opposition anyway—a side has a greater than 85 percent chance of winning. The question then is whether there is a pattern to the other 15 percent. What Hughes's statistics do not show is the possibility Taylor accepts, the possibility that feels intuitively true, that direct soccer can take a team only so far, that there comes a cer-tain level of opposition capable of keeping the ball, capable of controlling possession, against which it is rendered ineffective. Brian Clough was typi-cally unequivocal. "I want to establish without any shadow of a doubt that Charles Hughes is totally wrong in his approach to football," he said. "He believes that footballs should come down with icicles on them."

That is an exaggeration, but the flaws were obvious enough. Chapman's direct approach worked because he lured teams out and encouraged them to leave space behind them that his team then exploited. Taylor's Watford, with their high-tempo pressing game, were vulnerable to just that kind of attack. Hughes's formula makes no distinction as to the style played against. Given that Taylor's direct approach foundered against a Sparta Prague side adept at retaining, possessing, and launching astute counterattacks, wouldn't Hughes's have too? Organization and energy, Taylor found, will carry a team so far, but only so far.

The irony is that although Taylor was well aware of the defects of the method, it was he who was left to reap the pitiful harvest after Hughes had implemented Reep's principles as FA policy. Yes, there were players missing through injury, but still, have England ever sent out a weaker team in a major championship than the one that lost 2–1 to Sweden in the final group game of Euro 92: Woods; Batty, Keown, Walker, Pearce; Daley, Webb, Palmer, Sinton; Platt; Lineker? To rub salt in the wound, when England then failed to qualify for the 1994 World Cup, they were knocked out by Norway, a side practicing a variant of the Reepian model.

The links between Britain and the Scandinavian game had always been strong. Soccer was introduced to Sweden through the usual route of British sailors, with a little help from Anglophile Danes. When the Swedish Football Federation (SvFF) decided to appoint their first professional coach after the Second World War, they sought advice from the FA and hired George Raynor, who had been reserve team coach at Aldershot. Under his guidance and advantaged by their wartime neutrality, Sweden won gold at the 1948 London Olympics, finished third at the 1950 World Cup, and then reached the final again in 1958. There, they played a typical W-M with man-marking, something that, largely because of the amateur ethos of the SvFF, did not change until the late sixties.

Professionalism was finally sanctioned in 1967, and, in the aftermath of Sweden's failure to qualify for the knockout stage of the 1970 World Cup, Lars Arnesson, a leading coaching instructor, was appointed to work alongside the national manager, Georg Åby-Ericson. Arnesson envisaged a unified playing style across Swedish soccer and decided it should feature a German-style *libero*. That seemed to be vindicated at the 1974 World Cup, as Sweden finished third in their second-phase group, effectively fifth in the tournament. Although there had not been sufficient time for his idea of uniformity across all levels of coaching to have taken effect, that success did prove that Sweden could be internationally competitive with the system.

Almost immediately, though, a countermovement sprang up, as Eric Persson, an aging autocrat who had been chairman-coach of Malmö FF, decided to resign to allow greater specialization of management roles at the club. A high-profile banker, Hans Cavalli-Björkman, was appointed as chairman, while for a manager, considering local coaches overly conservative, the club turned to a twenty-seven-year-old Englishman called Bobby Houghton.

Houghton had played at Brighton and Fulham but decided early on to become a coach. He came through Wade's training course at the FA with top marks and, in 1971–1972, was appointed player-manager at Maidstone United. There he signed as player-coach a former classmate, Roy Hodgson, who had also shown promise on Wade's coaching courses.

Wade was a modernizing force who argued repeatedly against coaching drills that were not directly related to match situations. His main concern was less individual skills than shape and the distribution of players on the field. It was those ideas Houghton instituted at Malmö. When, two years later, he installed Hodgson at Halmstads BK, a division was created between their modern English school and those who favored the *libero*. Houghton and Hodgson employed a zonal defense, pressed hard, and maintained a high offside line. They counterattacked not in the way of the Dutch or Dynamo Kyiv but with long passes played in behind the opposition defense. "What Bobby and myself introduced to Sweden was less 'English football,' the long ball game and so on, than a different style of defending," Hodgson explained. "Instead of playing with a team that was very spread out from one end of the field to the other, with a *libero* who stays in his penalty area and a centre-forward who never tracks back, we set up a system of zonal defence, a back four, people pushing up and, of course, getting the ball forward into the final area much more quickly. And the Swedes didn't like the idea that their game was dominated by two English guys."

According to the Swedish academic Tomas Peterson, Houghton and Hodgson "threaded together a number of principles,. which could be used in a series of combinations and compositions, and moulded them into an organic totality—an indivisible project about how to play football. Every moment of the match was theorised, and placed as an object-lesson for training-teaching, and was looked at in a totality."

That, according to Arnesson, "stifles initiative, and turns players into robots," and, as critics dismissed the English style as "dehumanising," the debate about the relative merits of beauty and success came to Sweden. Peterson compared it to listening to Charlie Parker after Glenn Miller or viewing Picasso after classical landscapes: "the change does not just lie in the aesthetic assimilation," he wrote. "The actual organisation of art and music happens on a more advanced level." Naivety is gone, and there is a second order of complexity.

Success Houghton and Hodgson certainly had. They won five out of six league titles between them, while Houghton took Malmö to the 1979 European Cup final, where they were narrowly beaten by Clough's Nottingham Forest. At the 1978 World Cup, though, Sweden finished bottom of a first-phase group that included Austria, Brazil, and Spain, a poor showing that was blamed on the corrosive influence of the English style (England themselves, of course, hadn't qualified). When Sweden then failed to reach the finals of the 1980 European Championship, the SvFF was moved to act and, on December 11, 1980, formally declared that the English style would not be played by the national team nor taught at any national institution.

As Houghton and Hodgson left to take up positions at Bristol City, it seemed that the *libero* might prevail, but their influence was carried on by Sven-Göran Eriksson, who as part of his coaching education had observed Bobby Robson at Ipswich Town and Bob Paisley at Liverpool. Eriksson had worked as a PE teacher in Örebro, playing at right-back for KB Karlskoga, a local Second Division side. There, his thinking on the game was heavily influenced by his player-manager, Tord Grip, who had himself become convinced of the merits of the English style. After his retirement as a player, Grip became manager of Örebro before moving on to Degerfors IF.

When, at the age of twenty-eight, Eriksson was badly injured, Grip asked him to join him as assistant coach. Grip was soon hired as assistant to Georg Ericsson with the national side, leaving Eriksson, in 1976, to take over at Degerfors. He twice led them to the playoffs, finally winning promotion to the Second Division in 1979, at which, to widespread surprise, he was appointed manager of IFK Gothenburg. "Here was this really shy man, who had been the manager of a little team called Degerfors," said the defender Glenn Hysén, "and now he was suddenly in charge of the biggest club in the country. We had never heard of him, as a player or as a coach, and it took us a while to get used to him and respect him."

Gothenburg lost their first three games under Eriksson, at which point he offered to quit. The players encouraged him to stay, their form improved, and Gothenburg finished runners-up in the league, winning the cup. That did not, though, make him popular. "Eriksson has been at variance with the ideals of the fans since, like most managers, he wants results before anything," the journalist Frank Sjöman wrote. "Before long, he had introduced more tactical awareness, work-rate and had tightened the old cavalier style. The result has been that while Gothenburg are harder to beat, they are harder to watch." Their average attendance fell by 3,000 to 13,320.

Eriksson, like Wade, was obsessed by shape. "Svennis would place us like chess pieces on the training pitch," the midfielder Glenn Schiller said. "'You stand here, you go there,' and so on. . . . The biggest problem was fitting all the pieces together and getting them to move in harmony. The defensive part was the key to it all. When we were attacking, there was a fair amount of freedom to express ourselves, but we had to defend from strict, zonal starting positions."

Gothenburg finished second again in 1981, but they settled the debate decisively the following year, winning the league and cup double and, improbably, lifting the UEFA Cup. Although Eriksson soon left for Benfica, the English 4–4–2 was firmly established. In Norway, the debate was less ferocious and more decisively won by the pragmatists. Wade and Hughes had visited repeatedly in the sixties and seventies, and Wade's *The FA Guide to Training and Coaching* became central to Norwegian coaching and thinking, as is evident from *Understanding of Football*, the manual written by Andreas Morisbak, the technical director of the Norwegian soccer federation, in 1978.

The Norwegian University of Sport and Physical Education (NUSPE) was established in 1968, and, in 1981, a lecturer there, Egil Olsen, who had won sixteen caps for Norway, dissected Wade's model and presented a revised version. He argued that Wade had made possession too much of a priority, almost an end in itself, whereas he believed attaining it should be the aim of defensive play, and the application of it to produce goals the aim of attacking play. That may seem obvious, but the slight semantic clarification was to have radical effects, as Olsen extended the thought. He believed that in Wade's model too little attention was paid to penetration, that it was more important to pass the opposition longitudinally than to retain possession.

His work came just as the Swedish debate between system and beauty spread to Norway, stimulated largely by Vålerenga's title success in 1983 under Gunder Bengtsson, a Swede who was convinced by Houghton and Hodgson's methods. He was followed at Vålerenga and FK Lyn by another Swede, Olle Nordin—Marching Olle, as he was mocked after the 1990 World Cup, at which his highly regarded Sweden lost all three games by the same score: 1–2, 1–2, 1–2—and Grip then became national manager.

Olsen and his colleagues at NUSPE had begun statistically analyzing games, the results of which led Olsen to a series of conclusions outlined in his master's thesis. He discovered that the probability of scoring before the ball goes dead again is higher when it is with the opposing goalkeeper than with your own. This in turn led him to postulate that position of the ball is more important than possession.

"If I have to describe the core of my philosophy, the most central element, it is that if your opponent is off-balance, even slightly off-balance, he shouldn't be allowed to regain his balance," he explained in an interview with Lars Sivertsen in Issue Three of the *Blizzard*.

And that probably sounds simple enough, but there are very few who work systematically according to that principle. Even when it comes to the best teams in the world—who probably assume that since they have the best players in the world they can play their way through any defence anyway so they don't have to exploit moments of imbalance, but I could refer you to research showing that this isn't correct. You have a considerably greater chance of scoring when the opposition is off-balance than when they are in balance. Especially when it comes to playing out from the back, from your own goalkeeper, when the opposition is in full balance. Playing your way through and scoring, that's exceptionally uncommon. It hardly ever happens. So because of that, as soon as there is the possibility of exploiting imbalance the ball should be played forwards. Play the ball into space, into the "*bakrom*" ["the backroom"—that is, the area behind the opponent's defensive line] very quickly, few touches of the ball and with lots of movement off it.

In 1987 Olsen presented a paper at the Science and Football conference in Liverpool. While there, he met George Wilkinson, who was a match analyst for Howard Wilkinson, then the manager of Leeds. Through them he came upon the work of Reep, which to his mind confirmed his own theories about the role of chance in soccer and the inutility of possession. Olsen met Reep in 1993, and the two maintained a friendship so close that when Olsen was made manager of Wimbledon in 1999, Reep, then ninety-five, offered to act as his analyst.

Olsen became Norway national coach in 1990. He implemented a 4–5–1 formation, often playing a target man—Jostein Flo—wide to attack the back post where he would habitually enjoy a height advantage over the full-back who was supposed to be marking him. Taylor, interestingly, did something similar with Ian Ormondroyd at Aston Villa, and the theory was at least partially behind the use of Emile Heskey wide on the left under Gérard Houllier at Liverpool and for Eriksson's England. Olsen, nicknamed Drillo because of his dribbling skills as a player, demanded balls be pumped into the *bakrom* as his own side followed up with attacking runs. The phrase *å være best uten ball*—"to be the best without the ball"—initially attached to the midfielder Øyvind Leonhardsen, became a signature. Olsen was stunningly successful. Norway had not been to a World Cup since 1938, but he led them to qualification in both 1994 and 1998 and, briefly, to second in FIFA's world rankings.

"I invented what I termed a *gjennombruddshissig* style, a long and heavy word I believe I coined," Olsen explained.

Today we prefer to call it "forward football"—it's shorter and it's a bit more provocative as a contrast to what I call "backwards football," or possession-oriented football as some call it, which seems to be trendy these days in many circles. There is no definitive answer in football, but there is probably some kind of efficiency threshold. You see, we can measure this by counting how many forward passes are played, and Norway are currently at between 60 and 65%. I imagine that the most efficient way of playing is somewhere around that, maybe a bit higher. When we beat Brazil in the 1998 World Cup they played 35% of their passes forwards and we had 65%, and I made the statement that if they had played 65% of their passes forwards we wouldn't have stood a chance.

That his side ended up playing a lot of long balls, he said, was purely because of Flo's aerial ability; his theory demanded only that the ball should be played forward; it made no stipulation about length of pass.

Presumably because of their historical lack of success, Olsen's philosophy seems to have been more widely accepted in Norway than the long-ball game was elsewhere. As Larson notes, under him Norwegian fans became used to dealing in "goal-chances": a 1–1 draw in a World Cup qualifier at home to Finland in 1997, for instance, did not prompt anguish because it was recognized that they had won 9–2 on chances; they then beat the same opponents away, having won just 7–5 on chances. The issue, though, as it should have been for Reep and Hughes, is the quality of the chances. An open goal from six yards is not the same as a bicycle kick from thirty: not all chances are equal.

More significant was the qualifying campaign for the 1994 World Cup. When Norway beat England 2–1 in qualifying for the 1982 World Cup, it was such a shock it sent the radio commentator Børge Lillelien into barely coherent delirium: "Lord Nelson, Lord Beaverbrook, Sir Winston Churchill, Sir Anthony Eden, Clement Attlee, Henry Cooper, Lady Diana, *vi har slått dem alle sammen, vi har slått dem alle sammen* [we have beaten them all, we have beaten them all]. Maggie Thatcher, can you hear me? Maggie Thatcher . . . your boys took a hell of a beating! Your boys took a hell of a beating!" When Norway beat England 2–0 in Oslo in 1993, a game that also produced a notorious catchphrase—Taylor's "do I not like that," it was entirely predictable.

The more damaging result, though, had been the 1–1 draw at Wembley, a game England had dominated and led until Kjetil Rekdal, a defensive midfielder, thrashed a thirty-yard drive into the top corner fourteen minutes from time. This, for the dice-rollers, was vindication. Did Rekdal really think he would score? Did he send screamers like that flying in on a regular basis? Or was he simply, as Hughes would have urged him to do, buying another ticket for the raffle? Either way, random chance, as Reep no doubt saw it, had its revenge on Taylor.

England 1 Norway 1, World Cup qualifier, Wembley, London, 14 October 1992

16

THE RETURN OF THE BACK THREE

Brazil's defeat to Italy in 1982 may have prompted Zico to lament the death of soccer while others proclaimed the victory of system over individuality, but the irony is that *il gioco all'Italiana* was itself dying. As it did, so closed the great schism that had opened up in European soccer—although its effects can still be felt—and so was reborn the three-man defense.

The triumph of Brazil and their 4–2–4 in 1958 had exposed the vulnerabilities of the W-M, and, as the rest of the world raced to adapt, European soccer was split down the middle. Some preferred a *libero* and some preferred a back-four and pressing. The north—Britain, the Netherlands, and, eventually, Scandinavia—went with pressing; the south—Italy and the Balkans—with the *libero*. Germany, which accepted pressing only in the midnineties, used a *libero* and so falls in, uncomfortably, with the south, while the USSR pressed with a *libero* and was never as wedded to the offside trap as northern European countries farther west.

It's tempting to speculate on the reasons why, particularly as, in Western Europe, the split so closely mirrors the Protestant-Catholic divide (even down to Germany's odd hybrid position). The German sociologist Max Weber argued that Protestantism, particularly Calvinism, by encouraging the idea that work was in itself virtuous, led to individuals accumulating surplus wealth that could then be invested, stimulating the spread of capitalism in northern Europe. Could it be that soccer follows a similar logic and that those brought up with a Protestant work ethic feel the need to be doing something at all times and so are more comfortable with the constant movement of pressing? That proactivity and the overt exertion somehow feels more worthy or more natural than the reactivity of a *libero* and defending deep?

But by the early eighties the age of the *libero*, *il gioco all'Italiana* in particular, was coming to an end. "It was effective for a while," Ludovico Maradei explained, and, by the late 1970s and early 1980s everybody in Italy was playing it. But that became its undoing. Everybody had the same system and it was rigidly reflected in the numbers players wore. The No. 9 was the centre-forward, 11 was the second striker who always attacked from the left, 7 the *tornante* on the right, 4 the deep-lying central midfielder, 10 the more attacking central midfielder and 8 the link-man, usually on the centre left, leaving space for 3, the left-back, to push on. Everyone marked man to man so it was all very predictable: 2 on 11, 3 on 7, 4 on 10, 5 on 9, 6 was the sweeper, 7 on 3, 8 on 8, 10 on 4, 9 on 5 and 11 on 2.

The match in which the shortcomings of *il gioco all'Italiana* were exposed came less than a year after it had beaten the Brazilian game, as Juventus lost the 1983 European Cup final to Hamburg. Three of Juventus's back-four had played for Italy against Brazil in Barcelona, with Claudio Gentile and Cabrini as the full-backs and Scirea as the sweeper, the only difference being the presence of Sergio Brio as the stopper central defender. Hamburg played with two forwards: a figurehead in Horst Hrubesch, with the Dane Lars Bastrup usually playing off him to the left. That suited Juventus, because it meant he could be marked by Gentile, while Cabrini would be left free from defensive concerns to attack down the left.

Realizing that, the Hamburg coach Ernst Happel switched Bastrup to the right, putting him up against Cabrini. That was something almost unheard of in Italian soccer. Their asymmetric system worked because everybody was equally asymmetric: the marking roles were just as specific as they had been in the W-M.

Giovanni Trapattoni decided to stick with the man-to-man system and moved Gentile across to the left to mark Bastrup. That, of course, left a hole on the right, which Marco Tardelli was supposed to drop back and fill. In practice, though, Tardelli was both neutered as an attacking force and failed adequately to cover the gap, through which Felix Magath ran to score the only goal of the game.

Fading it may have been, but *il gioco all'Italiana* contained the seed of the system that would come to replace it. Pull the *tornante* back, shuffle the marking right-back a little more into the center and the marking centerback a touch to the left, and advance the left-back a little, and what is left is 3–5–2. By the nineties that was where the strand of the Italian game that had not followed Arrigo Sacchi had ended up. It suited the mentality of the Italian game that, since the days of Brera, had distrusted wingers, preferring

Hamburg 1 Juventus 0, European Cup final, Olympiako, Athens, 25 May 1983

to pack the center and turn matches into tight tactical battles. The 3–5–2 offered the possibility of attacking width through the wing-backs while still leaving a core of eight players down the center of the field. From the northern side of the schism, others came to the same formation; a return to the back three closing the gulf—in terms of shape and not necessarily style—that the move away from it had opened up two decades earlier.

Carlos Bilardo, meanwhile, had nothing to do with the European schism but devised the 3–5–2 as the solution to an entirely different problem: how to fit a playmaker into a system that was defensively coherent. It was a question being asked around the world: In a game in which a systematized approach had become almost universal, could there still be any place for the free-spirited epitome of the artistry of soccer, the number 10? Was it still possible to give him "the full rights of democracy" that Viktor Maslov had given Andriy Biba?

France, under Michel Hidalgo, and blessed with a side almost as talented as Brazil's, shifted shape according to the opposition, with Michel Platini playing sometimes as a center-forward, sometimes in the hole, and sometimes more as a *regista*. He was an exceptional player, and Hidalgo's use of him was probably unique, but what is significant is that he asked the playmaker to adjust to the demands of the system, rather than building the side around him. In that he was helped by the quality of the players around him: Alain Giresse and Jean Tigana were world-class playmakers in their own right, and Hidalgo's task was simply to find the right balance between creativity and structure; he could reasonably expect chances to arrive.

With Argentina in 1986, Bilardo had no such luxuries. Hardly surprisingly, given that he had grown up under Osvaldo Zubeldía, he adopted a more pragmatic approach. In any team, he said, seven outfield players were needed to defend, three to attack. It helps, of course, when one of those three is Diego Maradona. Presenting one of the most system-driven managers of all time with arguably the greatest individual player of all time could have been one of soccer's great jokes; as it turned out, it simply inspired Bilardo to the last great formational change, although he claims to have experimented with a 3–5–2 for the first time at Estudiantes in 1982. If, indeed, it was Bilardo who invented it; as with the back-four, the 3–5–2 is a formation with many fathers.

The trend through history had been to add defenders, from the two of the pyramid to the three of the W-M to the four of pretty much everything post-1958. Bilardo took one away. If there were no wingers any more, he reasoned, why bother with full-backs? Since Nílton Santos, full-backs had become more offensive, so why not redesignate them as midfielders and play them higher up the field? And so was born the 3–5–2. The defensive shape, of course, was very different from the M of the W-M: in the M, the defensive three was stretched, the two outside players having responsibility for the opposing wingers with the two deeper midfielders operating inside, marking the opposing inside-forwards; in the 3–5–2, the back three stayed relatively central, usually with a spare man and two markers picking up the opposing center-forwards, while the deeper midfielders flanked them. If those wide players were midfielders—that is, played with attacking full-backs, as for instance West Germany did in 1990 with Stefan Reuter and Andreas Brehme or Croatia in 1998 with Mario Stanić and Robert Jarni—it was a little more defensive. Played with orthodox full-backs, the shape was—although managers habitually denied it—a 5–3–2. The pyramid had been inverted.

Bilardo retired from playing in 1970 and succeeded Zubeldía as manager of Estudiantes the following year. While coaching, he also helped run his father's furniture business and practiced gynecology, only retiring from medicine in 1976, when he moved to Deportivo Cali in Colombia. He then had spells with San Lorenzo, the Colombia national team, and Estudiantes before being hired to replace César Luis Menotti as manager of the Argentina national side after the 1982 World Cup. At that stage, although the two clearly represented fundamentally opposed philosophies of the game, their relationship was relatively cordial.

At least initially, Bilardo spoke glowingly of Argentina's performance in winning the World Cup in 1978. After he succeeded Menotti, they met in the Arena Hotel in Seville in March 1983. Menotti told him there that Estudiantes had set back the development of Argentinian soccer by ten years, but they still parted on good terms. Bilardo, however, then ignored his predecessor's advice and benched Alberto Tarantini and Hugo Gatti from his squad for his first game, a friendly against Chile, to which Menotti reacted by writing a highly critical piece in *Clarín*. The detente over, they became implacable enemies.

While Menotti spun his visions of *la nuestra* revisited, Bilardo simply got on with the business of winning. "I like being first," he said. "You have to think about being first. Because second is no good, being second is a failure. . . . For me it's good that if you lose you should feel bad; if you want you can express it crying, shutting yourself away, feeling bad . . . because you can't let people down, the fans, everyone, the person who signed you. I'd feel very bad if we lost a match and that night I'm seen out eating calmly in some place. I can't allow it. Football is played to win. . . . Shows are for the cinema, for the theatre. . . . Football is something else. Some people are very confused."

In the early part of his reign, Bilardo himself was widely perceived as being confused. His start was disastrous, as Argentina won just three of his first fifteen games, a run that included a humbling exit from the Copa América and a defeat to China in a minitournament in India. By the time Argentina embarked on a tour of Europe in September 1984, Bilardo's position was under severe threat. "We were at the airport about to leave, when José Maria Muñoz, the commentator for Radio Rivadavia, came up to me," Bilardo remembers. "'Don't worry,' he said. 'If we win these three games, everything will be calm again.'"

That, though, seemed far from likely, and when Bilardo read out his team to face Switzerland in the first game of the tour, his reputation had sunk so low that it was widely assumed he had made a mistake. "They told me I was wrong, that I'd named three central defenders," he said. "But I told them I was not confused, that they should not panic, that everything was well. We were going to use three defenders, five midfielders and two forwards. We had practised it for two years, and now I was going to put it into practice in tough games."

Switzerland were beaten 2–0, as were Belgium, and then West Germany were beaten 3–1. "The system worked out, and afterwards we used it in the 1986 World Cup, where the entire world saw it," said Bilardo. "When we went out to play like that, it took the world by surprise because they didn't know the details of the system." Perhaps, like Alf Ramsey in 1966, Bilardo deliberately decided to shield his new formation from spying eyes; perhaps the truth is that his achievement was rooted less in any grand plan than in strategic tinkering as and when necessary (as, to an extent, was Ramsey's).

Yet Argentina weren't the only side in Mexico to play with a back three. Bilardo's interpretation of the system and his use of a playmaker within it may have been unique, but adding a third central defender wasn't.

There are those who insist the 3–5–2 was the creation of Ćiro Blažević at Dinamo Zagreb, foremost among them Ćiro Blažević. Even in his seventies he remained exhaustingly energetic, foul-mouthed, and hilarious, a man who had at least one opinion about everything and had no qualms about expressing it. "My son, let me tell you the truth," he said. "3–5–2 was invented in 1982 by Ćiro Blažević."

Blažević was born in 1937 in the Bosnian town of Travnik. He was a Yugoslav youth champion in skiing and then became a right-winger for Dinamo Zagreb, Sarajevo, Rijeka, and the Swiss side FC Sion, where a knee injury brought his career to a premature end. He stayed on in Switzerland, working as a coach and supplementing his income by taking a job in a watch factory. One day in 1968, shortly after he'd been appointed coach of Vevey, an old woman found him sweeping out the locker room.

"Why are you doing this?" she asked. "It's not your job. You're our head coach."

"Yes, I'm the head coach," Blažević replied, "and one day I will become national coach of Switzerland."

The old woman laughed. "Yes, of course," she said. "And one day, I will become Miss Switzerland."

Blažević, after stints at Sion and Lausanne, was right; the old woman wasn't.

He returned to Yugoslavia with Rijeka in 1979 and a season later took over a Dinamo Zagreb in decline. Blažević rejuvenated the squad and introduced an attacking style based on starting the game at a furious pace. They finished fifth, and then, as Blažević adopted a "lucky" white silk scarf, Dinamo won their first league title in twenty-four years. The following year, Dinamo lost out to Partizan in a three-horse race for the title but lifted the Yugoslav Cup.

The move to 3–5–2 began, Blažević said, as soon as he arrived in Zagreb. "To make a decision on which formation and tactics to play, you have to take three factors into account. 1) The attributes of the players you have at your disposal. 2) Tradition. 3) Putting factors 1) and 2) into the current system of play. Only a poor coach comes to a new club and says, 'I will play with this system' without respecting the attributes of the players he has in his squad. Only a poor coach becomes a victim of a system."

It seems more likely, though, that the transition began in spring 1982. Most Yugoslav sides until then had tended at that point to play in the German style: a 4–3–3 with a *libero* and man-marking, and tactical discussion in the media was extremely limited (with the notable exception of Tomislav Ivić, although he tended to talk about pressing rather than shape). Two players, the creative forward Zlatko Kranjčar and the powerful center-back Ismet Hadžić, had just returned from compulsory military service. Blažević realized that with Hadžić back, he could get more out of the popular and technically gifted Velimir Zajec, a natural leader with a reputation for slapping underperforming players, who operated either as a *libero* or at the back of midfield, and he decided to deploy three men on the center of defense—Zajec as the *libero*, with Hadžić to his right and either Srećko Bogdan or Borislav Cvetković to his left. Gradually he replaced the fullbacks, Zvjezdan Cvetković and Milivoj Bračun, with more attacking players, Petar Bručić and Drago Bošnjak, creating the 3–5–2.

It was primarily a system designed to catch opponents by surprise. Again and again that season, Dinamo went a goal or two up in the opening twenty minutes as opponents failed to react to the unfamiliar shape. Bručić and Bošnjak pushed high, and Zajec had the freedom to carry the ball out from the back, knowing always that he had two men behind him as cover. Once they had the lead, Dinamo tended to drop deeper, the full-backs falling back to create a 5–3–2, looking to check the opposing wingers rather than push forward themselves.

Blažević—of course, for no man is more sui generis than he and none more determined to be so—insisted the 3–5–2 was entirely his idea, calling Bilardo "a prick" for suggesting it was his idea. His story is that there was no evolution, that the formation leapt fully formed from his head: "I was never influenced by anybody." Perhaps not, but Blažević was coming from a tradition that favored the *libero*; advancing the full-backs to become midfielders and withdrawing a central midfielder as a marker were logical evolutionary steps.

Too opinionated and too restless ever to hold down a job for long, Blažević's relationship with his directors deteriorated in his third season, and he moved on, returning to Switzerland with Grasshoppers. He won the title in the first of two seasons there, then wandered through Greece, Kosovo, Croatia, and France, winning a promotion with Priština and then the Croatian league and cup in a third stint at Dinamo. In 1994, as an independent Croatia was accepted into UEFA, he was the obvious choice to be national manager. Croatia reached the quarterfinal of Euro 96, losing to Germany, and then took a side still brimming with patriotic pride to the semifinal of the 1998 World Cup. "I'm not saying he was a bad coach or a great coach," said the defender Slaven Bilić, who later became national coach, "but he was the ideal coach for us. He would gradually motivate you. He knows every day in his head that he's going to make a small incident to wake everybody up a bit, and then he's going to do this, then he's going to tell them to go out to a nightclub."

Blažević tended always to be scornful of talk of systems and formations—unless, of course, he is emphasizing his own role in the creation of one. For him, compression and the manipulation of space are key. "Nowadays we speak more about concepts—an offensive style of play, a defensive style of play—than systems. Nowadays you have all the time the transformation of players. Players from the defensive line go forwards. Players from the offensive line go backwards and defend. Everything has become fluid. Everything takes place within a space of 30m: practically everybody has to play in every position and everybody has to know how to play everything."

He is aware too that the most carefully prepared tactical system is worth nothing if the players don't have the faith in their manager to follow the game plan or if they lack motivation—and it is there that his real genius lies. "I spent the whole night thinking about theory," he said of his preparation for the 1998 World Cup quarterfinal against Germany.

I had a problem with [Oliver] Bierhoff, because I didn't have a skilled player who could beat him in the air, so I had the idea of stopping the crosses coming in. I was thinking about telling the players the story about Rommel and Montgomery. Rommel was much, much better in strategy, but he didn't have fuel. So the tanks couldn't move and Montgomery wins.

Then that morning, the guy who was with me said [the Croatia president Franjo] Tudjman was calling, and Tudjman said "Ćiro, you must win." I was on my way to the dressing room with my theories, and there are a lot of mirrors in every dressing room. I looked at myself in the mirror and I was a kind of green colour. So I thought, "Oh my God, am I going to die?"

I went to the room where the players were waiting for me—Šuker, Boban, Bokšić . . . and I had everything drawn on my paper, but I didn't start to talk about anything. I couldn't, because I was thinking was I going to die or not? I was looking at the players and there was silence in the dressing room, and after a few moments I saw that they were the same green colour as me.

My theory was seven or eight minutes long, and I knew I wouldn't be able to keep their attention so long. I didn't start to talk about my theory. They were more and more green. So I crumpled my theories and threw them down, and after seven minutes I had said nothing about them. Fuck the theory. So I just said, "You have to go outside and die today for the Croatian flag and all the people who have given their lives." No dealing with Bierhoff, nothing. And we won 3–0. You have to understand the psychology of the players. You have to have that sort of relationship with the team, so you can communicate your state of soul.

The back three also emerged from northern Europe in the form of Denmark, an international side who captured the imagination as the Dutch had a decade earlier. As Rob Smyth and Lars Eriksen wrote in an extraordinary paean to that Danish side in the *Guardian*, they were "both derivative and thrillingly futuristic. Although they had the Total Football hallmarks—spatial awareness, ceaseless movement and imagination of passing—they were like a fast-forwarded version of that Holland side. No team has ever had such a collection of jet-heeled dribblers."

And like the Dutch of the seventies, there was something appealing about the character of the Danes, perhaps simply because theirs was the first great Danish side; they had no critics bleating on about past glories and no real expectations. Rather there was a sense of disbelief about their progress from players and fans alike, a gratitude that they were being allowed to join in with the rest of the world, and an incredulity that they kept on winning. There was no pressure, because there was nothing to live up to. "They were unique, refreshing and life-affirming," Smyth and Eriksen wrote. "And even though time has not been kind to their array of tomboy mops, matted thatches and cock-rock mullets, they were seriously cool in a languorous, quintessentially Scandinavian way."

After reaching the semifinal of Euro 84, the coach Sepp Piontek allowed them a night out with a curfew of 5:00 a.m.; he brought discipline, but not too much. They were all guys together, having a laugh, something that came across clearly in "Re-Sepp-Ten," their magnificently kitsch World Cup song. Even Allen Simonsen, who won two UEFA Cups with Borussia Mönchengladbach and a Cup-Winners' Cup with Barcelona and was named European Player of the Year in 1977, didn't take himself particularly seriously. He played dead for several seconds during an international friendly in 1977, for instance, to provide footage for the thriller *Skytten*, the plot of which centered on a sniper who was targeting him. When Simonsen suffered what was effectively a career-ending broken leg during Euro 84, the rest of the squad went on television to sing a song of tribute. The fans, the Roligans, were part of it too; in the worst era of hooliganism, they were the happiest drunks in the world. Around sixteen thousand Danes went to France in 1984, including a young Peter Schmeichel, who made the thirty-eight-hour round trip despite having to play for Hvidovre against Brøndby the next day (they lost 8–1).

"Self-deprecation was the norm, and they revelled in their role as underdogs," Smyth and Eriksen said. "This was the beauty and the beast of Danish Dynamite: it was a love affair with chain-smoking, beer-drinking everymen who were actually top professionals at some of Europe's biggest clubs, but the considerable joy was tinged with the subconscious fear that the folksy, light-hearted Danish attitude was always going to stop them getting right to the top."

In terms of soccer, Denmark had been early adopters, but after taking silver at the 1908 and 1912 Olympic Games, they had slipped into obscurity. They won bronze at the 1948 Olympics and silver again in 1960— and a hugely fortuitous draw saw them reach the semifinal of the European Championship in 1964 by beating Malta, Albania, and Luxembourg—but it was only after the prohibition on professionals was abolished in 1971 that the game began to grow. The introduction of a professional league in 1978 was another major step, as was a sponsorship deal with Carlsberg that allowed the appointment of the German Sepp Piontek as national manager in 1979.

His predecessor had been Kurt Nielsen, a likeable and cheery man with extraordinary muttonchops but not a coach to drag Danish soccer into modernity. The documentary *Od Det Var Danmark* showed him before a game being asked whether he had any particular tactical plans. "No," he said. "Tactically it's still about scoring goals." Under him, the players hung around at a Copenhagen nightclub that became known as the clubhouse. As Smyth and Eriksen said, "Denmark were an international team in name, and a pub team in nature."

Tough and blessed with a dry wit, Piontek was thirty-nine when he was hired and had already managed Werder Bremen, Fortuna Dusseldorf, Haiti, and St. Pauli. He was not optimistic. "'I can't do anything with this team,' I thought," he said. "I only saw them six times, three days a year. There were limits to what I could achieve. How could I get them to work as a team?"

He found himself fighting against that culture of amateurishness. "Danes don't like the word 'discipline,'" he said. "'Nobody bosses us around. We're no good anyway.' I had to change that." The first-choice goalkeeper, Birger Jensen, was dropped, almost as a symbolic sacrifice. Slowly, the ethos changed. The year 1981 gave a hint of what was to come as Denmark won eight games out of nine, beating Italy 3–1 in World Cup qualifying, the Azzurri's only defeat on their way to lifting the trophy the following summer.

Symbolically at least, the key change was Piontek's decision to move the training camp to the Idrættens Hus, the headquarters of the Danish Confederation of Sport, a bleak concrete compound surrounded by barbed wire, with neither telephone nor television in players' rooms. Piontek was determined that the Danes should take soccer seriously, and, by the World Cup in 1986, he was holding three-hour tactical meetings and having his players train at altitude in oxygen masks in sessions that could last from 8:00 a.m. to 11:30 p.m.

In origin, Denmark's stylistic influence was Dutch. Frank Arnesen, Søren Lerby, Jesper Olsen, and Jan Mølby all moved to Ajax between 1975 and 1982, and that meant they came under the influence of Johan Cruyff. "He was like a king holding court," Mølby wrote in his autobiography, *Jan the Man*. "He knew everything and you couldn't help but listen. At times you'd want him to shut up, but he wouldn't."

As Piontek's Denmark matured, though, the Danish mode of play took on a character of its own. "No, no—we didn't play at all like Holland," Elkjær said.

We had a lot of players that played in Holland in that time, but the system was on our own: it was 3–5–2, and in Holland they play 4–3–3. I think the spirit was a bit like Holland: we want to have the ball, we

Denmark

want to play the ball around, we want to let the others run. The spirit is like they play in Spain today, or Holland back then, but the way we did it was our own. It was a positive style, because we were not able to only defend—of course we go back when we don't have the ball but we didn't go back with ten players.

It was the positional awareness and boldness of the experienced *libero* Morten Olsen that allowed the tactical radicalism. Elkjær spoke of 3–5–2, and certainly that was what the system became, but it stemmed from the 1–3–3–3 of Total Football. Søren Busk and Ivan Nielsen operated as the two central defenders, with the holding midfielder Jens Jørn Bertelsen able to drop in between them to create the *libero* plus three defensive shape of the Dutch. Two players—Søren Lerby and Klaus Berggreen at Euro 84— would then sit deep in midfield, flanked by Frank Arnesen and Jesper Olsen or John Sivebæk, with Elkjær and Michael Laudrup as a mobile front two. The identity of the wide players perhaps gives the best indication of the nature of the side: although Sivebæk could play as an orthodox full-back, both Arnesen and Jesper Olsen were genuine attacking wide midfielders, something that did occasionally get them into trouble. In the 4–2 win over the USSR in qualifying for the 1986 World Cup, the game widely regarded as the high point of Piontek's team, for instance, Olsen had to be replaced at half-time by the more defensive Per Frimann because of the damage Anatoliy Demyanenko was doing on that flank.

Piontek believes his was the first side in Europe to play that way. "The reason was I had many good midfield players," he explained.

Seven or eight—but I didn't have many good defensive players. At that time the opponents were only playing with two or one in attack, so why should I have four players in the back? Also if they were offensive they would have to run 80m forward and 80m back. That is very hard work. Where is the most work in the football game? In the midfield. They are involved in attack and defence. I played two markers [Nielsen and Busk], very strong, good in the air, and Morten was the third, behind. Also sometimes he came with the ball, and if it was necessary somebody could drop back from the midfield. So it was a very good system, and Germany were world champions using this system in 1990. It's also economical . . . they can always change who goes in the attack. One takes a rest, and then another goes.

The key was fluidity—what Piontek called the contra system—and a willingness to switch positions, as exemplified by, for instance, Sivebæk's goal against Ireland in 1985 when, after the ball had been calmly worked out of defense, the right-back found himself in the Irish half, paused, assessed his options, and kept running before finishing with a left-footed chip. Possession was prioritized to the extent that their goalkeeper almost never kicked the ball long, and the result was a number of goals scored from moves of bewildering simplicity. The goal against Scotland at the 1986 World Cup, to take just one example, came from six very simple passes straight down the middle of the pitch.

The biggest difference between the Danish and Dutch models, though, was less shape than style. Although the attacking ethos and the focus on possession may have been similar, Denmark's was far more of a dribbling game than the relentless passing of the Dutch, with Arnesen, Laudrup, Elkjær, and both Olsens gifted at running with the ball.

Morten Olsen and Søren Busk suggested pressing and playing with the high offside line. Piontek, recognizing his players' strength was their game intelligence and ability on the ball rather than necessarily their ability to win the ball, soon agreed. "He came with a lot of German discipline but also knew he had Danish players—they also need some of their own responsibility and he found a good balance between discipline and freedom," said Morten Olsen. "We couldn't play as a German team, we had to play as Danes. He knew that and that was very, very clever."

With their gleeful attacking style, Denmark became the world's second team, loved for their swagger and their style as arguably no national side has been since. When Jesper Olsen's blind square pass to nobody let in Emilio Butragueño to equalize for Spain in their second-round meeting at the 1986 World Cup, precipitating their collapse to a 5–1 defeat, the commentator Svend Gehrs lamented, "But Jesper, Jesper, Jesper, that's lethal. . . . " It was a cry of pain heard and felt around the world.

An Olsen error ended the Danish golden age—a dreadful burden for a player of such fragile brilliance to carry—but it had been he who had begun it, against England in the opening qualifier for Euro 84. England, in their first game under Bobby Robson, were almost overwhelmed but led 2–1 thanks to a Trevor Francis double. A defense that had conceded just twice in its previous eleven games seemed like holding out for an improbable victory when Olsen, capitalizing on a decoy run from Lerby, swerved through and slotted a finish under Peter Shilton. A 1–0 win at Wembley confirmed Denmark's qualification after a highly impressive campaign.

In France, a 1–0 defeat to the hosts was followed by a thrillingly open 5–0 win over Yugoslavia, meaning Denmark had only to draw against Belgium in their final game to qualify. Denmark went 2–0 down in an ill-tempered game before coming back to win 3–2, Elkjær rounding off the win with a stunning solo goal. The semifinal, against Spain, was another classic. Arnesen and Elkjær both hit the post in a 2–2 draw that Spain ended up winning on penalties. Elkjær missed the vital penalty, walking sadly away with his backside clearly visible through shorts ripped by a Spanish challenge earlier in the game, an image that managed to be both ridiculous and poignant.

The fear was that the success wasn't sustainable, particularly without Simonsen, but, if anything, Denmark got even better, reaching their peak in the 4–2 win over the USSR in 1985. It's the only game Mølby owns on video. "I was on the bench," he said, "and it's the best match I've ever seen."

Yet Denmark were never consistent, the element of risk in their play perhaps leaving them vulnerable. In the months leading up to the Euros, they lost 6–0 and 4–0 in friendlies against Holland and East Germany. In 1985, they played eight games: in four they failed to score; in the other four they ran in seventeen. Admittedly, two of those games were goalless draws against Switzerland in which they hit the woodwork a total of five times and missed a penalty, but it meant that with two qualifiers remaining there was a serious possibility they might miss out on Mexico 86, particularly when they went in at half-time in the first of those 1–0 down to Norway. Five second-half goals got them back on track, and qualification was confirmed with a 4–1 win over Ireland in Dublin.

Come the World Cup, Piontek was not prepared to compromise. "In Mexico we shall attack, like we always do," he promised, and they did. Elkjær got the only goal of an edgy 1–0 win over Scotland but Denmark then thrashed Uruguay 6–1. Admittedly, Uruguay had Miguel Bossio sent off after twenty minutes with the score at 1–0, but this was a domination that led to a red card rather than a red card that led to domination. That guaranteed Denmark's progress but meant they went into their final game, against West Germany, knowing defeat would set up a last-sixteen game against Morocco, while a draw or a win would mean an ostensibly tougher tie against Spain. Others might have sought to throw the game, but the Danes had beaten West Germany only once, in a friendly in 1971 when West Germany fielded an amateur side, and felt aggrieved their southern neighbors had refused to play them since. Piontek, besides, was desperate to make his mark against his homeland. Denmark, again, were almost casually brilliant, winning 2–0. Crucially, though, they had Arnesen sent off for kicking out at Lothar Matthäus. They missed him badly against Spain.

Denmark took the lead in that last 16 match through a Jesper Olsen penalty but then, just before half-time, the goalkeeper Lars Hogh threw the ball out to Olsen. He jinked by Julio Salinas and then, inexplicably, played a blind pass across the top of his own box. Hogh, presumably the intended recipient, was nowhere near and Butragueño rolled the ball in. Gehrs was right: it was lethal and his commentary became the epitaph for that generation. Denmark fell apart in the second half and Spain won 5–1.

Some suggested the collapse came because the intensity of Denmark's style couldn't be maintained in the heat and altitude of Mexico. Piontek blamed the Danish mentality. "This Danish attitude started creeping in [after the group stages in Mexico] where players thought, 'Oh well, we've made it this far, we've done brilliantly and nobody can blame us,'" he said. "At the end, there was something missing in their frame of mind. This transition to, 'We can and we must!' Perhaps it hadn't succeeded as well as I thought."

Denmark left Mexico having delighted the world. The FIFA technical report said that they "played the most spectacular football during the tournament . . . their readiness to risk something, linked to a full physical commitment, provided the Danish game with an exceptional dynamism." But they never did so again. Denmark lost all three group matches at Euro 88 and failed to qualify for Italia 90. Piontek quit in 1990, some said to take advantage of advantageous tax rates in Turkey, where he was appointed national manager, although he claimed it was in anger at tabloid stories about a secret bank account in Liechtenstein, reports he always denied. And then, just when the thought of success seemed to have gone, Denmark won Euro 92 having been called up as a late replacement for Yugoslavia. That team, coached by Richard Møller Nielsen, could hardly have been more different in style from the team of the eighties; some of the spirit may have been the same, but it was essentially functional and pragmatic.

With Denmark fallen in the last sixteen, the road was clear for Argentina to go on and win the 1986 World Cup, yet they did not go to Mexico with any great optimism. They won their last warm-up game 7–2 against Israel, but that was their first victory in seven games. As Maradona put it in his autobiography, fans watched their opening game against South Korea "with their eyes half-closed," fearing the sort of humiliation that was eventually inflicted upon them by Cameroon four years later. "They didn't even know who was playing," he went on. "[Daniel] Passarella had left; [Jorge Luis] Brown, [José Luis] Cuciuffo and [Héctor] Enrique had come into the squad. We trusted, we trusted, but we had not yet a single positive result to build on. . . . All Bilardo's meticulous plans, all his tactics, his obsession with positions, suddenly it all fell into place."

Cuciuffo and Enrique, though, did not play in that opening game. Rather, Argentina began with a 4–4–2, with Brown playing as a *libero* behind Néstor Clausen, Oscar Ruggeri, and Oscar Garré, and Pedro Pasculli alongside Jorge Valdano up front. Argentina won that comfortably enough, but against Italy, Bilardo decided Cuciuffo would be better equipped to deal with the darting Italy forward Giuseppe Galderisi. Ruggeri took care of Alessandro Altobelli and so, as in *il gioco all'Italiana*, the left-back, Garré, was left free to push on and join the midfield. The same system was retained for the third group game against Bulgaria and the second-round victory over Uruguay.

It was only against England in the quarterfinal that Bilardo settled upon the eleven that would go on to beat Belgium in the semifinal and West Germany in the final (in 1966, Ramsey, of course, had only settled on his final eleven in a quarterfinal against Argentina). In Brown he had a *libero* who seemed a throwback to the days of uncomplicated sweepers like Picchi. In front of him were the two markers, Ruggeri and Cuciuffo, who picked up the opposing center-forwards. Sergio Batista operated in front of them as a ball-playing ball-winner, with Julio Olarticoechea—preferred to the more defensively minded Garré—and Ricardo Giusti wide. Jorge Burruchaga, as a link between midfield and attack, was a certainty, as, obviously, were

Valdano and Maradona, which left just one position left to fill. Pasculli had scored the winner against Uruguay in the previous round, but Bilardo decided to drop him, deciding instead to pick Enrique. "You can't play against the English with a pure centre-forward," he explained. "They'd devour him, and the extra man in midfield will give Maradona more room."

So Maradona played as a nominal second striker, but he was given the freedom to roam wherever he saw fit by the defensive platform behind him. His first goal, after fifty-one minutes, was an example of *viveza* at its worst; his second, four minutes later, quite breathtaking. Called upon to attack by the two-goal deficit, the England manager Bobby Robson threw on two wingers in John Barnes and Chris Waddle, and the defensive weaknesses of Bilardo's system were immediately exposed. Gary Lineker converted a Barnes cross to pull one back and was a hair's breadth away from a repeat in the final seconds.

Would a side with wingers have overrun Argentina? Possibly. It could be argued that their central midfield three of Batista, Enrique, and Burruchaga would have dominated possession, but they failed to cut out the supply to Barnes and Waddle even against a central midfield duo as lacking in ferocity as Glenn Hoddle and Steve Hodge. Carlos Tápia replaced the more attacking Burruchaga with fifteen minutes to go, but Barnes still ran riot.

It hardly mattered. Belgium had no wide players of any note—who is to say they would have had the courage to play them even if they had?—and restricted their semifinal to a midfield battle, only to be beaten by more Maradona brilliance. In the final, Argentina met a West Germany side going through their own uneasy transition to a wing-back system.

After defeat in the 1966 World Cup final, West German soccer followed a similar evolution to the game in the Netherlands. The two nations may be traditional rivals, but the evolution of the game in each has much in common. Like the Netherlands, West Germany benefited from having few set theories as to how the game should be played. It had a more successful soccer tradition, of course, but a national professional league was established only in 1963. Soccer in Germany in the sixties was undergoing enormous change, and that made it receptive to new ideas.

In its own way West Germany's 3–1 win over England in the first leg of the European Championship quarterfinal in 1972 was as dramatic as Hungary's 6–3 win at Wembley had been nineteen years earlier. The English newspapers the following day glumly made the comparison, stunned by an opening half hour in which a West Germany side inspired by Franz Beckenbauer and Günter Netzer played brilliant bewildering soccer, interchanging positions and moving the ball at pace. *L'Équipe* hailed the West German style as "football from the year 2000," while English observers were quick to recognize the symbolic significance of the moment: at the time England and West Germany had each won one World Cup; since then Germany have lifted three further World Cups and three European Championships, while England have won nothing. "Defeat by this magnitude," Albert Barham wrote in the *Guardian*, "always has been on the cards since the World Cup–winning style of 1966 was copied and improved upon, while England remained content—work-rate being the great god to which the rest was subservient."

That game was the death of England's World Cup winners—Geoff Hurst never played another international and Alf Ramsey coached only one further tournament game. The assessment of Helmut Schön, West Germany's coach, resonated with unwelcome truth. "They seem to have stood still in time," he said. "Of course, they gave us a fight, but we were far superior technically." That progress had its roots at two clubs, neither of whom were founding members of the Bundesliga: Bayern Munich and Borussia Mönchengladbach. Bayern hired the Yugoslav Zlatko Čajkovski as manager in 1963; Gladbach hired Hennes Weisweiler in 1964. Both, in their own ways, were progressive, and both developed from within, focusing on youth. The Gladbach side that won promotion in 1964–1965 had an average age of just twenty-one and a half.

The effect of youth is twofold. On the one hand, as the expansive Romanian Mircea Lucescu has long argued, young players have fewer preconceived ideas and lack the experience that breeds caution. They are more biddable and less fearful (the stolid, unimaginative soccer produced by Ramsey's experienced England provides a neat counterpoint). And on the other hand, players who play together from an early age develop an understanding, grow organically together to accommodate each other's quirks. When one advances, another will cover; if one moves left, another moves right; positions were interchanged in a fluent, almost subconscious, way. Such sophistication can only come from profound mutual understanding, and that is most easily generated at a young age.

There were differences between the approaches—Gladbach tended to play on the counter, while Bayern preferred to control possession—and neither employed the ferocious pressing and aggressive offside trap of the Dutch (strangely, as Christoph Biermann shows in *Der Ball ist Rund*, it wasn't until the nineties that pressing was really accepted in Germany), but both promoted fluidity, encouraging players to find their own roles on the field, with reference to other players on the team rather than to fixed points.

As in the Netherlands, so in Germany soccer was part of a wider cultural movement: as Wolfram Pyta explained in his essay "German Football: A Cultural History," the "traditional emphasis on values and corresponding ways of life such as the bourgeois family lost their validity to such a degree that an increase in cultural autonomy led to a pluralism of lifestyles. Netzer and Beckenbauer, in this respect, were very much children of their time and exponents of the 1970s' cultural experimentation." The question, then, is why similar social forces did not have a similar impact on English soccer, and the answer is probably that they did, but only in isolated cases—the Mavericks of whom Rob Steen wrote—and that they thus never provided much of a challenge to the deep-seated traditions of the English game, traditions that had, after all, brought success only a few years earlier (for nothing, of course, breeds conservatism more surely than success).

Netzer in particular, Pyta wrote, "became the darling of left-wing German intellectuals who saw in him someone who broke with German cultural traditions on and off the pitch because [he] celebrated a way of playing that represented a radical break from the supposed German 'football virtues' of competitive strength and eagerness; in private because he was regarded as a nonconformist." In truth, although Netzer was the more overtly rebellious, particularly in terms of hairstyle and fashion sense, it was Beckenbauer who had the more turbulent private life. His image, though, thanks to his public support for the conservative CSU party—and the fact he played for Bayern—was perceived as the more conventional.

The final stage in West Germany's development probably came in the 1970 World Cup, when they played their group games, and the 3–2 quarterfinal victory over England in the intense heat of León. With chasing and harrying to win back the ball restricted, retaining possession was prioritized. In the *Guardian,* David Lacey suggested that West Germany made a conscious effort there to play the game, as far as possible, in the shadow of the main stand, further developing their awareness and their capacity to manipulate the game into the pattern that suited them. The result, when allied to a pragmatism the Dutch seemed almost willfully to eschew, was a style of soccer that dominated the European game at national and club level through the early and midseventies.

Beckenbauer was as central to West Germany's development as Cruyff had been to the Dutch. He had played as a *libero* for Bayern Munich from the late sixties, encouraged by Čajkovski, who had grown up in an environment that saw the value in having ball-playing central defenders (it's no coincidence that the first great Ajax *libero*, Velibor Vasović, was produced by the same culture). Beckenbauer himself always insisted his attacking style resulted from him playing in midfield for West Germany, where Willi Schulz remained the *libero*, which meant he was less prone to the discomfort defenders commonly felt when advancing with the ball.

Whatever the origins, a 1–3–3–3 with man-marking and the *libero* as a true free man became the default in German soccer, and, with the minor modification of one of the forwards being withdrawn into a playmaking role, it was still essentially that system that Beckenbauer, by then their coach, had West Germany use in Mexico in 1986. In the quarterfinal, for instance, when they beat the hosts on penalties, Ditmar Jakobs played as the sweeper with, from right to left, Andreas Brehme, Karl-Heinz Förster, and Hans-Peter Briegel in front of him. Thomas Berthold, Lothar Matthäus, and Norbert Eder made up the midfield, with Felix Magath as the play-maker behind Karl-Heinz Rummenigge and Klaus Allofs.

For the semifinal against France, though, which was won 2–0, West Germany also went with three central defenders, as Eder dropped in along-side Förster and Wolfgang Rolff came into midfield to perform a man-to-man marking job on Michel Platini. Beckenbauer instructed Förster to remain deep, and so, as the defender said, "we ended up playing zonal marking almost by default." It would be another decade before the debate was properly addressed in German soccer.

With Rolff standing down for the return of Berthold from suspension, the job of man-marking Maradona was given to Matthäus in the final. West Germany stuck with the 3–5–2 and Maradona was kept relatively quiet, but he also neutralized Matthäus, dragging him so deep that it was as though West Germany had four central defenders. With two holders in front of the back line, that deprived them of creativity and left Magath iso-lated, with the result that he was barely involved.

West Germany's narrowness—and their system didn't even allow the full-backs to push on—played into Argentina's hands. Brown headed them in front after Schumacher had flapped at a corner, and when Valdano calmly added a second eleven minutes into the second half, the game seemed won. Only then was Matthäus released from his marking duties, and only then did West Germany begin to play, exposing a weakness that had tormented Bilardo. Set plays were supposed to be his specialty, but he was so anxious about his side's ability to defend them that, at 4:00 a.m. on the morning of the final, he burst into Ruggeri's room, pounced on him, and, with the de-fender disoriented and half-asleep, asked who he was marking at corners. "Rummenigge," came the instant reply, which Bilardo took as evidence that Ruggeri was sufficiently focused.

With sixteen minutes to go, though, and with Brown nursing a frac-tured shoulder, Rudi Völler glanced on a corner for Rummenigge to score. Eight minutes later, Berthold headed another corner back across goal and Voller leveled. Perhaps having done so, West Germany should have gone back into the negativity their system seemed to demand, but they did not. The momentum was with them and, at last, they left space in behind their defense. It took Maradona just three minutes to exploit it, laying a pass be-yond Briegel for Burruchaga to run on and score the winner.

Looking back, their success seems almost freakish and, although the jibes they were a one-man team were unfair, the dangers of being quite so

Argentina 3 West Germany 2, World Cup final, Azteca, Mexico City, 29 June 1986

reliant on Maradona were seen as Argentina won only six of the thirty-one games they played between the end of that World Cup and the start of the next one. They went on, somehow, to reach the final.

Bilardo did not win many games as national coach, but he did have a habit of winning the ones that mattered. Moreover, his thinking came to seem axiomatic. By Italia 90, three at the back was a common sight. Brazil used the formation, as did West Germany, who went on to win the tournament with Klaus Augenthaler, Guido Buchwald, and either Berthold or Jürgen Kohler providing the foundations for a midfield trio of Matthäus plus two of Buchwald, Thomas Hässler, Uwe Bein, Pierre Littbarski, and Olaf Thon, depending on the circumstance. That was the beauty of the system—it allowed changes of tone to be made simply, without great wrenches of shape. Against Holland in the second round, for instance, Buchwald, usually a central defender, was used as a midfielder to help break up the Dutch passing game.

More surprisingly, even England adopted the *libero*, almost as a last resort after they began the competition with a 1–1 draw against the Republic of Ireland so bad that the *Gazzetta dello Sport* reported it under the headline "No Soccer, Please, We're British." With Mark Wright as a sweeper, flanked by Terry Butcher and Des Walker, England considered themselves able to deploy the attacking talents of Chris Waddle, David Platt, and Paul Gascoigne in the same midfield. They may have been fortuitous at times, but the outcome was that, in a paradox that seemed to blind England fans to the wider truths of that tournament, they played with greater adventure than they had for years and reached a semifinal for the first time since 1966. There, they were good enough to match West Germany before losing on penalties.

Still, that was not a good World Cup. Goals were down to a record low of 2.21 per game; red cards up to a record high of sixteen. Even West Germany, clearly the best side there, managed just three goals in their final three games: two penalties and a deflected free kick. Theirs was a team built predominantly on muscle, something the 3–5–2 seemed to encourage. Johan Cruyff despaired of it, later speaking of the replacement of the winger with the wing-back as the "death of football."

This was the result of the other facet of Bilardo's thinking coming into play: that the best place for a playmaker was perhaps not in the midfield, but as a second forward. His insistence on three players and seven runners may have been extreme, but the balance certainly tipped in that direction. Even Holland in 1988 ended up deploying Ruud Gullit, who would surely once have been a deeper-lying player, as a second striker behind Marco van Basten in a 4–4–1–1.

As players became fitter and systems more organized, defenses became tighter. The idealism of the Brazilians faded, and the playmaking second striker morphed into a fifth midfielder. After the sterility of the 1990 World Cup, the low point came in the European Championship of 1992, a festival of dullness that yielded an average of just 2.13 goals per game. Even as FIFA desperately changed the rules to outlaw the backpass and the challenge from behind, soccer seemed to have embarked on an endless march away from the aesthetic. With the game so well analyzed and understood and defensive strategies so resolute, by the early nineties the great question facing soccer was whether beauty could be accommodated at all.

17

THE COACH WHO WASN'T A HORSE

It was AC Milan's success in Europe in the sixties that introduced the *libero* as the Italian default, and, a quarter of a century later, it was AC Milan's success in Europe that killed it off. Hamburg's victory over Juventus in the 1983 European Cup final may have alerted coaches and pundits to the flaws in *il gioco all'Italiano*, but Juventus's 1–0 victory over Liverpool amid the horror of Heysel two years later confirmed its predominance.

There were efforts to move away from the *libero* and man-marking, but they were isolated. Luis Vincio introduced zonal defense at Napoli in 1974, but the experiment fizzled out, and then the former Milan forward Nils Liedholm employed a form of zonal marking with Roma, a tactic that got his side to the European Cup final in 1984. He moved on to Milan, but it was only after Arrigo Sacchi had succeeded him in 1987 that Italian soccer was awakened to the possibilities of abandoning man-marking altogether and adopting an integrated system of pressing.

"Liedholm's zone wasn't a real zone," Sacchi said. "My zone was different. Marking was passed on from player to player as the attacking player moved through different zones. In Liedholm's system, you started in a zone, but it was really a mixed zone, you still man-marked within your zone." It is probable no side has ever played the zonal system so well as Sacchi's Milan. Within three years, he had led them to two European Cups, and yet, when he took charge, he was a virtual unknown and the club appeared to be stagnating.

Born in Fusignano, a community of seven thousand inhabitants in the province of Ravenna, Sacchi loved soccer, but he couldn't play it. He worked as a salesman for his father's shoe factory and, as it became apparent he wasn't even good enough for Baracco Luco, his local club, he began coaching them. Not for the last time, he faced a crisis of credibility. "I was twenty-six, my goalkeeper was thirty-nine and my centre-forward was thirty-two," he said. "I had to win them over."

Even at that stage, though, for all the doubts he faced, Sacchi had very clear ideas about how the game should be played. "As a child I loved the great sides," he said. "As a small boy, I was in love with Honvéd, then Real Madrid, then Brazil, all the great sides. But it was Holland in the 1970s that really took my breath away. It was a mystery to me. The television was too small; I felt like I need to see the whole pitch fully to understand what they were doing and fully to appreciate it."

Those four sides were all great passing sides, teams based around the movement and interaction of their players. Honvéd, Real Madrid, and Brazil—with varying degrees of self-consciousness—led the evolution towards system; the Holland of Rinus Michels were one of the two great early exponents of its possibilities. Tellingly, when watching them, the young Sacchi wanted to see not merely the man on the ball, not merely what most would consider the center of the action, but also the rest of the team; he approached the conclusion Valeriy Lobanovskyi had come to, that the man out of possession is just as important as the man in possession, that soccer is not about eleven individuals but about the dynamic system made up by those individuals.

Most simply, though, Sacchi warmed to attacking sides, and that alone was enough to set him apart from the mainstream of a soccer culture conditioned by the legacy of Gipo Viani, Nereo Rocco, and Helenio Herrera. "When I started, most of the attention was on the defensive phase," Sacchi said. "We had a sweeper and man-markers. The attacking phase came down to the intelligence and common sense of the individual and the creativity of the number ten. Italy has a defensive culture, not just in football. For centuries, everybody invaded us."

That was what led Gianni Brera to speak of Italian "weakness," to argue that defensive canniness was the only way they could prosper, an idea reinforced by the crushing defeat of the Second World War, which seemed to expose the unreliability of the militarism that had underlain Vittorio Pozzo's success in the Mussolini era. Sacchi, though, came to question such defeatism as he joined his father on business trips to Germany, France, Switzerland, and the Netherlands. "It opened my mind," Sacchi said.

Brera used to say that Italian clubs had to focus on defending because of our diets. But I could see that in other sports we would excel and that our success proved that we were not inferior physically. And so I became convinced that the real problem was our mentality, which was lazy and defensive.

Even when foreign managers came to Italy, they simply adapted to the Italian way of doing things; maybe it was the language, maybe it was opportunism. Even Herrera. When he first arrived, he played attacking football. And then it changed. I remember a game against Rocco's Padova. Inter dominated. Padova crossed the halfway line three times, scored twice and hit the post. And Herrera was crucified in the media. So what did he do? He started playing with a *libero*, told [Luis] Suárez to sit deep and hit long balls and started playing counterattacking football. For me, *La Grande Inter* had great players, but it was a team that had just one objective: winning. But if you want to go down in history you don't just need to win, you have to entertain.

That became an abiding principle, and Sacchi seems very early to have had an eye on posterity, or at least to have had a notion of greatness measured by something more than medals and trophies. "Great clubs have had one thing in common throughout history, regardless of era and tactics," he said.

They owned the pitch and they owned the ball. That means when you have the ball, you dictate play and when you are defending, you control the space.

Marco van Basten used to ask me why we had to win and also be convincing. A few years ago, *France Football* made their list of the ten greatest teams in history. My Milan was right up there. *World Soccer* did the same: my Milan was fourth, but the first three were national teams—Hungary '54, Brazil '70 and Holland '74. And then us. So I took those magazines and told Marco, "This is why you need to win and you need to be convincing." I didn't do it because I wanted to write history. I did it because I wanted to give ninety minutes of joy to people. And I wanted that joy to come not from winning, but from being entertained, from witnessing something special. I did this out of passion, not because I wanted to manage Milan or win the European Cup. I was just a guy with ideas and I loved to teach. A good manager is both screenwriter and director. The team has to reflect him.

The sentiment is one with which Jorge Valdano, these days the eloquent philosopher prince of aesthetic soccer, is in full agreement. "Coaches," he said,

have come to view games as a succession of threats and thus fear has contaminated their ideas. Every imaginary threat they try to nullify leads them to a repressive decision which corrodes aspects of football such as happiness, freedom and creativity. At the heart of football's great power of seduction is that there are certain sensations that are eternal. What a fan feels today thinking about the game is at the heart of what fans felt fifty or eighty years ago. Similarly, what Ronaldo thinks when he receives the ball is the same as what Pelé thought which in turn is the same as what Di Stéfano thought. In that sense, not much has changed, the attraction is the same.

As Gabriele Marcotti pointed out in an article in the *Times*, for Valdano that attraction is rooted in emotion. "People often say results are paramount, that, ten years down the line, the only thing which will be remembered is the score, but that's not true," Valdano said.

What remains in people's memories is the search for greatness and the feelings that engenders. We remember Arrigo Sacchi's AC Milan side more than we remember Fabio Capello's AC Milan side, even though Capello's Milan was more successful and more recent. Equally, the Dutch Total Football teams of the 1970s are legendary, far more than West Germany, who beat them in the World Cup final in 1974, or Argentina, who defeated them in the 1978 final. It's about the search for perfection. We know it doesn't exist, but it's our obligation towards football and, maybe, towards humanity to strive towards it. That's what we remember. That's what's special.

Even as Sacchi entered his thirties, though, his quest for perfection was beginning. From Baracco Luco, he moved on to Bellaria before, in 1979, joining Cesena, then in Serie B, where he worked with the youth team. That was a Rubicon. "I was still working for my father's business, so that was a real lifestyle choice," Sacchi said. "I was paid £5,000 a year, which is roughly what I made in a month working as a director for my father's company. But in a way that freed me. I never did the job for money because thankfully I never had to think about it." It was a gamble that was to bring an improbably rapid return.

After Cesena, Sacchi took over at Rimini in Serie C1, almost leading them to the title. Then came his great breakthrough as he was taken on by Fiorentina, a Serie A club at last, where Italo Allodi, once the shadowy club secretary of Inter and Juventus, gave him the role of youth coach. His achievements there earned him the manager's job at Parma, then in Serie C1. He won promotion in a first season in which they conceded just fourteen goals in thirty-four matches—his attacking principles were always predicated on a sound defense—and the following year took them to within three points of promotion to Serie A. More importantly for Sacchi, though, Parma beat Milan 1–0 in the group phase of the Coppa Italia, and then beat them again, 1–0 on aggregate, when they were paired in the first knockout round. Parma may have gone out to Atalanta in the quarterfinal, and they may not have won a single game away from home in the league that season, but Silvio Berlusconi, who had bought Milan earlier in the year, was impressed by what he had seen. He, too, had dreams of greatness and seems to have bought into Sacchi's idealism.

"A manager," Sacchi said, "can only make a difference if he has a club that backs him, that is patient, that gives confidence to the players and that is willing to commit long-term. And, in my case, that doesn't just want to win, but wants to win convincingly. And then you need the players with that mentality. Early on at Milan I was helped greatly by Ruud Gullit, because he had that mentality."

Still, the problem of credibility remained. Sacchi admitted he could barely believe he was there but responded tartly to those who suggested somebody who had never been a professional soccer player—Berlusconi, who had played amateur soccer to a reasonable level, was probably a better player—could never succeed as a coach. "A jockey," he said, "doesn't have to have been born a horse."

Sacchi addressed the issue straightaway, reputedly telling his squad at their first training session, "I may come from Fusignano, but what have you won?" The side may have been expensively assembled, but the answer was, not a lot. Milan had lifted the *scudetto* just once in the previous twenty years and were still struggling to reestablish themselves after their relegation to Serie B in 1980 as part of the Totonero match-fixing scandal. The previous season they had finished fifth, edging past Sampdoria to the last qualification slot for the UEFA Cup only in a play-off.

Sacchi's resources were bolstered by the arrival of Gullit from PSV Eindhoven and Marco van Basten from Ajax for a combined fee of around £7 million, but still there was no great expectation, particularly as van Basten suffered a series of injuries, required surgery, and ended up playing just eleven league games, most of them toward the end of the season. They lost their second game of the campaign, 2–0 at home to Fiorentina, but that was one of only two defeats they suffered that season as they won the *scudetto* by three points.

That summer, Frank Rijkaard became the third Dutchman at the club. He had walked out on Ajax the previous season, having fallen out with their head coach, Johan Cruyff, and had joined Sporting in Lisbon. Signed too late to be eligible for them, though, he ended up being loaned out to Real Zaragoza; when Sacchi insisted on signing him, there was a distinct element of risk, particularly as Berlusconi was convinced that the best option was to attempt to resurrect the career of the Argentina striker Claudio Borghi, who was already on the club's books but had been loaned out to Como. Sacchi was vindicated, emphatically so, as Rijkaard's intelligence and physical robustness helped Milan to their first European Cup in twenty years.

"The key to everything was the short team," Sacchi explained, by which he meant that he had his team squeeze the space between defensive line and forward line. Their use of an aggressive offside trap meant it was hard for teams to play the ball behind them, while teams looking to play through them had to break down three barriers in quick succession. "This allowed us to not expend too much energy, to get to the ball first, to not get tired. I used to tell my players that, if we played with twenty-five metres from the last defender to the centre-forward, given our ability, nobody could beat us. And thus, the team had to move as a unit up and down the pitch, and also from left to right."

They were not, though, defensive, although as with so many innovations, those who sought to copy the system frequently became so. "I always demanded, when we had possession, five players ahead of the ball," Sacchi said. "And that there would always be a man wide right and a man wide left. But it could be anybody. It wasn't always the same people."

Sacchi's first experience of European competition had ended with an embarrassing UEFA Cup second-round defeat to Espanyol, but it was Europe that would prove his greatest stage. By the time of the European Cup final in 1989, Milan seemed unstoppable but, as Sacchi's detractors always point out, they had a huge stroke of luck in the second round. Vitosha of Bulgaria (the club that is now Levski) were beaten 7–2 on aggregate, but Crvena Zvezda of Belgrade were far tougher opponent and held Milan to a 1–1 draw at the San Siro.

Zvezda led the second leg at the Marakana 1–0 through a Dejan Savićević goal and, with Milan down to nine men after the dismissals of Pietro Paolo Virdis and Carlo Ancelotti, they seemed sure to go through. Fog, though, has a tendency to gather where the Danube meets the Sava, and, as it thickened in the second half, the game was abandoned after fifty-seven minutes. The sides returned the following day. Van Basten and Dragan Stojković exchanged goals, but the game was overshadowed by the horrific injury suffered by Roberto Donadoni as he was fouled by Goran Vasilijević. As Donadoni lay unconscious on the pitch, his life was saved only by the quick thinking of the Zvezda doctor, who broke his jaw to create a passage for oxygen to reach his lungs.

Gullit, still far from fit following a knee operation but on the bench, insisted on being allowed to take his place. Milan should have won it when Vasilijević deflected the ball over his own line, but neither referee nor linesman gave the goal, and they ended up progressing only by means of a penalty shoot-out.

There was controversy too in their quarterfinal against Werder Bremen. In the first leg in Germany, Werder had a goal ruled out for a far from obvious foul on the goalkeeper Giovanni Galli, while Milan were again left pointing to a shot that seemed to cross the line without being given as a goal and believed they should have had two penalties. In the second leg, it was a debatable penalty converted by Marco van Basten after Donadoni—back in action after the winter break—had gone down under challenge from Gunnar Sauer that gave Milan a 1–0 aggregate victory. At that stage Milan seemed merely fortuitous, but what happened in the semifinal confirmed their brilliance.

Poor Real Madrid: Twenty-three years from their last European triumph, it had come to feel that they existed merely for other teams to prove their excellence against. Benfica had seized the mantle from them in the 1962 final, Ajax had confirmed they were the best side in Europe by hammering them in the semifinal in 1973, and Sacchi's Milan similarly gave notice of their ascension into the pantheon with a superlative performance and a 5–0 win. Perhaps it is simply their reputation that inspires pretenders against them, but perhaps it is also the case that their historical insistence upon the individual renders them prone to destruction by well-drilled teams. Potent as their strike force of Emilio Butragueño and Hugo Sánchez were, there was an imbalance in their midfield, with the arrival of Bernd Schuster from Barcelona forcing the incisive Michel into a deeper role.

Milan had the better of the first leg in the Bernabéu but conceded a late equalizer and were held to a 1–1 draw. Madrid's coach, the Dutchman Leo Beenhakker, opted to start the second leg with Paco Llorente, a rapid right-winger who was usually used as a substitute. The idea was presumably that his pace could undo Milan on the break, but the effect was rather to weaken the midfield. Schuster was not quick enough to make any impression on Milan's central midfield pairing of Rijkaard and Ancelotti, and Butragueño ended up being dragged right to shore up the right flank, disabling his partnership with Sánchez.

Perhaps Beenhakker got it wrong, but that is not to detract from the excellence of Sacchi's side. "Milan's performance," Brian Glanville wrote, "was a compound of technical excellence, dynamic pace and inspired movement. Gullit, playing up front with Van Basten, can seldom have been better, seldom have shown such an irresistible combination of power, skill and opportunism." Ancelotti got the first after eighteen minutes, working space for himself with a couple of neat sidesteps before smacking a thirty-yard drive into the top corner. Even his presence in the side, never mind the goal, was a vindication of Sacchi's methods. When he had arrived in 1987 from Roma, he was twenty-eight, and he took time to adapt to the new coach's approach. "He struggled at first," Sacchi said. "Berlusconi said we had an orchestra director who couldn't read sheet music. I told him I would teach him to sing in tune with our orchestra. Every day, I would make him come an hour before training with some kids from the youth team and we would

AC Milan 5 Real Madrid 0, European Cup semifinal, San Siro, Milan, 19 April 1989

go through everything. Eventually he sang in perfect tune." And never better than in that semifinal.

Rijkaard converted a right-wing cross from Mauro Tassotti to make it two, and Gullit added a third before half-time with a characteristic header from Donadoni's clip from the left. The three Dutchmen combined for the fourth, four minutes after half-time, Gullit heading down Rijkaard's pass for van Basten to crash into the top corner. Donadoni rounded off Madrid's humiliation with a fifth, scudded in at the near post from the edge of the box. "It is hard to play like that," said Franco Baresi, "but when we do we are unbeatable."

Steaua Bucharest offered little resistance in the final and were beaten 4–0, Gullit and van Basten getting two goals each. "I was exhausted by the end," said the Steaua goalkeeper Silviu Lung. "In all my life I'd never had so many shots to deal with." That, Sacchi said, was as near as he got to the perfection he sought, the nearest he came to fulfillment. "The morning after we beat Steaua Bucharest I woke up with a feeling I had never experienced before," he said. "It was one which I have never experienced since. I had this unusual, sweet taste in my mouth. I realised it was the apotheosis of my life's work."

A decade after leaving the shoe factory, in two great performances, Sacchi saw his vision made flesh. "Many believe that football is about the players expressing themselves," he said. "But that's not the case. Or, rather, it's not the case in and of itself. The player needs to express himself within the parameters laid out by the manager. And that's why the manager has to fill his head with as many scenarios, tools, movements, with as much information as possible. Then the player makes decisions based on that. And it's about being a player. Not just being skilful or being athletic. I didn't want robots or individualists. I wanted people with the intelligence to understand me, and the spirit to put that intelligence to the service of the team. In short, I wanted people who knew how to play football."

In that, he differs from Valdano, whose romanticism is of a less pragmatic bent. "There is room for all theories, but individual expression on the pitch is something I don't think we can give up," Valdano said. "The brain of one manager can't compete with the infinite possibilities of eleven thinking brains on the pitch. Ultimately, while the concept of team is very important, you need individuals to go to the next level."

For Sacchi, though, the system was the most important thing. "Football has a script," he said. "The actors, if they're great actors, can interpret the script and their lines according to their creativity, but they still have to follow the script." There is no doubt that in his conception the scriptwriter was the manager, and the script itself was to be interpreted, not improvised upon. "I was the only one who could guide them and get them to develop a collective game which would maximize their potential as a unit," he said. "My philosophy was teaching players as much as I could, so they would know as much as possible. This would then enable them to make the right decision—and to do so quickly—based on every possible scenario on the pitch."

There is a sense in which his greatest triumph was persuading the great players and the great egos in his Milan squad of that. "I convinced Gullit and Van Basten by telling them that five organised players would beat ten disorganised ones," Sacchi explained. "And I proved it to them. I took five players: Giovanni Galli in goal, Tassotti, Maldini, Costacurta and Baresi. They had ten players: Gullit, Van Basten, Rijkaard, Virdis, Evani, Ancelotti, Colombo, Donadoni, Lantignotti and Mannari. They had fifteen minutes to score against my five players, the only rule was that if we won possession or they lost the ball, they had to start over from ten metres inside their own half. I did this all the time and they never scored. Not once."

Pressing was the key, but there was no sense of hounding the man in possession as Dynamo Kyiv or Ajax had done. "Many things influenced me," Sacchi said.

> Dutch football for one. But I think they were different from us, they were based more on athleticism; we were more about tactics. Every player had to be in the right place. In the defensive phase, all of our players always had four reference points: the ball, the space, the opponent and his teammates. Every movement had to be a function of those four reference points. Each player had to decide which of the four reference points should determine his movement.
>
> Pressing is not about running and it's not about working hard. It's about controlling space. I wanted my players to feel strong and the opponents to feel weak. If we let our opponents play in a way they were accustomed to, they would grow in confidence. But if we stopped them, it would hurt their confidence. That was the key: our pressing was psychological as much as physical. Our pressing was always collective. I wanted all eleven players to be in an "active" position, effecting and influencing the opposition when we did not have the ball. Every movement had to be synergistic and had to fit into the collective goal.
>
> Everybody moved in unison. If a full-back went up, the entire eleven adjusted. People think we had these big, strong players, but we had guys like [Alberigo] Evani and Donadoni, who are slight. No, they became big, strong players because of their positioning and movement. That's what made them seem big.
>
> And we had several types of pressing, that we would vary throughout the game. There was partial pressing, where it was more about jockeying; there was total pressing which was more about winning the

ball; there was fake pressing, when we pretended to press, but, in fact, used the time to recuperate.

It was based on a back-four who played, radically for Italy, not with a *libero*, but in a line—a sliding arc that was only flat when the ball was in the center of the field—and it was practiced relentlessly, as it needed to be. "Before he came to Milan, the clash between two opposing players was always the key, but with him it was all about movement off the ball, and that's where we won our matches," said Paolo Maldini. "Each player was as important defensively as he was in attack. It was a side in which players and not positions were the key." So crucial was mutual understanding between players that when Sacchi, as Italy national manager, gave his squad a day off during the 1994 World Cup, Baresi asked for a training session so the process of integration would not be checked.

A key part of coaching pressing was shadow play, which had been common in England from the sixties but was revolutionary in continental Europe. "On match-days, in the morning," Sacchi said, "we had a special training session. Butragueño told me that, before the semi-final against Real Madrid, they sent a scout to watch our session. The scout reported back: 'They played a game with a full eleven on a full-sized pitch against nobody and without the ball!' We would line up in our formation, I would tell players where the imaginary ball was and the players had to move accordingly, passing the imaginary ball and moving like clockwork around the pitch, based upon the players' reactions."

As Gullit suffered a series of knee injuries and underwent a string of operations, Milan never achieved quite the same heights again under Sacchi. Again they beat Real Madrid, this time in the second round, when the efficacy of their offside trap, marshaled by Baresi, was particularly obvious. Mechelen of Belgium were unconvincingly overcome in the quarterfinal, beaten 2–0 in extra time in the second leg after Donadoni had been sent off for retaliation, and they needed extra time in the semifinal as well, as they beat Bayern Munich on the away goals rule. That set up a final against Benfica, who had surprisingly—and undeservedly—eliminated Marseille in their semi, thanks in no small degree to a goal handled over the line by Vata Garcia. There was no repeat of the exhibition of a year earlier, and the game was won by a single goal, elegantly shaped home with the outside of his right foot by Rijkaard.

Milan had retained the European Cup, an increasingly rare feat, but they had been less convincing than the previous year, and Sacchi ran into further difficulties the following season. He fell out with van Basten and, with the Italian federation making little secret of their desire to make him national coach, Fabio Capello was appointed to work alongside him. Milan finished the season second in Serie A, but the more lasting impression was made by their disgraceful exit from the European Cup. Having drawn the home leg of their quarterfinal against Marseille 1–1, Milan were 1–0 down when the floodlights failed with two minutes of the second leg remaining. The players went off, the lights came back on, and Milan refused to return to the field. The game was awarded 3–0 against them and they were banned from European competition for a season.

Sacchi, as expected, left to take charge of the national side, but his career, after an astonishing rise, had already reached its peak. Like Lobanovskyi, he found the rhythm of coaching a national team difficult, because he could not spend every minute of every day schooling his players, working on their understanding. "It's impossible," he said. Added to which, his insistence that good footballers did not necessarily make good players meant an uneasy relationship with some of Italy's more vaunted players, most notably Roberto Baggio.

The two issues came together in Italy's second game in the 1994 World Cup. After losing their opener 1–0 to the Republic of Ireland, Sacchi made three changes to the side, the most significant of which turned out to be the replacement of Tassotti with Antonio Benarrivo. "Baresi and Costacurta attacked the Norwegian centre-forward," Sacchi explained. "Benarrivo, who was not used to playing with us, did not follow them. So he played an opponent onside, [the goalkeeper Gianluca] Pagliuca had to come out and commit a foul outside the box, getting himself sent off."

Sacchi had to sacrifice a player to bring on his substitute goalkeeper, Luca Marchegiani, and, to general amazement, chose to take off Baggio. Baggio himself was shown on television looking aghast as Sacchi signaled him off, clearly asking, "Has he gone mad?" A scrappy 1–0 win did little to resolve the argument either way, but it make clear Sacchi's attitude to marquee players, something that remained constant through his career. "When I was director of football at Real Madrid I had to evaluate the players coming through the youth ranks," he said.

> We had some who were very good footballers. They had technique, they had athleticism, they had drive, they were hungry. But they lacked what I call knowing-how-to-play-football. They lacked decision-making. They lacked positioning. They didn't have that subtle sensitivity of football: how a player should move within the collective. And, for many, I wasn't sure they were going to learn. You see, strength, passion, technique, athleticism, all of these are very important. But they are a means to an end, not an end in itself. They help you reach your goal, which is putting your talent at the service of the team, and, by doing this, mak-

ing both you and the team greater. So, in situations like that, I just have to say, he's a great footballer, but perhaps not a great player.

Italy reached the final of that tournament, losing on penalties to Brazil, but that was not enough to stem the criticism, and when they were bundled out of Euro 96 in the group stage, Sacchi's fate was sealed. He returned to Milan but could not replicate his earlier success and left after a season. He had a similarly brief spell with Atlético Madrid, where he struggled against interference from the club's president, the notorious Jesús Gil. A subsequent spell with Parma lasted only twenty-three days, encompassing three games before he quit, citing stress. "The difference between Milan and elsewhere was that at Milan I had quality players, at other clubs they obviously weren't as good," he said. "And you can only do it of you have a great club behind you. If Berlusconi hadn't backed me, not just in public, but with the players as well, I don't think I could have succeeded. I don't know that the players would have listened to me. When you try to do something new, when you try to do things differently, you need a tremendous amount of support."

It is just as easy to believe, though, that having achieved his apotheosis so quickly, Sacchi, like Viktor Maslov, found it impossible to summon the emotional energy to impose his vision again. Perhaps too, towards the end of his first stint at Milan, there was an element of Béla Guttmann's three-year rule kicking in: the exhausting, repetitive training sessions could be endured only for so long.

Certainly Milan soon proved not as moribund as Sacchi had believed them to be when he left. "I thought they were a great side near to their sunset boulevard, reaching the end of an unrepeatable cycle of success," he said. "Obviously, I was wrong. Managed by Capello, Milan won the Champions League and four league championships in five years, one of which passed without any defeats."

Sacchi, of course, must take some of the credit for laying the groundwork, but Milan were substantially different under Capello. Although the 4–4–2 principle remained the same and although they continued to press, Capello's Milan were far less fluid, far more defensive, often featuring an out-and-out holder like Marcel Desailly at the back of the midfield, something that was anathema to Sacchi's doctrine of universality. That trend reached its peak when Milan completed a hat trick of *scudetti* in 1994, despite scoring only thirty-six goals in thirty-four games; the strength was that same back-four of Tassotti, Baresi, Costacurta, and Maldini, which conceded just fifteen.

Yet that season they also produced one of the indelible European performances, arguably the greatest in a final since Real Madrid's 7–3 victory over

AC Milan 4 Barcelona 0, Champions League final, Spiros Louis Stadium, Athens, 18 May 1994

Eintracht Frankfurt in 1960, as they hammered Johan Cruyff's Barcelona 4–0 in Athens. It was a game wholly incongruous with the rest of the season. For one thing, Dejan Savićević, whose individualistic brilliance was out of keeping both with Sacchi's team-centered ideals and with Capello's pragmatism, played; for another, Baresi and Costacurta, both suspended, did not.

The game was billed as another allegory: the attacking of Johan Cruyff's Barcelona, with their total footballing heritage and their maverick strike force of Romário and Hristo Stoichkov, against the defense of Milan. Barcelona had won a fourth straight Spanish title that year, but they were hopelessly outclassed. Milan were already well on top when they took a twenty-second-minute lead, Savićević gliding by Miguel Ángel Nadal before hooking the ball across goal for Daniele Massaro to knock in. Their second was a sumptuous team goal, Savićević, Boban, and Cristian Panucci working the ball to Donadoni, whose cut-back from the byline was whipped into the far corner by Massaro. Savićević then added a wonderful lob and hit the post in the move that led to Desailly curling a glorious fourth. "They were just perfect," said the Barcelona goalkeeper, Andoni Zubizarreta.

"The press, especially the foreign media, had given us no hope," said Maldini. "Barcelona were certainly a good side, but we knew they had weaknesses and how to exploit them and we went for it, ruthlessly. We played an almost perfect game. We completely stifled difficult opponents and gave them almost nothing."

Sacchi, though, was never convinced, and Maldini acknowledged that the 1989 side was the best he ever played for. "Football is born in the brain, not in the body," Sacchi said. "Michelangelo said he painted with his mind, not with his hands. So, obviously, I need intelligent players. That was our philosophy at Milan. I didn't want solo artists; I wanted an orchestra. The greatest compliment I received was when people said my football was like music."

18

TOTAL RECALL

As the rest of the world caught up with what Ajax and Holland had done in the early seventies and systematization took hold, the home of Total Football was forced to confront the question of what came next. Evolution never stops: to keep doing the same thing over and over is to wait for extinction. For a time, Ajax struggled to develop, worn down by the usual clashes of personalities, the difficulty of maintaining their level without a huge budget, and the fact that other sides were working out how to play their way.

The return of Johan Cruyff as coach for three fractious years at least ended their European drought, as the Cup-Winners' Cup was won in 1987, but it wasn't until the appointment of Louis van Gaal in 1991 that Ajax took their place once again among the tactical avant-garde. Van Gaal was red faced, dogmatic, and given to crudeness and sudden outbursts of temper. At one point when he was Bayern Munich manager, for instance, he made the point that he was unafraid of his big-name players by dropping his trousers in the dressing room. "The coach wanted to make clear to us that he can leave out any player, it was all the same to him because, as he said, he had the balls," said the forward Luca Toni. "He demonstrated this literally. I have never experienced anything like it, it was totally crazy. Luckily I didn't see a lot, because I wasn't in the front row."

At Ajax, Van Gaal was violently unpopular among those who yearned for the romance of two decades earlier. They saw his reimagining of Total Football as dully mechanistic in its emphasis on system over creativity, on the retention of possession over the taking of risks. But Van Gaal had a vision, and he had the personality to rise above the club politicking and impose it.

Born in Amsterdam, Van Gaal had been briefly on Ajax's roster as a twenty-year-old, but he never made an appearance for them, spending the bulk of his career as a midfielder at Sparta Rotterdam. "As a professional soccer player," Henry Kormelink and Tjen Seeverens noted diplomatically in their book on his coaching philosophy, "he was known for his confidence in his own opinions, his abilities to convince players and coaches alike that he was right, and above all for his tactical insight." He was, in other words, exactly the sort of opinionated, tactically astute player in which Ajax specialized—which was perhaps why he was given the job of youth coordinator there in 1988, when he was thirty-six. When Kurt Linder departed after only a few months as head coach, Van Gaal and another youth coach, Spitz Kohn, were appointed on a temporary basis. The board felt Van Gaal was too inexperienced to take the job on permanently and so appointed Leo Beenhakker, who won the title in his first season before quitting to take up a more lucrative position at Real Madrid.

Van Gaal, having served as Beenhakker's assistant, was again placed in control, although it was widely assumed he was filling in until Cruyff was available once again. The forty-year-old, though, seized his opportunity. When he off-loaded a number of established and popular players—such as Wim Jonk, Jan Wouters, Brian Roy, and Dennis Bergkamp—fans and the media were outraged. By the time he followed Cruyff's path to Barcelona six years later, though, he had restored Ajax to the very pinnacle of the European game.

Players were initially just as skeptical as fans and journalists when Van Gaal imposed a strict disciplinary code. "Football," he said, "is a team sport and the members of the team are therefore dependent on each other. If certain players do not carry out their tasks properly on the pitch, then their colleagues will suffer. This means that each player has to carry out his basic tasks to the best of his ability and this requires a disciplined approach on the pitch. In my opinion this can only be achieved if there is also discipline off the pitch." For Van Gaal, that meant punctuality, eating together, and looking after physical fitness.

Discipline, though, was only one strand of his trinity of core beliefs, along with communication and team building. To encourage players to discuss soccer issues, Van Gaal, having noticed that players tended to chat unselfconsciously while seeing the team physician, even extended medical treatment sessions. Team building, to an extent, followed discipline and communication: Van Gaal wanted players to have an understanding of the strengths and weaknesses of their teammates to make it easier for them to cover. That was reinforced by a series of drills, perhaps the most notorious of which saw the players holding hands in a circle while heading the ball to keep it off the ground.

In terms of shape, Van Gaal made clear what had long been implicit in Ajax's 4–3–3, which was that, with one of the central defenders stepping out to be a holding midfielder, it was really a 3–4–3: a back three that marked zonally, two wingers flanking a striker, and a diamond shape in midfield. "In modern football," Van Gaal said, "the players in the middle of the back four...have really become playmakers." They, he explained, had space, whereas the number 10, the advanced central midfielder, had become too restricted to control the tempo of the game. When Ajax won the UEFA Cup in 1992, Van Gaal's first major trophy, he had Wim Jonk as his number 4, the center-back turned holding midfielder. In a side of extraordinary technical ability, the two full-backs in that lineup were Frank De Boer and Danny Blind. Sonny Silooy was a defensive center-back, but the other three in Van Gaal's back four all played as midfielders later in their careers. Van Gaal then brought Frank Rijkaard back from AC Milan to play as the 4; while at Euro 96, when Guus Hiddink used a similar system, he opted for a player who wasn't a defender in any sense, Clarence Seedorf.

Giving playmaking duties to the number 4, though, meant a change of role for the player who operated behind the central striker. "The Ajax number 10," Kormelink and Seeverens wrote, "...has to set an example by pursuing his opponent." For Van Gaal, who initially used Bergkamp in the role and then Rob Alflen, his ideal was always the industrious and skillful Finnish player Jari Litmanen, who joined the club in summer 1992. "When Ajax lose possession," Kormelink and Seeverens said, "he immediately carried out his defensive tasks, and when Ajax are in possession, he chooses the right moment to appear alongside the centre-forward as the second striker."

In turn the duties of the center-forward changed, and Van Gaal was always quick to dismiss those who criticized strikers such as Stefan Pettersson or Ronald De Boer for their comparatively poor goals return: "They were skilled at playing one-twos and creating space for their colleagues. Because Ajax play in a small area of the field, the mobile midfielders and, in many cases, the defenders can cover the ground quickly to get in scoring positions."

Where Van Gaal's philosophy differed from the Total Football that had emerged in the seventies, though, was that he was adamant midfielders should not run beyond their wingers to create overlaps. That was partly for defensive security, so that a missed attempt at an overlap did not expose the full-back, but also so that the winger always had space ahead of him to move into. The midfielder was there for support and to ensure that, if necessary, the ball could be switched quickly from one flank to the other.

Training focused heavily on passing drills, setting up scenarios to encourage both pressing and retaining possession under pressure. One of Van Gaal's favorites was known as 5:3, although oddly he was failed on it when he took his coaching badge on the grounds that it didn't relate to "a real football situation." It involved four players working along the sides of a rectangle, with another player on their team in the center surrounded by three defenders. The team of five had to retain possession, with the central player permitted to play only one-touch passes to keep the ball away from the other three. Van Gaal would also, on a half field, play a game of six against seven, the catch being that the seven had no goalkeeper so had to press rapidly to prevent being caught out by long shots.

Van Gaal's Ajax beat Torino in the UEFA Cup final of 1992 and went on to win the league three times. Their crowning glory, though, came in the Champions League final in 1995 against Fabio Capello's Milan, which had hammered Cruyff's Barcelona 4–0 in the final the previous year. Milan played the familiar 4–4–2, with Zvonimir Boban more advanced than Marcel Desailly in central midfield, but there were also tweaks to try to shut Ajax down. The center-forward Daniele Massaro, for instance, pulled right whenever Blind or Rijkaard had the ball to try to prevent the pass out to the left-back Frank De Boer—or at least to make sure than when he received possession he couldn't play the ball back infield. With Boban occupying Rijkaard, that meant most of Ajax's play in the first half came through the right-back, Michael Reiziger, a less adept long passer than De Boer. That, in turn, meant the service to Ronald De Boer—for Van Gaal had no qualms about long passes hit from deep to the center-forward—tended to be misplaced, frustrating Seedorf as he tried to get forward on the right side of midfield. As Desailly stifled Litmanen, Blind again and again was left to hit long balls out to Finidi George on the right.

At half-time, Van Gaal told Rijkaard to drop deeper, away from Boban, and play more as part of a back four. That gave him more time and space and allowed him to dictate the game, particularly when Kanu came on for Seedorf eight minutes into the half and Frank De Boer moved to the right side of midfield, pushing higher than Seedorf had done and so driving Demetrio Albertini back. Ajax began to dominate, controlling 60 percent of second-half possession and, after Patrick Kluivert had come on for Litmanen, Kanu, playing as the 10, began to gain the advantage over a weary Desailly. It was his pass, after a move initiated down the left by Marc Overmars, that set Kluivert up to score the only goal of the game with five minutes remaining.

Given Ajax's relative lack of resources and the youth of the team, that was a remarkable triumph, an extraordinary vindication of Van Gaal's philosophy. It carried Ajax to the final again the following year, but they were beaten on penalties by Juventus, and after that the break-up of the side was inevitable. Van Gaal replaced Bobby Robson at Barcelona, furthering the Total Football influence there, even if he and Johan Cruyff did

Ajax 1 AC Milan 0, Champions League final, Ersnt-Happel-Stadion, Vienna, 24 May 1995

constantly squabble like two Marxist theorists debating obscure doctrinal details. Ajax, meanwhile, undermined by the Bosman ruling of 1995 and by the way Champions League revenues are distributed, have never quite been the same.

Van Gaal, perhaps, has equally never been the same. Although he won two league titles at Barcelona, his battles with Cruyff and his natural bluntness meant he never quite seemed at home there. A stint with the Netherlands national team didn't work out, and neither did a return to Barça, nor a spell as a sporting director at Ajax. Only after dropping down a level to manage AZ did Van Gaal begin to be successful again—and that required a change of approach, as he adopted a far more attacking style. Improbably, he led AZ to the Dutch title in 2009. That earned him a move to Bayern, where he laid the foundations for the later successes of Jupp Heynckes and Pep Guardiola before, again adopting a counterattacking approach, he took the Netherlands national side to third place at the 2014 World Cup. But in a subsequent spell at Manchester United, Van Gaal tried to return to what he saw as the true Ajax principles. Perhaps his players couldn't grasp the positional demands he was making of them, or perhaps the increased pace of the modern game had exposed his interpretation of Total Football as too mannered, too risk averse, too obsessed with ball retention—which was what his critics had said all along. The result was a series of performances in which United passed the ball around some distance from their opponent's goal and got nowhere. An FA Cup success in his second season couldn't save him, and he left the job in 2016.

———

On the other side of the Atlantic, an equally driven coach was also exploring the possibilities of Total Football. But where Van Gaal had prioritized possession, Marcelo Bielsa was more interested in pressing. What is strange, given how profound the impact of the Dutch side of 1974 on South American soccer was, is that it took so long for any South American coach to try to employ Michels's principles themselves. When one finally did, he took its ethos so much to heart that he even replicated the sense of overreaching idealism that lay at its core. No coach this millennium has been so influential as Bielsa but, since taking gold with Argentina at the 2004 Olympics, he has won nothing. The way has become more important than the winning.

Innovation often comes from those who approach a subject from a different angle. Bielsa desperately wanted to be a soccer player, even leaving home when he was fifteen to move into accommodations at the Rosario club Newell's Old Boys—he lasted two days before being kicked out because he refused to leave his two-stroke Puma motorcycle outside—but his background was academic. Most of his family members were politicians or lawyers, or both, and it's said his grandfather had more than thirty thousand books in his home. Knowledge, the young Bielsa learned, was something to be treasured; information something to be collected and categorized. "I am a student of football," he said. "I watch videos, read, analyse, but beneath all my technical talk the great principle is not to concede too much space."

He subscribes to "over forty" international sports magazines. He has a collection of thousands of videos and DVDs. When he turned up for his interview with Vélez Sársfield in 1997, he brought fifty-one videos with him to explain his ideas to the club's directors. When he took the job there, he insisted on an office with a computer with the capacity to take screenshots from videos—something that was revolutionary at the time. Once, when asked how he planned to spend the Christmas and New Year's vacation, Bielsa explained that he intended to do two hours of physical exercise each day and spend fourteen hours watching videos.

As a boy, Bielsa had his mother buy him copies of *El Gráfico* and then index them. That wasn't all she did for him: she also instilled a ferocious determination. "The influence of my mother was fundamental in my life," he said. "For her, no effort was sufficient." As his players acknowledge, in that regard Bielsa is very much his mother's son. "At first he seems tough and he may even annoy you with his persistence and don't-take-no-for-an-answer resilience, but in the end he is a genius," said the forward Fernando Llorente, who played for him at Athletic. "He convinces you to keep working and running and it can be seen in his teams' games and practices. He knows more than anyone in the world, he is elite. Once you get used to him you love him."

Although (or perhaps because) his father was a fan of Rosario Central, Bielsa grew up a fan of their rivals, Newell's, and it was them he joined as a thirteen-year-old. As a player he was good on the ball but slow and not particularly good in the air. Although he did eventually play four times for the club, by the time Bielsa was twenty-one, it had become obvious that he had no future as a professional player, and he left.

He studied agronomy and then physical education before, at the age of twenty-five, moving to Buenos Aires to take up a position coaching the city university's soccer team. He approached the job with typical thoroughness, watching three thousand players before selecting his twenty-man squad. Immediately it was obvious he was not just another coach: he carried a thesaurus with him on the training field and addressed players using the formal pronoun *usted*. He became a youth coach at Newell's under José Yudica before succeeding him in 1990.

His basic soccer philosophy had already taken shape. "He changed our tactics of course," said the midfielder Juan Manuel Llop,

> but there was a big change between the 1980s and the 1990s anyway. The more experienced players looked at him out of the corner of their eyes because he was not an established coach, he was not well known, so you waited to see what he did because you weren't sure what to expect. Tactically it was a radical change: he altered the fitness preparation enormously, he worked set pieces very thoroughly and paid close attention to all details. That was the main change. Marcelo's philosophy took place within changes taking place between two decades. The style was very practical. It was a very aggressive style, looking for every man to win his personal duel—when that happens, it shifts a match in your favour and that was how Marcelo planned games. It was adding up the sum of winning individual battles, along with controlling possession as well as always looking to go forward and attack. Of course we had to balance that with defence but that was the idiosyncrasy of Marcelo's style.

Where Argentinian soccer had long been divided between *bilardisme* and *menottisme*—or between the Estudiantes of 69 and the Hurácan of 73, as Bielsa put it—he found a third way. "I spent sixteen years of my life listening to them: eight to Menotti who is a coach who prioritises inspiration and eight to Bilardo who is a coach who prioritises functionality," he said after becoming national coach in 1998. "And I tried to take the best from each."

Menotti and Bilardo responded according to type. "Bielsa is a young man with concerns," said Menotti, ever the café theorist willing to expound at length on minor philosophical details. "He has ideas and he knows how to develop them. But we do not agree on the starting point: he thinks football is predictable and I do not." Bilardo, pragmatic as ever, claimed Bielsa was simply repeating what he had done. "I share his thinking because it seems to me that we did that in 1986," he said. "They have many videos to study opponents, as I did back then."

Bielsa's obsessive video analysis was part of a wider pattern of meticulousness. By the time he led Athletic to the Europa League final in 2012, it had been noticed that he would always cross the technical area with thirteen steps, even if that meant taking absurdly short strides. While youth coach at Newell's, he decided there were probably players from the interior who were being missed by the big clubs. He divided his map of Argentina into seventy sections and then visited each to watch players, driving over five thousand miles in his Fiat 147 because he was afraid of flying.

Decisions once made, if he believed he'd made them for the right reasons, were rigorously adhered to. When he took the Argentina job in 1998, he decided, based on his experience in Mexico with Club América, a team owned by TV executives, that he would give no one-on-one interviews. He wanted the smallest provincial paper to have the same access as the biggest multinational television station and so decided to deal with the media only through press conferences. Given he would take questions from anybody and would answer in great and labyrinthine detail, that often meant his press conferences went on for several hours, but, having reached his conclusion as to what was fair, he maintained the practice.

Equally, he ensured he never got too close to his players by refusing to talk to them about anything other than soccer: they must remain to him bundles of attributes to be deployed appropriately rather than personalities. "I'm going to be your friend the day you retire from football," he told the Newell's midfielder Cristian Domizzi. He would drill those players relentlessly, running them through preplanned moves repeatedly, almost as though to minimize the human factor; that was what Menotti was complaining when he spoke of Bielsa believing the game too predictable.

The drills may have been *bilardista*, but the basic thrust of Bielsa's play was far more towards the *menottista* end of the spectrum. Bilardo saw the ideal way of playing as being with seven players to defend and three to attack; Bielsa's approach was far, far more aggressive. "I am obsessive about attack," he said. "When I watch videos it's for attacking not for defending. My football, in defence, is very simple: 'We run all the time.' I know that it's easier to defend than create. To run, for example, is a decision of the will, to create you need an indispensable amount of talent."

Defending for Bielsa was about proactivity; it wasn't a question of packing men behind the ball and entering a bunker. For him the key was to win the ball back as high up the field as possible, to stifle the opposition's attacks almost before they had begun. "While the opponent has the ball," he explained, "the whole team presses, always trying to cut off the play as close as possible to the opponent's goal; when we get it we look to play with dynamism and create the spaces for improvisation."

His philosophy, he said, could be broken down to four terms, *concentración permanente, movilidad, rotación, y repenitización*: the first three are relatively easy to translate—permanent focus, mobility and rotation; the fourth, though, is a classic Bielsa term. In music, *repenitización* is used for the practice of playing a piece without having rehearsed it first: it's not extemporization as such in that it involves sight reading, and yet in soccer it clearly has some sense of improvisation. It carries a sense of urgency, too. In a sense it's the key to the whole Bielsa philosophy: it demands players repeatedly do things for the first time, a paradox that perhaps suggests the glorious futility of what he is trying to achieve. "The possible is already done," Bielsa said during his time at Newell's. "We are doing the impossible."

That gives his project, his dedication to his theories, a quasi-religious aspect that perhaps explains the way that those who follow him can at times seem almost like a cult. To be *bielsista* requires faith, for his style is one that seems often counterintuitive. In February 1992, his own faith was sorely tested, but he emerged from the wilderness more convinced that what he was doing was right than ever before.

Although Newell's had beaten Boca Juniors in the play-off to be champions in 1990–1991, they'd won only six games in the *clausura*. That might have been put down to fatigue—and the tournament structure didn't exactly encourage a team who'd won the *apertura* to give their all in the *clausura*—but Newell's also began 1991–1992 abysmally, winning only three games in the *apertura*: thirty-eight league matches in 1991 had brought just nine wins. "We had two poor seasons because of the level that was demanded of us to fight for the title," Llop explained. "We had a small squad too. All players from the squad were from the youth system, so Marcelo was extremely demanding and along with the pressure of challenging for the title it made a certain easing off inevitable. It's a phase you go through." Newell's did start the *clausura* with a win, beating Quilmes 2–0, but then they faced a Copa Libertadores tie at home to San Lorenzo. They lost, 6–0.

Bielsa was distraught. The team went on to Santa Fe for that weekend's league game against Unión and it was there, in the Hotel Conquistador, that something extraordinary happened. "I shut myself in my room, turned off the light, closed the curtains and I realised the true meaning of an expression we sometimes use lightly: 'I want to die.' I burst into tears. I could not understand what was happening around me. I suffered as a professional and I suffered as a fan."

He phoned his wife, Laura, "and presented an argument that for many would be irrefutable: 'For three months our daughter was held between life and death. Now she is fine. Does it make any sense that I want the earth to swallow me over the result of a football match?' The reasoning was brilliant but, nonetheless, my suffering from what had happened demanded immediate vindication." This was his crisis: what had happened against San Lorenzo wasn't just a defeat; Bielsa wasn't just questioning his capacity as a coach. His choice of words was telling: it wasn't merely a solution he was looking for; it was vindication for the entire philosophy by which he played his soccer and lived his life.

Bielsa called his players together. "If we have to rethink the project," he said, "we will do it together. We will seek a new way of doing things if we

Newell's Old Boys 1992

don't feel able to achieve what we set out to do at the start of preseason." Newell's drew 0–0 against Unión, but Bielsa was set on his new path. It wasn't, he decided, that what he'd done before had gone too far; rather, it hadn't gone far enough. "Still under the emotional shock," he said, "there was born a new manner of understanding the tactics of the team. For quite some time I had had some ideas about individuality and its contribution to the joint effort, which I hadn't put into practice because they involved too many rotations in the field. We came through our failings to refresh the structure and a seemingly unfortunate situation allowed us to relaunch the general idea, through a series of changes of position."

Julio Saldaña tended to play as a right-back—but Bielsa switched him to the left. He became the image of the toughness and dedication of that Newell's side: his wife was killed in a car crash that year but he played on, finding strength in Bielsa and the team unit. Eduardo Berizzo, subsequently a devoutly *bielsista* coach at Celta Vigo and Sevilla, went from playing on the left side of defense to the back of midfield. Fernando Gamboa, a natural *libero*, went to the right, although with a brief to tuck in

behind the defense if the center-back Mauricio Pochettino was drawn forward by the man he was marking.

"I was playing full-back and we went to Unión de Santa Fe and he put
me in the centre of midfield, and that game was the change," said Llop.

That was the moment when we took off and when he took off as coach.
it was what set us on the way in that championship. Marcelo used me
in many different positions. I was mostly central midfield but also
played out wide, or as the stopper, or libero; to a large extent I was the
utility player. He looked to give players a certain versatility. It wasn't
a problem changing positions because we were convinced by what we
were doing. When you see the results, when you win two titles, when
you beat Boca away, reach the Copa Libertadores final you can see that
it is working and you are willing to do what he tells you.

The 3–4–3 was the basic shape but, Bielsa explained "the scheme always
depended on the characteristics of our opponents." Position and formation
became secondary. As Sacchi had determined, for players to hold their positions was a reactive way of playing; with a proactive outlook, positions have
value only relative to other positions; far more important are the principles
by which players adopt their positions. Bielsa's tutor in that regard was the
Uruguayan Oscar Washington Tabárez, a coach whose pragmatism seems
oddly incongruent with his own idealism. "Football," Bielsa said, "rests on
four fundamentals, as outlined by Oscar Tabárez: 1) defence; 2) attack; 3)
how you move from defence to attack; 4) how you move form attack to
defence. The issue is trying to make those passages as smooth as possible."

Bielsa was helped in that by the *polifuncionalidad*—versatility—in the
Newell's squad, something that allowed his players to adapt to the game
and made them unpredictable from an attacking point of view. If, for instance, Gerardo Martino, the attacking central midfielder, found himself
facing two holding players, Alfredo Berti could push forward so Martino
didn't face "an unequal struggle." That had consequences elsewhere, of
course. "What do we do with Berizzo when he remains alone against two
creative midfielders?" Bielsa asked. "Llop has to go up to the position that
Berti left or Saldaña goes into the position of Berizzo, *el Toto* [Berizzo]
thus running to the original demarcation of Berti.... Both possibilities are
valid, and which to apply is left to the judgment of the players." That players should take responsibility was a central tenet; Bielsa was a workaholic
and a perfectionist, but he was never as controlling as, say, Rafa Benítez.
Rather he would assign young players homework, asking them to analyze
their next opponent or their previous match to encourage them to think
about the game and plan tactical strategies.

Certain principles remained sacrosanct. "We can't have anybody in the squad who thinks they can win games on their own," Bielsa said. "The key is to occupy the pitch well, to have a short team with no more than 25m from front to back and to have a defence that is not distracted if somebody moves position." In that, of course, Bielsa sounds very much like Sacchi.

The new approach was hugely successful. Newell's won four and drew three of their remaining seven group games to reach the last sixteen of the Libertadores. They lost just once in winning the *clausura*. They beat Defensor Sporting of Uruguay in the Libertadores to set up a quarterfinal against San Lorenzo. This time they hammered them 4–0 in Rosario, 5–1 on aggregate, to reach the semis, in which they edged by América de Cali on penalties.

The final, against São Paulo, also went to penalties, and this time Newell's lost. Bielsa, seemingly exhausted by the emotional strain of coaching a team he supported to play in the style he envisaged, resigned and accepted an offer from Atlas in Mexico. He moved on to América before returning to Argentina in 1997, winning another title with Vélez. Since then, all he has won is an Olympic gold with Argentina in 2004. Near misses and beautiful failure have become his narrative, so that there is something of the alchemist about Bielsa, forever questing vainly after the absolute. His comment at Newell's that he was straining for the impossible was perhaps more literal than anybody realized at the time. In that, Bielsa inclines far more to Menotti than Bilardo: his medal haul—three Argentinian titles and an Olympic gold—is not particularly impressive, but he will be remembered for the way his sides played. More than that, he inspired a generation.

Fatigue has always been the curse of the Bielsa side. The intensity he demands seems unsustainable over any protracted period. His first season at Athletic, 2011–2012, was typical. After an awkward start as players took time to adapt, Athletic hit an irresistible patch of form in March, demolishing Manchester United home and away in the Europa League. By May, though, weariness had set in, and they lost tamely 3–0 to Atlético in the Europa League final before succumbing to Barcelona in the final of the Copa del Rey. When the center-forward Fernando Llorente arrived to train with Spain before the European Championship, he was so exhausted that the national coach, Vicente Del Bosque, said he knew immediately he would play no part in the tournament. By the start of the following season, Javi Martínez had left; Llorente, still apparently shattered, had made clear he wanted to go; and Bielsa had fallen out with members of the board who objected to his criticism of construction work at the training ground. It was all grimly predictable: Bielsa's vision undermined by such earthly concerns as money, ambition, and builders missing deadlines. "If players weren't human," he had said almost fifteen years earlier, "I would never lose."

The perfection Bielsa sought might have been glimpsed only in flashes, but many who followed him were more moderate, allowed their idealism to be tempered by pragmatism, and had greater success as a result. Some, such as Jorge Sampaoli, were overt disciples. In 2011, his Universidad de Chile side were untouchable, winning both *apertura* and *clausura* and sweeping all before them on their way to the Copa Sudamericana, becoming the first Chilean side in two decades to win a continental championship. After winning another *apertura* in 2012, Sampaoli was appointed national coach, continuing the legacy established by Bielsa in his time in the job between 2007 and 2011, and winning Chile's first ever Copa América in 2015. In the final, Chile beat an Argentina side managed by Gerardo Martino, who had taken Paraguay to the final of the 2011 Copa América. Martino had been part of Bielsa's team at Newell's and had clearly taken much from him. But the most successful *bielsista* coach is Pep Guardiola, the latest in a philosophical line stretching back 140 years.

19

GHOSTS AND THE MACHINE

The classical winger was all but dead, butchered in the sixties by Viktor Maslov, Alf Ramsey, and Osvaldo Zubeldía. By the midnineties, it seemed that all *fantasistas* might go the same way, sacrificed before that great bugbear of Willy Meisl, the fetishization of speed. Arrigo Sacchi may have found a beauty in system, but more generally the effect of pressing was to stifle creativity. As had happened throughout history, after Herbert Chapman, after Helenio Herrera, after Ramsey, the defensive elements of tactical innovation took root far more readily than the attacking ones. Blanket five-man midfields became commonplace; muscularity seemed to matter more than finesse; the aesthetic fell before the pragmatic. West Germany's less than inspiring success in the 1990 World Cup—excellent as they had been in the group stage—was followed by victory for an overwhelmingly functional Denmark in Euro 92. Brazil won the 1994 World Cup by that least Brazilian of methods—a penalty shoot-out following a goalless draw—and with a team that featured two midfield destroyers in Dunga and Mauro Silva. The future seemed negative. And yet, come the turn of the millennium, soccer was as attacking as it had been for two decades.

Euro 2000 was arguably the best tournament of the modern era. Germany, torpid, physical, and outdated, went home without winning a game; England, despite squeezing Steve McManaman, Paul Scholes, and David Beckham into their midfield, were made to look almost as sluggish and failed to progress from the group stage; and although Italy proved defensive soundness will never go out of fashion, battling with their modified 3–4–1–2 to reach the final almost despite themselves, there was much that was joyous.

France, the champions, fielded not merely Thierry Henry as a graceful and unorthodox center-forward but also Youri Djorkaeff, Zinédine Zidane, and Christophe Dugarry. The two losing semifinalists were almost

Germany 1996 (2–1 (AET – Golden Goal) v Czech Republic, Euro 96 final, Wembley, London)

France 2000 (2–1 (AET – Golden Goal) v Italy, Euro 2000 final, De Kuip, Rotterdam)

as blessed. Holland fitted Boudewijn Zenden, Dennis Bergkamp, and Marc Overmars behind Patrick Kluivert, while Portugal found room for three of Luís Figo, Manuel Rui Costa, Sergio Conceicão, and João Pinto behind Nuno Gomes. There were even swan songs for two of the great creative players of the previous decade, Gheorghe Hagi and Dragan Stojković, although both were slower and played deeper than they had in their heyday. Compare that to the Germany side that won the tournament in 1996 with a back five protected by Dieter Eilts, and the contrast is astonishing. It wasn't just that playmakers had been preserved; over the span of four years, wingers had been resurrected as well.

In a sense, the very defensiveness of the soccer led to the call for players capable of unpicking opposing defenses, who were often themselves given very little defensive responsibility. This was particularly true in Italy—hence their 3–4–1–2 formation in the Euro 2000 finals—where what was known as the "broken team" developed. There would be an attacking three (occasionally joined by a wing-back or a midfielder) and a defensive seven. Alberto Zaccheroni's *scudetto*-winning AC Milan of 1997–1998, for instance, played a 3–4–1–2 that featured a front two of George Weah and Oliver Bierhoff, with Leonardo just behind. Occasionally Thomas Helveg or Christian Ziege would get forward from wing-back to support, but the two central midfielders, Demetrio Albertini and Massimo Ambrosini, were largely defensive. At Juventus, similarly, Zinédine Zidane, Alessandro Del Piero, and Filippo Inzaghi were backed up by the industry of Edgar Davids, Didier Deschamps, Angelo Di Livio, and Antonio Conte. The role of the playmaker became increasingly necessary, increasingly exalted, and increasingly impossible; and by 2000 Italian soccer was heading down a cul-de-sac from which they arguably didn't escape until Carlo Ancelotti, at Milan, deployed Andrea Pirlo, a modern *regista*, deep in midfield.

Other countries, though, reacted to the negativity with greater adventure, fielding as many as three *fantasistas*. FIFA, rightly, accepted the credit for the rule changes that followed the 1990 World Cup—abolishing the backpass and outlawing the tackle from behind—but it wasn't quite as simple as that, for these artists were not the same as the artists of old. As Adolfo Pedernera pointed out at the beginning of the era of pressing and of the dominance of system, in such an age there can be no place for bohemians. Yet there is, clearly, a place for artistry; it can't all be about physical effort and defensive positioning. "There's a right-wing football and a left-wing football," said César Luis Menotti. "Right-wing football wants to suggest that life is struggle. It demands sacrifices. We have to become of steel and win by any method...obey and function, that's what those with power want from the players. That's how they create retards, useful idiots that go with the system."

Menotti had a particular ideological drum to beat, and his sides were always rather more systematized than he cared to admit, but here, surely, there is a truth (although the left-wing/right-wing dichotomy is unhelpful: for one thing, the Soviets played highly systematized soccer—"right-wing" by Menotti's definition; and for another, if political terms are to be ascribed to playing styles, is there not a reflection of social democracy in the egalitarian but largely flair-free 4–4–2s of Scandinavia?). Gianni Brera, in his quest for perfect goalless draws, may have appreciated the idea of a team without such fallible flamboyances as artistry, but few others would: even Zubeldía had Juan Verón, even Herrera had Sandro Mazzola, even Carlos Bilardo had Diego Maradona. A compromise between the two is necessary. As Marcelo Bielsa put it, "Totally mechanised teams are useless, because they get lost when they lose their script. But I don't like either ones that live only on the inspiration of their soloists, because when God doesn't turn them on, they are left totally at the mercy of their opponents."

The question then becomes how that artistry is to be incorporated into a system, without becoming systematized to the point of predictability. It is in Argentina, presumably because the eternal conflict between the *bilardistas* and the *menottistas* brings the issues to the surface, that the debate has been most fierce. There, the playmaker, the number 10, is revered as he is nowhere outside the Balkans. Italians divide playmakers into *trequartistas*, who play in the hole behind the attack (Francesco Totti, for instance), and *registas*, who are deeper lying (Pirlo). In Argentina, though, the playmaker is the *enganche*—literally "the hook"—who always operates between midfield and attack.

Juan Carlos Lorenzo popularized the position in the 4–3–1–2 he instituted with Argentina at the 1966 World Cup, with Ermindo Onega in the role. There is a certain irony in that, given Lorenzo's reputation as a pragmatist, which is indicative of how significant the changes that followed the switch to four at the back were. Lorenzo saw artistry had a place, incorporated it within his system, and was seen as opposing romance; today romantics in Argentina demand his formation be preserved.

Others followed Lorenzo's lead and, even quarter of a century after Bilardo's success with a 3–5–2, 4–3–1–2, and 3–4–1–2 remained the most common formations in domestic Argentinian soccer. Miguel Russo was part of Bilardo's Estudiantes side of the seventies and is temperamentally inclined to his way of doing things, but in his time as coach of Boca, which ended in December 2007, he felt unable to do away with the *enganche*. "Boca have a tradition of their own, their own structure, and you don't change things when they've won so much," he said. "Even if I want to change it I have to do it slowly."

Onega may have been the first to be deployed in the hole behind two strikers—a development, essentially, on the *ponta da lança* position, itself a development of the inside-forward—but he was certainly not the first playmaker, not even in Argentina. Arguably River Plate in the days of la Máquina had five. Independiente became famous for them. The most notable, perhaps, was Ricardo Bochini, who won the Libertadores every year between 1972 and 1975 and again in 1984. He was described by the journalist Hugo Asch as "a midget, ungainly, imperturbable, without a powerful shot, nor header, nor charisma," and yet still a wonderfully imaginative player. Elsewhere, most wondrously, there was Diego Maradona, and after him, a host of new Maradonas: Ariel Ortega, Pablo Aimar, Javier Saviola, Andres d'Alessandro, Juan Román Riquelme, Carlos Tévez, and Leo Messi.

Are such players relevant to the modern game? Of course they are. Or rather, of course Tévez and Messi are. But then neither are really playmakers in the traditional sense. Tévez is a support forward who can play on the wing, while Messi, having been a winger who cut infield, has become the image of a false nine. His use as an *enganche* at the 2010 World Cup was generally regarded as a failure, although that probably had more to do with a lack of balance in midfield than any great failing on his part.

It was Riquelme, mournful of demeanor, graceful of movement, and deft of touch, who best embodied the old-style *enganche* until his retirement in 2012. When Eduardo Galeano drew the comparison between soccer artists and the devotees of *milonga* clubs, it was to players like Riquelme he was referring, and it is upon him that the debate about the future of such players has focused. Riquelme has become less a player than a cipher for an ideology.

"In the pause," the columnist Ezequiel Fernández Moores wrote in *La Nacion*, quoting a phrase common in the blues tradition of Argentina, "there is no music, but the pause helps to make the music." He went on to recount an anecdote about Charles Mingus walking into a bar to see an impetuous young drummer attempting a frenetic solo. "No," Mingus said, "it's not like that. You have to go slowly. You have to say hello to people, introduce yourself. You never enter a room shouting. The same is true of music."

But is it true of soccer? Nostalgists and romantics would like to believe so, and Jorge Valdano raises the intriguing point that the incessant urgency of the modern game may lie in its packaging for television. "Football is no longer mysterious," he said.

We no longer experience it according to our own imagination because the cameras are everywhere. Pictures on a screen can't compete with the pictures you can form in your head. And it's impacting the way the game is played.

I heard [the boxer] Carlos Monzón's trainer, Amilcar Brusa, explain that when a boxer fights on television, it's crucial he throws many punches, regardless of where they land. That's because television demands activity. It's the same with football. The game has become more intense than it needs to be. In South America we have the concept of the "pause" in football, the moment of reflection which foreshadows an attack. It's built into the game, like music, which also needs pauses, drops in intensity. The problem is that this doesn't work in the language of television. A moment of low intensity in a televised football game is seen by some as time to change channels. So the game is getting quicker and quicker because television demands it.

The problem is that when two highly energetic systems clash, it can create games like the 2007 Champions League semifinal between Liverpool and Chelsea, which, for all its dynamism and physical exertion, produced little if anything of beauty and was notoriously described by Valdano as resembling "shit on a stick." That is not exactly good for ratings either.

Whether television is to blame or not, it did not help Riquelme, who stood outside the prevailing perception that urgency is essential. Moores argued that Riquelme would have to change, that he would have to learn, like Messi, a directness. Can the game today cope with a player who does not charge and hustle and chase, but exists apart from the hurly-burly, as the still point of an ever-turning world, guiding and coaxing through imagination rather than physique? "Riquelme's brains," Valdano went on, "save the memory of football for all time.... He is a player of the time when life was slow and we took the chairs out on the streets to play with the neighbours." Perhaps his melancholic demeanor reflected his knowledge that he was born out of his time. Then again, perhaps his lack of pace would have found him out whichever era he played in: he is, after all, not a paradigm for theoretical debate but an individual with many very great gifts and one very obvious weakness.

In Argentina, Riquelme was adored and despised in equal measure; the depth of feeling he provoked was indicative of how central the playmaker is to Argentinian notions of soccer. The *enganche*, Asch wrote in a column in *Perfil* in 2007, is "a very Argentinian invention, almost a necessity." The playmaker, he went on "is an artist, almost by definition a difficult, misunderstood soul. It would, after all, hardly seem right if our geniuses were level-headed"; it is as though they must pay a price for their gifts, must wrestle constantly to control and channel them. Certainly there is that sense with Riquelme, who eventually frustrated the Villarreal coach Manuel Pellegrino to the extent that he exiled him from the club.

"We are not," Asch wrote, "talking necessarily about a leader. Leaders were Rattín, Ruggeri, Passarella or Perfumo, intimidating people. No. Our man is a romantic hero, a poet, a misunderstood genius with the destiny of a myth.... Riquelme, the last specimen of the breed, shares with Bochini the melancholy and the certainty that he only works under shelter, with a court in his thrall and an environment that protects him from the evils of this world." Perhaps, Asch said, he should never have left Boca.

Well, perhaps, but it was not that Riquelme could not prosper away from the club he clearly adored—nor, as his unhappy time under Julio César Falcioni demonstrated, that Boca would always play in the way he demanded. He struggled at Barcelona, but he was the major reason Villarreal reached a Champions League semifinal in 2005–2006, and his intelligence was central to Argentina's sublime progress to the quarterfinal of the World Cup later that summer. And yet he took blame for his sides' exits from both competitions. He missed a penalty against Arsenal in the Champions League and was withdrawn after seventy-two anonymous minutes against Germany. Some cited Riquelme's supposed tendency to go missing in big games, but what is striking is that the coach José Pekerman replaced him not with a *fantasista*, despite having Messi and Saviola available, but with the far more defensive Esteban Cambiasso, as he switched to a straight 4–4–2. Pekerman said he had seen signs of fatigue from Riquelme and that he was worried about Germany's height advantage, but many argued that he had lost his nerve completely and, with it, faith in the formation because of Riquelme's ineffectiveness. Little wonder that Riquelme has commented—as a matter of fact, rather than from bitterness—that when his side loses, it is always his responsibility.

And this, really, is the problem with a designated playmaker: he becomes too central. If a side has only one creative outlet, it is very easy to stifle—particularly when modern systems allow two holding midfielders without significant loss of attacking threat. That is true of the 4–3–1–2, its close cousin the diamond, and the 3–4–1–2. All three can also suffer from a lack of width. Significantly, under Bielsa, Argentina played at times with a radically attacking 3–3–1–3, a formation almost unique at that level. Bielsa had already experimented with a 3–3–2–2, using Juan Sebastian Verón and Ariel Ortega behind Gabriel Batistuta and Claudio López, with Javier Zanetti and Juan Pablo Sorín as wing-backs and Diego Simeone as the holding midfielder in front of three central defenders. That was essentially a variant of the 3–4–1–2, with one of the central midfielders becoming an additional *trequartista*, but it was just as prone to the lack of width as the more orthodox version. Shifting one of the center-forwards and one of the *trequartistas* wide and converting them into wingers, though, alleviated that. The playmaker was provided with a wealth of passing options and the formation was so unusual it was difficult to counter.

"In the defensive phase," the Argentinian coach Cristian Lovrincevich wrote in *EF Deportes*, "the collective pressing method was adopted, with all lines pushing forwards to recover the ball as close as possible to the opposition goal. In essence it was very similar to the Total Football of the Dutch. In the offensive phase, once the ball had been recovered, the team tried to play with depth, avoiding unnecessary delays and the lateralisation of the game. In attack, five or six players were involved; only four positions were mainly defensive—the three defenders and the central midfielder."

The problem with both variants, whether pressing or not, is that once possession is lost, regaining it can be difficult and the team is necessarily vulnerable to the counter. Argentina employed the 3–3–2–2 at the 2002 World Cup and, after the group stage, they had had more possession, created more chances, and won more corners than any other side. Unfortunately, they were also on their way home, having managed just two goals and four points from their three games, raising questions both about defensive weaknesses and about the quality of the chances created. When attacks are funneled down the center, the defending side can simply sit deep, watch the opponents pass the ball around in deep areas, and restrict them to long-range efforts. In the 4–3–1–2 or the 3–4–1–2, width can be provided by good movement from the forwards, or by the shuttling midfielders pulling wide, or by attacking full-backs, but when the system goes wrong, the problem tends to be either a lack of attacking width or the holes left defensively by trying to provide it.

That is not to say that neither formation has any merit, merely that they are restricted in their application. In October 2002, for instance, in a Euro 2004 qualifier in Naples, Yugoslavia fielded a flattened diamond to try to frustrate Italy. Goran Trobok sat in front of the back-four, with Siniša Mihajlović to his left, Nikola Lazetić to his right, Dejan Stanković as a deepish *trequartista*, and Predrag Mijatović dropping off Mateja Kežman. Playing defensively, the plan worked, as Alessandro Del Piero found his space limited, and Yugoslavia arguably had the better of a 1–1 draw. At home in Belgrade against Finland four days later, though, Yugoslavia adopted a similar system—tipped towards attack by the use of Mijatović in midfield and the inclusion of Darko Kovačević as an additional forward—and struggled. With the onus on them to create, rather than relying on breaks, they lacked attacking width, and they struggled defensively as their full-backs were repeatedly isolated against Mika Nurmela and Joonas Kolkka, the two wide players in Finland's 4–4–2. At half-time it was 0–0, at which point Yugoslavia switched to a 3–4–1–2, with

342

Yugoslavia 2 Finland 0, Euro 2004 qualifier, Marakana, Belgrade, 16 October 2002

Mihajlović stepping out from the back three to become an additional mid-fielder. Nurmela and Kolkka suddenly found themselves having to deal with wing-backs, which both gave them a defensive responsibility and diminished the space in which they had to accelerate before meeting a defender; Yugoslavia, with a spare man both in the middle at the back and in the middle of midfield, began to dominate possession, and ended up winning by a comfortable 2–0.

That, perhaps, is the major reason the diamond slipped out of fashion. Of the thirty-two sides who reached the Champions League group stage in 2007–2008, only Mircea Lucescu's Shakhtar Donetsk deployed it in its classic form, and they ran into the classic problems. Particularly in their opening game, at home to Celtic, but also in their second, away to Benfica, they were superb, Razvan Raţ and Darijo Srna flying forward from full-back with the holding midfielder Mariusz Lewandowski dropping back to protect them (the diamond becoming effectively a 3–4–1–2), and the slight Brazilian Jádson operating as a playmaker behind a front two. In their next two games against AC Milan, though, their weakness high up

Shakhtar Donetsk 2007–2008

Shakhtar 2012–2013

the field in wide areas was exposed. They were well beaten in both and, as confidence waned, failed even to qualify for the UEFA Cup.

Shifting to a 3–4–1–2 worked for Yugoslavia against Finland largely because it negated the impact of the opposing wingers, but it is just as liable to render a side one-dimensional, as Croatia found at the 2006 World Cup, where they persisted with three at the back long after the rest of Europe had abandoned it. When they finished third at the World Cup in 1998, Ćiro Blazević had managed at times to squeeze three playmakers into their lineup. Fielding Zvonimir Boban, Robert Prosinečki, and Aljosa Asanović together in central midfield defied logic—it was, as Slaven Bilić said, "the most creative midfield ever"—and yet somehow it worked. That, though, was a one-off, aided by the fact that their back three included, in Bilić and Igor Štimac, two stoppers who were also comfortable on the ball—plus either Dario Šimić or Zvonimir Soldo, both of them equally capable of playing in midfield, who would step out to become a midfielder when necessary. It is notable too that the 3–0 quarterfinal victory over Germany, their best performance of the tournament, came when

Prosinečki was absent, leaving Soldo to operate as a holding midfielder in what was effectively a 3–3–2–2—another of those simple shifts of balance the 3–5–2 permits.

By the time of the 2006 World Cup, their coach, Zlatko Kranjčar, who had been part of Blažević's original 3–5–2 experiment at Dinamo Zagreb in 1982, had gone down the route of Italy in the late nineties. He decided that to play with an out-and-out playmaker—his son Niko Kranjčar—it was necessary to bolster the midfield with two holding players, a formation not dissimilar to that adopted by West Germany in the later stages of the 1986 tournament. However aggressive Srna and Marko Babić were as wing-backs, it couldn't disguise the fact that with Igor Tudor, often a center-back with Juventus, and Niko Kovač—a more complete midfielder but somebody who had become decreasingly creative as his career had gone on—at the back of the midfield, they were effectively playing with seven defenders.

That was enough to earn a battling 1–0 defeat to Brazil, but when Croatia had to take the initiative, as they did against Japan and Australia in their other two group games, they were tiresomely predictable, reliant for creativity either on the forward surges of the wing-backs or on an out-of-sorts Kranjčar. They played stodgy, tedious soccer, and, as their frustration got the better of them, they became overphysical and boorish. The only silver lining for Croatia was that Serbia-Montenegro had an even worse tournament, but it did not go unnoticed how impressive Serbia-Montenegro had been in qualifying, having switched away from the traditional Balkan three at the back. In ten qualifying games, they had conceded only one goal, with their quartet of defenders—Goran Gavrančić, Mladen Krstajić, Nemanja Vidić, and Ivica Dragutinović—attracting the nickname the Fantastic Four. Serbia-Montenegro could blame injuries and disintegrating team morale for their embarrassment in Germany; Croatia's problems seemed to be rooted in the very way they played the game: Serbia had at least begun their process of evolution.

The debate about the merits of 3–5–2, or 3–4–1–2, had dogged Croatian soccer for years. Bilić ended it at a stroke when he replaced Zlatko Kranjčar as coach after the tournament. His side, he announced, would play four at the back, preferably, but not necessarily, in a Dutch-style 4–3–3. The fear among traditionalists was that that would mean the end of the playmaker, but Bilić found a way of accommodating not just one, but two. It might not have been quite the heady days of Blazević's 3–3–2–2, but it was far better than anyone had hoped, far better than Kranjčar's reign.

Bilić supplemented his back four with Niko Kovač as a deep-lying midfielder and found room for not merely two forwards but also Kranjčar on the left, with Luka Modrić in the middle, and Srna on the right. With his

1998 (3–0 v Germany, World Cup quarterfinal, Stade Gerland, Lyon, 4 July 1998)

2006 (2–2 v Australia, World Cup Group Phase, Gottlieb-Daimler Stadium, Stuttgart, 22 June 2006)

2007 (2–0 v Estonia, Euro 2008 qualifier, Maksimir, Zagreb, 8 September 2007)

slight, almost fragile build, Modrić resembles the traditional playmaker, but there is more to his game than that. "My role in the national team is very different to the one I perform with Dinamo," he said in 2007. "Here I have a freer role, but I also have more defensive responsibilities." Significantly, Zlatko Kranjčar had praised his "organizational" qualities when he first called him into the national squad ahead of the World Cup.

Modrić came to represent the new style of playmakers—a *fantasista* with a certain robustness and also a sense of tactical discipline. As his career has gone on, Modrić has tended to play more as a *regista* at the back of the midfield, and he was a hugely influential presence in the 4–3–3 with which Real Madrid became the first side to retain the Champions League in 2017. "Nobody wants playmakers, nobody buys them," Asch explained, speaking of the traditional number 10, the sort of player the young Modrić had been. "Why? Do they hate poetry, do they hate colour?"

It comes back, it would seem, to Tomas Petterson's point about a second order of complexity. Once the systems are understood, once soccer has lost its naivety, it is no longer enough simply to be beautiful; it must be beautiful within the system. "It happens that nobody in the world plays with a playmaker anymore," Asch added. "Midfielders are multifunctional and forwards are blend of tanks and Formula One cars." Maybe so, and the playmaker will be missed, but just as the winger was superseded and phased out by evolution before undergoing a reinvention, so too will the traditional playmaker be reconstituted for a new age. Riquelme was a wonderful player. Before injuries took hold, he prospered again at Boca, to whom he returned at the beginning of 2008. He was, though, the last of a dying breed, a glorious anachronism.

The Nigerian cult of Kanu—which slightly mystifyingly saw him not as a second striker, as he was used throughout his career in Europe, but as a *trequartista*—regularly forced him into the playmaking role for his country, but that has served only to highlight its redundancy. For a time at Portsmouth, Kanu worked because he had in Benjani Mwaruwari a partner who charged about with an intensity that rather cloaked the intelligence of his movement. Benjani did the running while Kanu strolled around in the space between midfield and attack: one was energy, one was imagination, an almost absolute division of attributes that—at Portsmouth's level at least—worked.

At the African Cup of Nations in 2006, Kanu was used to great effect as a substitute. Once the pace of the game had dropped, he would come on, find space, and shape the game. Eventually the pressure from the Nigerian press grew until their coach, Augustin Eguavoen, felt compelled to start him against Côte d'Ivoire in the semifinal. Kanu barely got a kick, shut out by the pace, power, and nous of Côte d'Ivoire's two holding midfielders, Yaya Touré and Didier Zokora. Two years later, in Nigeria's opening game in Sekondi, also against Côte d'Ivoire, their new coach, Berti Vogts, threw him into exactly the same trap. Against one anchorman, perhaps Kanu could have imposed his will and thrived; against two, it was impossible. To say it was to do with his age is to miss the point. The playmaker belongs to an era of individual battles: If he could overcome his marker, he could make the play. Against a system that allows two men to be deployed against him, he can't. Yes, by deploying two men against the playmaker the defensive side is potentially creating space for another, but zonal marking is designed to counter precisely that sort of imbalance. There exactly is the deficiency of the 4–3–1–2: stop the designated playmaker and the flow of creativity is almost entirely stanched.

So how then can a playmaker be used in the modern game? Early versions of Bilić's system—such as that played by Croatia when they beat England 2–0 in Zagreb in October 2006—included Milan Rapaić, a forward-cum-winger on the right; Srna, as a wing-back who is also a fine crosser of the ball, gave them rather more balance. Still, Bilić's Croatia employed five attacking players, something that was highly unusual at the time, which may explain why they conceded three away to Israel and two at Wembley in qualifying for Euro 2008.

Fielding a single creator raises the danger of becoming one-dimensional, but there are other reasons why, in the early years of the twenty-first century, three at the back went through a decline in popularity in every major soccer country apart from Brazil. José Alberto Cortes, head of the coaching course at the University of São Paulo, believes the issue is physical. "With the pace of the modern game," he said, "it is impossible for wing-backs to function in the same way because they have to be quicker and fitter than the rest of the players on the pitch."

Most others, though, saw the turn against three at the back as the result of the effort to incorporate skillful players by bolstering the midfield. There is, of course, an enormous irony here, in that Bilardo's formation in 1986 both popularized three at the back and included a playmaker as a second striker, the very innovation that led to the decline of three at the back. Bilardo's scheme had two markers picking up the opposing center-forwards, with a spare man sweeping behind. If there is only one center-forward to mark, though, that leaves two spare men—one provides cover, a second is redundant—which in turn means a shortfall elsewhere on the field. "There's no point having three defenders covering one centre-forward," explained Miroslav Djukić, the former Valencia defender who became Partizan Belgrade coach in 2007.

Nelsinho Baptista, the experienced Brazilian coach who took charge of Corinthians in 2007, has developed software to explore the weaknesses of

Decline of 3–5–2

○ —simple cancellation

[i] —✗ wing-backs forced back to deal with ○ wingers

[ii] —3✗ defenders dealing with one ○ forward

[iii] —○ full-backs spare—can provide extra man at back;
drive down flank or help out in midfield

one system when matched against another. "Imagine Team A is playing 3–5–2 against Team B with a 4–5–1 that becomes 4–3–3," he said.

> So Team A has to commit the wing-backs to deal with Team B's wingers. That means Team A is using five men to deal with three forwards. In midfield Team A has three central midfielders against three, so the usual advantage of 3–5–2 against 4–4–2 is lost. Then at the front it is two forwards against four defenders, but the spare defenders are fullbacks. One can push into midfield to create an extra man there, while still leaving three v two at the back. So Team B can dominate possession, and also has greater width.

One of Team A's central defenders could, of course, himself step up into midfield, but the problem then is that Team A has four central midfielders, and still lacks width. And if a defender is going to step into midfield, why not simply play a defensive midfielder in that role anyway?

Egypt won a hat trick of African Cups of Nations with a 3–4–1–2 between 2006 and 2010, but that was probably largely because straight 4–4–2 still tended to dominate the thinking in Africa. In 2008, in fact, aside from Egypt—and at times Cameroon—only Guinea and Morocco, both of whom used a 4–2–3–1, did not set up in some form of 4–4–2. Significantly, the majority of the genuine contenders had strong spines and deficiencies wide and, in a generally excellent tournament, the one consistent disappointment was the standard of crossing. That could be a generational freak, or it could be related to the fact that when European clubs are looking to sign African talent, they tend to have what Manchester United's former Africa scout Tom Vernon calls "the Papa Bouba Diop template" in mind. The African players who have succeeded in Europe in the past have usually been big and robust, and so clubs look only for something similar. Players called up by European clubs at a young age develop faster and have a higher profile, and so it is they who make it into the national teams.

Vernon, who ran an academy in the hills above Accra, also believes the way the game is first played by children—at least in Ghana—has a tendency to shape them as central midfielders. "Look at how kids play," he said. "They have a pitch maybe twenty or thirty yards long, and set up two stones a couple of feet apart at either end, often with gutters or ditches marking the boundaries at the sides. So it's a tiny area. The game becomes all about receiving the ball, turning and driving through the middle." The result in the 2008 tournament was that every West African team—and this was particularly true of Côte d'Ivoire—had at least two good central strikers, so they tend to play them with little width that could have unsettled Egypt's two excellent wing-backs, Ahmed Fathy and Sayed Moewad.

Egypt 4 Cameroon 2, African Cup of Nations group, Baba Yara Stadium, Kumasi, 22 January 2008

Egypt 1 Cameroon 0, African Cup of Nations final, Ohene Djan Stadium, Accra,
10 February 2008

In their first game in the 2008 Cup of Nations, Egypt hammered Cameroon 4–2. They went on to add a further ten goals in disposing of Sudan, Zambia, Angola, and Côte d'Ivoire before meeting Cameroon again in the final. In that first game, Cameroon's coach, Otto Pfister, had his players a 4–4–2; in the final, he opted for a 4–2–3–1, and, for the first time in the tournament, Egypt struggled for fluency. The defender Wael Gomaa looked like a spare part, anxiously and uncertainly wandering into midfield, and, although Egypt bossed possession, they ended up beating a limited side only because of an individual error from Rigobert Song. Similarly, in 2010, the only side that really troubled Egypt was Ghana, partly, of course, because they had better players than any of Egypt's other opponents, but also because they set up with Asamoah Gyan as a lone striker.

More recently, the back three has enjoyed a resurgence. Initially its application seemed to be restricted to three basic situations. After Napoli's and Udinese's success with the formation in 2010–2011, as many as thirteen of the twenty Serie A sides used the system at some point in 2011–2012, including the champions Juventus. For Italian sides, which had seen the lack of width of Internazionale and AC Milan humiliatingly exposed by Tottenham and Schalke 04 in the Champions League the previous season, it offered a means of including wide players higher up the field without sacrificing players in the center. It provided width without a winger, whose role has always been distrusted in Italy.

For others, the back three was an overtly defensive system: after all, if a team is looking to sit deep and absorb pressure, accepting the opposition will dominate possession, having two spare men at the back is a useful extra precaution. When Estudiantes, under Alejandro Sabella, went to Vélez Sarsfield in October 2010 intent on securing a draw that would preserve their two-point lead at the top of the table, they played with a back three and four players very deep in midfield. Most of the game was played in Estudiantes' half, and Vélez controlled possession but were restricted by and large to long-range shots. Estudiantes, having secured the draw they desired, went on to win the *apertura*.

And for others, those of a *bielsista* persuasion, the back three is a way to get more players high up the field to try to win the ball back as early as possible. It was that variant that, by 2016, would come to have a profound impact.

———

Bilardo suggested teams should be split with three attackers and seven defenders; Bilić opted for five and five, but the general move in the nineties was towards a middle ground, with four attacking players and six defensive.

When the 4–5–1 first became popular in Western Europe in the late eighties and early nineties, it was widely seen as a defensive system: "the right of the weak," like early *catenaccio*, to be employed against stronger sides to try to frustrate them. Until remarkably recently, it was not unusual to read or hear pundits complaining of sides who refuse to use "two up," yet 4–5–1 was always as implicit in 4–4–2 as 4–4–2 was in 4–2–4.

At least in a British context, strike partnerships in a 4–4–2 tend to fall into two categories: the big man–quick man (John Toshack and Kevin Keegan, Mark Hateley and Ally McCoist, Niall Quinn and Kevin Phillips) or the creator-goalscorer (Kenny Dalglish and Ian Rush, Peter Beardsley and Gary Lineker, Teddy Sheringham and Alan Shearer). In the former, there genuinely were two strikers, but in the latter, did the creator not drift deeper, linking the space between midfield and attack? The remarkable impact on English soccer of Éric Cantona and Gianfranco Zola was largely the result of their ability to drop off and play between the lines, confusing English center-backs just as surely as had Matthias Sindelar and Nándor Hidegkuti. The issue, then, seems one of notation: nobody would have thought of describing, for instance, Sunderland's promotion side of 1989–1990 as playing 4–4–1–1, but with Eric Gates tucked behind Marco Gabbiadini, that is assuredly what it was. And once the instinctive recoil against 4–5–1 has been bypassed, it becomes apparent that it is just as flexible, just as easily recalibrated according to circumstance, as the 3–5–2.

It is arguable, in fact, that the first team to deploy a 4–5–1 to international success was the great Flamengo side of Paulo César Carpegiani, which beat Liverpool 3–0 to win the Intercontinental Cup in 1981 and could not be described as being even remotely negative. Faced with the problem of choosing between four *fantasistas*—Lico, Zico, Adília, and Tita—Carpegiani did exactly what Brazil would do at the 1982 World Cup: he played them all. Rather than laying them out behind two strikers, though, Carpegiani opted to play with Nunes as a lone front man, with Victor Andrade operating as a holding midfielder behind them in what would now be called a 4–1–4–1.

The fluent Tottenham side that finished third in the league and lost in the FA Cup final under David Pleat in 1986–1987 played a similarly attacking variant, with Osvaldo Ardiles holding, Paul Allen and Steve Hodge shuttling, Chris Waddle in one wing, and Glenn Hoddle as a playmaker behind Clive Allen. But more commonly in the eighties, five in midfield was a defensive system. Everton were especially adept at switching to a 4–5–1 for away games in European competition. In the first leg of the quarterfinal of the Cup-Winners' Cup away to Bayern Munich in 1985, for instance, Howard Kendall left out the center-forward Andy Gray, bringing Alan Harper into midfield in his place and leaving Graeme

Flamengo 3 Liverpool 0, Intercontinental Cup, National Stadium, Tokyo, 13 December 1981

Sharp as a lone striker. After a 0–0 draw, Everton restored Gray and won the home leg 3–1. Gray admits that there was nothing particularly subtle about their play that night: they realized the Bayern defense was uncomfortable against the aerial threat they posed and so set out to exploit it.

Generally speaking, the more direct a side, the more defensive they will be in a 4–5–1. The aim for them is simply to plant nine men between the opposition and the goal, then look for the center-forward to battle for possession, hold the ball up, and either lay it off to breaking midfielders or win a dead ball. Ian Wright performed the role to perfection for George Graham's Arsenal in a number of European ties in the early nineties. Once the game becomes about possession and short passing, though, a five-man midfield becomes a far more subtle tool.

In Spain, 4–2–3–1 was common by 2000, and within a couple of years had become almost a default. Perhaps that is not surprising, for it was in Spain that the formation first developed as something distinct from 4–4–2. Once sides had started using their playmaker as a second striker—a trend that emerged with Carlos Bilardo's deployment of Diego Maradona at the 1986 World Cup—the coming of 4–2–3–1 was inevitable. Initially a holding midfielder would be detailed to pick him up—hence the late-nineties boom in players capable of playing what became known as the Makélélé role—at which point the deep-lying forward would start drifting wide to find space. If the holding player followed him, that created space in the middle, so an additional player would be dropped deeper as cover, with consequences for the more attacking midfielders.

Or the evolution could come from the other direction: a side playing 4–4–2, with the wingers pushed high and one of the center-forwards dropping deep, is effectively playing a 4–2–3–1. When Manchester United beat Barcelona in the 1991 Cup-Winners' Cup final, for instance, they had Bryan Robson and Paul Ince holding, with Lee Sharpe and Mike Phelan wide and Brian McClair dropping off Mark Hughes. Everybody still referred to it as 4–4–2, but it was in effect a 4–2–3–1. Arsenal did similarly in Arsène Wenger's first full season in England, with Emmanuel Petit and Patrick Vieira deep, Marc Overmars and Ray Parlour wide, and Dennis Bergkamp behind Nicolas Anelka—although Parlour could tuck in and Overmars push on to produce something more akin to an old-style 4–3–3.

The first to deploy the new formation self-consciously, though, at least according to the Spanish coaching magazine *Training Fútbol*, was Juanma Lillo, later a mentor for Pep Guardiola, while he was in charge of the Segunda Division side Cultural Leonesa in 1991–1992. "My intention was to pressure and to try to steal the ball high up the pitch," he explained. "It was the most symmetrical way I could find of playing with four forwards. One of the great advantages is that having the forwards high allows you to play the midfield high and the defence high, so everybody benefits. But you have to have the right players. They have to be very, very mobile and they have to be able to play when they get the ball. You have to remember that they're pressuring to play, not playing to pressure."

At Leonesa, Lillo had Sami and Teofilo Abajo as his two pivots (the system in Spain is known as the *doble pivot*, with Carlos Nuñez, Ortiz, and Moreno in front of them and Latapia as the lone forward). Seeing the success of the system, Lillo took it to Salamanca. There, according to an editorial in *Training Fútbol*, the players reacted with "faces of incredulity because they thought it was a strange way to play; they responded to the positions they were told to adopt and the distribution of each line of the team with the same sense of strangeness and surprise as someone who had just come face to face with a dinosaur." Nonetheless, it took them to promotion.

The formation rapidly spread. Javier Irureta had been using it with Deportivo la Coruña for a couple of seasons before they won the league title in 2000, and when John Toshack returned to Real Madrid in 1999, he deployed Geremi and Fernando Redondo as his holding midfielders, with Steve McManaman, Raúl, and Elvir Baljić in front of them and either Anelka or Fernando Morientes as the lone striker.

The formation's transfer to England—at least in terms of its recognition as something distinct from 4–4–2—came with Manchester United's 3–2 home defeat by Real Madrid in the Champions League in 1999–2000, which convinced Sir Alex Ferguson that the more orthodox 4–4–2 he had employed to win the treble the previous season had had its day in European competition.

The 4–2–3–1, though, is just one variant of the five-man midfield. One of the attacking midfielders can be sacrificed for an additional holder, producing either a 4–3–2–1—the Christmas tree—or the modern 4–3–3. Co Adriaanse seems to have been the first exponent of the 4–3–2–1 at Den Haag in the late eighties, and Terry Venables experimented with it with England ahead of Euro 96, but it was at the 1998 World Cup that a side using it achieved its first notable success and it entered the mainstream.

The France manager Aimé Jacquet's problem was accommodating Zidane, one of the greatest playmakers the world has known, but a player of limited pace and almost no defensive instinct. Jacquet's solution was to give him effectively a free role, but to do that without destabilizing his team defensively, he followed the Italian convention and fielded three midfielders whose function was primarily defensive: Didier Deschamps, Emmanuel Petit, and Christian Karembeu. Youri Djorkaeff was included as a further creative presence, with Stéphane Guivarc'h as the lone center-forward. He was much derided—and it may well be that, from a technical point of view, he is the worst center-forward ever to win a World Cup—but he performed his function, which was, broadly speaking, to provide a focal point and hold the ball up for the creators behind (once that has been accepted, the possibility opens up that Serginho's role in Brazil's 1982 World Cup side could be open to reinterpretation). By 2000, Jacquet had more confidence—and in Patrick Vieira a superb and mobile defensive midfielder—and felt able to align the three creators behind Henry in a 4–2–3–1.

AC Milan under Carlo Ancelotti are the best twenty-first-century exponents of the 4–3–2–1, although theirs was rather more attacking than France's had been. Kaká and Clarence Seedorf operated as the advanced midfield presences, with Andrea Pirlo playing as a *regista* behind them, flanked by the snapping and snarling of Gennaro Gattuso and the unfussy efficiency of Massimo Ambrosini. Again, though, the key is fluidity, for both Pirlo and Ambrosini were comfortable advancing and Seedorf, equally, could play in a more defensive role.

More common is the 4–3–3, which bears little resemblance to the 4–3–3 as practiced by the Brazil of 1962. Theirs was a lopsided 4–2–4, with Mario Zagallo dropping deep from the wing to become an extra midfielder. With some exceptions, most notably in the Netherlands and Germany, it remained asymmetric through to the eighties when, for instance, Newcastle would set out a 4–3–2, then deploy Chris Waddle on one or other flank according to which of the opposing full-backs looked weaker. The modern 4–3–3, as practiced by José Mourinho's Chelsea and many others, though, is really a modified 4–5–1.

Here, perhaps, the most significant recent shift in the understanding of tactics becomes clear: the notion that there are only three bands—defense, midfield, and attack—is gone, its dissolution hastened by the ongoing liberalization of the offside law since 1990. It has become increasingly difficult, particularly since the definition of interfering with play was changed in 2005, for teams to play a hard-pressing game with a high offside line, and so the effective playing area has been stretched from around 35–40m to around 55–60m.

That has had two major effects. First, there is more time and space in midfield, and less physical contact, which has allowed the reemergence of slight, creative presences—such as Messi, Xavi, Andrés Iniesta, and Mesut Özil—and the recognition that midfielders no longer have to be muscular athletes. And, second, trying to use a single-band midfield as anything other than a defensive tactic has become increasingly difficult, because with space in front of it and behind it, it is relatively easy to pierce for players playing in the spaces. For that reason, the most notable aspect of the 2010 World Cup from a tactical point of view was the replacement of 4–4–2 with 4–2–3–1 as the default formation.

There is a general recognition now that each of those basic categories of defense, midfield, and attack can be subdivided into smaller bands, although as that process goes on, it may be that the bands are so narrow as to cease to be meaningful. "It's about the movement of your players, up and down, left and right," Bilić said. "There are no lines any more." Mourinho didn't go quite so far, acknowledging that lines still exist, while maintaining that his players' job, at least when going forward, was to break them.

Under Mourinho's management, Chelsea's back four was relatively orthodox. Claude Makélélé sat immediately in front of them, with Frank Lampard and Tiago—or, later, Michael Essien and Michael Ballack—operating as shuttling runners ahead of him. Didier Drogba was the single center-forward, with two wide men—some combination of Damien Duff, Joe Cole, and Arjen Robben—operating both as wingers and auxiliary midfielders; not quite forwards, but not midfielders either. Sometimes it was 4–1–2–3, sometimes it was 4–1–4–1, but it became more easily understood as 4–3–3.

Mourinho's Chelsea

It remains debatable just how new the breaking of the lines is. There have, after all, always been defensive midfielders and attacking midfielders, while the notion of the field being divided into four bands was there in the W-M. Perhaps, as much as anything else, as with Flávio Costa's diagonal, what has changed is rather the notation. As that becomes increasingly sophisticated and more adept at representing the reality, so those realities become easier to grasp. Certainly today the term *4–5–1* is so vague as to be almost useless to describe how a team lines up on the field. It is rather a generic term, describing a family of formations.

As late as 2008, Arrigo Sacchi was adamant that there had been no innovations since his Milan and, while there was a self-interest in his claims, there was also a large degree of truth to them. Perhaps more significant, though, was his attitude to the likes of Makélélé. Sacchi was skeptical about the 4–2–3–1 and the modern 4–3–3 with its designated holder because, to him, they were too restrictive. "Today's football is about managing the characteristics of individuals," he said. "And that's why you see the proliferation of specialists. The individual has trumped the collective. But it's a sign of weakness. It's reactive, not pro-active." The likes of Barcelona under Pep Guardiola and Borussia Dortmund under Jürgen Klopp have helped reverse that trend.

Reactivity, Sacchi believed, was the fundamental flaw in the *galácticos* policy at Real Madrid, where he served as director of soccer between December 2004 and December 2005 as the club signed a host of stars and tried to balance them with hard runners from the youth setup. "There was no project," he explained.

> It was about exploiting qualities. So, for example, we knew that Zidane, Raúl and Figo didn't track back, so we had to put a guy in front of the back four who would defend. But that's reactionary football. It doesn't multiply the players' qualities exponentially. Which actually is the point of tactics: to achieve this multiplying effect on the players' abilities.
>
> In my football, the *regista*—the playmaker—is whoever had the ball. But if you have Makélélé, he can't do that. He doesn't have the ideas to do it, although, of course, he's great at winning the ball. It's become all about specialists. Is football a collective and harmonious game? Or is it a question of putting x amount of talented players in and balancing them out with y amount of specialists?

The power of those talented players, of course, is enhanced by modern celebrity culture; it may even be that clubs feel a need for obvious stars, the more peacock-like the better, to be able to market their brand in the emerging markets of Asia, Africa, and the United States.

When he returned to AC Milan in 1996 after his stint in charge of the national team, Sacchi ensured that Marcel Desailly, who had been used in midfield by Fabio Capello, was returned to the defensive line. Like Valeriy Lobanovskyi, for whom he professes a great admiration, Sacchi believes in the benefits of universality, in players who are not tied by their limitations to certain roles but can roam, taking as a reference for their positioning their teammates, their opponents, and the available space as much as the field. When that is achieved, the system is truly fluid.

That, of course, is precisely what the new breed of wingers and play-makers offer. They are not merely creators, but also runners and, to a degree, defenders. As *fantasistas* have evolved, so other positions have changed. It is very rare, for instance, to find a top side that plays with two stopper central defenders. There is a need always for at least one who can pass the ball or advance with it into midfield. More strikingly, the sniffer center-forward has all but vanished. "Those half-chances that poachers used to seize on don't exist any more," explained Zoran Filipović, once a striker with Crvena Zvezda, later their coach, and then the first manager of an independent Montenegro. "Defences are organised better, players are fitter. You have to create chances; you can't rely on mistakes."

Filippo Inzaghi was among the last of a dying breed, but at least obso-lescence crept up on him towards the end of his career; Michael Owen was in his midtwenties when it became apparent that, however good he was at sitting on the shoulder of the last defender or darting across the near post, it was not enough in modern soccer. "I've definitely developed my game, coming off and holding the ball up better and trying to link a bit more, but I've got to keep the main thing which is scoring goals and trying to get in behind people," he said. "The main aim at the end of the day is to put the ball in the back of the net."

The attitude is typically English and one that is a great source of frus-tration to managers. "I can't believe that in England they don't teach young players to be multi-functional," Mourinho said. "To them it's just about knowing one position and playing that position. To them a striker is a striker and that's it. For me, a striker is not just a striker. He's somebody who has to move, who has to cross, and who has to do this in a 4–4–2 or in a 4–3–3 or in a 3–5–2."

Owen was highly critical of the then–England coach Kevin Keegan's efforts to expand his repertoire in the buildup to Euro 2000, but the reality may be that putting the ball in the back of the net is no longer sufficient—or, at least, not at the very highest level, something Owen finally acknowl-edged after the 2010 World Cup. "It hurts me to say it as a striker who almost needs to play up front with another, but the days of 4–4–2 against a good team are going," he wrote in his column in the *Telegraph*.

Owen became one of those players who wins teams the occasional game—as he did in the Manchester derby at Old Trafford in 2009–2010, coming off the bench and scoring a late winner—but prevents them from playing good soccer (which means that he may prove extremely useful to mediocre sides, or even to a good side playing badly, but rarely if at all to a good side playing well). Even allowing for his history of injuries, it is surely significant that when he left Real Madrid in 2005, no Champions League qualifier was prepared to take him on, and he ended up at Newcastle. When he left there, there was almost an embarrassed silence before Manchester United picked him up on a free transfer. He appeared a player left behind by the tactical evolution of the game, and he played only infrequently for United before moving to an equally bench-bound role at Stoke City.

The modern forward, rather, is far more than a goalscorer, and it may even be that he can be successful without scoring goals. The example of Guivarc'h has already been mentioned, but at Euro 92, Denmark's two center-forwards, Flemming Povlsen and Kim Vilfort, were both widely perceived as having had excellent tournaments but scored between them only one goal—and that not until the final. Their job was rather to challenge for long balls, retain possession if they won it, and lay it off for Henrik Larsen and Brian Laudrup, the two more attack-minded midfielders. That seemed at the time an aberration, but it was a sign of things to come.

Goals are obviously part of it—a particularly valuable part—and the nonscoring forward a particular case, but many modern forwards appear rather as a hybrid of the old striker partnerships. The likes of Didier Drogba, Emmanuel Adebayor, and Fernando Llorente are both target men and quick men, battering rams and goalscorers, imposing physically and yet also capable of finesse. A Thierry Henry, Luis Suárez, or David Villa mixes the best qualities of the creator and goalscorer, capable of dropping deep or pulling wide, as adept at playing the final ball as taking chances himself. Somewhere in between the two extremes, at their peak, were Falcao, Andriy Shevchenko, Zlatan Ibrahimović, Samuel Eto'o, and Fernando Torres. Cristiano Ronaldo, for all the doubts about his defensive discipline when operating in wide areas, is extraordinarily complete—physically robust, technically supreme, and a superb finisher.

Simply to be a creator is no longer enough, simply to be a goalscorer is not enough; the best modern forwards have at least an element of universality and—crucially—they have to be able to function within the system.

20

PRESSING AND POSSESSING

By the final whistle, the 2011 Champions League final had long since become an exhibition. The ball zipped from *blaugrana* shirt to *blaugrana* shirt as Manchester United chased and chased, reduced in the end simply to admiring the filigree patterns of Barcelona's passing. Two years earlier, in Rome, Barcelona had beaten United 2–0 in the final; this time the margin was the same, 3–1, but the gulf between the teams was far greater. This was Barcelona absolutely at the top of their game, devastating the Premier League champions. "Nobody's given us a hiding like that but they deserve it," said the United manager Sir Alex Ferguson. "They play the right way and they enjoy their football. They do mesmerise you with their passing and we never really did control Messi...In my time as manager, it's the best team I've faced."

That performance against United wasn't even Barcelona's best; the pinnacle probably came in the 5–0 win over Real Madrid in November 2010, José Mourinho's first *clásico* as manager of Madrid. Wayne Rooney, who watched the game on television, admitted he found himself spontaneously standing up and applauding. He wasn't the only one: Barcelona's style was praised across the world.

Ferguson hadn't changed his opinion of Barcelona by January 2012. "The Barcelona team at the moment is by far the best team," he said. "We have experienced three years of it and sometimes in football you have to hold your hand up and say 'they are better than us.' It's not a crime or a weakness, just a plain fact that the Barcelona team now, particularly with Lionel Messi in the side, are just an extraordinary team." When the best player in the world plays for the best team in the world, there's not a lot the rest of the world can do.

Barcelona did not simply happen. This wasn't the result of a handful of great players all happening to be in the same place at once, or of one visionary coach leading a revolution. The Barcelona that won two

Barcelona 3 Manchester United 1, Champions League final, London, 28 May 2011

Champions Leagues in four years, narrowly losing in the semifinal on the other two occasions, is the result of four decades of evolution.

––––––––––

The sixties were a grim decade for Barcelona. They became the first team to eliminate Real Madrid from continental competition when they beat them in the semifinal of the European Cup in 1961, but that was about as good as that decade got. They went on to lose to Béla Guttmann's Benfica in the final and had added only two Copas del Generalísimo and a Fairs Cup when they faced Slovan Bratislava in the 1969 Cup-Winners' Cup final in Basel.

Barça lost 3–2, prompting a spate of gloomy soul-searching that led to a proposal that Helenio Herrera should be restored as manager. The prospect split the club. The president, Narcis de Carreras, and the coach, Salvador Artigas, quit, and the former Barcelona player Josep Seguer was appointed as interim manager. By January 1970, the club lay tenth in the league and was struggling. Radical action was needed and was taken, and an appointment was made that would change the course of the club, establishing a tradition that would still be bearing fruit four decades later.

Yet Vic Buckingham, with his creased face and neatly parted hair, didn't look much like a messiah, even if Ivan Ponting wrote of his "natural elegance and flamboyant personality" in his obituary in the *Independent*. He had played alongside Arthur Rowe and Bill Nicholson in Peter McWilliam's Tottenham team of the late thirties and had gone on to become West Bromwich Albion's longest-serving manager, winning the FA Cup in 1954. He was an "astute tactician," Bobby Robson, who played under him at the Hawthorns, wrote in his autobiography. "[He was] not afraid to take on board the hard lessons learned from the Hungarians and to experiment with our style of play."

Buckingham had had two spells as coach of Ajax, winning the league in his first and giving a debut to Johan Cruyff in his second, while laying the foundations for the great team of Rinus Michels. By the time Barcelona approached him, though, he had been out of soccer for more than a year, disillusioned by the match-fixing scandal that had overwhelmed Sheffield Wednesday shortly after his departure and by three acrimonious seasons in charge of Fulham. A brief stint in Greece with Ethnikos had begun to revive him, but it was at Barcelona that he ensured his legacy.

Charly Rexach, who spent twenty-two years at Barcelona as a player and a further twenty-two on the coaching staff, is in no doubt about Buckingham's significance. "There are certain managers in the history of soccer who have stolen an excessive limelight, but Buckingham was not one of those who pretended that the team didn't exist without him and it was only thanks to him that it won or lost," he explained. "But he was the first coach I worked under who taught us the importance of (1) having good players, (2) having discipline in the changing room, and (3) having a game plan."

With his taste for tweed jackets and silk ties, his love of cocktails, golf, and horse racing, Buckingham was seen as a perfect English gentleman. But there was a harshness beneath the charm, and he swore copiously—particularly at players he didn't rate. "There were six or seven players who if he found anywhere near the changing room, he'd simply tell to fuck off," said Barcelona's then-captain Josep Fuste. He would also swear at the opposition, on one occasion writing "BETIS" on the blackboard in the dressing room then asking, "Who are Betis? Fuck Betis," and kicking the blackboard to the ground.

"He had some very clear professional concepts," said José-Maria Minguella, who worked as his interpreter. "He used to say that once a match got under way, it was like a film that constantly changed scenes. Each player had to think of himself as an actor in that film, constantly adapting to the change of scene, moving his position to deal with each move that was played."

Buckingham led Barça to fourth and then, in his first full season, they finished a point behind Valencia in the championship before beating them in the final of the Copa del Generalísimo. A severe back problem, though, meant he returned to England that summer. Barça turned to the man who had taken on Buckingham's principles at Ajax and used them to form a European Cup–winning team: Rinus Michels.

Initially, the move was not a success. Michels was unpopular, nicknamed El Señor Marmol, "the Man of Marble," for his apparent humorlessness. Although Barça did win the Fairs Cup in September 1971, beating Leeds in the final, many insisted the credit was due less to the Dutchman than to Buckingham.

Buckingham had insisted on discipline, but Michels was even stricter. An incident after a cup defeat to Second-Division Sevilla in 1972–1973 became notorious. Seven players, including Rexach, tried to wind down over a game of cards in the hotel. They ordered two bottles of cava on room service, but Michels intercepted them and hurled the bottles at the players, screaming at them about the lack of discipline in Spanish soccer. He admitted later it had been an overreaction, one that said much about the mood of frustration that hung over the club.

It was lifted only by the arrival of the third of the three figures who transformed Barcelona in the early seventies, Johan Cruyff. Buckingham had made an approach to bring him from Ajax, even though foreigners were still banned from playing in the Spanish league. The deal was done within a few weeks of that prohibition being lifted in May 1973. When Cruyff arrived, Barcelona had gone fourteen years without a league title, but he provided the jolt that resurrected the club.

That season, 1973–1974, stands as perhaps the most extraordinary in Barcelona's history. Franco was ailing, and nationalist activity was increasing after the appointment of the hardline admiral Luis Carrero Blanco as president. He was killed that December by a bomb planted by ETA, a Basque nationalist and separatist organization. With the center weakening, a wave of Catalonian pride was unleashed, carrying along the soccer team and being reinforced by it. Cruyff's league debut came in a 4–0 win over Granada. The impact he had, the impression he made, was immediate. "Cruyff not only plays for the rest of the team; he makes the team play," a piece in *Barça* magazine explained the week after the game. "His quality brings out the best in those other Barça players whose quality was never in doubt but who sometimes stumbled rather than showing the true measure of their worth. The team has turned into a homogenous unit, full of ideas and at ease with itself. And what all this means is that football has become fun again. It's recovered that special grace which makes it the favourite sport of the masses."

Better was still to come. The 1973–1974 *clásico* at the Bernabéu was scheduled for February, on the same day Cruyff's son was due to be born. Cruyff's wife, Danny, had a caesarean so Jordi was born a week early, allowing Cruyff to play in the game. He was mesmerizing in a 5–0 victory. Joan Laporta and Sandro Rossell, both of whom would go on to become presidents of Barcelona, watched the game as schoolboys.

Barça went on to win the league that season, finishing eight points clear of Atlético but, although Johan Neeskens arrived that summer, they never quite recaptured the same form. Michels, having had a year away when he was replaced by Hennes Weisweiler (who had practiced a less stringent version of Total Football at Borussia Mönchengladbach), left the club for the final time in May 1978, prompting a period of instability. Although Josep Lluís Núñez, who was elected to the presidency that same year, did follow Cruyff's advice in establishing la Masía, the club's renowned youth academy, he also pursued a policy of bringing big names to Camp Nou— and that meant instability. Between Michels's departure and the arrival of César Luis Menotti in March 1983, Barcelona went through six other managers. Although the theories espoused by Buckingham and Michels continued to underpin the academy, at first-team level the sense of Barcelona as heirs of the Total Football tradition was lost. Menotti, certainly, had very different ideas about how the game should be played, and the rumor was that he had been appointed to replace Udo Lattek (who had overseen the Total Football revolution at Bayern) as much to try to get the best out of signing Diego Maradona as anything else.

Menotti's conception of soccer as an updating of *la nuestra* had survived the *junta* and Bilardo, but at Barcelona he faced another threat: the final flowering of *la furia*. The storm was centered where it had begun, in the Basque country. Real Sociedad won the title in 1981 and retained it the following year, but it was in Bilbao where the style was taken to extremes.

Athletic hadn't won the league since 1956 and, after a couple of third-place finishes in the midseventies, had slipped back into midtable when, in 1981, they turned to Javier Clemente. His playing career with Athletic had been curtailed by injury, and he had served his coaching apprenticeship with the local side Getxo and then Biskonia, Athletic's reserves. He was Basque to the marrow—feisty, quick tempered, unafraid to speak his mind. He smoked constantly, swore frequently, and seemed to exist in a haze of perpetual fury. He's widely credited with having coined the term *tiki-taka*, but he meant it as a scornful dismissal of passing for passing's sake, to be set in contrast with his own more direct style of soccer. As Sid Lowe noted, Clemente will "forever be associated with the phrase '*patapún y p'arriba*'—'bish-bosh, up it goes,' a kind of Spanish ''Ave it!'—and with defensive, devious and downright dirty football."

Clemente's soccer was the opposite of tiki-taka. His sides were resilient, pragmatic, and muscular, playing a high-intensity game based around the *bloque*—two holding midfielders screening the back four. Infamously, when manager of the national side, he once played Miguel Ángel Nadal and Fernando Hierro, two players who were primarily central defenders, together in midfield. At Athletic, he inherited a side that included Andoni Goikoetxea, Manu Sarabia, and the captain Dani, to whom he added the goalkeeper Andoni Zubizarreta, the full-back Santi Urkiaga, the midfielders Ismael Urtubi and Miguel de Andrés, and the winger Estanislao Argote, all of them drawn from Athletic's *cantera*. He forged them into a tough, fiercely competitive unit.

At Barcelona, Menotti's reign began well as the side won the 1983 Copa del Rey, a last-minute header from Marcos Alonso giving them a 2–1 victory over Real Madrid in the final in Zaragoza. They were already, though, too far adrift in the league. Madrid led Athletic by a point going into the final day, but they lost 1–0 in Valencia while Athletic won 5–1 away to Las Palmas to claim the championship. The following season, the title race was even closer, and it was then that Spanish soccer witnessed the great clash between the high-octane pragmatism of Athletic and the romantic aestheticism of Barcelona.

There had been tension since a game in December 1981, the first in which Clemente had coached Athletic against Barcelona, when a challenge from Goikoetxea left Bernd Schuster with a ruptured anterior cruciate ligament, causing him to miss the World Cup six months later. The antipathy was intensified by the prevailing political situation. ETA carried out forty-three assassinations in 1983, while the governing socialist party established clandestine Anti-Terrorist Liberation Groups—effectively death squads—which were responsible for at least twenty-seven political killings before being disbanded after exposure by *El Mundo*. But what really gave the rivalry its edge, as Scott Oliver demonstrated in issue four of the *Blizzard*, was a protracted spat between Menotti and Clemente, whose personalities seemed somehow to lie at the heart of their teams' style of play.

Menotti dismissed Clemente as "authoritarian"—a particularly barbed word given that dictatorships had only recently ended in both Spain and Argentina—and described his team as "defensive and destructive"; Clemente hit back by calling Menotti "a hippy and a womaniser." Clemente was a committed Basque nationalist, even while manager of Spain. His habit of referring to his people as *"una raza especial"*—a special race— seemed self-consciously to evoke Francoist notions of Spanish purity (for Franco had seen the Basque country as the heart of the true Spain, despite his hatred of Basque nationalism) and *la furia*; certainly it was enough for Menotti to brand him "a fascist." (Menotti's politics were rather harder to pin down: although his self-conscious bohemianism seemed to align him with the left, in 1994 he sought selection to run for the governorship of the province of Santa Fe for the Justicialist Party, which had been founded on authoritarian-populist lines by Perón in 1947 to replace the Labour Party, but by the midnineties, under Carlos Menem, it had become a center-right neoliberal party.)

The rivalry between the two managers was still bubbling four years later when they met again, Clemente as manager of Espanyol and Menotti of Atlético Madrid (with Goikoetxea in his squad; there was a rarely acknowledged streak of expediency in Menotti). The Argentinian condemned Clemente's tactic of narrowing the field for a UEFA Cup tie against Internazionale, prompting Clemente to call Menotti a "bluffer who gets by on jibes and metaphors" and a soccer "parasite" or "scrounger" whom "everyone in football knew" had only won a World Cup because the "president had bought it for him." Menotti hit back, claiming Clemente demonstrated "attitudes and postures of fascist character" and insisting he had issues that "ought to be resolved by psychiatric means.... I don't understand Clemente's reaction, unless he admires or is envious of me." That may have been little more than playground posturing, but the wider point Menotti made about the psyche of Spanish soccer was profound. "The day Spain decides to be a bullfighter rather than a bull on the pitch," he said, "it will play better football."

The first meeting of Menotti and Clemente on the field came at the Camp Nou on September 24, 1983. Athletic had won their first three games of the season but were 3–0 down just before the hour when Schuster fouled Goikoetxea; revenge, many assumed, for the foul in 1981. The crowd had been chanting Schuster's name and, Maradona claimed in his autobiography, Goikoetxea had clearly been agitated even before the foul, hissing, "I'm going to kill that guy." Maradona tried to calm him down but only succeeded in enraging him further. The result was one of the most notorious fouls in history as Goikoetxea clattered into Maradona's standing leg, snapping the lateral malleolus in his left ankle and rupturing the ligaments. Maradona was carried off; Goikoetxea wasn't even sent off, although he subsequently received an eighteen-game ban that was reduced to six on appeal. Athletic showed no remorse: Clemente suggested after the game that Maradona had exaggerated the seriousness of the injury, while Goikoetxea, who insisted there'd been no intent, kept the boot with which he'd committed the foul in a glass case in his living room.

Athletic and Barça met again in the Supercopa, Menotti's side winning 3–2 over two legs. Barcelona then won the second league meeting between the sides, 2–1 at San Mamés. It wasn't enough. The absence of Maradona had unsettled them, particularly when Schuster then picked up another injury three weeks later, and, despite winning eight and drawing one of their final nine games of the season, they finished level with Real Madrid, a point behind Athletic.

There was still one game to come, though, the Copa del Rey final, and it was then that the acrimony boiled over. Clemente and Maradona traded barbs before the game, and the atmosphere at a damp Bernabéu was soured further when Athletic fans whistled during a minute's silence for Barça fans killed in a coach crash on the way to Madrid. There were numerous bad fouls on both sides, while Schuster lobbed missiles that had been thrown at him back into the crowd. Endika scored early for Athletic, chesting the ball down and finishing neatly, and, having gone ahead, Athletic sat back, spoiled, and looked to counter. A frustrated Barça rarely looked like finding an equalizer and, at the final whistle, as Athletic's coaching staff ran onto the field to celebrate the double, Maradona flipped, kneeing the unused Bilbao substitute Miguel Ángel Sola in the face as he knelt on the field and knocking him unconscious. Maradona later claimed he'd been provoked by a V-sign from the Athletic defender José Núñez but, whatever the cause, what followed was one of the most disgraceful brawls in soccer history, with players from both sides flying in with high kicks. Riot police joined substitutes, journalists, backroom staff, paramedics, and fans on the field, and there were still scuffles going on as a horrified King Juan Carlos II presented the cup to Dani. It was the culmination of an odd and short-lived rivalry rooted in stylistic difference as much as anything else, and it was also the final triumph of *la furia*. No team since in Spain has been successful with a way of playing so insistently physical.

Menotti left Barcelona that summer, returning to Argentina following the death of his mother, while Maradona was sold to Napoli. Barça, to widespread surprise, appointed the Queen's Park Rangers manager Terry Venables. As he admitted, they wanted an English manager to hammer the team into shape and improve fitness levels, but he had at least spent three years playing under Bill Nicholson at Tottenham and so was part of the tradition established by McWilliam. Venables got rid of the sweeper favored by Menotti and restored the pressing game. "I worked hard for them to press the ball, hustling the man in possession with three to four players at one time and trying to rob him in parts of the field where we could counter-attack quickly, efficiently and effectively instead of falling back and only winning it when their whole team was in front of us," he said. He was rewarded with a league title.

Clemente stayed at Athletic for two more seasons, taking the club to third and fourth. He returned to the club in 1990 but was sacked shortly after a 6–1 home defeat to Barcelona, who by then had returned to the Total Football principles that had guided them in the seventies and appointed Johan Cruyff as manager.

Cruyff the player had had an extraordinary impact on Barcelona; as a manager it was even greater. At Ajax his record as coach was mixed: no league titles in three seasons, but two cups and, crucially, the Cup-Winners' Cup, ending a thirteen-year European drought. At Ajax, he had insisted on picking Stanley Menzo in goal—maintaining his ball-playing ability and capacity to initiate attacks while operating as a sweeper-keeper outweighed concerns about his technical merits. Only with a goalkeeper who could occupy the space behind the defensive line could the rest of the side push up as high as Cruyff demanded while remaining compact and not leaving space behind the defense for opponents to exploit with balls over the top. This would become a defining characteristic of the new orthodoxy. The story of the goalkeeper's reintegration into the side as a quasi-outfield player (something discussed in far more detail in my book *The Outsider*), had begun with Gyula Grosics in Hungary's *Aranycsapat* and was continued by the likes of Tommy Lawrence at Liverpool and Edwin van der Sar at Ajax before reaching a peak with Victor Valdés and Manuel Neuer under Pep Guardiola at Barça and Bayern.

Cruyff had also prioritized players from the youth academy—those brought up in the Ajax way. At Barcelona, he discovered that the academy he had advised Núñez to establish was bearing fruit, and that encouraged his radicalism. "It just happened that when I arrived there was a new crop of local players who had come up through the *cantera* and were ready to join the first team," he said.

There was the kind of availability that comes at the end of a cycle, every five or six years. But there is another situation that I understood. Fans the world over like to see good players who share their mentality, and preferably come from their country, and if a coach has to choose between a foreign and a local with equal abilities, he should go for the local. That way the fans are less likely to whistle him if things go wrong. At Barça, fans like seeing players from the *cantera* in the first team; it makes them feel that a coach is somehow more a part of Barcelona that way.

Success took time. In Cruyff's first season, Barça finished five points adrift of Real Madrid but won the Cup-Winners' Cup, beating Sampdoria 2–0 in the final. With Cruyff adopting the classic Ajax 4–3–3-cum-3–4–3, Gary Lineker operated as part of a front three with Julio Salinas and Txiki Begiristain, but he was never happy at having to operate wide on the right at times. That summer, Lineker was off-loaded as Barça signed Ronaldo Koeman and Michael Laudrup.

Koeman was vital as the sweeper who was comfortable stepping into midfield. "He had a fantastic touch," Cruyff said. "With one of his passes he could get all the forward players to work playing one to one with that one pass, and then there was real rhythm of play, and all sorts of possibilities opened up." Laudrup, meanwhile, operated as a highly mobile center-forward, perhaps the closest thing the world has known to Cruyff—although Cruyff always lamented his lack of edge. "Had Michael been born in a poor ghetto in Brazil or Argentina with the ball being his only way out of poverty he would today be recognised as the biggest genius of the game ever," he said. "He had all the abilities to reach it but lacked this ghetto-instinct, which could have driven him there."

In terms of his role, Laudrup was perhaps the forerunner of Lionel Messi; the term false nine wasn't in common usage then but that was essentially what he was, just as G. O. Smith of Corinthians, Nolo Ferreira of Estudiantes, Nándor Hidegkuti of Hungary, and Cruyff himself had been. Real Madrid again won the title in 1990, but Barcelona's critics were kept at bay by victory over Real in the Copa del Rey final. That summer, Hristo Stoichkov was brought in from CSKA Sofia, adding his blend of combustible intensity and deft technique. At that stage, there were major concerns about the throughput of players and the inconsistency of Cruyff's selection, particularly when the coach suffered a heart attack. But the club stayed loyal to the Dutchman, and he stayed loyal to his philosophy.

"When Cruyff and I arrived to take over at Barça," said Rexach, who served as assistant coach,

> we decided to install the football that inspired us; the football of Rinus Michels. Make no mistake—it cost us to achieve. We inherited a culture at the Camp Nou where the fans whistled and jeered at a defender if he passed the ball back to his keeper, or at a winger if he reached the by-line but didn't cross the ball—whether there was anybody there to take advantage of the chance or not. Our first task was to find and sign players who had the correct philosophy and skill set and to educate the ones we inherited, but a by-product was that we educated our fans. Everything flowed once we taught everyone that there was a baseline philosophy and we would not bend from it.

Cruyff's cardiac problems forced him to give up cigarettes but, sucking furiously on lollipops, he oversaw the emergence of a team that encapsulated his vision. Barça won the league in 1990–1991 and went on to win it in each of the next three seasons as well. Even more importantly, in 1992, the Dream Team, as it became known, became the first Barcelona side to win the European Cup. Stoichkov happily played wide in that lineup, usually on the left but occasionally on the right; Laudrup by then was playing at the tip of the midfield diamond, with Julio Salinas as the central striker and José María Bakero on the other flank.

By 1994, when Barcelona again reached the European Cup final, the system had evolved one step further. The Brazilian Romário operated at center-forward, a fine goalscorer himself but also a player capable of dropping deep or pulling wide, while Stoichkov tended to play on the right with Begiristain on the left, each cutting infield onto their stronger foot into space created by Romário, enhancing their goalscoring potential. They weren't the first inverted wingers, but they were probably the first to be used so systematically with such a mobile forward.

After two seasons without trophies and a falling-out with Núñez, Cruyff left in 1996, replaced by Bobby Robson, who won the Copa del Rey and the Cup-Winners' Cup but was only ever seen as a stopgap until Louis van Gaal was available. Van Gaal's slightly more mechanized variant of Total Football was successful, bringing two league titles and a cup, and emphasizing the link between la Masía and the first team, but after his (first) departure in 2000, the club lost its way.

By 2003, Barcelona had won nothing for four years and had mounting debt. They considered Guus Hiddink and Ronaldo Koeman as managers but, deciding both were too expensive, turned, on Cruyff's recommendation, to Frank Rijkaard. Given his limited managerial experience—his Dutch national side had been beaten on penalties by an Italy reduced to nine men in the Euro 2000 semifinal, and he had then led Sparta Rotterdam to their first relegation—his appointment was a remarkable statement of faith in the philosophy of Total Football.

At first, it seemed it had backfired. By January 2004, Barça were thirteenth, having taken ten points from nine home games. When they lost 3–0 at Racing Santander a few weeks after losing 5–1 at Malaga, the expectation was that Rijkaard would be sacked. But Cruyff, who remained the conscience of the club even though he'd held no salaried post since 1996, insisted the corner had been turned. Sure enough, Barcelona won fourteen and drew three of their next seventeen matches and ended up finishing second, ahead of Real Madrid. Rijkaard went on to lead the club to two league titles and the Champions League. His preference was for an orthodox 4–3–3, although the Mexican center-back Rafael Márquez was capable of stepping into midfield alongside a more orthodox holder such as Edmílson; his soccer had the virtues of Total Football, but perhaps not the radicalism of Van Gaal or Cruyff.

By 2008, though, there was a sense that Rijkaard had run out of steam and that certain elements in the squad had become disruptive, particularly after the departure of Henk Ten Cate, Rijkaard's assistant, in summer 2006. There was talk of appointing José Mourinho, who had worked at the club as a translator under Bobby Robson, but that move was vetoed by Begiristain, who had risen to become director of soccer. His policy was one of philosophy over personality, and so he promoted from within, giving the job to Pep Guardiola, who was thirty-seven and whose only managerial experience was with Barça's reserve team. It was an inspired appointment.

Guardiola was steeped in Barcelona and the tradition of Cruyff and Michels. A boyhood fan, he had learned the game at la Masía, gaining a reputation as a slight but intelligent midfielder. When, in 1990, Ronald Koeman suffered an Achilles injury, Cruyff considered signing Jan Mølby to replace him before being told by Rexach of Guardiola's potential. Cruyff went to a reserve match to watch him and was baffled that Guardiola remained on the bench all game, despite being widely acknowledged as the best player in the youth team. Cruyff was told that Guardiola wasn't considered robust enough; he replied that if a player was good enough his physique didn't matter, a philosophy that has run through the club ever since. "Guardiola had to be clever," Cruyff explained. "He didn't have any other choice back then. He was a bit like me. You must have a lot of technique, move the ball quickly, avoid a collision—and to avoid it you must have good vision. It's a domino effect. You soon get a sharp eye for detail, for players' positions. You can apply this when you are a player and a coach too. Guardiola learnt that way—thanks to his build—and he was lucky enough to have a coach who had experienced the same thing."

Guardiola played three matches as Barça won the first of their four successive titles and soon became a regular in that key position that was part center-back, part central midfielder. "Guardiola could control the ball quickly and pass it quickly," Cruyff said. "He could deliver the ball in good condition so that another player could do something with it."

A year before Rijkaard's departure, Guardiola had returned to the club, insisting on managing the reserve side, then in the Third Division, after being offered an apparently more prestigious role as director of the academy. What he wanted to do, he said, was coach. He took to the role with extraordinary self-confidence. Rijkaard may have played a relatively conservative 4–3–3 with the first team, but, immediately, Guardiola imposed a Cruyffian 3–4–3. The reserve side thrived, winning promotion in Guardiola's only season with them before he was elevated to the senior side.

Inexperienced as a coach Guardiola may have been, naïve he was not. Like Van Gaal, he realized his philosophy demanded discipline and wholehearted commitment from everybody. Each player was told their ideal weight, and there were punishments for those who missed targets. For every five minutes a player was late for training or a meeting, there would be a €500 fine. Aliaksandr Hleb, for instance, was often late, and so, for all his ability, he was off-loaded. Ronaldinho was seen as a disruptive influence and traded. Later, the failure of Samuel Eto'o and Zlatan Ibrahimović to conform led to them being traded, in both cases for fees that seemed well below the market rate. "Little details matter a lot now and, psychologically, we are undergoing a Masters degree with Pep," Xavi said in Guardiola's first season. "Everything is controlled and well-prepared. We spend a lot of time on strategy, tactics and how the opponent is going to play against us."

The emphasis on the *cantera* was clear: Victor Valdés, Carles Puyol, Gerard Piqué, Sergio Busquets, and Xavi were all Catalans who had come through la Masía, while Pedro, Lionel Messi, Andrés Iniesta, and Thiago Alcantara had all been scouted and taken there very young. Most of the coaching staff, including Guardiola and his assistant Tito Vilanova, who would succeed him, had come through the *cantera*.

Before taking the job, Guardiola consulted a number of coaches, including Marcelo Bielsa, with whom he shared an *asado* and a discussion that went on into the early hours. In the emphasis on passing and winning the ball back high up the field, Barça's style, although an evolution of their own model, clearly mirrored Bielsa's approach—and that was made easier by the fact that the players had all been trained from an early age in the virtues of pass and move. As Rexach observed, "Other teams can try to copy us, of course, but we've got 30 years of a head start."

Bielsa's main role, perhaps, on Guardiola's research tour was to confirm the Barcelona man in his beliefs. Cruyff, who was his manager for six years, was clearly a huge influence, but so too was Juanma Lillo, who had coached Guardiola during his brief stint in Mexico with Dorados. And so, despite the widespread assumption that they didn't get along, was Van Gaal and, in particular, his Ajax side. "That Ajax team always gave me the impression that they tried to and could do all of the following: play, sacrifice themselves as a team, shine individually and win games," Guardiola said. "All the players of different quality, without exception, were aware of their mission on the field of play. They demonstrated a tactical discipline and enormous capacity to apply all of that at just the right time."

The essence of Guardiola's philosophy was simple. "In the world of football there is only one secret: I've got the ball or I haven't," he said. "Barcelona have opted for having the ball although it is legitimate for others not to want it. And when we haven't got the ball we have to get it back because we need it." The core of technical training was the *rondo*, in which a ring of players seek to keep possession from two others. "They taught us to know who was around us before the ball arrived and to be prepared to use a flick or a cushion or a volley in tenths of a second to keep the circulation of the ball flowing," Xavi explained to Graham Hunter in *Barça*. Even more than before, the focus was on the creation and exploitation of space, generated by movement off the ball and by technique good enough that defenders could be lured towards a forward before a pass would be released.

But there was also tactical training. To instill his ideas about positional play, Guardiola divided the training field into twenty sections. The lines marking the penalty areas were extended for the full length and width of the field, while the vertical lines marking the sides of the six-yard box were picked up again at the edge of the eighteen-yard box and extended to the edge of the other eighteen-yard box. The zones nearest the touchlines were then split again, halfway between the eighteen-yard and halfway lines.

The idea was that players would adjust their position according to which zone the ball is in. But that was just the foundation: ideally players should be flexible enough to fill a zone that would, in the initial template, be filled by somebody else, creating a level of rotation to overman key areas while maintaining a structure that should both offer passing options and maintain a defensive shape that can react effectively to the loss of possession and a counterattack by being immediately prepared to counterpress.

At its simplest level, the zone principle should mean that no more than three players are in a line horizontally and no more than two vertically: if a player moves into a zone that means four in the same horizontal line are occupied, one of the other three should automatically move. That should ensure that the man on the ball always has two or three passing options and allows possession to be retained—the endless *rondos* that Guardiola favors in training making his players supremely adept at giving and receiving the ball in tight spaces—which is why his sides regularly have so much of the ball.

When it is not aimed directly at the opposition goal, passing is designed to allow the team to generate the right structure, whether to mount an attack or to be prepared to counterpress. Guardiola has said it takes fifteen passes for that structure to be created. This is not, Guardiola insisted, tiki-taka, which he interprets as passing for passing's sake, but *juego de posición*.

While the system produced vast quantities of goals, there was also a defensive element. Barça's pressing was supreme, founded on tremendous fitness and organization. Like Van Gaal, Guardiola insisted that if the ball wasn't won back within three seconds, his side should drop back and assume their defensive positions. "While we attack, the idea is always to keep your position, always being in the place you have to be," he said. "There is dynamism, mobility, but the position has always got to be filled by someone. So if we lose the ball it will be difficult for the rival to get us on the counter-attack—if we attack in formation it becomes easier then to hunt down the opposite player with the ball when we lose possession."

At first, Guardiola's shape was a variant of 4–3–3, with Messi used to the right of the forward line and Thierry Henry to the left, on either side of Samuel Eto'o. Sergio Busquets, whose promotion to the first team was Guardiola's first gamble in terms of personnel, could drop back to become almost a third center-back, giving himself time to become the playmaker Van Gaal demanded his number 4 should be, setting the tempo for the rest of the side, and also freeing up the full-backs to attack.

In having wingers on the "wrong" side, that is, using a left-footer on the right or vice versa, Barça were part of a much wider trend. With a lone center-forward, of course, there is a need for the advanced midfielders to provide goals (and, conversely, it may be that many of the players now operating as wide forwards would in a previous age have been second strikers), particularly if that forward drops deep, operating as a false nine in a strikerless system. That, perhaps, to an extent explains the modern directness, the tendency for wide men to run at the goal rather than making for the goal line and looking to cross.

But as Herbert Chapman pointed out, it's far from obvious why the belief had developed that the most lethal cross was a ball dragged back from the goal line. It can be dangerous, of course, raising doubt in a goalkeeper's mind as to whether he should come to claim or not, but there seems to be no reason why it should be more threatening than an inswinger delivered at pace. In fact, intuitively, it would seem a ball whipped towards the far post that requires just a touch to divert it in, or that will sneak in if nobody touches it, is more dangerous. It also feels as though that sort of goal has become more common over the past decade or so. That may itself be a result of an increasing number of inverted wingers, or it may be a result of the increased spin that can be imparted on modern balls, or even perhaps of the liberalization of the offside law which forces teams to defend deeper—an inswinger curving into the far post is obviously more dangerous if players are running into it six yards out rather than fifteen yards out, both in terms of angle and the time a goalkeeper would have to react to a touch.

There are other advantages to a wide player coming inside. For one thing, given most full-backs still play on the traditional side, a winger attacking him on the inside is attacking his weaker foot. For another, a wide player drifting infield is opening up space for an overlapping full-back, of whom there are an increasing number. The linkup of Robert Pires and Ashley Cole at Arsenal was an early example of that; more recent examples include Ivan Rakitić and Danijel Pranjić for Slaven Bilić's Croatia and Steven Gerrard and Ashley Cole for Fabio Capello's England. The most obvious and effective example, though, was that of Messi and Dani Alves.

And then there is the issue of acceleration room. A full-back pushed tight on a wide forward does not allow him to accelerate down the line, but by cutting inside onto his stronger foot, the forward opens up room on the diagonal, something at which Messi was particularly adept. But gradually Messi and Eto'o began to swap positions. Moving into a central role and dropping deep, Messi confounded defenders just as surely as Nándor Hidegkuti had confounded England in 1953. The false nine had entered the mainstream.

His arrival had been foretold. At a conference in Rio de Janeiro in 2003, Carlos Alberto Parreira, who led Brazil to victory in the 1994 World Cup, spoke of the possibilities of a 4-6-0. "You'd have four defenders at the back although even they'd be allowed to run forward," Andy Roxburgh, the former UEFA technical director, explained. "Then six players in midfield, all of whom could rotate, attack and defend. But you'd need to have six Decos in midfield—he doesn't just attack, he runs, tackles covers all over the pitch. You find him playing at right-back sometimes."

Yet what was Deco but a classic example of Valeriy Lobanovskyi's and Arrigo Sacchi's notion of universality? It is notable that in 2005–2006, although Frank Rijkaard often deployed the combative Mark van Bommel or the converted central defender Edmílson in midfield in the Champions League, in la Liga he often used Deco, Xavi, and Andrés Iniesta, all of whom were under 5'9" and none of whom were exactly terrifying physical presences. Industrious and technically gifted players properly organized don't need to dominate by size. Under Guardiola, it came to seem that 5'7" was the ideal height for a passing midfielder.

Barça benefitted, of course, from various law changes. The tackle from behind, that traditional weapon for intimidating creative players, was outlawed, while any physical contact is now likely to be penalized. At least as significant were the changes to the offside law, which began to be liberalized as a response to the negativity of the 1990 World Cup. When the definition of interfering with play had been amended in 2005, the offside trap was virtually decommissioned as a general way of playing. That forced teams to defend deeper, which in turn meant the effective playing area—that is, the area between the two defensive lines—increased. More space equals less physical contact, and that in turn means less need for muscular or robust players.

Slowly, Parreira's vision became reality. In 2006–2007, for instance, Luciano Spalletti's Roma played a 4–1–4–1, but with Francesco Totti, the archetypal *trequartista*, as the lone striker. David Pizarro operated as the holding player, with Taddei, Simone Perrotta, Daniele De Rossi, and Mancini in front of him. What regularly happened, though, was that Totti dropped deep into the *trequartista* position in which he'd spent so much of his career, creating a space into which one or more of the attacking midfielders advanced. As the distinction between center-forward and attacking midfielder dissolved, Roma's formation became, if not a 4–6–0, then certainly a 4–1–5–0. Spalletti took the system to Zenit St. Petersburg, who won back-to-back titles in 2010 and 2011–2012 with Aleksandr Kerzhakov operating as a false nine.

Roma's experiment was taken on, slightly surprisingly, by the team that had beaten them 7–1 in the previous season's Champions League: Manchester United. With Cristiano Ronaldo, Wayne Rooney, Carlos Tévez, and Ryan Giggs or Nani slung in front of a holding pair of two from Owen Hargreaves, Michael Carrick, Anderson, and Paul Scholes, United regularly had no obvious front man, with the front four taking it in turns to become the de facto striker. It is a system that requires much work to develop a mutual understanding, but when it does click it can produce exhilarating soccer.

Spain's version of strikerlessness in the European Championship in 2012 was more radical still. Vicente Del Bosque's side had won the World Cup two years earlier, scoring just eight goals in seven games, and the

Roma 2006–2007

Manchester United 2007–2008

accusations of negativity were even louder in Poland and Ukraine. At least in South Africa he had usually had a striker on the field; at the Euros, in part because of injury to David Villa and Fernando Torres's loss of form, he tended to use Cesc Fàbregas as his most advanced player.

Fàbregas, though, seemed less a false nine than a midfielder used in a center-forward's role, so he actually dropped deep comparatively rarely. Of course, when players did break beyond him, he was ideally equipped to slide through balls to them, but his role was really more one of ball retention. A center-forward is usually selected for his finishing or his pace or his aerial ability; Fàbregas seemed to be selected because he could pass. He was there at the front of the attack for the ball to be bounced off of, to provide more angles for the midfield, playing almost as a target man, just receiving balls on the ground rather than in the air. Spain's second goal in the final against Italy, in fact, came from a long ball from the goalkeeper Iker Casillas out to Fàbregas on the left wing. The likes of Flemming Povlsen and Stéphane Guivarc'h, Serginho even, have long shown that center-forwards

Spain 2012

can be effective without offering much of a goal threat. Fàbregas's role seemed a fusion of that tradition with that of the false nine.

By using Fàbregas like that, Spain were better able to hold possession, something that gave them the "control" Del Bosque kept saying he desired. For him and for Spain, matches and tournaments were not won by creating chances but by dominating possession to the extent that the opponent is stifled. Have thirty chances and allow the opposition five, and there is a chance that the opponent will win; have five and restrict the opponent to none, and the worst-case scenario is a penalty shoot-out. It is a method attritional in ethos and yet proactive; in a sense it is the logical end product of the philosophy of Total Football. Hadn't Ajax, after taking an early lead in the 1973 European Cup final against Juventus, opted to hold possession, defending their lead by keeping the ball away from the Italians? Hadn't the very invention of passing by Queen's Park in 1872 been a defensive measure designed to keep the ball away from the more physically imposing English players?

As numerous Spanish players pointed out, if opponents packed men behind the ball and looked to frustrate Spain, why were they the ones blamed if the soccer sometimes lacked sparkle? Del Bosque spoke repeatedly of how his side kept being denied *profundidad*—depth of field of play—by teams sitting deep. As soon as a team did alter their approach and try to press Spain high up the field, as Italy did in the final, the space they left was ruthlessly exploited and they were beaten 4–0. This, surely, was Spain playing as Menotti had demanded, as the bullfighter not the bull. The irony is that it was Barcelona who taught Spain to play that way. As David Winner pointed out in a piece outlining the similarities between tiki-taka and bullfighting in issue four of the *Blizzard*, the bull is the symbol of Spain, not of Catalonia, which is why in 2007 separatists destroyed the last Toto de Osborne—the huge silhouette statues that once advertised sherry—that had remained in the region.

Although Arsène Wenger did protest about Barça's "sterile domination," Guardiola's side largely avoided the accusations of boringness, something helped by scoring 412 league goals in four seasons. They kept evolving—a couple of players arriving each summer, Messi moving in from the right—and they kept winning: in Guardiola's first three seasons, they won three league titles and two Champions Leagues. Only a semifinal defeat to José Mourinho's magnificently dogged Internazionale—aided by an Icelandic volcano that meant Barça had to travel to Milan by bus—prevented them winning a hat trick of European titles.

Guardiola seemed always aware of the dangers of complacency and stasis, determined, perhaps, to avoid the problems Béla Guttmann highlighted in his comment that the third year is fatal. In that sense, his final season at Barcelona became like a Greek tragedy—the hero aware of his fate yet unable to avert it, even creating, perhaps, the conditions in which his destiny could be fulfilled by his attempts to avoid it. Ibrahimović had been signed, as much as anything, to offer variety of attack, but his disruptiveness meant he had to be off-loaded. Guardiola's next idea was the back three, not a Van Gaal style three with a holding midfielder always ready to make it a four, but an aggressive *bielsista* three. When, in December 2011, a switch from four to three turned a *clásico* in which Real Madrid appeared to have the edge, it seemed a vindication for his revisions. There were accusations even then that Guardiola had overcomplicated things, that the measures he had taken to avert his destiny were precisely those which ensured it came to pass. He was worried by teams sitting deep against Barça, worried that his team would become predictable, and so he devised a way of getting more players, Dani Alves in particular, higher up the field to try to outflank blanket defenses. All that did, though, was to make Barça more predictable: it is easier to mark a player who starts high than one coming from deep.

That wasn't the sole cause of that odd flatness Barça demonstrated in the final minutes of the second leg of the Champions League semifinal against Chelsea, but it did explain why they never had players bursting at pace through the defensive lines: everybody was too near the box already—they couldn't build up enough pace to be traveling at speed when they ran onto the ball. And so, as against Inter two years earlier, Barça were undone in the last four of the Champions League by a team that packed men behind the ball, played with great spirit and concentration, had a little luck, and took their chances when they arrived.

By then, it seemed that Guardiola, clearly contemplating the end as Mourinho's Real Madrid won la Liga, was in the grip of a fatalistic idealism—that he was determined his team should have the most Barça-ish identity of all Barças, come what may, particularly in the moment at which his Barça faced its dissolution. His determination to play with fewer and fewer defenders became a form of martyrdom: as Samuel Weber, in his rereading of Freud, asked, what better way for the ego, when facing its own dissolution, to assert mastery than to dissolve itself by following to the ultimate the philosophy from which it derived meaning? Rather than just let his Barça fade away, rather than face the prospect of their philosophy being overcome, rather than risk the intervention of random events, Guardiola sought to stave off the entropic imperative by exaggerating what had made Barça great, by holding possession even longer, by getting even more men forward. It was failure, but at least it was failure on his terms. And, of course, by any realistic measure it wasn't failure. Of the nineteen trophies Guardiola could have won in his four years as Barcelona manager, he claimed fourteen, a remarkable run of success. He also provided the players and a basic blueprint that, with some modifications, inspired Spain to two European championships and a World Cup over a four-year period, an unprecedented run of domination in the international game.

More than that, his side also fulfilled Sacchi's requirement for greatness: they will be remembered for their style as much as for their victories, for taking the idea of passing, as conceived in Glasgow in 1872, and developing it to hitherto undreamed-of heights. Bob McColl took passing from Queen's Park to Newcastle in 1901; Peter McWilliam learned from him and took the theory to Tottenham in 1912; there he instructed Vic Buckingham, who influenced Rinus Michels and Johan Cruyff, paving their way at both Ajax and Barcelona. Guardiola and his Barcelona are worthy heirs to that line. There are many ways of playing, but theirs is the great tradition.

21

THE POST-CRUYFFIAN WORLD

The Spanish hegemony, their domination of the pass, came to an end in April 2013. Barcelona's defeat to Chelsea in the semifinal of the 2012 Champions League could be written off as a blip, as could Bayern's penalty shoot-out victory over a Real Madrid still hamstrung by their dependence on Cristiano Ronaldo (in no sense had either club been outplayed), but what happened in the semifinals the following year was rather different.

On April 23, Barcelona, by then managed by Tito Vilanova, were hammered 4–0 by Bayern Munich—the side Pep Guardiola, who had quit to take a sabbatical in New York, was set to take over when Jupp Heynckes's contract expired the following summer. The next night, Jürgen Klopp's Borussia Dortmund savaged Real Madrid, beating them 4–1. In both cases, the German side had less possession. But they weren't clinging on, holding out against the siege, and stealing something on the break: in both cases, the German side looked quicker, stronger, and sharper. This was a systematic approach based on counterattacking, and it had finalized the process begun by Internazionale in 2010 and Chelsea in 2012: it ended the obsession with ball retention.

There were predictable snide comments—the age of social media, after all, was fully upon the world—about Bayern's folly in appointing as their new manager the high priest of a style their outgoing manager had just exposed, but that was to miss the point. It was reasonable to feel sympathy for Heynckes, who would end up being ousted having won a treble, but the new German style was less an antidote to the Spanish game than a variant of it. What clouded the issue was the focus on possession. Barcelona at their best, like Ajax before them, had excelled not merely at keeping the ball but at winning it back. Guardiola's Barça were probably the greatest side at holding onto the ball there has ever been, but they also excelled at pressing, and it was that aspect that the new German style prioritized.

Germany's attitude towards pressing was always a little perplexing. Bayern and Borussia Mönchengladbach in the seventies played a possession game, but it was never predicated on pressing. Rather, West German soccer retained a man-marking structure in which the *libero* became the effective playmaker as the other nine players on the field dealt with their direct opponent.

The Austrian Ernst Happel did introduce zonal marking during his stint with Hamburg, but he never had them press as hard as he had, for instance, the Feyenoord team with which he won the European Cup in 1970. In the Netherlands, he had been a pioneer of pressing, almost as though he and Rinus Michels, who was at Ajax at the time, drove each other to greater and greater heights. The similarity in approach was sufficient for Happel to seem the obvious choice to lead Holland at the 1978 World Cup. Happel used the style with some success at Club Brugge as well, taking them to a European Cup final in which they were beaten by Liverpool, but by the time he became the first manager to win the European Cup with two different sides (with Hamburg in 1983), he had tempered his approach. A difficult spell with Sevilla in 1973–1974, perhaps, had taught him that the same approach doesn't necessarily work everywhere; West Germany in the early eighties simply might not have been ready for pressing.

As the decade went on, 5–3–2 became a viable alternative to 4–3–3, but zonal marking was still generally regarded as needless foreign overcomplication. Games were to be won by character and by the efforts of the *Führungsspieler*—the Franz Beckenbauer or Lothar Matthäus figure who could inspire his men to glory. And for a long time, it worked: between 1972 and 1996, (West) Germany won two World Cups and three European Championships, while losing in three major finals.

But there were doubters, foremost among them Ralf Rangnick. Born in 1958, the defensive midfielder began his career at VfB Stuttgart but never made it beyond their amateur side. He studied English and sports science at the University of Stuttgart, a course that included a year at the University of Sussex, where he became a devout Anglophile. One of his classmates in Stuttgart played professional volleyball for Feuerbach, and he was struck by how much training she did: ten hours a day, including gym work and two hours purely on tactics. He came to wonder whether soccer was stuck in its ways, a little backwards in that regard.

Rangnick drifted through Germany's lower leagues before, at the age of twenty-four, becoming player-manager of the sixth-tier side Viktoria Backnang. In February 1983, they played a friendly against Valeriy

Lobanovskyi's Dynamo Kyiv, who were staying at Sportschule Ruit for a winter training camp. It was, he later said, "an epiphany." When the ball went out of play for a throw-in early on, Rangnick counted the Dynamo players, half believing they'd sneaked an extra man onto the field. They hadn't; but such was the ferocity of their pressing that it felt like they had. Rangnick had never experienced anything like it before. Dynamo kept coming to Ruit and Rangnick kept studying them.

In 1985, Rangnick became coach of VfB Stuttgart's amateur side. At around the same time, he met Helmut Groß, a structural engineer who had essentially taught himself tactical theory and was part of a think tank trying to pass ideas on to younger coaches. While manager of the sixth-flight side SC Geislingen, he had observed how efficient zonal marking was in terms of energy conservation. That excess energy, he reasoned, could be employed to press higher up the field. Groß had no soccer background, which meant he was treated with a certain skepticism, but he was far from a crank. With the fifth-division side Kirchheim, he twice won the Baden-Württemberg championship and once even held Dynamo to a 1–1 draw. In 1984, his successor at Geislingen, Jakob Baumann, led his side to a shock 2–0 victory over Happel's Hamburg SV in the DFB Cup.

Groß and Rangnick became good friends, sitting up late into the night to discuss tactics and watch videos they had shipped from Italy of Arrigo Sacchi's Milan. In 1989, Groß was put in charge of VfB Stuttgart's youth setup and made pressing mandatory for all development sides. Rangnick, who had been convinced that players of any level could prosper by pressing after implementing the system at SC Korb in the German seventh flight, soon followed him to the club, after being appointed reserve-team coach.

Slowly zonal marking and pressing began to spread throughout Germany. Volker Finke, another coach who had had no professional playing career to speak of, took charge of Freiburg in 1991. He led them to promotion to the Bundesliga in 1993. They narrowly avoided relegation the following season but made their mark with a number of emphatic wins against top sides: 3–1 over Bayern, 4–1 over Dortmund, 4–0 at Stuttgart. The following season was even better, as they hammered Bayern 5–1 on the second weekend and went on to finish third. Yet Finke still wasn't taken entirely seriously and, when economic reality hit and Freiburg began to slide, it seemed to confirm the wisdom of the conservative establishment.

Gradually, though, a revolution was brewing. Wolfgang Frank had been a Bundesliga striker for Eintracht Braunschweig in the seventies, but his biggest influence was Sacchi. When he was appointed coach of Mainz in the second division in September 1995, they had one point and no goals from eight games. He explained his ideas and set about implementing them, benefiting from taking over a side that essentially had nothing left to lose. It was hard, boring work: learning positioning, walking around in prearranged patterns on the training field. "But," said the team's center-back, Jürgen Klopp, "we thought if Gullit and Van Basten had to learn that at Milan, we could put up with it as well." They stayed up and the next season finished fourth.

Rangnick, meanwhile, went to Reutlingen and then Ulm, whom he led to promotion to the second flight in 1997–1998. That summer, Germany were embarrassed at the World Cup, playing grim, functional soccer before being outplayed by Ćiro Blažević's Croatia in the quarterfinal. Success at Euro 96 (with a drab, clanking squad), it quickly became accepted, had been some-thing of a freak. But just because there were doubts over the old ways didn't mean there was any consensus on which way German soccer should turn.

The following season, Ulm began with sixteen games unbeaten. In December 1998, Rangnick was invited on *ZDF Sportstudio*, a Bundesliga highlights show, to discuss zonal marking and a flat back-four which, if the tone of the presenter is anything to go by, seemed to be regarded by the wider soccer public less as basic tactical concepts and more as kabbal-istic mumbo jumbo. In ninety cogent seconds, the slim and bespectacled Rangnick explained his system, pointing out that the focus on a *libero*, a free man, made little sense in a world that had largely abandoned man-marking. Germany, though, perhaps still wasn't ready to hear the message. There was a backlash from the establishment, and Rangnick was derided as "a professor" and "a theorist."

Subsequent events gave his critics ammunition. Rangnick left Ulm for Stuttgart in March 1999. Ulm went on to win promotion, but Rang-nick faltered at the bigger club. That he was their fifth manager in a year perhaps should have been a warning. More practically, the transition to Rangnick's approach was always going to be difficult for a side used to playing through a playmaker in the fan-favorite Krassimir Balakov. Rang-nick's relationship with the Bulgarian was never easy, but it collapsed com-pletely when Balakov swore at him after being substituted in a league game against 1860 Munich. Balakov was suspended but, with results disappoint-ing, Rangnick was soon sacked. Could his methods, it was asked, really work with higher-profile players who might not be prepared to subjugate their egos to the needs of the team?

Yet while there were doubts about Rangnick, there were even bigger doubts about the way German soccer as a whole was going. The 1998 World Cup had been a wake-up call. Berti Vogts was hounded out of his job the following September and replaced by Erich Ribbeck. At sixty-one, he was not a man likely to lead a revolution. Far more significant, it turned out, were reforms the DFB had begun to introduce to youth coaching. Alarmed that a lack of players, forwards in particular, had led to the South

African Sean Dundee and the Brazilian Paulo Rink being naturalized to cover a dearth of German strikers, the DFB appointed the former Kaiserslautern, Eintracht Frankfurt, Fortuna Düsseldorf, and Egypt coach Dietrich Weise to oversee the establishment of 121 regional centers across Germany. Euro 2000, in which Germany were eliminated in the group stage, even losing to Kevin Keegan's England, confirmed just how bad things had become. Germany played what became derided as *Rumpelfußball*: the team was old, they lumbered around, and in 2001 they lost a World Cup qualifier 5–1 at home to England.

But this was a very German crisis. Bayern still won the Champions League in 2001 and, making the most of a fortunate draw, Germany, by then managed by Rudi Völler, reached the final of the World Cup in 2002. They were still, by and large, disciplined; still tough enough to win tight games; and, in Oliver Kahn, had a highly gifted goalkeeper who fit the ethos of the team perfectly. By 2002, Germany had become about "Kahn, *Kampf und Kopfball*"—Kahn, struggle, and heading—a pastiche of the *Turniermannschaft*—tournament side—identity of which they'd once been so proud.

It was then that the wisdom of the post-1998 review really began to be seen. Graduates of Weise's development centers started to come through. The clubs were cajoled into establishing their own academies. Changes in 2001 made it easier for immigrants and their children to secure German citizenship, making it possible for thousands of potential players to play for Germany who would otherwise have been lost—as Yıldıray Baştürk, Ümit Davala, and İlhan Mansız, all of whom were born in Germany but played for Turkey, had been.

The revolution wasn't only bottom-up but also top-down, as Jürgen Klinsmann was appointed manager of the national side, assisted by Jogi Löw, who had worked with Groß at Stuttgart. Klinsmann's insistence on living in California and his habit of speaking business jargon inflected with vague New Age pretension didn't endear him to everybody, but his time playing in Italy, France, and England had opened his eyes to other ways of approaching the game. He introduced systematic pressing, got the players fitter, and made them work in a far more structured way on transitions. He also dropped Kahn for Jens Lehmann—a mobile goalkeeper more in step with the post-Cruyffian demand that the goalkeeper should be able to operate at times as a quasi-outfielder—and in so doing enacted a radical change in the template of the German goalkeeper, leading ultimately to Manuel Neuer, the ultimate sweeper-keeper.

Quite how adept Klinsmann was as a manager is debatable—subsequent spells with Bayern and the United States didn't work out well—and there is a sense that Germany's success at the 2006 World Cup, when they finished third having played much brighter, slicker soccer than they had in years, was the result as much of the generally euphoric home atmosphere as of anything the coaching staff did. What is clear is that he opened the door to a new era in German soccer, one on which Löw capitalized. He replaced Klinsmann after the World Cup and, after defeats in the final of Euro 2008 and the semifinals of the 2010 World Cup and Euro 2012, lifted the World Cup in 2014, by which time twenty-one of the twenty-three-man squad had come through the academy system. The speed of the national side had increased significantly: in 2005, an average of 2.8 seconds passed between a player controlling and passing the ball; by 2010, that gap was less than a second.

The confirmation that the new ways of press-and-possess had been fully adopted came in 2005 when Klopp, who had replaced Frank as manager of Mainz and, after two near misses, had in 2004 led them to promotion to the Bundesliga for the first time, was invited by ZDF to be a studio pundit for their coverage of the Confederations Cup. He designed a video tool to help explain tactical issues and, in the same studio where Rangnick had alienated the establishment seven years earlier, became a huge success. Perhaps Rangnick was simply preaching his message too soon, or perhaps Klopp's charisma and his self-deprecating wit made it easier for the audience to relate to him, but what was clear was that the national mood had changed. Soccer was no longer merely about personalities and leadership; tactical discussion, which by then meant zonal marking and pressing, had entered the German mainstream.

Rangnick led Schalke 04 to second in the league in 2004–2005 and then achieved astonishing success with Hoffenheim, where he employed Groß as his advisor and the former national hockey coach Bernhard Peters as his assistant. Two promotions took the village club to the Bundesliga and, in 2017, under another young coach who favored a pressing game, Julian Nagelsmann, they qualified for the Champions League play-offs for the first time. Returning to Schalke, Rangnick got them to a Champions League semifinal, but it was Klopp who became the face of the new style.

Mainz were relegated in 2007 and, having failed to gain promotion the following season, Klopp resigned. He was appointed at Borussia Dortmund, who had just finished thirteenth, and he led them to sixth and then fifth, before winning the title in both 2011 and 2012. His style, *Gegenpressing*, began to draw attention from across Europe. *Gegenpressing*, Klopp said, "is the best playmaker in the world." Win the ball back quickly, high up the field, when the opposition is disoriented, and the chances almost created themselves.

But it wasn't kick-and-rush. It wasn't just about tempo and energy. "When three players chase in a swarm after a ball that's just been lost, it can sometimes look chaotic," Groß said. "But this is chaos of a controlled and highly creative kind." Klopp had learned from Frank and so in that sense was influenced by Sacchi. Having been born in Stuttgart, he is often seen as part of a Swabian school with Rangnick and Löw, and he is open in his admiration of Lobanovskyi. In his desire to win the ball back quickly high up the field, Klopp is like Bielsa or Guardiola. Klopp himself has never made any secret of his love for English soccer and the way it dominated Europe in the late seventies and early eighties with a form of pressing game. When Klopp was appointed Liverpool manager in 2015, there was a strange sense that he was selling back to its creator, in slightly modernized, more sophisticated form, the English game of thirty years earlier—before the Heysel ban and the loss of confidence, before the vain scrabble through the Dutch, French, Spanish, and German games for some imagined secret formula that could reinvigorate English soccer.

Klopp's success at Dortmund confirmed the new style could be effective at the highest level. As a new generation of coaches—the likes of Roger Schmidt, Thomas Tuchel, and Tayfun Korkut—began to be appointed to Bundesliga jobs, *Gegenpressing* began to diversify. Klopp's sides would essentially encircle the man in possession, giving him no space to play a pass.

Klopp's Dortmund (DFB–Pokal final, 2012)

When Heynckes adopted *Gegenpressing* in 2012–2013, the season Bayern won the double, he preferred a man-oriented variant. One player would go to the opponent with the ball, while others would seek to mark possible recipients of a pass, cutting down the options of the man in possession. Nagelsmann's sides tended to focus on the passing lanes, looking to insert themselves between the man on the ball and potential recipients of a pass, relying more on interceptions than on making tackles. That perhaps required more thought from the players, but it meant that when possession was regained, the man winning the ball should have more time and space to initiate an attack.

———

It wasn't just Germany where *Gegenpressing* took hold. This, though, was a new style of tactical revolution. Neoliberal economics had changed soccer utterly. Where previously a great club had risen with a group of great players playing the perfect soccer for that group of players, only to fall away as their secrets were understood, age sapped their zip, success drained their hunger, and the emotional attrition of constant exposure to one another eroded the bonds of team spirit, by 2013 soccer had entered the era of the super-clubs. The elite by then were so much richer than the rest, the financial structures of soccer so rigged to perpetuate the flow of wealth, that it became impossible for the biggest clubs to fall any great distance. In the season in which they lost 7–0 over two legs to Bayern and the style they had made their own ceased to be dominant, Barça won the league.

Illness forced Tito Vilanova to quit that summer. His replacement, Gerardo Martino, had been a key part of Bielsa's Newell's side in the early nineties and had made significant progress using a cautious interpretation of his pressing style with Paraguay, leading them to the final of the 2011 Copa América. He never really settled, though, and was gone within a year, replaced by Luis Enrique. Persuading the midfielder to leave Real Madrid for the Camp Nou had been just about Johan Cruyff's last act as manager of Barcelona, and Luis Enrique became a teammate of Guardiola during the extraordinary period when Louis van Gaal was manager and Ronald Koeman and José Mourinho were his assistants. From a tactical point of view, modern soccer was forged during that period at Barcelona.

Luis Enrique ended his first season in charge by winning a treble, yet in January 2015, he had seemed on his way out, with Barça apparently mired in crisis. That, perhaps, is also a feature of the age of the super-club: success becomes so expected that the slightest dip in form or results prompts panic, and long-term thinking becomes all but impossible—something that makes tactical radicalism far less likely.

Barça had signed Neymar for a basic fee of around £50 million in 2013 and Luis Suárez for £65 million a year later, deals that seemed simultaneously to excite and unsettle fans. The players' quality was not in doubt, but equally the signings seemed to signal a move towards a *galáctico* model similar to that employed by Real Madrid, and thus away from the team ethic and the reliance on the *cantera* that represented Barça's self-image. It's hard to claim to be *més que un club* when you're just signing celebrities like everybody else.

When the season began disappointingly, that unease became anger. Luis Enrique had declared "hunting season" open in November 2014 after Barcelona's first ever home defeat to Celta Vigo. When they lost 1–0 at home to Real Sociedad in the first game back after the winter break, his future seemed very uncertain indeed, particularly given that he had left Messi out of that game. Messi had been on the bench for his first game back after spending Christmas in Argentina in both of the two previous seasons, but this time it was perceived as evidence of a rift between player and coach. Rumors of a breakdown in their relationship were only fueled when Messi then skipped a training session, blaming gastroenteritis, which Xavi had unhelpfully revealed the previous week was the excuse usually given when a player has other reasons not to train. The defender Jérémy Mathieu admitted Messi and Luis Enrique had clashed.

Off the field, Barcelona's image had been sullied by a transfer ban imposed because of irregularities in how they'd signed Under-16s and by ongoing allegations over the signing of Neymar. The club legend Andoni Zubizarreta was dismissed as director of soccer and his assistant, Carles Puyol, the former captain, soon followed. Luis Enrique admitted his position had been "weakened,"' and a poll suggested 68 percent of fans wanted him gone.

But then Barça scraped a win over Atlético that suggested some fight remained in the side. Messi returned to the middle and a false nine role, with Luis Suárez shifting to the right. That brought greater fluidity, and Barça won thirty-one of their final thirty-five games of the season, including a 3–1 victory over Juventus in the Champions League final. Yet was it Luis Enrique's doing? Suárez let slip that the switch that got the front three performing so well was something that happened almost organically during a game, when the Argentinian eventually told him to stay where he was after he had drifted into the middle.

But to suggest Luis Enrique was nothing more than a figurehead—somebody who is wise enough to know when to shut up and let the players get on with it, although that is in itself a skill—would be misleading. His management of Xavi's decline could hardly have gone better, although he found Xavi a far more biddable soul that he himself had been as Frank

Rijkaard eased him out of the side in 2003–2004. And, most significantly, he oversaw the transition to a more varied style, which was perhaps not surprising: after all, he was not as steeped in Barça's traditions as Guardiola was; he came through not at la Masía but at Sporting de Gijón's academy.

Six of the Barça side that played against Juventus in Berlin in that 2015 final had also played against Manchester United in Rome in 2009. In one sense, that represents a remarkable level of continuity; only four players who played for Real Madrid in the 1956 European Cup final—Marquitos, José María Zárraga, Francisco Gento, and Alfredo di Stéfano—also played when they won it for a fifth time in a row in 1960. Continuity, though, will take you only so far. After Guardiola's departure, there had been a sense of drift. Perhaps Barça had lost their desire; perhaps Vilanova and Martino simply hadn't been able to inspire them. Certainly they looked fitter under Luis Enrique. But there was also a feeling that they had become too harmonious, that their constant passing, their reluctance to play the risky ball or attempt the dribble that might lose possession, made them at times predictable. A devout Cruyffian might even have suggested that they had become too much like a Van Gaal side. Inter and Chelsea may have ridden their luck to beat them in the Champions League semifinals in 2010 and 2012, but they had shown the way: after those games everybody knew that the best chance of beating Barça was to sit back and deny them space and the possibility of verticality, making them pass the ball horizontally across the field. Where teams would once have been terrified by the prospect of having only 20 percent possession in a game, that became accepted as the most effective way against such a radical possession side.

That's why the signings of Neymar and Suárez were so significant. Their individual ability meant they could disrupt marking structures by beating a couple of men with a dribble, making it far harder for opponents simply to sit deep against Barça. Messi, of course, had always offered that element of chaos, but three soloists are far harder to defend against than one: the statistics showed that Barça dribbled three times more frequently in 2014–2015 than they had in 2010–2011. Ivan Rakitić, similarly, offered a new aspect in midfield: quicker, riskier, and more direct forward passes—looking to release that front three, rather than being a sophisticated lubricant in the way Xavi had been. Perhaps the Barça of 2015 was not as pure as that of 2011, they were not a distillation of post-Cruyffianism, but those impurities made them harder to stop.

But there was a cost. Two years later, Barça, having survived a remarkable last-sixteen tie in the Champions League against Paris Saint-Germain—in which they lost 4–0 in the first leg—were well beaten by Juventus in the quarterfinal. As they finished second behind Real Madrid in the league, a mood of general dissatisfaction hung over the club. The

Luis Enrique's Barcelona (Champions League final, 2015)

remnants of Guardiola's great side were aging, new signings hadn't worked out, the production line from la Masía had slowed, and Neymar, who had been lined up as Messi's successor, left for PSG. Worse, the sense of Barcelona as something unique, as the manifestation of a philosophy, had gone. They were just another wealthy club, struggling to cope with the transfer market. Wealth insulated them and there was no dramatic decline, but the specialness had gone. Perhaps that was inevitable—no academy can simply produce great players to order—but it didn't dull the pain. The appointment of Ernesto Valverde, who had played under Cruyff at Barça in the late eighties, felt like a conscious attempt to drag the club back to its principles, although the result was an oddly insipid 4–4–2 that was good enough to win la Liga but the defensive inadequacies of which were exposed by Chelsea in the Champions League even before the surrender of a 4–1 first-leg lead in the Champions League quarterfinal against Roma.

Those Champions League defeats to PSG and Juventus were the continuation of the process begun in the 2013 Champions League semifinals. Barça, in part sustained by the finances of modern soccer, had not gone away. They had not collapsed or sunk into the sort of decline suffered by Inter after their defeat to Celtic in 1967 or by Ajax after the departure of Cruyff. They were still there at the top table, habitual challengers in the Champions League, just about able to conceive of finishing third in la Liga, but certainly no lower. Their style, though, whether referred to as tiki-taka, a term Guardiola abhors, or *juego de posición*, is no longer hegemonic. Spain, too, suffered their defeats, savaged 5–1 by a series of counterattacks at the 2014 World Cup as Louis van Gaal's Holland played against type. They were then harried and pressed to a 2–0 defeat by Jorge Sampaoli's Chile and eliminated. At Euro 2016, after an unconvincing group stage, sluggish going forward and unable to deal with their rapid transitions, Spain were undone by Antonio Conte's Italy.

All three key defeats came against sides playing a back three. "When Italy need to come out with the ball, having three at the back and two wide players means they have five possible people to carry it out—which makes it difficult for Spain to press as they would like," Xavi had explained in *La Gazzetta dello Sport* before the meeting in Paris. "Then, playing with two strikers complicates things further forward, because it occupies both of our centre-backs and then one of the two full-backs has to step forward to close down [Antonio] Candreva or [Alessandro] Florenzi—leaving you with only three at the back. At the World Cup in Brazil, both Holland and Chile chose to use a 3–5–2 against us and it put us in great difficulty."

Shape, assuredly, was part of it—and getting the extra man into midfield, getting the full-backs higher up the field as wing-backs, was a major reason why the back three began to return to fashion. But there was also a sense of Spain following Barça—understandably, given how many of the players were the same—in becoming a little stale and so unable to deal with the ferocity of opponents who, smelling blood, pressed against them. It's perhaps not so much that the style of 2011 has been superseded as that the second final against United was an apotheosis: a core of players who had grown up together playing a radical style that was perfect for them.

For teams who wanted to press high up the field, or even teams who wanted to counter that pressing, the back three had begun to make a comeback. Gian Piero Gasperini, for instance, had begun to use a back three in that way during his time at Genoa and took Atalanta to a fourth-place finish in Serie A in 2016–2017, overwhelming teams by pressing with five midfielders.

The most striking use of a back three that season, though, was at Chelsea. Spooked into a change of formation having gone 3–0 down at Arsenal in their sixth game of the season, their manager Antonio Conte switched to a 3–4–2–1 at half-time and, although they lost that game, they won their next thirteen in the league and went on to win the title, becoming the first side to do so in England while fielding a back three since Everton in 1962–1963. Harry Catterick's side featured Brian Labone at center-half flanked at the back by Mick Meagan and either Alex Parker or George Thomson, the last hurrah in England of the W-M. The following year, Bill Shankly's Liverpool, operating a back four, won the league, and it was his thinking and that of Don Revie and Alf Ramsey that would dominate for half a century.

The immediate impact of the switch to a back four was to neuter the winger, but there was a corollary to that, which was the release of the full-back. Nílton Santos and Silvio Marzolini pioneered the idea of attacking from deep-lying wide areas and that strategy, uneasily and unevenly, spread. When England, belatedly, adopted the notion of a formation with three central defenders at the 1990 World Cup, they still clung to the notion that a full-back, as the name suggested (not that that had bothered them with center-halves), should be a defender. Their interpretation of

Conte's Chelsea (2016–17)

a 5–3–2 featured not midfielders in the wide positions but Paul Parker and Stuart Pearce as full-backs who could get forward. But Brazil's use of Leandro and Júnior at the 1982 World Cup, to take just one example, had shown another way. In other cultures, the *lateral* was simply a player who operated wide; there was no preconception he should be first and foremost a defender.

By the late nineties, the back three was retreating in the face of single-striker systems. Once the full-back had tasted freedom, though, there was no turning him back. The advent of 4–2–3–1 and return to popularity of 4–3–3 pushed wide creators higher up the field, but full-backs remained an attacking presence.

That has become increasingly the case with the growing trend for inverted wingers. If a left-footed forward plays on the right, his effectiveness is significantly enhanced if he has a full-back overlapping outside him, presenting the full-back with the dilemma of defending on the inside—anticipating the forward coming onto his stronger, left, foot—or remaining in a neutral position in case the ball is pushed right to a full-back coming on the outside.

Conte took that further. There were times during the Euro 2016, notably against Spain in the last sixteen, when the Italy wing-backs, Mattia De Sciglio and Alessandro Florenzi, were pushed so high that the shape was almost 3–3–4 rather than 3–5–2. Guardiola, in his first season at Manchester City, at times deployed a back three, with Raheem Sterling and Leroy Sané or Nolito as his wide men, in what was effectively a 3–2–4–1. He took the idea that full-backs were to be regarded as midfielders more than defenders further than anybody. At Bayern, he would have David Alaba and Philipp Lahm tuck in to operate as central midfielders, forming the same trapezium with the back three that had been there in the defensive M of the W-M. He perhaps didn't have the personnel for that in his first season at City, but by the second he had Kyle Walker and Benjamin Mendy or Fabian Delph working the whole flank and often coming inside their winger, changing the angle of attack and exploiting the join between the opposing full-backs and central defenders.

But in 2016–2017, it was Conte, using a back three, who had the greatest success. For him, a back three was paradoxically more defensive than a back four, the insertion of David Luiz between César Azpilicueta and Gary Cahill offering protection that allowed Victor Moses and Marcos Alonso, the wing-backs, to act as midfielders. Their provision of attacking width in turn had an impact higher up the field. N'Golo Kanté and Nemanja Matić provided an extra layer of protection in front of the back four, that familiar trapezoid shape. With that platform in place, there was then freedom for Eden Hazard and Pedro (or Willian), operating essentially as inside-forwards behind a lone striker. Playing in that awkward niche between the opposing holding midfielders and the full-backs, unopposed as they once would have been by wing-halves, they frequently found themselves in pockets of space.

Chelsea weren't the first to use the shape: Brendan Rodgers had done so at Liverpool two seasons earlier (having been impressed by Paulo Sousa's use of it with Basel), and it could even be argued Roy Evans's Liverpool had played a similar shape in the midnineties. But Conte's side were the first to combine that shape with a ferocious pressing game, and in some ways they were the most successful. As opponents sought to work out a way of dealing with them, no fewer than thirteen of the twenty Premier League sides used some variant of a back three at various points in the season. That, perhaps, was simple geometric sense: playing that M shape at the back, using the trapezoid block as the basic defensive unit, does offer two holding midfielders who can operate as wing-halves once did, and so at least occupy the space sought by the inside-forwards.

Conte's other great strength is his work on positioning, which he practices using the shadow-play popularized by Arrigo Sacchi, but which was seemingly developed by Alan Brown at Sunderland in the early sixties. There again the influence of Lobanovskyi is felt, with Conte so concerned to keep the preprogrammed moves of his side secret that while Italy coach he forbade all but the closest members of his coaching staff to watch practice. "We work a lot of tactical positions and we know exactly what we have to do on the pitch, where I have to go and where the defenders have to go," the Chelsea winger Eden Hazard said, explaining the major differences between Conte and his predecessor at Stamford Bridge, José Mourinho. "We know exactly what to do. With Mourinho, he put in a system but we didn't work lots. We know what to do because we play football, but maybe the automatisms were a little bit different....It's not always nice as a forward as you have to run, defend and everything, but at least at the weekend, you know exactly what to do, you can even close your eyes and play."

––––––––

Conte's success was significant in that it brought together two of the biggest trends in soccer over the past couple of decades: the liberation of the full-back and the insistence on pressing. What marked him out as modern, though—or, at least, if Hazard is to be believed, more modern than Mourinho—was his work on coordinated attacking moves. In itself, of course, that is nothing new—managers as diverse as Herbert Chapman and Valeriy Lobanovskyi implemented clear structures of attacking play—and nor should such an approach be seen as prescriptive. Rather it is a theme on which great artists can extemporize, designed though familiarity to speed up attacking play by making complex moves semiautomatic. (This is also one of the reasons international soccer so often seems wanting in the modern age; national managers simply don't have the time with their players to generate the sort of mutual understanding from which true fluency derives.)

Hazard wasn't the only one to find Mourinho wanting in that regard: the most consistent criticism of him at Real Madrid, from a tactical point of view, was that he left the forwards to improvise rather than drilling them in how to break down the massed defenses they regularly came up against. Guardiola, similarly, in his obsession with *juego de posición*, is a manager who likes his sides to attack in preset ways.

But that's a detail, a preference—an evolution, perhaps, and something that will presumably only become more sophisticated as data analysis and computer modeling improves, but nothing as revolutionary as what Guardiola achieved with Barcelona. In the years since 2013 and the recognition that that style of radical possession was no longer hegemonic, what has followed is, broadly speaking, a multiplicity of Barça-inflected approaches.

There are exceptions, of course. Mourinho, since Guardiola got the Barcelona job ahead of him in 2008, seems almost willfully to be playing an anti-Barça style of soccer, using the lessons he learned working under Louis van Gaal in the late nineties to undermine the philosophy, almost reveling in winning games with minimal possession. The side he began the season with at Manchester United in 2017–2018 was the tallest in any of the top five leagues in Europe, demonstrating a preference for physical power over technique. The way his side bullied Peter Bosz's post-Cruyffian Ajax in the 2017 Europa League final was a prime example of how effective that way of playing can be.

Or there's Diego Simeone, brought up in an entirely different tradition: his first youth coach when he joined Veléz Sarsfield was Victorio Spinetto, and he has clearly absorbed many of his principles about the need for *fibra*. To say he practices *anti-fútbol* in the way it has been interpreted since Osvaldo Zubeldía's Estudiantes would be unfair, but equally he seizes whatever advantage he can, even if that means instructing ballboys to throw additional balls onto the field to stop opposing attacks. At the same time, though, he has clearly been conditioned by his time playing at Atlético and in Italy.

This blurring of influences, perhaps, is the most notable feature of the modern game: managers and players move far more than ever before, constantly testing their ideas in new environments. What worked for Guardiola at Barça, for instance, had to be amended when he went to Bayern, and there was need of an even more significant rethink after he took the Manchester City job.

And then there's money, or rather its distribution. Elite soccer is dominated now as it never has been before by a handful of super-clubs. For many of them, winning their domestic title has come to be regarded almost as a formality. There are vast imbalances within leagues, and that, of course, conditions the tactical approach teams take. If you expect to win most games comfortably, everything becomes focused on attacking, which can cause problems for the super-clubs on the rare occasions they come up against team at around their level: they forget not merely how to defend but also how to fight. The standard of defending has declined alarmingly among elite clubs, something that's not just to do with a shift to a more attacking focus. In the eight seasons from 2009 to 2010, 21 of 104 games in the quarterfinals or later finished with a winning margin of three or more; in the eight seasons before that, there were only eight. In 2017–2018, there were even more: Liverpool against City, Real Madrid against Juventus, Barcelona against Roma, then Roma against Barcelona, and Liverpool against Roma. Never has a three-goal lead seemed less secure.

The need to generate revenue, meanwhile, has led to an increasing focus on the individual. Perhaps that's a natural consequence of an era that has enjoyed two players as ludicrously gifted as Lionel Messi and Cristiano Ronaldo, but it also feels that the nature of the game has changed, that the soap opera culture that funds modern soccer requires stars and celebrities. Guardiola, at Barcelona at least, when he had an academy that produced players already inculcated with his style, stood in opposition to that; he has found it harder to succeed without spending since. The attitude of players, in turn, seems to have changed. It's hard to quantify, of course, but when Paul Pogba, on joining Manchester United in 2016, spoke less of hoping to win the league or the Champions League than of striving for the Ballon d'Or, it felt like a key moment. Players now ask at least as much what a club can do for them as what they can do for the club—and that means their willingness to submit themselves to a tactical system can be limited. That, allied with the constant pressure for results, inhibits experimentation and leads to tactical conservatism.

At the same time, soccer has never been as systematized as it is now; it's often how effectively managers resolve that contradiction that determines whether or not they are successful. The tension can produce positive results: it's a matter of taste more than anything else, but there were many who preferred the Barcelona side that won the Champions League under Luis Enrique in 2015 to the Guardiola model. Certainly, by having three soloists, in Messi, Luis Suárez, and Neymar, they had greater variety to their attack, more ways of breaking down a packed defense, even if the whole felt less pure, less of an expression of an ideal, than the team of four years earlier.

Soccer, by 2018, was in a distinctly post-Cruyffian age, and the influence of those who had played or coached at Barcelona in the late nineties was everywhere to be seen. But that style was never entirely dominant. Even when Guardiola's Bayern and Manchester City sides were dominant in their domestic leagues, they retained a vulnerability that ended up undoing them in the Champions League. In each of his three seasons in Germany, Guardiola won the championship with ease, breaking records and essentially ending the title race as a contest long before Christmas. In 2013–2014, Bayern conceded twenty-three goals in thirty-four games. The following season, they let in eighteen, then seventeen. It was a similar story in his second season in England, in 2017–2018, when City wrapped up the league with five games remaining, conceding roughly two-thirds of a goal per game. That suggests defensive stability, and yet in 2014 Bayern went out of the Champions League in the semifinal, losing 1–0 and 4–0 to Real Madrid, and in the 2015 semi they lost the first leg of their semifinal 3–0 to Barça as they suffered a 5–3 aggregate defeat. In 2018, City lost 3–0 and 2–1 to Klopp's Liverpool in the Champions League quarterfinal. They were defensively strong, in other words, apart from in certain games when they collapsed. His sides had a habit, in big games, of leaking three goals in twenty-minute spells: City had also let in three in quick succession in their 4–3 league defeat at Anfield in 2017–2018. Even in a league game against Leicester in 2016–2017, they'd gone 3–0 down in twenty minutes.

What was significant about the opponents wasn't just their quality but their style, or at least the style they adopted in the key moments of those games. Bypass the press, attack at pace, and Guardiola's sides were not just vulnerable but prone to panic. There's not only a psychological dimension—does the obsessive focus on the system perhaps deny players the individuality that would allow them, in difficult circumstances, to demonstrate the initiative to yank a game back their way? Do Guardiola's players, as Zlatan Ibrahimović claimed, become in some way little more than obedient schoolchildren?—but also a tactical one. It's no coincidence that the manager with by far the best record against Guardiola is Klopp, with eight wins in fourteen meetings. To say Klopp's high-tempo *Gegenpressing* style is the best or only countermeasure to Guardiola's positional game is oversimplistic—City, after all, while losing three games out of four to Liverpool in 2017–2018, won the other one 5–0—but it does seem a way of taking it on that exposes its vulnerabilities.

It may be that this is always the way after an ideological revolution. Once the first blast of the new way's radicalism is over, what remains feels necessarily like a compromise. While there is a general sense of the pre-eminence of pressing, there is no side dragging football in a direction it feels like everyone else must follow. False nines are accepted and understood but far from common. The back three has returned to fashion but is not universal. Most but not all top sides play with a high line. Goalkeepers now are expected to be able to play with their feet, to be comfortable outside the box. The Real Madrid side that won three Champions Leagues in four years were obviously hugely talented, but they won't be remembered for any tactical innovation. This second decade of the twenty-first century feels like a period of retrenchment rather than radicalism. Nobody has been capable of playing in quite the same way as Guardiola's Barça, but equally nobody could ignore the lessons they had taught.

EPILOGUE

It would be easy to survey modern soccer and insist there can be nothing new. Roberto Mancini, in fact, did just that at a lecture he gave in Belgrade in 2007, arguing that future advances in soccer would come not in tactics but in the physical preparation of players. To an extent he is probably right. Soccer is a mature game that has been examined and analyzed relentlessly for almost a century and a half, and, assuming the number of players remains constant at eleven, there probably is no revolution waiting to astonish the world. Even if there is, even if some coach in some unlikely corner happens upon some radical departure, it will not have the stunning impact that, say, Hungary's withdrawn center-forward had in the early fifties. Even that was, as I hope this book has demonstrated, part of a continuum, drawing directly from Matthias Sindelar's interpretation of the center-forward's role in the Austrian *Wunderteam*, and having a parallel in Martim Francisco's work with Vila Nova.

England could not deal in 1931 with Sindelar dropping off, British sides struggled to cope with Vsevolod Bobrov doing the same when Dinamo Moscow toured in 1945, and they were humiliated by Nándor Hidegkuti in 1953. Lessons, evidently, should have been learned, but that they were not is explicable by the fact that those three examples were isolated and spread over twenty-two years. These days, Hungary's *Aranycsapat* would not have come to London as a mystery: their successes would have been seen on television, videos would have been picked over, and the movement of their players would have been analyzed by computer. A tactical innovation will never again spring up as a surprise.

Besides which, a talented Hungarian coach such as Gusztav Sebes would almost certainly not be working in Hungary, but would have followed the money to Western Europe. As cross-pollination between different soccer cultures increases, so national styles become less distinct. We are not yet homogenized, and probably never will be, but the trend is in that direction.

And yet there are always imaginations ready to defy expectation. For a long time, a promoted side, particularly one with limited resources, would usually adopt a defensive style. Spoil the game, the logic goes, restrict the influence of skill, reduce the number of goals likely to be scored, and a weaker team increases its chances of stealing a draw or a 1–0 win. Yet in 2006–2007, Pasquale Marino, having led Catania to promotion to Serie A the previous season, had his side play a 4–3–3 with attacking full-backs and no holding midfielder. They were encouraged not to play the percentages, but to try the outrageous and the difficult. Occasionally they came unstuck—they were hammered 7–0 by Roma, for instance—but exuberance proved just as hard to play against as dourness. Following the murder of a policeman during rioting at the derby against Palermo in February, Catania were banned from playing games at their home stadium, but they still finished as high as thirteenth. It wasn't a new system, but it was a revolution of style, a rebellion against convention. Since then the Premier League has seen the likes of Norwich City and Swansea City succeed while defying the stereotype.

Old styles can be successfully reintroduced in new contexts, particularly in the shortened form of major tournaments. Greece, for instance, at Euro 2004, were the only team who played without a zonal-marking back four. Their coach, Otto Rehhagel, employed a *libero* with three man-markers and then added further solidity with a five-man midfield and a lone striker. "Rehhagel won because he posed a problem people had forgotten how to solve," said Andy Roxburgh. "It wasn't fashionable but it was effective. They controlled matches without having control of the ball. Otto's view was: why should he try a watered-down version of somebody else's system? Whatever you say about his system, you have to admit that Greece got the ball into attack very quickly every time they had possession."

France, in particular, seemed to struggle against Greece, losing 1–0 to them in the quarterfinal. "They needed to get the ball to Thierry Henry faster," Roxburgh said. "Henry is at his most dangerous running into the centre from the left or running just left of centre. Against Greece, he drifted too wide because he wasn't getting any space. That's one of the things you want to do: push a threat to the touchline. Greece's opponents weren't used to being marked so tightly. The old method turned out to be a novelty."

When Spain won Euro 2012 playing often without a striker, it didn't come as a shock; it was seen merely as the progression of trends that had been traced over the previous few years. Barcelona's excellence, similarly, was revolutionary in degree rather than in conception; they simply did what others had done before but better and more so.

At the moment, use of strikerless formations is restricted to a tiny handful of elite clubs. Perhaps the 4–6–0 will, in time, become just as much the orthodoxy as 4–4–2 was in England until the midnineties, or the *libero* was in Italy until the late eighties; perhaps it will prove merely a passing fad. Certainly its emergence hints at the death of the old-fashioned striker in favor of something more versatile, and the move to universality, it can be said with some confidence, is an ongoing trend—even Robert Lewandowski, who resembles Ian Rush and has the physique an old fashioned target man, is comfortable pulling wide and dropping deep. Then again, perhaps that simply proves Mancini's point, and all that is actually happening is that the technicians of old are, thanks to improved nutrition and better training methods, becoming physically more imposing; if everybody is fit and powerful, then there is necessarily less demand for those players who offer little beyond their physique or their engine. If strikers are heading the way of old-school wingers and playmakers, though, then the question is who next? Center-backs, maybe? After all, if there is no center-forward to mark, the second center-back in a 4–4–2 would seem as redundant as the third in a 3–5–2 playing against a lone forward.

It is hard to believe, equally, that the increasingly detailed analysis afforded by technology will not also make a difference. Computers and a knowledge of cybernetics helped Valeriy Lobanovskyi devise his system, and it stands to reason that the more sophisticated technology becomes, the more sophisticated systems will become. The biggest obstacle to that, in fact, are the egos of players. Puffed up by years of immense wages and celebrity status, are they willing, as Lobanovskyi and Arrigo Sacchi demanded, to sacrifice themselves utterly to the collective? The experience of Real Madrid in the *galácticos* era suggests not.

That, perhaps, is the other side of the paradox at which Jorge Valdano hinted when he spoke of television's influence on the modern game: that it is the very popularity of soccer that prevents its advancement. Fans, arguably, are complicit in that. Terraces tend to conservatism, and the example of Sweden in the seventies indicates that there is a love of individualism—of soccer of first-order complexity, to use Tomas Petterson's term—that exceeds the demand for victory. Argentina's experiences as the period of *la nuestra* came to an end show just how damaging that decadence—of thought, if nothing else—can be. That said, globalization is a built-in defense; if nobody is progressing, then nobody is being left behind, so a wake-up like Argentina's 6–1 defeat to Czechoslovakia in 1958 is unlikely, unless a country outside the soccer mainstream is suddenly blessed with a hugely gifted generation of players who can resist the lures of Western

European materialism long enough to submit themselves to the system of a tactically astute coach. South Korea's success in reaching the semifinal of the 2002 World Cup is evidence of what can be achieved with rigorous organization, even with essentially average players.

When he left Real Madrid, Sacchi said he found it "remarkable, worrying" that there had been no significant tactical development since the radical systematized approach of his Milan, but he remained convinced evolution would continue. "As long as humanity exists," he said, "something new will come along. Otherwise football dies." What came along was Barcelona. "Like my Milan," Sacchi said, "this team mark a 'before' and 'after' in world football."

The immediate time after was characterized by Bayern Munich and Borussia Dortmund, two teams who took the essential Van Gaal/Bielsa principles—from Van Gaal himself in Bayern's case—and sped them up. It is a truth—hinted at by Menotti's dictum that the point of training is to increase the speed at which a team can be precise—that seems written in the internal rhythms of soccer: each new form is developed and modified, made faster, until it reaches a maximum pace at which a new innovation arises to replace it. What Bayern Munich did was to take the Barcelona model and improve it, not so much with technical innovation as with physical.

What Barcelona had done with their phalanx of 5'7" geniuses, Bayern did with players who were bigger, faster, and more direct. Bayern perhaps didn't hit quite the same levels of filigree passing as Barça at their peak, but they were not far off, and what was striking in that Champions League semifinal was how tired—how weak—Barcelona looked. Of course, it's not entirely fair to compare a team on the rise with one coming to the end of its cycle—one is hungry, desperately eager for success, and the other is sated, lacking the drive to suffer to stay in a game—but equally it can hardly be denied that Bayern's players were bigger than Barça's.

Guardiola's Barça felt like a pinnacle that would not be surpassed in a long time—if ever—and yet, within two years of their peak at Wembley, Bayern, on the stage, completed a Champions League victory that suggested that they were capable of even greater heights. They never quite scaled them, not even under Guardiola. His Manchester City, similarly, has seemed brilliant but flawed. It would take a peculiarly one-eyed view of the world not to acknowledge Guardiola's genius, and yet it increasingly seems that the Barcelona of 2011 may have been his finest side. After all, no matter how great a manager, he is still to an extent reliant on circumstance, and then he was working with an exceptional squad, the majority of whom had grown up at the club and been schooled in the Barça style.

And so what remains is not one hegemonic style, but a multiplicity of approaches, in part conditioned by Guardiola's Barça. And so, the wider soccer world joins Sacchi in awaiting the next great step. It may take time, but it will come. Many before have hailed the end of history; none have ever been right.

BIBLIOGRAPHY

BOOKS AND JOURNALS

Alabarces, Pablo, Ramiro Coelho, and Juan Sanguinetti, "Treacheries and Traditions in Argentinian Football Styles: The Story of Estudiantes de la Plata," in Armstrong and Giulanotti, *Fear and Loathing in World Football.*

Alcock, Charles W., *Football: The Association Game* (George Bell & Sons, 1902).

Aleinikov, Sergei, and D. I. Belenky, *I zhizn, I slyozy, i futbol* (Polymya, 1992).

Allison, Malcolm, *Soccer for Thinkers* (Pelham, 1967).

Andersen, Jens, *Frankie Boy* (People's Press, 2008).

Archer, Ian, and Trevor Royle (eds.), *We'll Support You Evermore: The Impertinent Saga of Scottish Fitba'* (Souvenir Press, 1976).

Archetti, Eduardo P., *Masculinities: Football, Polo and the Tango in Argentina* (Global Issues, 1999).

———, "Masculinity and Football: The Formation of National Identity in Argentina," in Giulianotti and Williams, *Game Without Frontiers.*

Armstrong, Gary, and Richard Giulanotti (eds.), *Entering the Field: New Perspectives on World Football* (Berg, 1997).

———, *Fear and Loathing in World Football* (Berg, 2001).

Assaf, Roberto, and Clóvis Martins, *Almanaque do Flamengo* (Abril, 2001).

———, *Campeonato carioca: 96 anos de história, 1902–1997* (Irradiação Cultural, 1997).

Auclair, Philippe, "Roy the Rover," *Blizzard*, Issue Five (June 2012).

Bakema, J. B., *Thoughts About Architecture*, ed. Marianne Gray (St. Martin's Press, 1981).

Ballard, John, and Paul Suff, *The Dictionary of Football: The Complete A–Z of International Football from Ajax to Zinedine Zidane* (Boxtree, 1999).

Bangsbo, Jens, and Birger Pietersen, *Soccer Systems and Strategies* (Human Kinetics, 2000).

Barend, Frits, and Henk van Dorp, *Ajax, Barcelona, Cruyff: The ABC of an Obstinate Maestro*, trans. David Winner and Lex den Dam (Bloomsbury, 1997).

Barnade, Oscar, and Waldemar Iglesias, *Mitos y creencias del fútbol Argentino* [Myths and beliefs of Argentinian football] (Al Arco, 2006).

Barthes, Roland, *Mythologies* (Éditions de Seuil, 1957, trans. Annette Lavers Vintage, 2000).

Bate, Richard, "Football Chance: Tactics and Strategy," in Reilly et al., *Science and Football* (Spon, 1988).

Bayer, Osvaldo, *Fútbol Argentino* [Argentinian football] (Editorial Sudamericana, 1990).

Ben-Ghiat, Ruth, *Fascist Modernities: Italy 1922–45* (University of California Press, 2001).

Blokhin, Oleh, *Futbol na vsyu zhyzn* (Veselka, 1988).

Booth, Keith, *The Father of Modern Sport: The Life and Times of Charles W. Alcock* (Parrs Wood, 2002).

Borges, Jorge Luís, and Adolfo Bioy Casares, *"Esse est percipi,"* in Kuper and Mora y Araujo, *Perfect Pitch: Dirt.*

Bottenburg, Maarten van, and Beverley Jackson, *Global Games* (University of Illinois Press, 2001).

Bowler, Dave, *Winning Isn't Everything: A Biography of Sir Alf Ramsey* (Victor Gollancz, 1998).

Bray, Ken, *How to Score: Science and the Beautiful Game* (Granta, 2006).

Brera, Gianni, *Herrera e Moratti* (Limina, 1997).

———, *Storia critica del calico Italiano* (Tascaballi Bompiani, 1978).

Buchan, Charles, *A Lifetime in Football* (Phoenix House, 1955).

Burgess, Ron, *Football: My Life* (Souvenir, 1955).

Burn, Gordon, *Best and Edwards: Football, Fame and Oblivion* (Faber and Faber, 2006).

Burns, Jimmy, *Barça: A People's Passion* (Bloomsbury, 1999).

———, *Hand of God: The Life of Diego Maradona* (Bloomsbury, 1996).

Buxton, Peter, *Stoke City Football Club: A Centenary* (Pyramid, 1963).

Caldas, Waldenyr, *O pontapé inicial: Memória do futebol Brasileiro (1894–1933)* (IBRASA, 1990).

Camus, Albert, *La chute* [The fall], trans. Justin O'Brien (Penguin, 1990, first published 1956).

Castillo, Juan José, *Ladislao Kubala* (Barcanova, 1998).

Castro, Ruy, *Garrincha: The Triumph and Tragedy of Brazil's Forgotten Footballing Hero*, trans. Andrew Downie (Yellow Jersey, 2004).

Chapman, Herbert, *Herbert Chapman on Football* (Garrick, 1934).

Clough, Brian, *Clough: The Autobiography* (Corgi, 1994).

———, *Cloughie: Walking on Water: My Life* (Headline, 2002).

Connolly, Kevin, and Rab MacWilliam, *Fields of Glory, Paths of Gold: The History of European Football* (Mainstream, 2005).

Connor, Jeff, *The Lost Babes* (HarperSport, 2006).

Cox, Richard, *The Encyclopaedia of British Football* (Routledge, 2002).

Crabtree, Stephen, *The Dons—the Amazing Journey 1982–87* (Baron, 1987).

Craig, Jim, *A Lion Looks Back* (John Donald, 1998).

Crampsey, R. A., *The History of Queen's Park, 1867–1967* (Nisbet, 1967).

Crerand, Paddy, *Never Turn the Other Cheek* (HarperSport, 2007).

Crick, Michael, *The Boss: The Many Sides of Alex Ferguson* (Simon & Schuster, 2002).

Csaknády, Jenő, *Die Béla Guttmann story: Hinter den kulissen des weltfussballs* (Verlag Blintz-Dohány, 1964).

Csanádi, Árpád, *Soccer*, trans. István Butykai and Gyula Gulyás, trans. rev. Charles Coutts (3rd ed., Corvina Kiadó, 1978).

Cullis, Stan, *All for the Wolves* (Rupert Hart Davis, 1960).

DaMatta, Roberto, *O que faz o Brasil, Brasil?* (Rocco, 1984).

DaMatta, Roberto, et al., *Universo do futebol: Esporte e sociedade Brasiliera* (Edições Pinakotheke, 1982).

De Galan, Menno, *De trots van de wereld* (Prometheus BV Vassallucci, 2006).

Di Giano, Roberto, *Fútbol y cultura política en la Argentina, identidades en crisis* (Leviatán, 2005).

Dickinson, Wendy, and Stafford Hildred, *For Pete's Sake: The Peter Taylor Story: Volume 1: The Backstreets to the Baseball Ground* (Matador, 2010).

Diéguez, Luis, and Ariel Scher, *El libro de oro del mundial* (Clarín, 1998).

Downing, David, *The Best of Enemies: England v Germany, a Century of Football Rivalry* (Bloomsbury, 2000).

———, *England v Argentina: World Cups and Other Small Wars* (Portrait, 2003).

———, *Passovotchka* (Bloomsbury, 1999).

Edwards, George, *Right Place, Right Time: The Inside Story of Clough's Derby Days* (Stadia, 2007).

Edwards, Leigh, and Andy Watson, *Mission Impossible: The Story of Wimbledon Football Club's Historic Rise from Non-League to the First Division* (Dons Outlook, 1986).

Edwards, Maurice, *Brian and Peter: A Right Pair; 20 Years with Clough and Taylor* (Derby Books, 2010).

Filatov, Lev, *Obo vsyom poporyadku* (Fizkultura I Sport, 1990).

Filho, Mário, *O negro no futebol Brasileiro* (2nd ed., Civilizaçao Brasiliera, 1964).

Finn, Ralph, *A History of Chelsea FC* (Pelham, 1969).

Foot, John, *Calcio: A History of Italian Football* (Fourth Estate, 2006).

Fox, Norman, *Prophet or Traitor: The Jimmy Hogan Story* (Parrs Wood, 2003).

Francis, Tony, *Clough: A Biography* (Stanley Paul, 1987, rev. ed., 1993).

Freddi, Cris, *Complete Book of the World Cup 2002* (CollinsWillow, 2002).

Freyre, Gilberto, *The Gilberto Freyre Reader* (Knopf, 2002).

Galeano, Eduardo, *Football in Sun and Shadow*, trans. Mark Fried (Fourth Estate, 1997).

Galinsky, Arkady, *Nye sotvori syebye kumira* (Molodaya Gvardiya, 1971).

Galinsky, Vitaly, *Valeriy Lobanovskyi: Chetyre zhyzni v futbolye* (Sport, 2003).

Gardner, Paul, *The Simplest Game: The Intelligent Fans' Guide to the World of Soccer* (Collier Books 1976, rev. ed. 1994).

Garland, Ian, *History of the Welsh Cup 1877–1993* (Bridge, 1993).

Gemmill, Archie, *Both Sides of the Border* (Hodder & Stoughton, 2005).

Giulianotti, Richard, *Football: A Sociology of the Global Game* (Polity, 1999).

Giulianotti, Richard, and John Williams (eds.), *Game Without Frontiers: Football, Identity and Modernity* (Arena, 1994).

Glanville, Brian, *Champions of Europe: The History, Romance and Intrigue of the European Cup* (Guinness, 1991).

———, *Cliff Bastin Remembers* (Ettrick, 1950).

———, *Soccer Nemesis* (Secker and Warburg, 1955).

———, *The Story of the World Cup* (Faber and Faber, 2001).

Goldblatt, David, *The Ball Is Round: A Global History of Football* (Viking, 2006).

Golesworthy, Maurice, *The Encyclopaedia of Modern Football* (Sportsman's Book Club, 1957).

Gorbunov, Alexander, *Trenerskoe naslediye: Boris Arkadiev* (Fizkultura i Sport, 1990).

Górski, Kazimierz, *Piłka jest okrągła* (Kazimierz Górski, 2004).

Gould, Stephen Jay, *Triumph and Tragedy in Mudville* (Cape, 2004).

Gray, Andy, with Jim Drewett, *Flat Back Four: The Tactical Game* (Boxtree, 1998).

Grayson, Edward, *Corinthians and Cricketers* (Sportsman's Book Club, 1957).

Green, Geoffrey, *The Official History of the FA Cup* (Naldrett, 1949, rev. ed. Heinemann, 1960).

———, *Soccer: The World Game—A Popular History* (Phoenix House, 1953, rev. ed. Pan, 1956).

———, *There's Only One United* (Hodder and Stourton, 1978).

Greenwood, Ron, *Yours Sincerely* (Willow, 1984).

Hamilton, Aidan, *An Entirely Different Game: The British Influence on Brazilian Football* (Mainstream, 1998).

Hamilton, Duncan, *Provided You Don't Kiss Me: 20 Years with Brian Clough* (HarperPerennial, 2008).

Handler, Andrew, *From Goals to Guns: The Golden Age of Football in Hungary 1950–56* (Columbia University Press, 1994).

Heizer, Teixeira, *O jogo bruto das Copas do Mundo* (Mauad, 1997).

Hermiston, Roger, *Clough & Revie: The Rivals Who Changed the Face of English Football* (Mainstream, 2011).

Herrera, Fiora Gandolfi, *Tacalabala, esercizi di magia di Helenio Herrera* (Tapiro, 2002).

Herrera, Helenio, *La mia vita* (Mondo Sport, 1964).

Hesse-Lichtenberger, Ulrich, *Tor! The Story of German Football* (WSC, 2002).

Hey, Stan, *The Golden Sky* (Mainstream, 1997).

Hidegkuti, Nándor, *Óbudától firenzéig* (Sport, 1965).

Holden, Jim, *Stan Cullis: The Iron Manager* (Breedon, 2000).

Holt, Richard, J. A. Mangan, and Pierre Lanfranchi (eds.), *European Heroes: Myth, Identity, Sport* (Frank Cass, 1996).

Honigstein, Raphael, *Harder, Better, Faster, Stronger: Die geheime Geschichte den englischen Fussballs* (Kiepenheuer & Witsch, 2006).

Hopkins, Stephen, "Passing Rhythms: The Modern Origins and Development of 'The Liverpool Way,'" in Williams, Hopkins, and Long, *Passing Rhythms*.

Horak, Roman, and Wolfgang Maderthaner, "A Culture of Urban Cosmopolitanism: Uridil and Sindelar as Viennese Coffee-House Heroes," in Holt, Mangan, and Lanfranchi, *European Heroes*.

Howard, Charles, (ed.), *The Encyclopaedia of Sport and Games* (Heinemann, 1911).

Hughes, Charles, *Football: Tactics and Teamwork* (EP, 1973).

———, *Soccer Tactics and Skills* (BBC and Queen Press, 1980).

———, *The Winning Formula* (Collins, 1990).

Hunt, David, *The History of Preston North End Football Club: The Power the Politics and the People* (Carnegie, 1992).

Hunter, Graham, *Barça: The Making of the Greatest Team in the World* (BackPage Press, 2011).

Inglis, Simon, *Football Grounds of Britain* (Collins Willow, 1996).

Iwanczuk, Jorge, *Historia del fútbol amateur en la Argentina* (Autores Editores, 1995).

Jackson, N. L., *Association Football* (Newnes, 1900).

Jakobsen, Joakim, *Tynd luft: Danmark ved VM i Mexico 1986* (Gyldendal, 2008).

James, Brian, *England v Scotland* (Sportsman's Book Club, 1970).

Johnston, Harry, *The Rocky Road to Wembley* (Sportsman's Book Club, 1954).

Johnston, William, *The Austrian Mind: An Intellectual and Social History* (University of California Press, 1983).

Jones, Ken, *Jules Rimet Still Gleaming: England at the World Cup* (Virgin, 2003).

Jones, Peter, *Wrexham: A Complete Record 1972–1992* (Breedon, 1992).

Joy, Bernard, *Forward Arsenal!* (Phoenix, 1952).

———, *Soccer Tactics: A New Appraisal* (Phoenix, 1957, rev. ed., 1963).

Kassil, Lev, *Vratar respubliki* (repr. Detgiz, 1959, first published 1938).

Keith, John, *Bob Paisley: Manager of the Millennium* (Robson, 1999).

———, *The Essential Shankly* (Robson, 2001).

Kelly, Stephen, *The Boot Room Boys: Inside the Anfield Boot Room* (Collins Willow, 1999).

Kormelink, Henny, and Tjen Seeverens, *The Coaching Philosophies of Louis van Gaal and the Ajax Coaches* (Reedswain, 1997).

Køster-Rasmussen, Janus, "Denmark 4 USSR 2," *Blizzard*, Issue Three (December 2011).

Kovacs, Ştefan, *Football Total* (Calman-Levy, 1975).

Kraul, Andreas, *Presenting Jesper Olsen* (Thaning & Appel, 2007).

Kucherenko, Oleg, *Sto let rossiyskomu futbolu* (Russian Football Union, 1997).

Kuper, Simon, *Ajax, the Dutch, the War: Football in Europe During the Second World War* (Orion, 2003).

———, *Football Against the Enemy* (Orion, 1994).

Kuper, Simon, and Marcela Mora y Araujo (eds.), *Perfect Pitch: Dirt* (Headline, 1999).

Lacey, Josh, *God Is Brazilian: Charles Miller, the Man Who Brought Football to Brazil* (NPI, 2005).

Larson, Øyvind, "Charles Reep: A Major Influence on British and Norwegian Football," *Soccer and Society* 2, no. 3, Autumn 2001, 58–78.

Lawson, John, *Forest 1865–78* (Wensum, 1978).

Lawton, James, *On Football* (Dewi Lewis Media, 2007).

Lawton, Tommy, *Football Is My Business* (Sporting Handbooks, 1946).

———, *My Twenty Years of Soccer* (Heirloom, 1955).

Lebedev, Lev, *Rossyiskiy futbol za sto let* (Russian Football Union, 1997).

Le Corbusier, *Vers une architecture*, trans. F. Etchells (Architectural Press, 1970, first published 1923).

Leite Lopes, and José Sergio, "Successes and contradictions in 'Multiracial' Brazilian Football," in Armstrong and Giulianotti, *Entering the Field*.

Lidbury, Michael, *Wimbledon Football Club: The First Hundred Years* (Ward and Woolverton, 1989).

Lobanovskyi, Valeriy, *Beskonyechnyy match* (IN Yura, 2003).

Lovejoy, Joe, *Sven-Goran Eriksson* (Collins Willow, 2002).

Mangan, J. A., *Athleticism in the Victorian and Edwardian School: The Emergence and Consolidation of an Educational Ideology* (Cambridge University Press, 1981).

Maradona, Diego, with Daniel Arcucci and Ernesto Cherquis Bialo, *El Diego*, trans. Marcela Mora y Araujo (Yellow Jersey, 2005).

Marples, Morris, *A History of Football* (Secker and Warburg, 1954).

Martin, Simon, *Football and Fascism: The National Game Under Mussolini* (Berg, 2004).

Mason, Tony, *Passion of the People? Football in South America* (Verso, 1995).

Matthews, Sir Stanley, *Feet First* (Ewen & Dale, 1948).

Mazzola, Ferruccio, and Fabrizio Calzia, *Il terzo incomodo: Le pesanti verità di Ferruccio Mazzola* (Bradipolibri 2004).

Mazzoni, Tomás, *O Brasil na taça do mundo 1930–50* (Leia, 1950).

———, *História do futebol no Brasil 1894–1950* (Leia, 1950).

McCarra, Kevin, *Scottish Football: A Pictorial History from 1867 to the Present Day* (Third Eye Centre and Polygon, 1984).

McCarra, Kevin, and Pat Woods, *One Afternoon in Lisbon* (Mainstream, 1988).

McIlvanney, Hugh, *McIlvanney on Football* (Mainstream, 1994).

———, *World Cup '66* (Eyre & Spottiswoode, 1970).

McKinstry, Leo, *Sir Alf* (HarperSport, 2006).

Meisl, Willy, *Soccer Revolution* (Sportsman's Book Club, 1956).

Melegari, Fabrizio, Luigi La Rocca, and Enrico Tosi, *Almanacco ilustrato del Milan* (Panini, 2005).

Menotti, César Luis, *Como ganamos la Copa del Mundo* (El Gráfico, 1978).

Menotti, César Luis, and Ángel Cappa, *Fútbol sin trampa* (Muchnik, 1986).

Merrick, Gil, *I See It All* (Museum Press, 1954).

Midwinter, Eric, *Parish to Planet: How Football Came to Rule the World* (Know the Score, 2007).

Mikes, George, and Nicholas Bentley, *How to Be an Alien: A Handbook for Beginners and Advanced Pupils* (Penguin, 1970).

Milan, Betty, *Brasil o pais da bola* (Berst, 1989).

Miller, David, *Cup Magic* (Sidwick and Jackson, 1981).

Mølby, Jan: *Jan the Man* (Orion, 1999).

Morales, Víctor Hugo, and Roberto Perfumo, *Hablemos de fútbol* (Booket, Planeta, 2007).

Morisbak, Andreas, *Fotballforståelse* (Norges Fotballforbund of Folkets Brevskole, 1978).

Motson, John, and John Rowlinson, *The European Cup 1955–1980* (Queen Anne, 1980).

Mourant, Andrew, *Don Revie: Portrait of a Footballing Enigma* (Mainstream, 1990).

Müller, Salo, *Mijn Ajax: Openhartige memoires van den talisman van Ajax in den gouden jaren '60 en '70* (Houtekiet, 2006).

Murphy, Patrick, *His Way: The Brian Clough Story* (Portico, 2004).

Murray, Bill, *The World's Game: A History of Soccer* (University of Illinois Press, 1996).

Oliveira, Cândido de, *A Evolução da táctica no futebol* (Capa de Pagarna, 1949).

———, *Sistema W-M* (Capa de Pagarna, 1950).

Oliver, Scott, "The Other Rival, Another Way," *Blizzard*, Issue Four (March 2012).

Olsen, Egil, "Scoringer i fotball," master's thesis (NUSPE, Oslo, 1973).

Panzeri, Dante, *Burgueses y gangsters en el deporte* (Libera, 1974).

——, *Fútbol, dinámica de lo impensado* (Paidós, 1967).

Papa, Antonio, and Guido Panico, *Storia sociale del calcio in Italia* (Il Mulino, 2002).

Paulo Emílio, *Futebol: Dos alicerces ao telhado* (Oficna do Livro, 2004).

Pawson, Tony, *100 Years of the FA Cup* (Heinemann, 1972).

Pelé, with Orlando Duarte and Alex Bellos, *Pelé: the Autobiography*, trans. Daniel Hahn (Pocket Books, 2006).

Perdigão, Paulo, *Anatomia de una derrota* (L&PM, 1986).

Persson, Gunnar, *Stjärnor på flykt: Historien om Hakoah wien* (Norstedts, 2004).

Peterson, Tomas, "Split Visions: The Introduction of the Svenglish Model in Swedish Football," *Soccer and Society* 1, no. 2 (Summer 2000): 1–18.

Pinto, Edson, *Flávio Costa: O futebol no jogo da verdade* (Cape, 1996).

Powell, Jeff, *Bobby Moore: The Life and Times of a Sporting Hero* (Robson, 1993).

Pozzo, Vittorio, *Campioni del mondi: Quarant'anni do storia del calcio Italiano* (Centro Editoriale Nazionale, 1960).

——, "Il fallimento del calcio Italiano," *Successo* 2 (1959): 107–108.

Puskás, Ferenc, *Captain of Hungary* (Cassell, 1955).

Radnedge, Keir, *50 Years of the European Cup and Champions League* (Carlton, 2005).

Rafferty, John, *One Hundred Years of Scottish Football* (Pan, 1973).

Ramsey, Alf, *Talking Football* (Stanley Paul, 1952).

Reep, Charles, and Bernard Benjamin, "Skill and Chance in Association Football," *Journal of the Royal Statistical Society*, Series A, 131, 581–585, 1968.

Reilly, T., A Lees, K. Davids, and W. J. Murphy (eds.) *Science and Football* (Spon, 1988).

Revie, Don, *Soccer's Happy Wanderer* (Museum, 1955).

Riordan, James, *Sport in Soviet Society: Development of Sport and Physical Education in Russia and the USSR* (Cambridge University Press, 1977).

Ronay, Barney, "The Bomb and the Bowler Hat," *Blizzard*, Issue Three (December 2011).

——, *The Manager: The Absurd Ascent of the Most Important Man in Football* (Sphere, 2009).

Rostron, Phil, *We Are the Damned United: The Real Story of Brian Clough at Leeds United* (Mainstream, 2009).

Sabaldyr, Volodymyr, *Vid matchu smerti do matchu zhyttya* (Lesya, 2005).

Sábato, Ernesto, *Sobre héroes y tumbas* (Súdamericana, 1961).

Saldanha, João, *Futebol & outras histórias* (Record, 1988).

——, *Histórias do futebol* (Revan, 1994).

Sarychev, Vasily, *Mig i sudba* (Pressball, 2004).

Sebes, Gusztáv, *Örömök és csalódások* (Gondolat, 1981).

Sivertsen, Lars, "The Mind Has Mountains," *Blizzard*, Issue Three (December 2011).

Smith, Stratton, (ed.), *The Brazil Book of Football* (Souvenir, 1963).

Smith, Stratton, and Eric Batty, *International Coaching Book* (Souvenir, 1966).

Soar, Phil, *And the Spurs Go Marching On* (Hamlyn, 1982).

Soar, Phil, and Martin Tyler, *Arsenal: The Official History* (Hamlyn 1998).

Soter, Ivan, *Enciclopédia da seleção1914–2002* (Folha Seca, 2002).

Souness, Graeme, with Bob Harris, *No Half Measures* (Collins Willow, 1985).

Starostin, Nikolai, *Futbol skvoz' gody* (Sovetskaya Rossiya, 1989).

———, *Zvyozdy bol'shogo futbola* (Sovetskaya Rossiya, 1969).

Steen, Rob, *The Mavericks* (Mainstream, 1994).

Stiles, Nobby, *Soccer My Battlefield* (Stanley Paul, 1968).

Studd, Stephen, *Herbert Chapman: Football Emperor* (Souvenir, 1981).

Syzmanski, Stefan, and Tim Kuypers, *Winners and Losers: The Business Strategy of Football* (Penguin, 2000).

Taylor, Chris, *The Beautiful Game: A Journey Through Latin American Football* (Victor Gollancz, 1998, rev. ed. Phoenix, 1999).

Taylor, Matthew, *The Leaguers: The Making of Professional Football in England 1900–1939* (Liverpool University Press, 2005).

Taylor, Peter, *With Clough by Taylor* (Sidgwick and Jackson, 1980).

Taylor, Rogan, and Klara Jamrich (eds.), *Puskas on Puskas: The Life and Times of a Footballing Legend* (Robson, 1998).

Todrić, Mihailo, *110 Years of Football in Serbia*, trans. Borislav Bazić and Marijan Franjia (Football Association of Serbia, 2006).

Torberg, Friedrich, *Die erben der tante jolesch* (DTV, 1978).

———, *Kaffeehaus war überall* (DTV, 1982).

Trapattoni, Giovanni, *Coaching High Performance Soccer* (Reedswain, 1999).

Valentim, Max, *O futebol e sua técnica* (ALBA, 1941).

Vargas, Walter, *Fútbol Delivery* (Al Arco, 2007).

Végh, Antal, *Gyógyíthatatlan?* (Lapkiadó-Vállalat-Ország-Világ, 1986).

———, *Miért beteg a magyar futball?* (Magvető, 1974).

Vialli, Gianluca, and Gabriele Marcotti, *The Italian Job: A Journey to the Heart of Two Great Footballing Cultures* (Transworld, 2006).

Vickery, Tim, "The Rise of the Technocrats," *Blizzard*, Issue Six (September 2012).

Vignes, Spencer, *Lost in France: The Remarkable Life and Death of Leigh Richmond Roose, Football's First Playboy* (Stadia, 2007).

Wade, Allen, *The FA Guide to Training and Coaching* (Football Association, 1967).

———, *Modern Tactical Development* (Reedswain, 1996).

Wagg, Stephen, *The Football World* (Harvester, 1984).

Wall, Sir Frederick, *50 Years of Football, 1884–1934* (Soccer Books, 2005).

Ward, Andrew, "Bill Shankly and Liverpool," in Williams, Hopkins, and Long, *Passing Rhythms*.

Weber, Max, *The Protestant Ethic and the Spirit of Capitalism*, trans. Peter Baehr and Gordon C. Wells (Penguin, 2002, first published 1904).

Whittaker, Tom, *Tom Whittaker's Arsenal Story* (Sportsman's Book Club, 1958).

Williams, John, Stephen Hopkins, and Cathy Long (eds.) *Passing Rhythms: Liverpool FC and the Transformation of Football* (Berg, 2001).

Williams, Richard, *The Perfect 10: Football's Dreamers, Schemers, Playmakers and Playboys* (Faber and Faber, 2006).

Williams, William Carlos, *Selected Essays* (Random House, 1954).

Wilson, Jonathan, *The Anatomy of England: A History in Ten Matches* (Orion, 2011).

———, *Behind the Curtain: Travels in Eastern European Football* (Orion, 2006).

———, *Nobody Ever Says Thank You: A Biography of Brian Clough* (Orion, 2011).

———, *The Outsider: A History of the Goalkeeper* (Orion, 2012).

Winner, David, *Brilliant Orange: The Neurotic Genius of Dutch Football* (Bloomsbury, 2000).

———, *"Corrida* of Uncertainty," *Blizzard*, Issue Four (March 2012).

———, *Those Feet: A Sensual History of English Football* (Bloomsbury, 2005).

Young, Percy M., *Football in Sheffield* (Sportsman's Book Club, 1964).

———, *A History of British Football* (Stanley Paul, 1968).

Zauli, Alessandro, *Soccer: Modern Tactics* (Reedswain, 2002).

Zelentsov, Anatoliy, and Valeriy Lobanovskyi, *Metodologicheskiye osnovy razrabotki modelyey trenirovochnykh zanyatiy* (Sport, 2000).

Zubeldía, Osvaldo, and Geronazzo, Argentino, *Táctica y estrategia del fútbol* [Tactics and strategy of football] (Jorge Álvarez, 1965).

WEBSITES

Russell Gerrard's searchable archive of international fixtures: www.staff.city
.ac.uk/r.j.gerrard/football/aifrform.html

Milos Radulović's searchable archive of European club fixtures:

www.dfb.de

www.englandstats.com

www.icyb.kiev.ua

www.playerhistory.com

www.rsssf.com

www.soccerassociation.com

www.soccerbase.com
www.thefa.com
www.uefa.com

MAGAZINES AND NEWSPAPERS (UK UNLESS STATED)

Aftonbladet (Sweden)
Arbeiter-Zeitung (Austria)
Brighton Evening Argus
The Boys' Champion Story Paper
Buenos Aires Herald (Argentina)
Champions
Clarín (Argentina)
Corriere della Sera (Italy)
Daily Mail
Daily Record
East Anglian Daily Times
Efdeportes (Argentina)
L'Équipe (France)
Evening Standard
FourFourTwo
Futbol (Russia)
Futbolnyy kuryer (Ukraine)
A Gazeta (Brazil)
El Gráfico (Argentina)
The Guardian
The Herald
Hol (Ukraine)
The Huddersfield Examiner
The Independent
Kievskiye vedomosti (Ukraine)
Konsomolskaya Pravda (Russia)
Kronen Zeitung (Austria)
Lance (Brazil)
Literaturnaya Rossiya (Russia)
Liverpool Echo

Manchete Esportiva (Brazil)
Manchester Evening News
O Mundo (Brazil)
La Nacion (Argentina)
News of the World
Neues Wiener Journal (Austria)
Pariser Tageszeitung (France)
The Punter
The Scottish Athletic Journal
Scottish Referee
Scottish Umpire
The Sheffield Independent
Sheffield Telegraph and Star Sports Special
Sovetsky Sport (Russia)
Sport (Serbia)
Sport Express (Russia)
Lo Sport Fascista (Italy)
Sport den za Dnyom (Ukraine)
Sporting Chronicle
Sports (Brazil)
Sportyvna Hazeta (Ukraine)
Lo Stadia (Italy)
The Standard (Argentina)
Sunday Times
Tempo (Serbia)
Ukrayinskyy Futbol (Ukraine)
Welt am Montag (Austria)
World Soccer

INDEX

Jonathan Wilson's *Inverting the Pyramid* was football book of the year in the UK and Italy and was shortlisted for the William Hill Sports Book of the Year Award. His other books include *Behind the Curtain: Travels in Eastern European Football*; *Sunderland: A Club Transformed*; *The Anatomy of England: A History in Ten Matches*; *Nobody Ever Says Thank You*, a critically acclaimed biography of Brian Clough; *The Outsider: A History of the Goalkeeper*; *Angels With Dirty Faces: How Argentinian Soccer Defined a Nation and Changed the Game Forever*; *The Anatomy of Liverpool* and *The Anatomy of Manchester United*. He also writes for the *Guardian, Sports Illustrated*, and *World Soccer*, and he is the editor of *The Blizzard*.